T0262750

Electric Vehicle Propulsion Drives and Charging Systems

This book covers the introduction, theory, development, and applications of hybrid and electric vehicles and their charging infrastructures. It also discusses the real applications of power converters and electric drives to give the readers a flavour of how to design propulsion drives and fast charging systems for electric vehicles. It further covers important topics such as static and dynamic wireless charging systems, battery management, and battery swapping systems for electric vehicles.

This book:

- Presents comprehensively different types of electric vehicles and their powertrain architecture.
- Highlights modern optimization techniques such as genetic algorithms, simulated annealing, particle swarm optimization, and ant colony optimization.
- Discusses different charging methods such as wired and wireless for a variety of batteries including lead acid, lithium-ion, and vanadium redox.
- Covers grid-to-vehicle, vehicle-to-grid, and vehicle-to-vehicle bidirectional power flow analysis.
- Showcases power 2X technologies such as power-to-ammonia, power-to-chemicals, power-to-fuel, power-to-gas, and power-to-hydrogen.

The text is primarily written for senior undergraduate and graduate students as well as academic researchers in the fields of electrical engineering, electronics, and communications engineering.

Electric Vehicle Propulsion Drives and Charging Systems

Edited by
Kundan Kumar, Ambrish Devanshu,
and Sanjeet K. Dwivedi

CRC Press
Taylor & Francis Group
Boca Raton London New York

CRC Press is an imprint of the
Taylor & Francis Group, an **Informa** business

Designed cover image: Shutterstock

First edition published 2024
by CRC Press
2385 NW Executive Center Drive, Suite 320, Boca Raton FL 33431

and by CRC Press
4 Park Square, Milton Park, Abingdon, Oxon, OX14 4RN

CRC Press is an imprint of Taylor & Francis Group, LLC

ISBN: 978-1-032-52811-3 (hbk)
ISBN: 978-1-032-77060-4 (pbk)
ISBN: 978-1-003-48106-5 (ebk)

DOI: 10.1201/9781003481065

Typeset in Sabon
by codeMantra

Contents

About the editors

Kundan Kumar is presently working as an Assistant Professor in the Department of Electrical Engineering, at NIT, Manipur. He received his B. Tech. from the Institute of Engineering and Technology, Mahatma Jyotiba Phule Rohilkhand University, Bareilly in 2008. He received his M. Tech. in Electrical Engineering from NIT, Jamshedpur, India, and the Ph.D. in Electrical Engineering from the University of Padova, Padova, Italy, in 2010 and 2016, respectively. Prior to NIT Manipur, he worked as an Assistant Professor at the School of Electrical Engineering, Kalinga Institute of Industrial Technology, deemed to be university, Bhubaneswar, India. Kumar was the recipient of the Silver Medal for securing the first position during his M. Tech. course. He has also been awarded a University Fellowship for Ph.D. course at the University of Padova, Italy. He has also been awarded as Best Presentation Recognition award at IECON, held in Japan in 2015. He has chaired and co-chaired the various Technical Sessions in the prestigious IEEE International Conferences such as IECON, PEDES, ICPEE, and GUCON. He has published more than 45 research articles in International Journals and Conference Proceedings and five book chapters. Presently, he is editing a book entitled "Electric Vehicle Propulsion Drives and Charging Systems" which will be published in Taylor & Francis, CRC Press. He has organized an IEEE International Conference on Power Electronics and Energy (ICPEE-2021) and International Conference on Sci./Tech. and Engineering (ICSTE-2023) with the capacity of organizing secretary. He has worked as a Conference Chair for the 2nd IEEE International Conference on Industrial Electronics: Developments and Applications, which was held at NIT Manipur from 29th to 30th September 2023. He is a senior member of the IEEE (USA) and an Associate Member of the Institution of Engineers (IE), India. He is the reviewer of IEEE Journals/Transactions such as *TIE*, *TPEL*, *JESTPE*, and various reputed conferences such as *IECON*, *PEDES*, *INDICON*, and *PEMC*. His research interests include electric vehicles and their charging infrastructures, propulsion drive systems for EVs, application of wide bandgap semiconductor devices (i.e. GaN & SiC), wireless power transfer systems, dynamic wireless charging systems, high-efficiency power converters, soft switching, multi-port converters, single-active bridge (SAB), and dual active bridge (DAB) converters.

Ambrish Devanshu received his B.Tech. in Electrical and Electronics Engineering from the School of Engineering, Cochin University of Science and Technology, Cochin, Kerala, India in 2011 where he had completed his major project in the lead center of Indian Space Research Organization (ISRO) under the Department of Space (DOS), Government of India, Vikram Sarabhai Space Centre (VSSC). From September 2011 to June 2014, he served as a Project Engineer in Wipro Technologies, Greater Noida, India. Thereafter, he joined as a full-time PhD research scholar in the Department of Electrical Engineering, Delhi Technological University (DTU), Delhi, India, and received his PhD in 2019. In 2020, he joined the National Institute of Technology Patna as an Assistant Professor. In 2022, he joined the National Institute of Technology Silchar and currently working there as an Assistant Professor. He has five SCI papers as a first and corresponding author on his name along with several conference papers in IEEE. He has also reviewed more than 50 research papers of many reputed peer-reviewed SCI journals including *IEEE Transactions*, and reputed journals belong to Taylor & Francis and Willey publishers. He has also delivered various expert talks in the different institutes of national importance. Recently, in 2021, he received "premier research award" in 4th Research Excellence Award Functions as a Certificate of Appreciation and INR 100k cash prize, organized by Delhi Technological University, Delhi, India. He was a member of the organizing committee of the First IEEE International conference ICPEICES-2016 organized by DTU. He has also attended several workshops, the faculty development programs, and GIAN Courses to enhance his skill but not limited to Electric Machine Drives, Power Electronics, Nonlinear Control, Electric Vehicle, and Renewable Energy.

Sanjeet K. Dwivedi is Fellow of IET (UK) & working as a senior Technology Manager in Green Hydrogen Danish MNC Everfuel A/S. Previously, he was senior Research Leader at Danfoss, Denmark from 2008 to 2021. Prior to this, Sanjeet was an Electrical Engineer in Larsen and Toubro, an infrastructure company in India (1991–1992), Electrical Engineer in CPWD, Government of India (GoI). He worked as a senior faculty member of the Department of Technical Education, MP, India (1993–2006) and Dean R&D, Government Engineering College SAGAR MP India (2006–2008) Sanjeet has awarded with two master degrees, first one from IIT Roorkee, ME (Gold Medal) in Power Apparatus and Drives and second one from South Denmark University, M.Sc. Engineering in Innovation and Business. He has completed his Ph.D. in Green Technologies from IIT Delhi India. Sanjeet also completed his executive leadership education from MIT Boston. He was honored with adjunct professor at Curtin University, Perth, Australia (2016–2018). Sanjeet is Member of Faculty board of South Denmark University in the Innovation and Business department. Dr. Sanjeet has authored more than 40 technical papers and holds 14 international patents, three business trade and three books engineering research books published from Academic Press (UK) and IET Press (UK). He is an advisory board member of *International Journal of Power Electronics (IJPE)*, Associate Editor of the *IEEE Transaction on Industrial Electronics (IEEE TIE)*. He has given invited presentations, organized and chaired special sessions in several IEEE and European Power Electronics conferences around the globe. Previously he worked as Technical Editor of *IEEE/ASME Transaction on Mechatronics,* Associate Editor of *IET (United Kingdom) Power Electronics Journal,* and Associate Editor of *Korean Journal of Power Electronics (JPE)*. He is a recipient of Merit Award from Institution of India IE(I) (2006) for his research publication on permanent magnet machines. He was also awarded with 9th Man on the Moon Global Innovation Award from the CEO and President of Danfoss (2015) and another prestigious recognition as winner of IETE-Bimal Bose Award (2017) for outstanding contribution in power electronics and drive.

Contributors

Fareed Ahmad
Department of Electrical
  Engineering
S. N. D. College of Engineering and
  Research Centre
Nashik, Maharashtra, India

Srikanth Allamsetty
Electrical Engineering Department
National Institute of Technology
  Silchar
Silchar, Assam, India

T. Anil Kumar
Department of Electrical and
  Electronics Engineering
Anurag University
Hyderabad, Telangana, India
and
Siksha 'O' Anusandhan Deemed to
  be University
Bhubaneswar, Orissa, India

Aurobinda Bag
Department of Electrical and
  Electronics Engineering
Anurag University
Hyderabad, Telangana, India

Sakshi Bansal
Department of Electronics and
  Instrumentation
National Institute of Technology
  Silchar
Silchar, Assam, India

Pratim Bhattacharyya
Electric Mobility and Tribology
  Research Group
CSIR-Central Mechanical
  Engineering Research Institute
  (CMERI)
Durgapur, West Bengal, India
and
Academy of Scientific and
  Innovative Research (AcSIR)
Ghaziabad, Uttar Pradesh, India

Mohd Bilal
Department of Electrical
  Engineering
S. N. D. College of Engineering and
  Research Centre
Nashik, Maharashtra, India

Vimal Singh Bisht
Electronics and Communication
  Engineering Department
Graphic Era Hill University
  Bhimtal
Bhimtal, Utrakhand, India

Tanmoy Roy Choudhury
Department of Electrical
  Engineering
NIT Rourkela
Rourkela, Orissa, India

Kantipudi V. V. S. R. Chowdary
School of Electrical Engineering
Kalinga Institute of Industrial
  Technology
Bhubaneswar, Orissa, India

Dipankar Debnath
Department of Electrical
  Engineering
IIT Kharagpur
Kharagpur, West Bengal, India

Ambrish Devanshu
Department of Electrical
  Engineering
National Institute of Technology
  Silchar
Silchar, Assam, India

Kosha Krishna Dutta
Electrical Engineering Department
National Institute of Technology
  Silchar
Silchar, Assam, India

Santu Kumar Giri
Electric Mobility and Tribology
  Research Group
CSIR-Central Mechanical
  Engineering Research Institute
  (CMERI)
Durgapur, West Bengal, India
and
Academy of Scientific and Innovative
  Research (AcSIR)
Ghaziabad, Uttar Pradesh, India

S. Hajari
School of Electrical Sciences
Indian Institute of Technology
  Bhubaneswar
Bhubaneswar, Orissa, India

Surya Kant
Electronics and Communication
  Engineering Department
Graphic Era Hill University
  Bhimtal
Bhimtal, Utrakhand, India

Ashish Khandelwal
Battery Researcher
San Ramon, California

Munmun Khanra
Department of Electronics and
  Instrumentation
National Institute of Technology
  Manipur
Imphal, Manipur, India

T. Koteswara Rao
Civil Engineering
Jawaharlal Nehru Technological
  University
Kakinada, Andhra Pradesh, India

Kundan Kumar
Department of Electrical
  Engineering
National Institute of Technology
  Manipur
Imphal, Manipur, India

Pradeep Kumar
Department of Electrical and
  Electronics Engineering
NIT Sikkim
Ravangla, Sikkim, India

Ngangoiba Maisnam
Department of Electrical
  Engineering
National Institute of Technology
  Manipur
Imphal, Manipur, India

Suman Majumder
Department of Electrical
  Engineering
NIT Mizoram
Aizawl, Mizoram, India

N. J. Merlin Mary
Department of Electrical and
  Electronics Engineering
National Institute of Technology
  Tiruchirappalli
Tiruchirappalli, Tamil Nadu, India

Arshad Mohammad
Department of Electrical
  Engineering
Aligarh Muslim University
Aligarh, Uttar Pradesh, India

Byamakesh Nayak
School of Electrical Engineering
Kalinga Institute of Industrial
  Technology
Bhubaneswar, Orissa, India

Piyush Pandey
Electrical and Electronics
  Engineering
Ajay Kumar Garg Engineering
  College
Ghaziabad, Uttar Pradesh, India

Pabitra Mohan Patra
Department of Electrical
  Engineering
Institute of Technical Education
  and Research
Siksha 'O' Anusandhan Deemed to
  be University
Bhubaneswar, Orissa, India

Dinanath Prasad
Electrical and Electronics
  Engineering
Ajay Kumar Garg Engineering
  College
Ghaziabad, Uttar Pradesh, India

Pratap Sekhar Puhan
Department of Electrical and
  Electronics Engineering
Sreenidhi Institute of Science and
  Technology
Hyderabad, Telangana, India

Subhranshu Sekhar Puhan
Department of Electrical
  Engineering
Siksha 'O' Anusandhan Deemed to
  be University
Bhubaneswar, Orissa, India

O. Ray
School of Electrical Sciences
Indian Institute of Technology
  Bhubaneswar
Bhubaneswar, Orissa, India

M. Rizwan
Department of Electrical
   Engineering
Delhi Technological University
Rohini, Delhi, India

K. Sateesh Kumar
Electrical and Electronics
   Engineering
National Institute of Technology
   Tiruchirappalli
Tiruchirappalli, Tamil Nadu, India

Shelas Sathyan
Department of Electrical and
   Electronics Engineering
National Institute of Technology
   Tiruchirappalli
Tiruchirappalli, Tamil Nadu, India

Vikram Kumar Saxena
Department of Electrical
   Engineering
National Institute of Technology
   Manipur
Imphal, Manipur, India

Raghu Selvaraj
Electric Mobility and Tribology
   Research Group
CSIR-Central Mechanical
   Engineering Research Institute
   (CMERI)
Durgapur, West Bengal, India
and
Academy of Scientific and
   Innovative Research (AcSIR)
Ghaziabad, Uttar Pradesh, India

Siddheswar Sen
Electric Mobility and Tribology
   Research Group
CSIR-Central Mechanical
   Engineering Research Institute
   (CMERI)
Durgapur, West Bengal, India
and
Academy of Scientific and
   Innovative Research (AcSIR)
Ghaziabad, Uttar Pradesh, India

Renu Sharma
Department of Electrical
   Engineering
Siksha 'O' Anusandhan Deemed to
   be University
Bhubaneswar, Orissa, India

Bhim Singh
Department of Electrical
   Engineering
Indian Institute of Technology
   Delhi
Hauz Khas, New Delhi, India

Sreejith R.
Department of Electrical
   Engineering
Indian Institute of Technology
   Delhi
Hauz Khas, New Delhi, India

Chapter 1

Impact of EVs and its business case studies for the automobile market

Tanmoy Roy Choudhury, Dipankar Debnath, and Suman Majumder

1.1 ELECTRIC VEHICLES: INTRODUCTION AND TYPICAL ARCHITECTURE

A vehicle that employs one or more electric motors for propulsion is known as electric vehicle (EV). There are four broad categories of such vehicles:

a. **Battery Electric Vehicle (BEV):** This type of vehicle is powered by electricity only and is more efficient compared to hybrid and plug-in hybrids. Examples of such vehicles include Tesla Model 3, Audi e-tron, etc.

b. **Hybrid Electric Vehicle (HEV):** They employ both the internal combustion engine (ICE) and the electric motor powertrain, which is powered by a battery. The battery is charged using the IC engine and also through regenerative braking. There is no option to charge the battery by plugging in an EV charger. These vehicles are generally not as efficient as fully electric or plug-in hybrid vehicles. Examples of such vehicles include Honda Civic Hybrid, Toyota Camry Hybrid, etc.

c. **Plug-in Hybrid Electric Vehicle (PHEV):** They employ both an IC engine and motor for propulsion wherein the latter uses power from a battery charged from an external socket (plug-in option available). PHEVs are generally more efficient than HEVs but usually less efficient than BEVs. Examples of such vehicles include Ford fusion energy, BMW 330e, etc.

d. **Fuel Cell Electric Vehicle (FCEV):** These are hydrogen-powered vehicles that use a similar system as a BEV for propulsion. Hydrogen is stored in a gas tank and converted to electricity by using 'fuel cells'; thus, electric energy is produced from chemical energy. Examples of such vehicles include Hyundai Nexo FCEV, Toyota Mirai, etc.

The rest of this chapter focuses on BEV, which is referred to as EV in general.

DOI: 10.1201/9781003481065-1

1.1.1 Typical configuration of electric vehicles

A typical EV configuration consists of three major subsystems: electric motor propulsion, energy storage unit, and auxiliary, and a simplistic illustration of the same is shown in Figure 1.1. The electric propulsion subsystem comprises the electric motor, voltage source converter with a suitable motor control strategy, vehicle supervisory controller, transmission unit, drive shaft, and differential and driving wheels. The energy storage subsystem consists of energy storage (typically a battery bank), the energy/battery management unit, and the energy refuelling unit. The auxiliary subsystem consists of various auxiliary loads of the vehicle, viz., power steering unit, the temperature control unit, and a suitable auxiliary power supply unit to cater to the auxiliary loads.

The driver actuates the control inputs, i.e., brake, accelerator, and forward/reverse command as per requirement, and these non-electrical signals are first converted to electrical signals by employing a suitable conversion system. Based on the aforesaid control inputs, the vehicle controller provides proper control signals to the motor control unit (MCU), which consists of a voltage source inverter along with its controller. The MCU

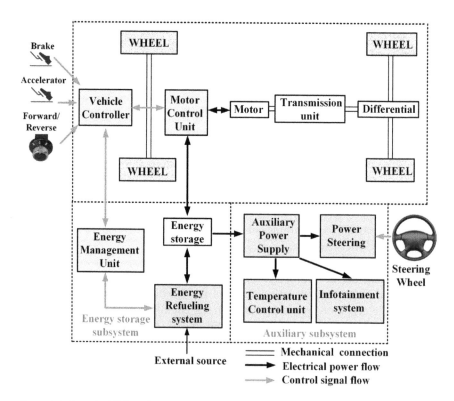

Figure 1.1 A typical EV configuration.

accordingly regulates the power flow between the electric motor and energy source. The power flow direction is from battery to motor during motoring mode of operation. The reverse power flow, i.e., power flow from motor to energy source, takes place during regenerative braking provided the energy source has the capability to absorb this power. The energy management unit helps to control the charging rate of the energy source, takes care of charge balance of individual units that form the complete energy source pack, and thus enhances the lifetime of the energy source. A comparative study (Table 1.4) of popular commercial models from several EV companies worldwide is provided in Annexure I. The comparison is made on several important aspects, viz. e-range, battery type and capacity, motor type, maximum power and torque rating of motor employed, top speed, acceleration time, etc.

1.2 HISTORY OF EV

Horses and buggies were the main form of transportation in the past, but scientists from the USA, Hungary, and the Netherlands dreamed of a small-scale EV for the future, which led to the creation of the first rudimentary EV by Robert Anderson in or around 1832. The practical EV, on the other hand, wasn't invented until much later, possibly in the 1870s or later. The successful EV debut in the USA reported during 1889–1891 was developed by William Morrison from Des Moines, Lowa. Owing to the advantages such as less audible noise, easy to drive, and no pollutant emission, the EV had attained larger popularity among the urban women residents. To improve the technology, in 1901, Thomas Alva Edison concentrated on upgrading the battery used to power the EVs.

The world's first HEV was invented by Ferdinand Porche in 1901 where the vehicle was powered by a battery and a gas engine. However, a decline in EVs seen during 1920–1935 due to the improved road quality and cheaper crude oil, and by that time, the gas-powered vehicles gained popularity in the American market. Over the next 30 years, the extensive use of fossil fuels leads to rising prices of gases and oil, thus creating interest in EVs again. In 1971, NASA's Lunar rover was driven by electricity on the moon and regained the profile of EVs. For the next few years, different companies have started exploring alternative fuel vehicles, among which EVs have got the maximum attention due to certain advantages, which are discussed in this chapter in successive sections. Many conventional ICE vehicle manufacturers turned their focus on the emerging EV sector leading to the first commercial electric vehicle launched in 2010 by General Motors. Soon after that, the era of vehicle electrification has been extensively witnessed across the globe during the second decade of 21st century. For minute to minute details, one can visit the source of this portion as mentioned in Ref. [1].

The contribution of EV in greenhouse gas (GHG) emission reduction has proved quite promising since the past decade. There are different types of mass transport systems used around the world. Some of them are metro rails, trolley buses, trams, pods, monorails, etc.

Evaluation of the mass transit options for urban cities shows that metro systems get more preference than road-based bus system because of their high-capacity accommodation. A metro rail is a high-capacity train that runs with high speed on an exclusive pathway and is independent from other traffic roads. The first rail-based metro line was completed in London in 1863 [2], the first elevated railway in New York City in 1868, and the first line of the Paris network in 1900 [3]. Around 148 cities have a metro system, and there are close to 540 lines in total and they carry over 150 million passengers per day [4]. Two-thirds of the world's metro systems are located in Asia and Europe [5]. Statistics shows that the length of world's metro lines is 11,000 km with 9,000 metro stations with an average distance of 1.2 km between the stations.

Second is trolleybus which is among one of the most common on-road urban transit systems and a readily available solution for reducing the city-level pollution. The trolleybus is a proven public transit system being operated in over 56 countries (310 cities worldwide), and more than 40,000 trolleybuses are in operation in the world [6]. The trolleybus uses the dynamic charging provided by the direct contact with the overhead supply lines.

Third is tram, which is electrically operated, pollution-free, with a high carrying capacity and lifetime, is the most feasible option for crowded cities. Populated cities of the world are reviving the Tramways system since it runs on electricity. The world's first electric tram line operated in Sestroretsk near Saint Petersburg, Russia. These were common in the late 19th century, but during the mid-20th century, they disappeared from many cities. Trams use overhead electric contact wires, and the current is drawn through trolley poles.

Monorail, as the name suggests, is a railway which has a single rail track, and it operates on elevated guideways. The guideway is a beam, a concrete structure that measures around 2 feet in width on which the vehicles either ride on or are suspended. Monorail vehicles use rubber tyres that provide traction and also make them quieter with respect to other modes of transport. The first monorail prototype was made in Russia in 1820 by Ivan Elmanov [7].

Maglev is among the futuristic technologies in the transport sector. Maglev vehicle employs electromagnets as a suspension and linear motors for its propulsion. The train's levitation capabilities due to the magnets and their control make it frictionless [8]. It uses the basic theory of magnetism i.e., like pole attract and unlike poles repel. Maglev can achieve high speed as it does not have any contact with the floor [9,10], and this has made the trains in Japan to exceed the speed of 600 km/h.

The last one is Hyperloop, a concept created by Elon Musk in 2012 [11], is a proposed mode of mass transit and would propel a pod-like vehicle through a reduced pressure tube. The vehicles would use linear induction motor to drive on the tracks using passive levitation and air compressors [12].

Implementing these existing and futuristic mass transit systems in developing countries has to overcome a number of challenges imposed due to limited space, weak grids, and high investments. The metro rail has the benefit of reduced congestion on road due to their underground and elevated construction. But the available road space fills up with motorised vehicles due to their increased demands. The capital cost of construction is also high, i.e., 20–30 times than that of bus transit system. Trams and trolleybuses have similar drawbacks of expensive investment at approximately 5–10 times of the bus transit system. They also have dependent infrastructure, which makes them inflexible, and Indian cities already have space issues. Monorail too imposes similar issues of dedicated space and a high investment in terms of million USD for per km of construction costs. The evolution of EVs during the last two centuries is summarised in Figure 1.2.

1.3 ADVANTAGES AND DISADVANTAGES OF EV

1.3.1 Advantages of EVs

a. **Reduction in CO_2 emissions:** Transportation sector uses approximately one-third of total energy worldwide. The major part of this transportation energy comes from petroleum products and, hence, is directly linked with harmful CO_2 emissions. Electricity-based transportation can help reduce CO_2 emissions. It is estimated that usage of 100% EVs can cut CO_2 emissions by half. This will further enhance if electricity, being used to charge the EV batteries, is generated from renewable energy sources.

b. **Low running and maintenance cost:** Though EV has higher capital cost, the overall life cycle cost is lesser than ICEV as EVs have low running and maintenance cost.

c. **Depleting nature of conventional fuel:** Recent studies suggest that the conventional fuel being employed in vehicles will be depleted in about 40 years if extracted at the present rate [13]. Thus, the transportation sector needs to focus on alternate fuels, which proffered EVs as one of the most promising solutions.

d. **Performance benefits:** EV users experience quieter and smoother operation, stronger acceleration, and less maintenance as compared to ICEVs.

e. **Overall efficiency is better than ICEV:** Electrical energy from grid to power at the wheels has typically 59%–62% efficiency for EVs, whereas energy stored in gasoline to power at the wheels has typically 17%–21% efficiency for ICEVs.

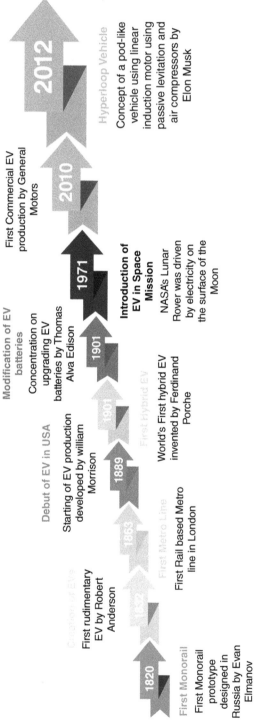

Figure 1.2 Evolution of electric vehicles in the last two centuries.

f. **Reduce energy dependency:** EVs require electricity which is a domestic energy source. Hence, it helps to reduce energy dependency, especially for those countries which need to depend on fossil fuel imports required for ICEVs.

g. **Friend to grid:** The energy stored in EV batteries clubbed with a bidirectional charger can be utilised to support the electricity grid when required. This mode of operation is known as Vehicle to Grid (V2G), and it can support the grid in various ways, viz. peak loading support, reactive power compensation, harmonic compensation, etc. Further, the EV battery back along with a bidirectional charger can also be configured to cater emergency loads in a household when there is a power cut. Such operation is termed as Vehicle to Home (V2H).

h. **Regeneration:** During braking, the kinetic energy of the vehicle can be partially transferred back to the battery, thereby enhancing the overall efficiency of the system and reducing wear and tear problems in the mechanical arrangements.

i. **Government support:** To enhance EV adoptions, several governments worldwide offer additional perks viz. tax reduction, reduced loan interest, toll fee reduction, green number plates, etc.

1.3.2 Disadvantages of EVs

a. **Lower driving range:** One of the major concerns for EVs over their IC engine counterpart is their e-range, which is on the lower side. Typically, the e-range is limited to 60–120 miles on a full charge, although a few models can go 200–400 miles, whereas the ICEVs have an average range of around 350–400 miles.

b. **Longer recharge time and unavailability of adequate fast charging stations:** Another disadvantage for EVs is their longer recharge time requirement. To fully recharge the battery pack in EV, it can take 4–8 hours. Even a 'fast charge' to 80% of the capacity can take 30 minutes. Further, the fast charging stations are not available frequently. On the contrary, to refuel an ICE vehicle, it takes a few minutes, and there are ample fuel stations already existing.

c. **Higher initial cost:** The initial cost of buying an EV in most of the countries is generally 1.5–2 times higher than ICEVs. This higher cost is due to the costly EV batteries and the use of high-end technologies.

d. **Maturity of technology:** The EV industry is still evolving, and hence, is having less maturity than ICEVs. In addition, the availability of fewer service stations equipped with required trained human power is also a demotivating factor for new EV buyers.

e. **Low resale value:** EV technology is en route rapid advancement, and the introduction of new feature rich EV models is on offer every now and then. As a consequence, the resale value of second-hand EVs is too low.

1.4 GOVERNMENT POLICY AND INITIATIVES ON EV

As per a recent global scenario, the transport sector is a major contributor to CO_2 emissions (around 24%) from fuel combustion, whereas, in some countries, it becomes the largest single source of GHG emissions [14,15]. The associated impact on air pollution, health hazards, climate change, etc. are the key contributions to the society leading to noncompliance with sustainable development goals (SGDs) 3 and 13. However, these issues can be combated with the appropriate inclusion of EVs on a larger scale. Most of the nations agreed to this point, and in fact, the developing countries like India have already set their mission to adopt around 30% vehicles to be EVs by 2030 [16]. Due to the huge capital investment required for these EVs and the lack of enthusiasm shown by the majority of citizens, this goal unintentionally confronts increased difficulties. In addition, fewer other factors, such as design constraints, limited driving range, unreliable technology, etc., seem to be further hindrance to the popularity of EVs [16,17].

As per World Bank data, the EV market is widespread in developed countries such as the USA, China, and Europe; however, in developing countries, the adoption seems indolent. Figure 1.3 shows the electric car sales data worldwide, which indicates higher EV adoption in developed countries rather than the developing countries. According to a study, developing countries across the continents can aspire to get economic benefits through adopting EVs [19]. In addition, the higher upfront cost can be optimised with reduced operating costs, a step towards reduced carbon footprint for a sustainable society.

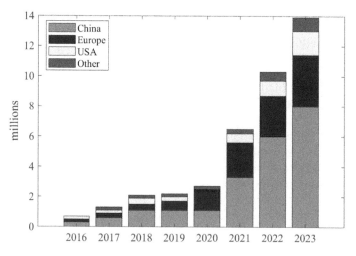

Figure 1.3 Electric car sales data country-wise during 2016–2023 published by IEA, Paris [18].

To prioritise the emerging EV market, the governments of various nations have taken several initiatives through enhanced budget allocation for infrastructure development, consumer and industry incentives, and amended regulations as per requirements [20,21]. For example, in the UK, the Government has planned to stop sales of conventional ICE vehicles (cars and vans) by 2030 and to adopt completely zero-emission vehicles by 2035. Meanwhile, the Government is also believed to set up a minimum of 300,000 charging stations within that time frame to cater to EVs [22]. Further to that, the trend of price reduction of EVs in comparison with ICE vehicles as reported in Refs. [22,23], which is almost 10%–14% for different segments of EVs, will be the topping to the ice cream. To speed up the market adoption of EVs, the Chinese government has adopted a range of incentives since 2009. These include financial incentives, privilege rewards, demonstration incentives, and charging incentives [24]. Policies that combine financial incentives with administrative restraints, such as purchase subsidies, purchase tax exemptions, and vehicle purchase limitations, are more effective in raising the short-term demand for EVs. On the whole, though, policies that mix privilege incentives, charging incentives, and demonstration incentives are more successful at hastening the adoption of EVs. Examples include removing restrictions on buying and driving, enhancing charging infrastructure, engaging in public procurement, and increasing the cost of fossil fuels [24]. Similarly, Government of India has started devising initiatives with the adoption of National Council for Electric Mobility (NCEM) since 2011. Indian Government initiatives excelled through the flagship scheme namely Faster Adoption and Manufacturing of (Hybrid and) Electric Vehicles (FAME) – Phases I and II with a collective investment of over INR 10,000 Cr. Under this scheme, the buyers are entitled to some incentives as mentioned in Table 1.1. In India, apart from the direct incentives, several other benefits are also provided to the customers in terms of loan on reduced rate, road tax and registration fee exemption, income

Table 1.1 Incentives offered by Government of India under FAME scheme to promote EV utilisation [25]

Sl. no.	Vehicle class	Approx. incentive/ kWh (in $)	Approx. size of battery (kWh)	Remarks
1	Two Wheeler (2W)	175	2	Almost 40% vehicle cost is covered
2	Three Wheeler (3W)	120	5	NA
3	Four Wheeler (4W)	120	15	NA
4	E – Buses	240	250	NA
5	E – Trucks	240	NA	NA

NA stands for Not Available.

tax benefits, scrapping benefits of older ICE vehicles, etc. [24,25]. The US Government has also implemented tax credit eligibility for EV customers (having a battery capacity 7 kWh or above) based on critical mineral requirements and battery component requirements with $3,750 each case [26]. As an example of local incentives, the authority of New Orleans, in partnership with Entergy New Orleans, planned to set up around 30 EV charging stations for residents to access free charging facility [27]. Many other examples can also be seen in the website of the US Department of Energy website, as mentioned in Ref. [27].

In addition to those policy advancements, the EV manufacturers of the USA, France, Germany, and the UK are now focused on extending the driving range of such EVs to a range of 300–350 km (may be with limited options). However, China is still fighting with a constraint of range extension which is restricted to 220 km only. Further, different nations, like the USA, Europe, Japan, Russia, etc., enhanced their investments towards research and development on battery technologies to become self-sufficient in the years to come [28]. Apart from such incentivised policies, some areas are declared to be low emission zones (LEZ) as adopted by the inhabitants of such favouring EVs. For instance, London and Milan have already implemented this concept, which has been in force for many years [28].

As per the recent reports of International Energy Agency (IEA), China is leading the EV market with around 60% of global EV sales, whereas the second and third positions are attained by Europe and the USA, respectively. Further, the worldwide sales growth of around 25% is seen during the first quarter of 2023 and expecting to cross 14 million units to be sold by the end of this year [28]. Even though the largest share of EVs can be seen in developed countries as mentioned above, substantial growth has been witnessed in India, Indonesia, and Thailand during 2022. In India, EV growth is reinforced by the Government's $3.2 billion incentive scheme, which further attracted $8.3 billion investments in this field. Apparently, Indonesia and Thailand are also developing their policies such that expertise can be shared with potential market places urging them to nurture EV implementation [28].

As the implications of EV policies are in force, a substantial amount of GHG emissions are projected to be reduced by 2030, which can be witnessed in Figure 1.4. During 2022, a mere amount of 80 Mt of GHG emissions were reduced through EVs, where only China has contributed around 30% of the global emission reductions through the electrification of passenger vehicles. In the Stated Policies Scenario (STEPS), by 2030 overall GHG emission can be avoided by 700 Mt CO_2 equivalent by implementing EV. However, at that time, electricity production to supply those EVs will lead to 290 Mt equivalent of CO_2 emission, which is still considerably less compared to CO_2 emissions (980 Mt) by the ICE vehicles. Similarly, in the Announced Pledges Scenario (APS), the overall GHG

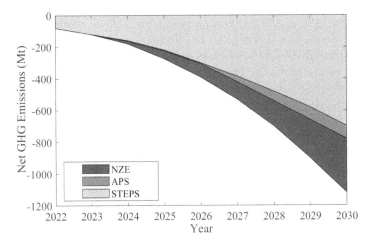

Figure 1.4 Net GHG emission reduction during 2022–2030 as reported in Ref. [28] in line with NZE=Net Zero Emissions, APS=Announced Pledges Scenario, STEPS=Stated Policies Scenario.

emissions to be reduced by 770 Mt CO_2 equivalent. With the ever increasing trend of EV, a further reduction in GHG emissions is just a matter to wait for [29]. As per studies in Ref. [17], the authors have claimed that on average, 1% deployment of EV results in 0.5% GHG emissions. Thus, the importance of EV in a future sustainable society is much understood from such studies. This will further boost attaining the UN SDGs (3 & 13) to a greater extent.

1.5 BUSINESS CASE STUDIES OF EV WORLDWIDE

The year 2022 seems to be a record year in terms of electric light duty vehicles (eLDV) sales even with issues with supply chain, economic and geopolitical uncertainties, higher price of energy and commodities. Even though the overall car sales have dipped by 3% in 2022, the growth of EV sales including BEV and PHEV is commendable across the globe. Substantial growth in EV sales is witnessed during the last 5 years (2017–2022) resulting in units sold as 1–10 million, whereas during the previous 5 years (2012–2017), it had jumped from 100,000 to 1 million only. In addition, the percentage of EV sales increased from 9% in 2021 to 14% in 2022, which is ten times greater than their stake in 2017 [28].

As per reports by IEA in the EV Outlook, China has outperformed in 2022 where almost 60% of the global eLDVs were registered accounting for 13.8 million units. This led to the early achievement of their national target, which is planned to achieve by 2025. In Europe, electric car sales have been extended by 15% in 2022 in comparison with 2021 to reach 2.77 million units. The European Union (EU) has shown consistent growth averaged to 40% during 2017–2019, whereas in 2021, it has reached 65% in terms of growth rate. Among the EU countries, Norway has held the baton with 88% of EV sales share, successively other countries such as Sweden 54%, the Netherlands 35%, Germany 31%, the UK 23%, and France 21% also maintained their position in the race. However, in a few of the EU countries such as Italy, Austria, Denmark, and Finland, the EV trend is slowed down due to certain reasons. The USA has reported their growth of 55% in 2022 relative to 2021 towards EV car sales. EV sales in India have also substantially grown, and an impressive three-wheeler sales figures to 425,000 units are sold in 2022. Keeping an eye on the increasing demand of worldwide EV sales, the manufacturers are also focusing on the availability of a higher number of models where in 2021 it was 450, whereas, in 2022, the options reached 500 [28].

If the average cost of the vehicle is a concern, here also China has the dominance where in 2022, the average cost of a small BEV is below $10,000, whereas in the USA, the same segment is available at $30,000. The Chinese car manufacturers have the intention to develop EVs in smaller and more affordable models ahead of their international competitors and reduce production cost. In contrast, the EV manufacturers of the EU and USA have mostly focused on luxury and/or larger segments of the vehicles leading to a higher cost. With higher cost of such vehicles, a better option of longer driving range is also attained through these EVs, which is not available in most of the Chinese vehicles. To compete with the global market, the manufacturers in the USA have also started reducing the cost of their vehicles. For example, Tesla has heavily reduced the price of its models on two occasions leading to a competitive price range that may be predicted in the near future. In the same order, the heavy duty vehicle industry is also gradually approaching towards the adoption of electrification in some countries [28].

There was a major constraint of the non-availability of sufficient models in the EV sector in the past; however, the data revealed in Global Drive to Zero Emission Technology Inventory (ZETI) database indicates that around 840 models of medium and heavy duty vehicles will be available in a near term, including current models [28,29]. The model variations are also in line with a wider development in terms of enhancing the battery capacity, as can be seen in Table 1.2, accessed through the ZETI tool [28,30]. It is apparent from the data analysis that the battery capacity enhancement, which in turn is useful for range extension, is also carried out looking into the recent market trend.

In addition to the above-mentioned advancement, public charging facilities are also required to be uplifted. The majority of charging requirements

Table 1.2 Summary of battery capacity development in medium and heavy duty vehicles during 2019–2022 [28,30]

Vehicle category	Average battery capacity (kWh)				
	2019	2020	2021	2022	Change 2019–2022
Shuttle bus	104	119	120	150	45%
Transit bus	264	322	225	345	31%
Yard tractor	150	184	160	197	31%
Medium duty step van	–	134	155	163	22%
Heavy duty truck	293	232	372	311	6%
School bus	155	141	207	137	−12%
Cargo vans	69	90	57	60	−13%
Coach	316	347	233	266	−16%
Medium duty truck	124	139	99	92	−26%

Source: Sourced from IEA analysis based on the Global Drive to Zero ZETI tool database.

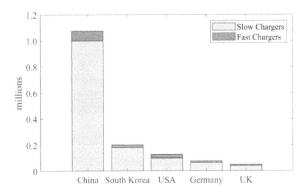

Figure 1.5 Number of publicly available EV chargers in 2022 as per records with statista.com [32].

are now met by home charging, but in order to increase the acceptance of EVs by a larger population, public charging infrastructure is urgently needed to make it as simple as refuelling traditional ICE vehicles. According to sources in Ref. [28], there were 2.7 million charging points installed globally by the end of 2022, with just 0.9 million of those installations occurring in that year. The global trend (through the major EV implementing countries) of EV charging stations (slow and fast chargers) can be viewed in Figure 1.5. However, in India, according to the data of Bureau of Energy Efficiency (BEE) and the Ministry of Power, as of June 2023, there are 8,738 operational EV charging stations available across the country, with a goal to install 46,397 charging stations by 2030 [31].

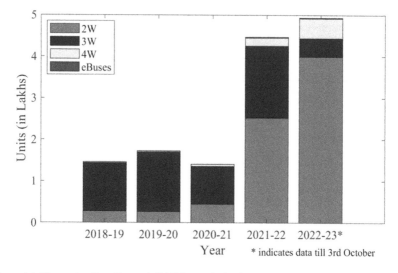

Figure 1.6 Year-wise (last 5 years) EV Sales in India for all major vehicle segments (*here 2W stands for 2 wheeler, and so on*).

As of date, the development of battery swapping entails the heavy duty vehicles, especially in China, replacing the drained battery with a charged one. This reduces the charging time in between, reducing short-range anxiety, and purchasing parity with conventional ICE vehicles. Further, the driver has the autonomy to choose the right capacity of the battery based on the trip distance, i.e., for a shorter distance, a low-capacity battery can be hired, whereas for a longer distance, larger battery can be procured leading to operating cost optimisation of such vehicles. However, this technology has so far been largely implemented for heavy duty trucks, but in the future, all segments of EVs can adopt this technique for better utilisation of the vehicles. Owing to the advancement of policies, infrastructure, environmental consciousness, etc. among the people, a sharp shoot in EV sales of all major segments (2W, 3W, 4W, and e-Buses) in India can be witnessed in Figure 1.6. The data presented here is adopted from the sources mentioned in Ref. [33]. The fall in sales during 2020–2021 may be due to the restrictions of COVID-19.

1.6 IMPACT OF EV AND ECONOMICS

1.6.1 Need for electrification of vehicle

Air pollution is an alarming concern worldwide, which results in global temperature rise and health hazards. Air pollution is caused by the emission of pollutants from various sources. Hence, emission reduction is a global mission, and countries worldwide are working towards this goal. Transportation system using ICEs are one of the major contributors towards emission. Since transportation needs rise with increasing population, emission intensity reduction steps should be implemented soon to affect global emission reduction. In this regard, transportation network electrification is a possible solution. However, electrifying only transit systems will not have much impact without energy policy evolution and renewable source share enhancement.

1.6.2 The global approach

Air pollution is presently a global concern, and the rapidly increasing air pollutant levels are conditioned into air quality deterioration. In 2018, countries such as India, Bangladesh, and many others across the world had a record of the lowest air quality [34]. The poor air quality due to the presence of air pollutants such as NO_x, SO_x, and particulate matter (PM) results in cardiovascular diseases and risks of cancer. Hence when in 2018, the world saw the poorest air quality index, and the World Health Organization (WHO) reported 600,000 deaths every year caused due to it.

In addition, along with environmental health risks, the GHGs, which are one of the primary air pollutants, resulted in global warming. During 2012, the global carbon footprint reached 55.6 Gt (of CO_2), which is 43% higher than that of 2000 levels. Thus, the year 2018 was the warmest year recorded in Europe, the Middle East, New Zealand, and parts of Asia [35]. A similar report by the IEA revealed that India emitted 2,299 Mt of CO_2 in 2018, which is 4.8% higher than the 2017 level. A further in-depth study states that 73% of the global carbon footprint is from the transport sector.

Many studies are conducting zero-emission public transport services. The Netherlands is working on the National Climate Agreement (NCA) that includes steps to reduce GHG emissions by 49% (in comparison with the levels in 1990) by 2030. In early 2016, there were 90,275 registered EVs in the Netherlands. Similarly, Germany has approximately 30 E-bus ongoing projects with various charging concepts. For example, Berlin (present fleet-size of 1,300 buses) procured 30 single decks and 15 articulated E-buses by 2019 (with inductive and pantograph charging). With these numbers, Germany aims to achieve a 55% reduction in GHG emissions by 2030.

North America has actively participated in the cause where the transport sector contributes 24% of the total emission in Canada. Canadian cities, such as Toronto, Montreal, and Vancouver, have committed to not buying diesel vehicles from 2020 onwards. The Government of Canada aims to achieve a 30% reduction in emissions by 2030 (in comparison with that in 2005). The Chicago Transit Authority (CTA) tested e-buses and reported that their use saved more than $24,000 in fuel costs and $30,000 in maintenance costs each year. CTA is currently working to achieve full-fleet electrification by 2040.

Asian countries are also working toward implementing E-mobility. Ministry of the Environment, Government of Japan, performed a long-term test of E-buses to assess their impact on the environment and energy costs [36]. The test report reveals that E-buses resulted in 28%–42% lesser emission and 57%–64% lesser energy cost compared to that of ICE vehicles. The studies conducted in the cities of China to analyse the environmental impacts of E-buses show that the E-buses are capable of reducing 30%–40% well-to-wheel GHG emissions.

1.6.3 Environmental impact

The above numbers from countries around the globe elaborate on the importance of transportation sector. Meanwhile, it should be noted that the source of electric vehicle, i.e., electricity and its generation, is not clean and therefore completely shifting towards EV is not an effective solution to emission reduction. Hence, generation of electricity by renewable energy sources like solar and wind, etc., should be opted for. Renewable sources for electricity generation will have two advantages. First, it will help in reducing emission from electricity production. Second, it will help reduce dependency on fossil fuel.

Looking into the major advantages of renewable energy-based transportation system on environment. It is well known that renewable energy sources have negligible emission. Hence, implementing the same in running the vehicles on road will significantly reduce the tail-pipe emission. The vehicular emissions mostly contribute towards CO_2 pollutants, and with clean fuel the GHG emission can be lowered and therefore help combat the drastic climate change. In addition, less emission will help improve the air quality and thereby reduce the health hazards caused by the same. Along with air pollution, electrification of vehicles also helps to reduce noise pollution as EVs are quieter than the conventional ICE vehicles. Thus, it aids towards reducing noise pollution in urban areas, resulting in a much pleasant environment.

1.6.4 Economic impact

The mass transition from ICE vehicles to EV would have both positive and negative impact on the nation's economy. The impact, in particular, depends upon factors such as characteristics of the region, government policies, and the rate of adoption of EVs. The positive economic aspects of EV are as follows:

a. **Job opportunities:** In this context, the EV manufacturing, related research and development will open doors for job opportunities. The production facilities regarding the constituents of an EV and development of charging infrastructure will provide new jobs.

Table 1.3 Summary of EV impact on environmental and economic aspects

Environmental aspects	Less/negligible tail-pipe emission
	Less contribution of pollutants like CO_2, SO_x, NO_x, and PM
	Slow down climate change
	Better air quality
	Less human health issues caused by pollutants
	Can help to reduce reliability on fossil fuel with implementation of renewable energy sources in energy sector
Economic aspects	Increase employment opportunities in EV production
	Increase research and development related to EV
	New jobs with establishment of charging infrastructure facilities
	Encourage investment in green fuel in energy and transport sector
	Innovation opportunities on battery and driving technologies
	Less health cost incorporated due to better air quality

b. **Energy sector:** Where EVs with integration of green energy will reduce fossil fuel dependency, the energy sector itself will have a hike in electricity demand. It will also promote the use of renewable generation, due to which green sources will require great investments.

c. **Technical advancements:** The EV technology will attract innovation in the area of battery technology, drive train, and connectivity between vehicles and consumers.

d. **Health cost:** EVs are popular due to their almost no emission policies. In this regard, with better air quality, there are possibilities to spend less on health issues caused by poor air quality.

A summary of the environmental and economic aspects is maintained in Table 1.3.

1.7 CHALLENGES AND RESEARCH OPPORTUNITIES

1.7.1 EV drivetrain is not yet a mature technology

Unlike ICEVs, the drivetrain of EV is not yet a very mature technology, and hence, there exists scope for further improvement and innovations. Figure 1.7a presents an EV drivetrain configuration having a motor (M), a clutch (C), a gear box (GB), and differential (D). This configuration is most common in ICEV converted EVs. The lower gears are used to run the vehicle at low speed and high torque, whereas higher gears are used during low torque and high-speed operation. The clutch box is required to

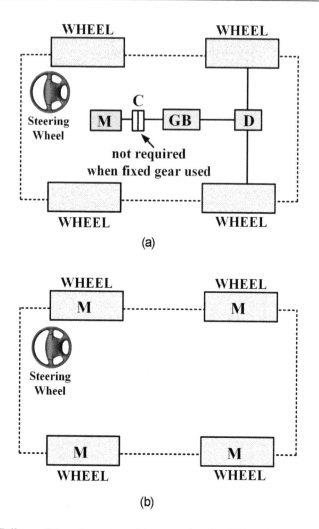

Figure 1.7 Different EV configurations: (a) conventional and (b) multi-wheel drive.

engage and disengage the motor from the rest of the drivetrain during gear shifting stages similar to ICEVs. With proper selection and/or design of the motor and associated control strategy, some of the mechanical components of the drivetrain can be avoided. This leads to enhanced efficiency and reduction in weight and volume. A configuration eliminating clutch, GB, and differential is shown in Figure 1.7b, for example, which belongs to the category all-wheel drive or multi-wheel drive. Such configuration requires an advanced control strategy and multi-disciplinary knowledge for proper distribution of torque on the multiple drive wheels.

1.7.2 Heavy dependency on electronics and requirement for various protections

EVs are heavily dependent on electronic components, some of which are subjected to harsh conditions as compared to their counterparts employed in favourable domestic applications. The tough conditions to which electronic components of EVs are subjected to include but are not limited to, noise and vibrations, chances of getting exposed to dust and water, wide variation in humidity, temperature and altitude, etc. To address these concerns, the electronic components need special automotive grade compliance and several protections to ensure required lifetime. Some of the required protections are as follows: (i) Accidental reverse polarity protection in regard to connection of the battery and power supply; (ii) inrush current protection; (iii) over voltage protection; (iv) overcurrent protection; (v) over temperature protection; (vi) shoot-through protection; (vii) protection from voltage spikes due to parasitic inductances; (viii) ingress protection (IP); (ix) sensor fault detection and mitigation strategy, etc.

The challenge to make EVs more robust and reliable has increased research opportunities in various fields, viz., fault studies and mitigation of electric motors and controllers (fault tolerant drives), functional safety, etc.

1.7.3 Concern regarding range anxiety and charging time

One of the major challenges for mass EV adoption is range anxiety. The longer time (around 4–8 hours) requirement for charging of the battery and the unavailability of adequate fast charging stations contribute adversely to this problem. However, it also brings opportunities for research. Some of the key research areas related to this concern are as follows:

a. Research on advanced battery chemistry/material and associated analysis for increasing power and energy density while reducing its cost. Making the battery manufacturing process more sustainable and eco-friendly is also one of the major areas of research. Some widely studied materials for battery are sodium, graphene, carbon nanotube electrode, cobalt free batteries, aluminium-air, etc.
b. Development of fast and slow chargers with high efficiency. The use of wide bandgap semiconductor devices in the power converter and higher dc voltage levels is gaining huge research interest.
c. Battery swap technique is another area where lots of research work is being carried out. It includes, but is not limited to, compact battery pack design for ease of removal and fitting, automatic battery swappable stations, optimum location selection, business model development, etc.

d. Design and development of various types of wireless charging methods, viz., inductive charging, capacitive charging, hybrid charging, etc. In addition to static wireless charging, research on dynamic wireless charging is gaining huge popularity. In dynamic wireless charging the vehicle can be charged when the vehicle is on the move. One set of coils is embedded on the road structure,and is energised with high frequency AC supply. The other coil, i.e., the receiving coil, is placed on the vehicle, which receives the energy and then transfers it to the battery of the vehicle through a suitable power electronic interface. As the vehicle battery can be charged when the vehicle is moving on road, the battery size can be reduced which leads to reduction of cost, weight, and volume. The dynamic wireless charging mechanism is shown using the block diagram representation in Figure 1.8.

1.7.4 Inadequate availability of charging stations

Even though the popularity of EVs is on the rise, the inadequate availability of charging stations is still a major concern that hinders mass EV adoption. More than technology itself, the challenge is on the planning and profitable business strategy development, which is attracting several researchers to carry out further research in this area.

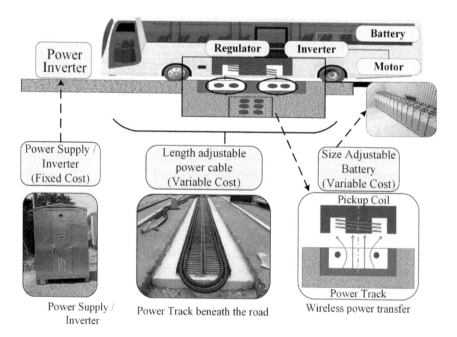

Figure 1.8 Demonstration of dynamic wireless charging [37].

1.7.5 Further reduction in CO_2 emission through electricity generation from non-polluting resources

Even though the EVs don't have tail-pipe CO_2 emissions, they are not entirely free from it as most of the electricity generated is from fossil fuel-based power plants. Thus, for further reduction in CO_2 emission, attention is being provided to promote electricity generation from non-polluting resources, viz., solar, sind, hydro, etc. However, most of these sources are intermittent in nature and hence need proper planning along with storage features for a reliable power supply. In addition, renewable energy-based charging stations are also getting wide attention from the research communities.

1.7.6 High penetration of charging stations may impact grid stability

With higher adoption of EVs, the installations of the charging stations are on the rise. As the charging stations require power electronic interface, they have associated concerns, viz., harmonic injection, reduced inertia, etc. The impact of such high penetrations of charging stations on the traditional power system brings in scope for research, planning, and optimisation.

1.7.7 Inadequate availability of rare earth magnet for permanent magnet motors

At present, the majority of the commercial EVs use permanent magnet synchronous motor (PMSM) for the propulsion. These motors employ rare earth permanent magnets, which are available only in very few countries, and their reserves are limited. As a result, their cost is increasing. Further, such motors are also at the risk of demagnetisation due to high-temperature operating conditions, high demagnetising current, etc. This opens up opportunities for research on motors ,which either do not require magnets or can be designed with less amount of magnets or non-rare earth magnets, for example, switched reluctance motors (SRM), synchronous reluctance motors (SyRM), etc. However, these motors come with their own challenges and hence brings along research opportunities.

1.7.8 Unavailability of adequately trained human power

As the EV industry is still evolving, the unavailability of adequately trained human power is still a major concern. This opens up opportunities for several educational institutions to create suitable courses to cater to the needs of the EV industry.

1.7.9 Availability and cost of lithium batteries

At present, the majority of the commercial EVs use lithium-based batteries as the energy storage medium. Unfortunately, they are available in only very few countries, and their reserves are limited. As a result, their cost is increasing. This calls for research in the alternate battery chemistry and manufacturing process.

1.7.10 Recycling and reuse of EV batteries after their end of life for EV application

When the State of Health (SoH) of EV batteries hits the 70%–80% mark, they are generally discarded from EV application. Such batteries can be recycled to extract the major materials, viz., lithium, cobalt, nickel, and other metals. However, this recycling method is a costly affair and also needs sophisticated arrangement. Fortunately, some of these discarded batteries can be still utilised for some other applications without recycling, for example, as a storage unit for solar photovoltaic systems. Such applications are termed as second life applications. However, these second life batteries differ from each other in several aspects, for example, ageing, state of charge, SoH, etc. Hence, developing an energy storage unit with such heterogeneous battery packs is a challenge and requires a smart power electronic interface with associated control mechanism.

1.7.11 Low resale values

At present, the second-hand EVs don't have a good market value. Attempts can be made to address this concern by making EV parts reusable after their first usage.

1.7.12 Need for highly efficient and compact power converters

EVs need power electronic converters for various purposes, viz., motor controller, battery charger, power supply for auxiliary loads, etc. There are several challenges and research opportunities in designing such converters, viz. (i) design of wide bandgap based solution operating at high switching frequency thereby leading to reduction in size, weight vehicle increasing efficiency, (ii) multi-level based architecture for vehicles which requires high-voltage DC bus/battery, (iii) compact multi-port converters to cater for different voltage levels instead of applying dedicated single stage converter for each voltage levels, (iv) integrated/multifunctional battery charger which can also serve other purposes, viz., motor controller, V2G operation, V2H operation, V2V operation, etc.

1.7.13 Enhancement of modern features

The EV industry is evolving at a high speed, and every now and then, new models are hitting the road with new features. This has created more expectations from the buyer who keeps on looking for the new features. Along with interesting features, there is ever increasing demand for safety enhancement. The present trend is to provide even low end or light duty vehicles with such features albeit in a cost-effective manner. Some of these features are listed below: (i) enhancement in Artificial Intelligence (AI)-enabled features, viz., pedestrian detection, remaining energy based route planning, predictive maintenance, etc., (ii) sleep eye/fatigue detection and suitable driver assistance for preventing accidents, (iii) lane departure/ frontal collision warning/ side collision prevention, (iv) night vision, (v) virtual side mirror (based on camera), (vi) augmented reality dashboard, (vii) reconfigurable/multipurpose vehicle, (viii) enhanced theft prevention, (ix) smart headlight (to automatic shift from beamer to softer light), etc.

REFERENCES

1. "The History of the Electric Car," Department of Energy, Federal Govt., 2014. https://www.energy.gov/articles/history-electric-car.
2. B. P. Y. Loo, J. R. Bryson, M. Song, and C. Harris, "Risking multi-billion decisions on underground railways: Land value capture, differential rent and financialization in London and Hong Kong," *Tunn. Undergr. Space Technol.*, vol. 81, pp. 403–412, 2018.
3. C. L. Galviz, "The polities of a new technology: Electricity and the city railway in London and Paris, c. 1880–1910," *Métropoles*, vol. 6, 2009. https://doi.org/10.4000/metropoles.3920.
4. X. Fu and Y. Gu, "Impact of a new metro line: Analysis of metro passenger flow and travel time based on smart card data," *J. Adv. Transp.*, vol. 2018, 13p, 2018. https://doi.org/10.1155/2018/9247102.
5. M. R. Killada and G. V. R. Raju, "World's top economies and their metro systems' ridership and financial performance," *Int. J. Traffic .Transp. Eng.*, vol. 7, no. 4, pp. 91–97, 2018. https://doi.org/10.5923/j.ijtte.20180704.03.
6. M. Połom, "Technology development and spatial diffusion of auxiliary power sources in trolleybuses in european countries," *Energies*, vol. 14, no. 11, p. 3040, 2021. https://doi.org/10.3390/en14113040.
7. Wikipedia contributors. Wikipedia contributors. https://en.wikipedia.org/w/index.php?title=Monorail&oldid=1206711886.
8. G. Yang and Z. Tang, "The analysis of high-speed wheel rail train and high-speed maglev train safety systems" *Proceedings of ICSSSM 05. 2005 International Conference on Services Systems and Services Management*, Chongquing, China, 2005, pp. 1403–1407, vol. 2.
9. L. J. Money, "The saga of Maglev," *Transpen. Res-A.*, vol. 18A, no. 4, pp. 333–341, 1984.

10. M. Kim, J. H. Jeong, J. Lim, and M. C. Won, "Design and control of levitation and guidance systems for a semi-high-speed maglev train," *J. Electr. Eng. Technol.*, vol. 12, pp. 117–125, 2017.
11. E. Musk, Hyperloop Apha. SpaceX. Retrieved August 13, 2013.
12. M. Garber, The real ipod: Elon Musks wild idea for a Jetson Tunnel from S. F to L.A, The Atlantic. Retrieved September 13, 2013.
13. When Fossil Fuels Run Out, What Then? https://mahb.stanford.edu/library-item/fossil-fuels-run/.
14. V. Singh, V. Singh, and S. Vaibhav, "Analysis of electric vehicle trends, development and policies in India," *Case Stud. Transp. Policy*, vol. 9, no. 3, pp. 1180–1197, 2021. https://doi.org/10.1016/j.cstp.2021.06.006.
15. Z. Chen, A. L. Carrel, C. Gore, and W. Shi, "Environmental and economic impact of electric vehicle adoption in the U.S," *Environ. Res. Lett.*, vol. 16, no. 4, 2021. https://doi.org/10.1088/1748-9326/abe2d0.
16. A. A. R. N. Avotra and A. Nawaz, "Asymmetric impact of transportation on carbon emissions influencing SDGs of climate change," *Chemosphere*, vol. 324, no. February, p. 138301, 2023. https://doi.org/10.1016/j.chemosphere.2023.138301.
17. D. L. McCollum, C. Wilson, M. Bevione et al., "Interaction of consumer preferences and climate policies in the global transition to low-carbon vehicles," *Nat. Energy*, vol. 3, pp. 664–673, 2018. https://doi.org/10.1038/s41560-018-0195-z.
18. "IEA, Electric car sales, 2016–2023," IEA, Paris, 2023. https://www.iea.org/data-and-statistics/charts/electric-car-sales-2016-2023.
19. "Electric Vehicles: An Economic and Environmental Win for Developing Countries," World Bank Feture Story, 2022. https://www.worldbank.org/en/news/feature/2022/11/17/electric-vehicles-an-economic-and-environmental-win-for-developing-countries#:~:text=A new World Bank report, on expensive imported fossil fuels.
20. C. Kanuri, R. Rao, and P. Mulukutla, "A Review of State Government Policies for Electric Mobility". WRI India Ross Center, available at https://www.wricitiesindia.org/sites/default/files/Full_report_EV_State_Policy.pdf
21. Y. Xue, Y. Zhang, Z. Wang, S. Tian, Q. Xiong, and L. Q. Li, "Effects of incentive policies on the purchase intention of electric vehicles in China : Psychosocial value and family ownership," *Energy Policy*, vol. 181, no. December 2022, p. 113732, 2023. https://doi.org/10.1016/j.enpol.2023.113732.
22. E. Hopkins, D. Potoglou, S. Orford, and L. Cipcigan, "Can the equitable roll out of electric vehicle charging infrastructure be achieved?" *Renew. Sustain. Energy Rev.*, vol. 182, no. May, p. 113398, 2023. https://doi.org/10.1016/j.rser.2023.113398.
23. IEA, "Global EV Outlook 2021- Accelerating ambitions despite the pandemic," *Global EV Outlook 2021*, p. 101, 2021. Available: https://iea.blob.core.windows.net/assets/ed5f4484-f556-4110-8c5c-4ede8bcba637/GlobalEVOutlook2021.pdf.
24. W. Li, R. Long, H. Chen, F. Chen, X. Zheng, and M. Yang, "Effect of policy incentives on the uptake of electric vehicles in China," *Sustainability*, vol. 11, no. 12, p. 103801, 2019. https://doi.org/10.3390/su10023323.

25. "National Level Policy," National Level Policy of Niti Aayog, Govt. of India. https://e-amrit.niti.gov.in/national-level-policy.
26. "Electric Vehicle (EV) and Fuel Cell Electric Vehicle (FCEV) Tax Credit," US Department of Energy, 2023. https://afdc.energy.gov/laws/409.
27. "Examples of Local Laws and Incentives," US Department of Energy, 2023. https://afdc.energy.gov/laws/local_examples.
28. International Energy Agency, "Global EV Outlook 2023," Geo, no. Geo, pp. 9–10, 2023.
29. A. M Elshurafa, "Electric Vehicle deployment and carbon emissions in Saudi Arabia: A power system perspective," *Electr. J.*, vol. 33, pp. 1–8, 2020, https://doi.org/10.1016/j.tej.2020.106774.
30. "Global Drive to Zero ZETI tool." https://globaldrivetozero.org/tools/zeti-data-explorer/.
31. "8738 public EV charging stations june minister," Mercom India, 2023. https://www.mercomindia.com/8738-public-ev-charging-stations-june-minister.
32. "Number of publicly available electric vehicle chargers (EVSE) in 2022, by major country and type," statista.com, 2023. https://www.statista.com/statistics/571564/publicly-available-electric-vehicle-chargers-by-country-type/.
33. smev.in, "EV Industries Sales Data." https://www.smev.in/statistics. Accessed on 08.10.2023.
34. A. Jabbar et al., Air quality, pollution and sustainability trends in South Asia: A population-based study. *Int. J. Environ. Res. Public Health*, vol. 19, p. 7534, 2022.
35. B. Clarke et al, "Extreme weather impacts of climate change: An attribution perspective" *Environ. Res.: Climate*, vol. 1, p. 012001, 2022.
36. K. Pietrzak and O. Pietrzak, "Environmental effects of electromobility in a sustainable urban public transport," *Sustainability*, vol. 12, no. 3, p. 1052, 2020. https://doi.org/10.3390/su12031052.
37. I. Hwang, Y. J. Jang, Y. D. Ko, and M. S. Lee, "System optimization for dynamic wireless charging electric vehicles operating in a multiple-route environment," *IEEE Trans. Intell. Transp. Syst.*, vol. 19, no. 6, pp. 1709–1726, 2018. https://doi.org/10.1109/TITS.2017.2731787.

ANNEXURE I

Table 1.4 Comparative study of electric vehicle models worldwide

Name	Price	Range (km)	Battery chemistry	Bat. Cap. (kWh)	V_B (V)	T_{ch} (hours)	Motor	P_{max_m} (kW)	T_{max_m} (N m)	T_{ACC} (s)	S_T (kmph)
Nissan Leaf (SV+)	30	340	Li-ion	60	360	11	PMSM	160	340	7.4(60)	170
Tesla Model X plaid	75	535	Li-ion	100	400	7	PMSyRM	760	NA	2.5(60)	262
Hyundai Ioniq i5	46	481	Li-ion	72.6	800	7	PMSM	160	350	5.2(100)	185
Audi E-tron GT	119	400	Li-ion	93.4	800	9	2x PMSM	390	640	4.1(100)	245
Tesla Model S plaid	80	637	Li-ion	95	350	7	PMSyRM with carbon sleeve	760	420	2(60)	322
Porsche Taycan	73	410	Li-ion	71	800	7.75	PMSM	300	345	5.4(100)	230
Hyundai Kona Electric	24	452	Li-ion	39.2	356	7	PMSM	100	395	9.7(100)	167
Volkswagen ID.4 GTX	60	400	Li-ion	77		8	PMSM	220	460	6.2(100)	180
Chevrolet Bolt EV	27.38	416.2	Li-ion	66	10	10	PMSM	150	360	7(100)	150
Tesla model 3	43	549	Li-ion	57.5	375	7	PMSyRM	239	420	4.2(96)	260
Ford Focus Electric	9	105	Li-ion	33.5	325	3.5	PMSM	107	250	9.9(96)	135
Tata Nexon EV (empowered MR)	18	325	Li-ion	30.2	320	8.5	3-ph PMSM	94.87	245	9.2(100)	120
Jaguar I pace	112.1	407	Li-ion	90	388	8.5	2x PMSM	294	696	4.8(100)	200

V_B = Nominal voltage of the battery, Price = Approximate price in INR (Lakhs), Bat. Cap. = Battery capacity in kWh, T_{ch} = Charging time in hours, P_{max_m} = Maximum Power rating of the motor employed in kW, T_{max_m} = Maximum torque rating of the motor employed in N m, T_{ACC} = time in seconds where number in parenthesis indicates speed in kmph from 0 kmph, S_T = Top speed in kmph, PMSM: Permanent Magnet Synchronous Motor, PMSyRM = Permanent Magnet assisted Synchronous Reluctance Motor, NA = Not available

Chapter 2

An overview of motors used in electric vehicle applications

Kosha Krishna Dutta, Ambrish Devanshu, and Srikanth Allamsetty

2.1 INTRODUCTION

Electric vehicles (EVs) are powered by rechargeable batteries for propulsion. EVs were invented in the 18th century, and the internal combustion engine (ICE) was developed in the 19th century by an American named George Brayton [1]. However, ICE-based vehicles became more successful than EVs due to their low cost. This prosperity of ICE-based vehicles continued until now. Nevertheless, concerns about environmental pollution and the crisis of fossil fuels have compelled the world to move toward alternative energy sources. Electric energy is considered the best form of energy, as it is very convenient to carry and handle. EVs offer certain extra benefits, such as increased volatility and enhanced stability control, in addition to being silent and producing zero CO_2 emissions [2]. Owing to these advantages, EVs have returned to the field of research as well as into the market. Now, all automobile industries are putting efforts into developing high-range, high-power, and highly reliable EVs.

The EV powertrain comprises several vital components that work together seamlessly to deliver a cleaner and more sustainable mode of transportation. At the core of the powertrain is the electric motor, which is responsible for converting electrical energy from the battery into mechanical power to drive the wheels and propel the vehicle. The battery pack serves as the energy reservoir, storing electrical energy in chemical form and providing power to the motor. Working in tandem with the motor and battery pack is the motor controller, a crucial electronic device that regulates the flow of energy between the battery and the motor, controlling speed, torque, and direction based on driver inputs and vehicle conditions. To ensure continued operation, the charging system allows the EV's battery to be replenished efficiently from external power sources. These components, along with additional systems for thermal management, power distribution, and various safety features, contribute to a greener and more environmentally friendly future, reducing greenhouse gas emissions and fostering sustainable mobility. Ongoing advancements in battery technology, electric motors,

DOI: 10.1201/9781003481065-2

27

and charging infrastructure will further propel the appeal and performance of electric vehicles, accelerating the transition toward a cleaner transportation landscape.

The main components of EVs are the battery, charger, and the vehicle's electric motor. The electric motor serves as the engine of the vehicle, and it can be of various types, such as direct current (DC) motors, brushless DC (BLDC) motors, permanent magnet synchronous motors (PMSM), induction motors (IM), and switched reluctance motors (SRM). While DC motors have been used in EVs since the 18th century due to their ease of control and simplicity compared to AC motors, modern EVs increasingly use AC motors like BLDC and PMSM due to their higher efficiency, reliability, and controllability. These motors are selected based on factors such as efficiency, reliability, cost, weight, and the overall system's maintenance requirements. One of the key features of EVs is regenerative braking, where the electric motor is used in reverse during braking, applying a braking force through electromagnetism. This concept helps to recover energy and extend the vehicle's range. Different EV types may offer specific driving modes with variable levels of regenerative braking. Compared to DC motors, AC motors, particularly BLDC and PMSM, are preferred for their higher reliability, controllability, and lower maintenance needs. They also exhibit higher power density, making them more suitable for EVs. Moreover, AC motors are brushless, eliminating the need for frequent brush replacement, which is typical in common DC motors [3]. This chapter presents a discussion on brushless motors, their parameters, and newly proposed design topologies for EV applications.

2.2 ELECTRIC VEHICLE

EVs are being developed with the aim of replacing ICE vehicles. There are some drawbacks of EVs, such as short travel range and the time taken to refuel, i.e., recharge, to which attention needs to be paid. These drawbacks can be overcome to a great extent by using different combinations of engines. According to the source of fuel, EVs are divided into four major classes: (i) battery electric vehicles (BEVs), (ii) hybrid electric vehicles (HEVs), (iii) plug-in hybrid electric vehicles (PHEVs), and (iv) fuel cell electric vehicles (FCEVs), as shown in Figure 2.1. Table 2.1 describes the details of different vehicles and their merits and demerits.

2.2.1 Battery Electric Vehicles

BEVs are simple powertrains, which run their electric motors only on batteries, without pollution, and have a lesser cost of fuel than any other type. Generally, the vehicle consists of electric components such as the motor,

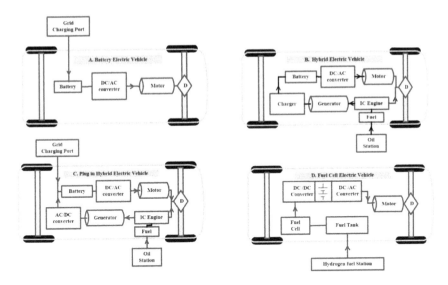

Figure 2.1 Different powertrain blocks of EVs.

DC-DC or DC-AC converter, controller, and power hubs. Further, direct torque control (DTC), field-oriented control techniques are being used to control the motors for EV. In addition, regenerating braking mode can be applied to the vehicles to save power [4]. EVs require a huge pack of batteries to run for a long distance and are not suitable to be used as heavy vehicles such as buses, trucks, or military vehicles. EVs' initial cost and the time taken to recharge their batteries are inconvenient.

2.2.2 Hybrid Electric Vehicles

HEVs are a combination of EVs and ICE-based vehicles (ICEVs). The disadvantages of ICEVs and EVs are conquered in HEVs for making them as commercial EVs. HEVs require two electric machines, i.e., motor and generator, for their run, and thus, there would be more energy loss due to two-stage energy conversion. Further, they also cause environmental pollution as they have ICEs. A few HEVs came up with new topologies, such as integrated with PV panels and ultra-capacitors [5,6]. Also, there are different architectures in HEVs according to the connection of sources, i.e., series, parallel, and complex (combination of series-parallel). In series condition, the power generated by ICEs propels the vehicle as well as charges the batteries. When the fuel gets over or the driver changes the mode to run as EV, the vehicle would be run by batteries, which are connected in parallel to cater to the sufficient driving range. HEVs suffer from larger sizes, higher costs, complex energy management, and control problems [6].

Table 2.1 EVs features and its merits and demerits [3,7]

Vehicles	Source	Propulsion	CO_2 emission	Advantage	Disadvantage	Example of EVs
EVs	Batteries	Motor	Zero	• Environment eco-friendly • Less maintenance • Low running cost	• High manufacturing cost • Short running distance • Time is taken in refueling. • Low power density	• Tesla Model S • BMW i3 • Nissan leaf
HEVs	Gasoline	Motor ICE	Low	• Less dependent on fuel • Long distance	• High CO_2 emission • Cannot charge the battery	• Honda Civic • Toyota Prius
PHEVs	Gasoline Batteries	Motor ICE	Low	• Long distance • Rechargeable battery • CO_2 Emission less	• High manufacturing cost • Difficult to maintenance	• Audi i3 • Ford Fusion • Chevy volt
FCEVs	H_2 Gas	Motor	Zero	• Beneficial for health (Especially in urban areas) • Power density is high	• High risk to Safety • High manufacturing cost • Operating cost (H_2)	• Honda Clarity • Toyota Mirai • Hyundai Nexo

2.2.3 Plug-in Electric Vehicles

PHEVs are modified versions of HEVs with a provision to charge the batteries externally through a plug point. These are highly efficient than HEVs but complex in manufacturing and maintenance [7]. PHEVs typically operate in one of the two energy management modes, a charge depleting (CD) mode, which utilizes only electricity for mobility and a charge sustaining (CS) mode which uses an alternative fuel for locomotion. As the battery bank size is increased and the ICE engine size is reduced, there are a few advantages with this type of EV such as low operation costs, reduced emission of gases, and reduced noise [3].

2.2.4 Fuel Cell Electric Vehicles

Hydrogen gas (H_2) is used as fuel for FCEVs. When positive ions of H_2 are separated using suitable catalysts, free electrons would be generated. Electrical energy can be produced by providing a path for these free electrons. After flowing through the load, these electrons again join the positive ions and oxygen and produce water as a by-product. FCEV is one of the good alternatives for HEV due to its high energy density, long-range, and zero CO_2 emissions [8]. The cost of hydrogen is too high, and there is a high risk to carry it, which makes FCEVs an uncommon choice compared to other EVs [9,10].

2.3 ELECTRIC VEHICLE POWERTRAIN AND CONFIGURATION OF EV MOTORS

An EVs powertrain is a system that delivers power from the battery to the wheels to propel the vehicle. It consists of various components: battery, electric motor, and controller. The powertrain of an EVs is significantly different from that of a traditional ICE vehicle. EV motors can be configured in different ways, depending on the vehicle's design and intended purpose. Common configurations include single motor rear-wheel drive (RWD) and dual motor all-wheel drive (AWD).

2.3.1 Dynamic power equation for EVs [1,11]

The force that propels the vehicle to move or accelerate is called tractive force, the components of which are shown in Figure 2.2. Tractive force (F_t) depends on the road conditions, the slope of the road, weather, wind, body structure, mass, and diameter of the wheel of the vehicles. Depending on the slope of the road (α), the mass of that vehicle (m), and gravitational force (g), a grading resistance force (F_g) acts on the vehicle. Another force, i.e. rolling resistance force (F_{rr}), acts in the same direction as that of F_g, due

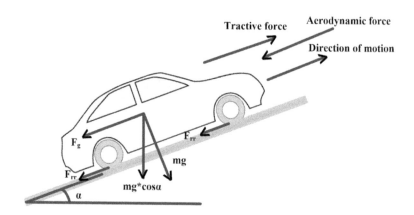

Figure 2.2 Dynamic force acting on the EVs.

to road conditions, the surface area of the wheel, and the material on the surface of the road such as oil, liquid substance, dust, etc. Aerodynamic force (F_a) acts as resistance due to the motion of the wind, the temperature of the weather, and the shape of the vehicle. The power (P_t) required for motion is equal to the product of force (F) and speed (V). When the different forces are described as given in the equations (2.1)–(2.3), the power can be calculated using (2.4).

$$F_{rr} = \mu_r mg \tag{2.1}$$

$$F_g = mg \sin\alpha \tag{2.2}$$

$$F_a = \tfrac{1}{2}fC_D A(V - V_b)^2 \tag{2.3}$$

$$P_t = \mu_r mg + mg\sin\alpha + \{\tfrac{1}{2}fC_D A(V - V_b)^2\} \tag{2.4}$$

where rolling coefficient (μ_r), air density (f), aerodynamic drag constant (C_D), opposite air velocity (V_b), and frontal area of the vehicle (A). f change from 1.514 kg/m³ (−40°) to 1.127 kg/m³ (+40°), the average air density is 1.25 kg/m³.

Tables 2.2 and 2.3 give the details about the aerodynamic drag constant for the vehicles of different shapes and the rolling coefficients (μ_r) of different road conditions, respectively.

Let us say the maximum speed of a car while traveling inside the city is 40 km/h. The weight of the car is 1,300 kg. The wind is blowing at 10 km/h. The dimensions of the car are 4,300×1,700×1,200. When the inclination of the road is 10°, the amount of mechanical torque used to accelerate it can be calculated as follows [12].

Table 2.2 Aerodynamic drag constant for the different vehicle

Body shape	C_D	Body shape	C_D
Open vehicle/van	0.5–0.7	Regular	0.4–0.5
Wedge	0.3–0.4	Bus/train	0.8–1.5
Stream-line	0.15–0.2	Motor cycle	0.6–0.7

Table 2.3 Rolling coefficient (μ_r) of different road conditions

Road condition	μ_r
Car-type concrete/asphalt	0.02
Rolled gravel (compress)	0.03
Field (loose)	0.1–0.35
Track-type concrete (racing)	0.006
Train rail	0.001

$\mu_r=0.02$ (road condition according to city), $V=40$ km/h, $m=1{,}200$ kg, $\alpha=10°$

C_D (regular body)$=0.4$, $f=1.25$ kg/m³, $V_b=10$ km/h, $g=9.8$ m/s$=35.8$ km/h

The frontal area of the car is the multiplication of 85% times the width and the height

$$A=(1.7\times1.2)\times85\% \ \text{m}^2=1.734\,\text{m}^2$$

From equation (2.4)

$$\text{Power}\,(P_t) = 0.02\times1{,}300\times35.8+1{,}200\times35.8\times\sin(10)$$

$$+\left\{\frac{1}{2}\times1.25\times0.4\times1.734\times10^{-6}\times(40-10)^2\right\}40^2$$

$P_t=930.8+7459.92+0.007=8390.727$

Torque $T_m=$ Power/ speed$=8{,}390.73/40=209.76$ N m

If slope is zero than $P_{t0}=930.8+0.007=930.80$ W

Torque $T_{m0}=930.8/40=23.27$ N m

So, at least more than 20 N m, load torque is required to start the vehicle.

2.3.2 Motor configuration in EVs [3]

EVs can employ various drivetrain configurations to convert the motor's power into motion. Electric bikes, for example, use a hub drive system, like the Bafang M500 motor, which integrates the motor directly into the wheel hub. This design eliminates the need for a separate transmission system or differential and is commonly used for pedal-assist or fully electric propulsion in e-bikes. Electric motorcycles, like the Zero Motorcycles SR/F, use a belt-driven system. The electric motor transfers power to the rear wheel through a reinforced rubber belt, connecting the motor's output shaft to a pulley on the rear wheel [13]. Most modern electric cars, like the Nissan Leaf, use a gear with a differential drive system. The electric motor's rotational force is transmitted to the wheels through a reduction gearbox and a differential. The gearbox adjusts speed and torque output, while the differential enables smooth turns by allowing the wheels to rotate at different speeds.

Different motor configurations that are being used in EVs are shown in Figure 2.3. EVs with a single motor consist of a singular assembly of an electric motor, with a fixed gear, and a differential gear system for rear or front-wheel drives, as shown in Figure 2.3a. Similarly, EVs with dual motors consist of fixed and differential gear systems to provide power to wheels on both sides as shown in Figure 2.3b. In Figure 2.3c, the triple motor configuration used is Tesla's new model. To implement the AWD system without using any additional mechanical parts, a new configuration has been suggested in Ref. [3] as shown in Figure 2.3d. The AWD system provides better acceleration on slippery roads, making them ideal vehicles for snowy and muddy conditions. AWD delivers power to all wheels, providing better traction and ultimately, better acceleration. An AWD system can be implemented in EVs either by a dual-motor system or by a four-motor system configuration [14].

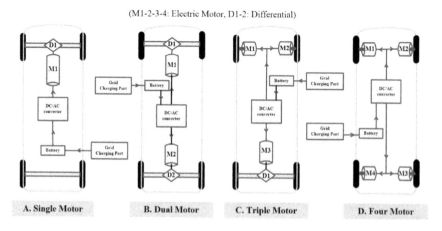

Figure 2.3 Different position configurations of motor in EVs.

Among all, the single-motor powertrain is compact and cheaper to build. Other configurations provide high power, good acceleration, and an additional degree of freedom to enhance traction and control stability but are complex to control.

Table 2.4 shows different vehicle configurations of various EV models and details such as vehicle range, electric motor, batteries, etc. Different vehicles use various types of motors according to their requirements in terms of power, efficiency, reliability, and size.

Automobile industries kept on working on developing different motor structures and improving their control strategies.

2.4 PROPULSION MOTORS FOR EVS

Research and development activities are essential to create the best propulsion motor for EV applications. Selecting the right motor for an EVs involves a careful assessment of various factors to ensure optimal performance and efficiency. First, the vehicle requirements must be determined, encompassing the total weight, desired top speed, acceleration capabilities, and the required range on a single charge. Next, the motor type should be chosen based on factors such as efficiency, power density, and suitability for the vehicle's size and performance needs. Cost, availability, and integration with the power electronics and battery system are also essential considerations [15]. The power and torque requirements must be calculated based on the vehicle weight and acceleration demands to ensure the motor can handle the necessary load and provide the desired speed and performance.

An electric motor that operates without the mechanical brushes and commutator, which are typically present in conventional brush motors, is called a brushless DC motor (BLDC). Despite having additional upfront expenses, it offers clear advantages over brushed motors and is also more cost-effective overall. BLDC motors are being used in various trenchless construction applications.

According to a recent report [5], there is a growing need for creating sophisticated traction motors for EVs despite having a lot of traction motors in the market. However, the choice is frequently between the IM and PMSM when considering the trade-offs based on performance, robustness, dependability, and cost. AC motor with a re-breaking generating system and driving cycle shows better performance than DC motor [16]. The high grade of core materials does not guarantee a better efficiency of an electric motor [17].

All comparisons depend on their construction parameters such as input voltage, current, flux, resistance, and reluctance. Here, the relation between these parameters has been discussed using mathematical modeling.

Table 2.4 EV companies and their vehicle configurations [3,12]

Name	Body style/ (type)	Electric motor (kW)	Transmission	Battery (kWh)	Range (km)	Wheelbase (mm)	Length (mm)	Width (mm)	Height (mm)	Curb weight (kg)
GM EV1	2-seat, 2-door coupe. (BEV)	Three-phase IM (102)	Single-speed reduction integrated with motor and differential	Lead acid (18.7)/NiMH (26.4)	Release 1 (112–160)/Release 2 (160–224)	2,512	4,310	1,765	1,283	1,400
Nissan Leaf	5-door hatchback (BEV)	PMSM (80)	Single-speed direct drive	Lithium-ion (24)	EPA (117)/NEDC(175)/Nissan (76–169)	2,700	4,445	1,770	1,550	1,521
Mitsubishi MiEV	5-door hatchback (BEV)	PMSM (7)	Single-speed reduction gear	Lithium-ion (16)	Release 1 (100–160)	2,550	3,680	1,475	1,600	1,080
Honda E	3-door hatchback (BEV)	Permanent magnet BLDC (113)	Single-speed fix gear	Lithium-ion (28.5)	Honda E (120–250)	2,538	3,894	1,752	1,512	1,855
Tesla Model S	5-door sedan liftback (BEV)	Three-phase IM (102)	Single-speed fix gear	Lithium-ion (75)	model S (401–417)	2,960	4,980	1,964	1,490	1,961
Tata Tiago	5-door hatchback (BEV)	Permanent magnet BLDC (45)	Single-speed Automatic	Lithium-ion (19.2)	XE (296)/XZ (315)	2,400	3,769	1,677	1,536	1,235
Honda Insight	3-door liftback (HEV)	Permanent magnet BLDC (10)	3 cylinder ICE (Parallel hybrid)	NiMH (1)	(1,100/40l)	2,400	3,955	1,695	1,355	834
Toyota Prius	4-door sedan (HEV)	PMSM (70)	4 cylinder ICE (Parallel hybrid)	NiMH (1.8)	Prius (1,100/44.7l)	2,550	4,310	1,695	1,460	1,254
Honda FCX	4-door 5-seater sedan (FCEV)	PMSM (100)	Single speed, direct drive	Fuel cell	FCX Clarity (432)	2,799	4,834	1,847	1,468	1,600

2.4.1 BLDC motor

The BLDC motor is an AC motor, and its rotor consists of a permanent magnet (PM). A Hall Effect sensor is used to sense the position of the rotor. Back EMF is generated due to the rotating PM, inducing current in the stator coil, which, in turn, generates regenerative braking energy in the motor [18]. The BLDC motor has a higher torque-volume ratio than the induction motor. When choosing BLDC motors, one can opt either for slotted or for slot-less motors. The characteristics of slotted and slot-less BLDC motors can be analyzed using the 2D finite element method. The slotted BLDC motor has higher torque than the slot-less BLDC motor. However, the power produced by both of them is almost the same, while the speed of the slot-less BLDC is ten times higher than that of the slotted BLDC. The slotted BLDC produces more ripple torque, resulting in higher vibration than the slot-less BLDC. The ripple torque of the slot-less BLDC motor is smoother than that of the slotted BLDC motor [17].

2.4.1.1 Mathematical model

A mathematical model can be developed as follows for the three-phase, start-connected BLDC. Phase variable model is more applicable than the d-q axis model for mathematical analysis. The EMF equations (2.5)–(2.7) refer that the mutual inductances between the stator and rotor are also considered. Magnetic circuit saturation and all losses are ignored. All semiconductor switches are considered to be ideal [19–21].

$$V_a = Ri_a + (L - M)\frac{di_a}{dt} + e_a \tag{2.5}$$

$$V_b = Ri_b + (L - M)\frac{di_b}{dt} + e_b \tag{2.6}$$

$$V_c = Ri_c + (L - M)\frac{di_c}{dt} + e_c \tag{2.7}$$

$$e_a = K \cdot \int(\theta) \cdot w_m, e_b = K \cdot \int\left(\theta - \frac{2\pi}{3}\right) \cdot w_m, e_c = K \cdot \int\left(\theta + \frac{2\pi}{3}\right) \cdot w_m \tag{2.8}$$

EMF function $\int(\theta)$ is given in equation (2.9)

$$\int(\theta)\begin{cases} 0 > \theta \geq 30 & 0 \\ 30 > \theta \geq 150 & 1 \\ 150 > \theta \geq 210 & 0 \\ 210 > \theta \geq 330 & -1 \\ 330 > \theta \geq 360 & 0 \end{cases} \tag{2.9}$$

The electromagnetic torques of BLDC motor are given in equations (2.10) and (2.11) [1,18]

$$T_e = T_l + J\frac{dw_m}{dt} + \beta w_m \tag{2.10}$$

$$T_e = \left(e_a i_a + e_b i_b + e_c i_c\right)/w_m \tag{2.11}$$

where V_a, V_b, V_c is phase voltage, i_a, i_b, i_c is phase current, e_a, e_b, e_c is phase back emf. R, L & M are resistance, self-inductance, and mutual inductance of the stator. T_e is electromagnetic torque. T_l is loading torque. W_m is rotating angular speed. β is the damping coefficient. θ is the phase angle. K is back emf constant (volt/rad/s). J is moment of inertia.

2.4.2 Induction motor

IMs are classified into two types: squirrel cage (SCIM) and wound rotor motors based on their rotor construction. SCIMs are known for their low maintenance and good running torque. Specifically, screw-type SCIM motors are known for their reduced locking tendency and harmonics. On the other hand, the wound rotor type IMs exhibit high starting torque but low efficiency and as they have more air gap, no-load current would be more than that of SCIM. Three-phase IMs are self-started, whereas single-phase IMs require auxiliary winding for getting started. The stator and rotor resistances of a wound rotor is adjustable by connecting external resistances through sliprings, whereas the squirrel cage resistive components are fixed [16,22].

The frequency alone does not regulate the speed because of the 'slip' caused by the torque in IMs. However, by measuring the angular speed and incorporating it into the feedback path, the frequency can be adjusted to achieve the required pace. The greatest force is determined by the intensity of the magnetic field in the gap between the rotor and the stator coils. The inductance of the coils, which has an impedance that is proportional to the frequency, causes the current to decrease as the frequency rises, when the voltage remains steady. Therefore, if the inverter is powered by a constant voltage, the highest torque that can be achieved is directly proportional to the speed [16,23].

2.4.2.1 D-Q transformation

Figure 2.4 shows the basic equivalent circuit diagram of the IM. The DQ transformation is applied to convert the three-phase to a two-phase model. Its main advantage is the conceptual simplicity of the model for

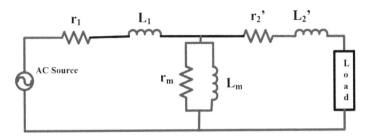

Figure 2.4 Induction motor circuit diagram [24].

understanding and thus, controlling the output of the motor. The transformation acts as a tensor in order to view the vector quantities of the three-phase motor as scalar quantities on the reference axis, and it is the product of two transformations: αβ–(Clarke) transformation and dq–(Park) transformation. Relation between the *abc* to *dq* transformation can be obtained as given in equation (2.12) [24]

$$
\begin{bmatrix} i_q \\ i_d \end{bmatrix} = \begin{bmatrix} \dfrac{2}{3} & \dfrac{1}{3} & \dfrac{1}{3} \\ 0 & \dfrac{1}{\sqrt{3}} & \dfrac{1}{\sqrt{3}} \end{bmatrix} \begin{bmatrix} i_a \\ i_b \\ i_c \end{bmatrix} \tag{2.12}
$$

2.4.2.2 Mathematical model

Several assumptions must be made to derive the dynamic model that consisting winding parameters on the stator and rotor. T_e is a critical variable that is required to determine the rotor speed; therefore, its origin cannot be ignored [25]. The three-phase motor can be modeled using the following equations.

$$
V_{d1} = i_{q1} r_1 + L_1 \frac{d}{dt} i_{q1} + L_m \frac{d}{dt} i_{q2} \tag{2.13}
$$

$$
V_{d1} = i_{q1} r_1 + L_1 \frac{d}{dt} i_{q1} + L_m \frac{d}{dt} i_{q2} \tag{2.14}
$$

$$
V_{q2} = L_m \frac{d}{dt} i_{q1} - w_r L_m i_{d1} + i_{q1} r_2 + L_2 \frac{d}{dt} i_{q2} - w_r L_2 i_{d2} \tag{2.15}
$$

$$
V_{d2} = L_m \frac{d}{dt} i_{d1} + w_r L_m i_{q1} + i_{d1} r_2 + L_2 \frac{d}{dt} i_{d2} + w_r L_2 i_{q2} \tag{2.16}
$$

From equations (2.13)–(2.16), it can be noted that the system input power, mechanical power, and stored magnetic energy are considered to derive the model. The product of the electromagnetic torque and rotor speed will give the air-gap power [26]. The electromagnetic force is described in (2.17)–(2.19).

$$T_e = \frac{P}{2} \times \frac{3}{2} L_m \left(i_{q1} i_{d2} - i_{q2} i_{d1} \right) \tag{2.17}$$

$$T_e = T_m + J \frac{dw_m}{dt} \tag{2.18}$$

$$w_2 = \frac{2}{P} w_m \tag{2.19}$$

where vector of voltage, current of stator, and rotor in dq axis are V_{d1}, V_{q1}, V_{d2}, V_{q2}, i_{d1}, i_{q1}, i_{d2}, i_{q2}, respectively. Voltage, and current in abc parameter are V_a, V_b, V_c, i_a, i_b, i_c. r_1, L_1 and r_2, L_2 stator and rotor resistance and inductance. L_m mutual inductance. P is pole, and J is moment of inertia. stator, rotor, and magnetized angular velocity are w_1, w_2, and w_m. T_e is electromagnetic torque. T_l is loading torque.

2.4.3 Switched Reluctance Motors

Linear SRM and rotary SRM are also known as servo motor and axial field SRM, respectively. They are classified according to their construction. The servo motor consists single-step stator and rotor. Stator of SRM is identical to that of the BLDC motor as per the construction of its winding. The absence of brush makes it run at high speed. HEV applications can be described as optimal for the SRMs. These motors have several benefits when utilized for traction applications such as a more extensive constant power-speed range than any other motor, high-speed capability, zero short-circuit current, and easy, simple, and durable construction [3,15]. However, special power electronics drive converters are needed for the SRM. The SRM's extended constant power-speed range more than makes up for its poor efficiency and torque density compared to some of the other motors. The number of stator poles is higher than that of the rotor as shown in Figure 2.5a, i.e. a 6/4 pole (6 stator poles, 4 rotor poles) setup. Rotor consists of simple laminated salient poles without windings, and thus, offers less copper loss. Silicon steel is preferred for its stampings, especially, in applications that require increased efficiency [27]

2.4.3.1 Mathematical model

Torque is developed in SRMs due to the tendency of the magnetic circuit to adopt the configuration of minimum reluctance. The magnetic behavior of

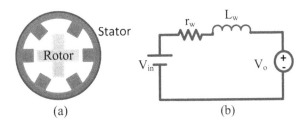

Figure 2.5 (a) Stator vs rotor construction of the SRM [28]. (b) Electrical circuit of phase winding of SRM [29].

the SRM is highly nonlinear. The static torque produced by one phase at any rotor position is calculated using the following equations:

The phase voltage of the Motor is : $V_p = r_{w1}i + L\dfrac{di}{dt} + e$ $\quad\quad$ (2.20)

Induce EMF $e = \dfrac{dL(\theta,i)}{d\theta}w_m i$ $\quad\quad$ (2.21)

Input power of the Motor $P_i = Vi = r_{w1}i^2 + i^2\dfrac{dL}{dt} + Li\dfrac{di}{dt}$ $\quad\quad$ (2.22)

Air gap power of the motor $P_a = w_m T_e$ $\quad\quad$ (2.23)

Electromagnetic torque $P_i = Vi = r_{w1}i^2 + i^2\dfrac{dL}{dt}$ $\quad\quad$ (2.24)

where Phase Voltage V_p, current i, r_{w1}, L_{w1} and r_{w2}, L_{w2} stator and rotor resistance and inductance. P_i is input power; P_a is air gap power. J moment of inertia. stator, rotor, and magnetized angular velocity w_m. T_e is electromagnetic torque. T_m is loading torque.

2.4.4 PMSM motor

The rotor of the PMSM is comparable with the stator of a typical three-phase synchronous magnetized motor. The fixed magnet produces an induced electromotive force that has the shape of a sine wave. The algebraic model of the PMSM starts with the following presumptions: core saturation can be ignored; eddy current and hysteresis loss can be disregarded; the induced electromotive force is sinusoidal; the rotor lacks a damping winding and the permanent magnetic field has no damping impact. The rotor speed is the rate of rotation of the reference locations for the rotor. Consider the orientation of the rotor as positive, anticlockwise.

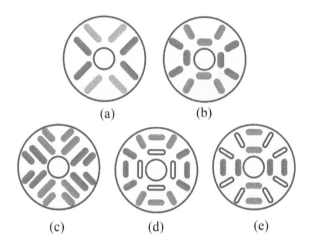

Figure 2.6 Schematic diagram of different rotor topologies. (a) V, (b) U, (c) Double V, (d) Delta, (e) Double tangential.

2.4.4.1 New rotor construction of the PMSM

Figure 2.6 demonstrates the Schematic diagram of different rotor topologies of PMSM are (a) V, (b) U, (c) double V, (d) delta, and (e) double tangential [30]. The highest magnetic density is found in the rotor magnetic bridge, which limits the development of magnetic leakage. A magnetic bridge is minimized to increase the performance. The V-shaped and double V-shaped topologies' stator teeth have the highest magnetic density of all the topologies. Furthermore, the magnetic densities of the double-layer topologies are more concentrated on the d-axis-aligned teeth. This topology decreases the harmonics [30].

2.4.4.2 Mathematical model

Figure 2.7 shows the basic d-q axis equivalent circuit diagram of the PMSM. The d-q axis voltage equation is

$$U_q = R_s i_q + \frac{d}{dt}\varphi_q + w_r\varphi_d \tag{2.25}$$

$$U_d = R_s i_d + \frac{d}{dt}\varphi_d + w_r\varphi_q \tag{2.26}$$

$$\text{Flux Linkage}: \varphi_q = L_q i_q, \quad \varphi_d = L_q i_q + \varphi_f \tag{2.27}$$

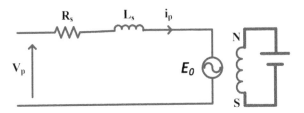

Figure 2.7 Electrical circuit diagram of PMSM.

Equation of motion of the motor, The electromagnetic Torque from (2.28) and (2.29)

$$T_e = \frac{d}{dt}\left(\varphi_d i_q - \varphi_q i_d\right) = \frac{d}{dt}\left\{\varphi_f i_q - \left(L_q - L_d\right)i_q i_d\right\} \tag{2.28}$$

$$T_e = T_m + Bw_r + J\frac{d}{dt}w_r \tag{2.29}$$

Commonly, control i_d at 0 is the complete solution of the steady state. In such cases, obtain i_q and w_r. State variable PMSM dynamic mathematical model may be obtained from equation (2.30)

$$\begin{bmatrix} i_q \\ w_r \end{bmatrix} = \begin{bmatrix} \dfrac{-R_s}{L_q} & \dfrac{-\varnothing_f}{L_q} \\ \dfrac{K}{J} & \dfrac{-B}{J} \end{bmatrix}\begin{bmatrix} i_q \\ w_r \end{bmatrix} + \begin{bmatrix} \dfrac{-U_q}{L_q} \\ \dfrac{-T_m}{J} \end{bmatrix} \tag{2.30}$$

where U_q, U_d, i_d, i_q d-q axes voltage and currents, Ψ_d, Ψ_q d-q axes flux linkages, Ψ_f PM flux linkages T_e is electromagnetic torque. T_m is loading torque. w_r electrical angular frequency. B is magnetic field, K is back emf constant (volt/rad/sec). J moment of inertia. R_s stator resistance, L_q, L_d d-q axes inductance.

2.5 CONTROL TECHNIQUE

Induction motors are widely used for industrial applications with different speeds and torque. The high performance of AC motors, in the form of control, efficiency, and maintenance, is far better than that of DC motors, as given in Table 2.5. Thus, AC motors are preferred to be used in industries. Further to control the dynamics of the motors, scalar and vector control techniques are being used. Table 2.5 gives a comparison between them.

Table 2.5 Characteristics of different motors

Characteristics	BLDC	PMSM	SRM	IM	DC
Type family	AC synchronous excited, PM	AC Separately excited	DC synchronous unexcited	AC induction slip ring squirrel cage	DC commutator, separately excited
Rotor power	PM	PM	Induced	Induced	DC
Stator power	Pulse DC	AC	Pulse DC	AC	DC
Cost	High	High	Medium	Medium	Low
weight	Low	Medium	Medium	Medium	Heavy
Maintenance	Little	No	No	No	Required
Commutation method	Internal electronics	External electronics	External electronics	External electronics	Mechanical commutation
Controller	More costly	Costly and complex	Required position sensing	Complex	Complex and weak
Process outcome using the controller	Good torque, fast response	High torque, better performance, more reliability, less noise	Low inertia	High efficiency	Bulky, complex for getting efficient output
Starting torque	>175% to rated	>200% to rated	Up to 200% to rated	high	>175% to rated
Speed range	Excellent	Controllable	Controllable	Controllable	Limited by brushed
Efficiency (only motor)	80	97	94	90	80
Efficiency (motor with electronics)	78	90	85	84	78
Control technique	FOC, DTC MPC, sensor less controller	FOC, DTC-SVM, MPC-PTC, SMC, sensor less controller	TSF, DTC, DITC, MPC, FOC, SMC	DTC, MPC, FOC, sensor less controller	Flux control, voltage control
Key challenge	High-cost magnet, reliability, less efficiency	Demagnetization, fault-tolerant, torque ripple	Low torque density, high noise	High core loss, low efficiency	Cost, brush wear, field weakening

2.5.1 DC motor

Field flux control and armature resistance control methods are traditional ways to control the speed of the DC motor. The basic DC motor EMF equation is as follows:

$$E_b = \frac{PnZ\varnothing}{60a} = V - I_a R_a \qquad (2.31)$$

Where E_b is EMF, V voltage, I_a armature current, R_a armature resistance, Z no. of conductor, $\varnothing$ is flux produced per pole, a is no. of parallel paths in armature.

$$\text{from equation} (2.31) \quad E_b \propto n \propto R_a \quad \text{or} \quad E_b \propto \varnothing \qquad (2.32)$$

From equation (2.31), it can be said that the voltage (E_b) is directly proportional to armature resistance (R_a). By changing R_a, or by changing the flux in the field, the speed of DC motors can be controlled as per the equation (2.32). [22].

2.5.2 AC motor

2.5.2.1 Scalar control

The steady-state model is the base for scalar control. The controller adjusts for changes in the magnitude of the frequency and ignores the coupling impact on the motor, or. The V/f ratio always be constant [28,31,32]. Scalar control achieved electromagnetic torque control by using the following techniques:

a. Varying magnitude of Stator Voltage, maintain frequency fixed.
b. Varying frequency of Stator Voltage, maintain magnitude fixed.
c. Varying both above parameters, the V_s/f ratio should be constant.

2.5.2.2 Vector control

The nonlinear dynamic model is used in vector control technique for a high dynamic performance drive system based on the angle and magnitude of flux, phase of current, or voltage. Two different techniques are used for vector control depending on the model transformation from the steady-state model to Clarke or Park transformations. There are (i) field-oriented control (FOC) and (ii) DTC [28,33]. Table 2.4 shows the difference between FOC and DTC. FOC gets applied to the rotor field of the motor. Torque and speed independently get controlled in FOC as a separately excited DC motor in a PMSM motor at low speed [34,35]. The dynamic response is faster than scalar control. DTC gets applied to the stator side of the motor.

Table 2.6 Difference between scaler control and vector control

Scalar control	Vector control
• Simple in mathematics	• Complex mathematics
• Poor dynamic performance	• Excellent dynamic performance
• Speed control ratio low	• Speed control ratio high
• High power dissipation	• Low power dissipation
• Harmonic present in the system	• Harmonic not present
• Slow response	• Faster response

Table 2.7 Difference between DTC and FOC and scaler control [35,36]

Characteristic	DTC	FOC	Scalar control
Dynamic response to torque	Quick	Fast	Slow
Coordinates frame	α, β (stator)	d, q (rotor)	V, f (stator)
Coordinate transformations	Not required	Required	Not required
Switching frequency	Variable	Constant	Constant
Controlled variables	Torque & stator flux	Vector component of torque & rotor flux current	Magnitude of stator voltage & frequency
Sensitivity of close loop parameter	d, q inductances with Stator resistance	d, q inductances with rotor resistance	V, f with field flux
Control tuning loops	Hysteresis band	PI controller gain	PI controller gain
Complexity	Lower	Higher	Simple
Rotor position	No	Yes	No

Input of error signal is a three-level hysteresis comparator between the estimated torque and the reference torque. While the Two-level hysteresis comparator is between the estimated stator flux and the reference stator flux magnitude [37]. Tables 2.6 and 2.7 give the comparative information about scalar and vector controlled used for AC machines with respect to different characteristics.

2.6 CONCLUSION

Different control strategies are being used to increase the efficiency and improve the power dynamic performance of AC drives, thus enhancing the overall performance of EVs. The electric motors are not only responsible for effective power quality and efficiency but also for the equipment used in

EVs. Electric motors are attracting particular attention due to the variety of topologies that can be considered for EV applications. In this chapter, a thorough review of different motors used in EVs has been presented. The performance of EVs can be improved with the right motor type selection and design, including discussions on efficiency and stability. According to the study's conclusion, there is a large market for AC motors and significant interest in the development of intelligent AC motors for EVs.

REFERENCES

1. J. Larminie and J. Lowry, *Electric Vehicle Technology Explained*. John Wiley & Sons, Chichester, West Sussex, 2012.
2. R. N. Tuncay, O. Ustun, M. Yilmaz, C. Gokce, and U. Karakaya, "Design and implementation of an electric drive system for in-wheel motor electric vehicle applications," In *2011 IEEE Vehicle Power and Propulsion Conference, VPPC 2011*, 2011. doi: 10.1109/VPPC.2011.6043070.
3. D. Mohanraj, J. Gopalakrishnan, B. Chokkalingam, and L. Mihet-Popa, "Critical aspects of electric motor drive controllers and mitigation of torque ripple - Review," *IEEE Access*, vol. 10, pp. 73635–73674, 2022. doi: 10.1109/ACCESS.2022.3187515.
4. X. D. Xue, K. W. E. Cheng, and N. C. Cheung, "Selection of electric motor drives for electric vehicles," In *2008 Australasian Universities Power Engineering Conference (AUPEC'08)*, Sydney, NSW, Australia.
5. K. V. Singh, H. O. Bansal, and D. Singh, "A comprehensive review on hybrid electric vehicles: Architectures and components," *Journal of Modern Transportation*, vol. 27, no. 2, pp. 77–107, 2019. doi: 10.1007/s40534-019-0184-3.
6. M. Ehsani, K. V. Singh, H. O. Bansal, and R. T. Mehrjardi, "State of the art and trends in electric and hybrid electric vehicles," *Proceedings of the IEEE*, vol. 109, no. 6, pp. 967–984, 2021. doi: 10.1109/JPROC.2021.3072788.
7. B. Das, P. K. Panigrahi, and C. K. Samant, "Impact analysis of plug-in hybrid electric vehicle on integration with micro grid -A review," In *Proceedings - 2020 IEEE International Symposium on Sustainable Energy, Signal Processing and Cyber Security, iSSSC 2020*, Institute of Electrical and Electronics Engineers Inc., Gunupur Odisha, India, Dec. 2020.
8. C. Jia, W. Qiao, J. Cui, and L. Qu, "Adaptive Model-Predictive-Control-Based Real-Time Energy Management of Fuel Cell Hybrid Electric Vehicles," *IEEE Transactions on Power Electronics*, vol. 38, no. 2, pp. 2681–2694, 2023, doi: 10.1109/TPEL.2022.3214782.
9. D. F. Pereira, F. D. C. Lopes, and E. H. Watanabe, "Nonlinear model predictive control for the energy management of fuel cell hybrid electric vehicles in real time," *IEEE Transactions on Industrial Electronics*, vol. 68, no. 4, pp. 3213–3223, 2021.
10. O. Castillo, R. Álvarez, and R. Domingo, "Opportunities and barriers of hydrogen-electric hybrid powertrain vans: A systematic literature review," *Processes*, vol. 8, no. 10, pp. 1–32, 2020. doi: 10.3390/pr8101261.
11. J. Mikolaj and Ľ. Remek, "Sustainable Maintenance of low-level road network," In *MATEC Web of Conferences*, EDP Sciences, Rostov-on-Don, Russia, Sep. 2018.

12. M. Yaich, M. R. Hachicha, and M. Ghariani, "Modeling and simulation of electric and hybrid vehicles for recreational vehicle," In *16th International Conference on Sciences and Techniques of Automatic Control and Computer Engineering, STA 2015*, Institute of Electrical and Electronics Engineers Inc., Monastir, Tunisia, Jul. 2016, pp. 181–187.
13. H. El Hadraoui, M. Zegrari, A. Chebak, O. Laayati, and N. Guennouni, "A multi-criteria analysis and trends of electric motors for electric vehicles," *World Electric Vehicle Journal*, vol. 13, no. 4, p. 65, 2022. doi: 10.3390/wevj13040065.
14. L. I. Farfan-Cabrera, "Tribology of electric vehicles: A review of critical components, current state and future improvement trends," *Tribology International*, vol. 138, pp. 473–486, 2019. doi: 10.1016/j.triboint.2019.06.029.
15. Z. Cao, A. Mahmoudi, S. Kahourzade, and W. L. Soong, "An overview of electric motors for electric vehicles," In *Proceedings of 2021 31st Australasian Universities Power Engineering Conference, AUPEC 2021*, Institute of Electrical and Electronics Engineers Inc., Perth, Australia, 2021. doi: 10.1109/AUPEC52110.2021.9597739.
16. K. Sedef, A. Maheri, A. Daadbin, and M. Yilmaz, "A comparative study of the performance of DC permanent magnet and AC induction motors in urban electric cars," In *2nd International Symposium on Environment Friendly Energies and Applications, EFEA 2012*, Newcastle Upon Tyne, UK, 2012, pp. 100–105. doi: 10.1109/EFEA.2012.6294077.
17. S. O. Kwon, J. J. Lee, B. H. Lee, J. H. Kim, K. H. Ha, and J. P. Hong, "Loss distribution of three-phase induction motor and BLDC motor according to core materials and operating," *IEEE Transactions on Magnetics*, vol. 45, no. 10, pp. 4740–4743, 2009.
18. W. Chen, S. Yang, F. Gao, X. Wang, and L. Wang, "The simulation analysis of the interaction between solid state power controller and brushless DC motor," In *2013 15th European Conference on Power Electronics and Applications, EPE 2013*, Lille, France, 2013.
19. M. M. Kelek, İ. Çelik, U. Fidan, and Y. Oğuz, "The simulation of mathematical model of outer rotor BLDC motor," In *SETSCI Conference Proceedings*, Samsun, Turkey, Jul. 2019, pp. 412–415. doi: 10.36287/setsci.4.6.106.
20. Universitas Gadjah Mada, Institute of Electrical and Electronics Engineers. Indonesia Section., and Institute of Electrical and Electronics Engineers, "Independent Speed Steering Control of Rear In-wheel BLDC Motor in EV Based on Fuzzy Logic Controller in GUI," In *2019 5th International Conference on Science and Technology (ICST)*, 30–31 July 2019, Eastparc Hotel, Yogyakarta, Indonesia. Proceedings, Ed., 2019.
21. Mouliswararao. R, Bhaskararao. K, Prasad. Ch, 2019, "Mathematical modeling of brushless DC motor and its speed control using pi controller," *International Journal of Engineering Research & Technology (IJERT)*, vol. 08, no. 05 (May 2019).
22. P. S. Bimbhra, *Electrical Machinery*. Khanna Publishers, Delhi, 2018.
23. K. T. Chau, C. Liu, and J. Z. Jiang, "Comparison of outer-rotor stator-permanent-magnet brushless motor drives for electric vehicles." In *2008 International Conference on Electrical Machines and Systems*.

24. W. Wasusatein, S. Nittayawan, and W. Kongprawechnon, "Speed control under load uncertainty of induction motor using neural network auto-tuning PID controller," In *2018 International Conference on Embedded Systems and Intelligent Technology and International Conference on Information and Communication Technology for Embedded Systems, ICESIT-ICICTES 2018,* Institute of Electrical and Electronics Engineers Inc., Aug. 2018. doi: 10.1109/ICESIT-ICICTES.2018.8442062.

25. A. Devanshu, M. Singh, and N. Kumar, "Nonlinear flux observer-based feedback linearisation control of IM drives with ANN speed and flux controller," *International Journal of Electronics,* pp. 1–23, 2020. doi: 10.1080/00207217.2020.1765416.

26. S. N. Manias, "Introduction to motor drive systems," In *Power Electronics and Motor Drive Systems.* Elsevier, 2017, pp. 843–967. doi: 10.1016/b978-0-12-811798-9.00012-3.

27. S. Oshaba, E. S. Ali, and S. M. Abd Elazim, "ACO based speed control of SRM fed by photovoltaic system," *International Journal of Electrical Power and Energy Systems,* vol. 67, pp. 529–536, 2015.

28. Z. Xu, T. Li, F. Zhang, Y. Zhang, D. H. Lee, and J. W. Ahn, "A review on segmented switched reluctance motors," *Energies,* vol. 15, no. 23, p. 9212, 2022.

29. H. Vasquez and J. K. Parker, "A new simplified mathematical model for a switched reluctance motor in a variable speed pumping application," *Mechatronics,* vol. 14, no. 9, pp. 1055–1068, 2004. doi: 10.1016/j.mechatronics.2004.04.007.

30. T. Song, Z. Zhang, H. Liu, and W. L. Hu, "Multi-objective optimisation design and performance comparison of permanent magnet synchronous motor for EVs based on FEA," *IET Electric Power Applications,* vol. 13, no. 8, pp. 1157–1166, 2019, doi: 10.1049/iet-epa.2019.0069.

31. J. Yu, T. Zhang, and J. Qian, "Modern control methods for the induction motor," in J. Yu, T. Zhang, and J. Qian (Eds) *Electrical Motor Products,* Woodhead Publishing Limited, Cambridge , 2011, pp. 147–172.

32. G. Kohlrusz and D. Fodor, "Comparison of scalar and vector control strategies of induction motors," *Hungarian Journal of Industrial Chemistry,* vol. 39, no. 2, pp. 265–270, 2011.

33. F. Patel, M. Tech, P. Ahir, B. Priyanka Patel, and I. Surat, "Control theory for permanent magnet synchronous motor-A review," *Asian Journal of Convergence in Technology,* vol. V, no. I, pp. 1–5.

34. T. Sun, J. Wang, C. Jia, and L. Peng, "Integration of foc with dfvc for interior permanent magnet synchronous machine drives," *IEEE Access,* vol. 8, pp. 97935–97945, 2020, doi: 10.1109/ACCESS.2020.2996948.

35. X. T. Garcia, B. Zigmund, A. Terlizzi, R. Pavlanin, and L. Salvatore, "Comparison between FOC and DTC strategies for permanent magnet synchronous motors." *Advances in Electrical and Electronic Engineering,* vol. 5, no. 1, pp. 76–81.

36. M. Hamouda Ali, "Parameters Estimation for Sensorless Induction Motor Drives Using Intelligent Techniques," *A Thesis of Master of Science in Electrical Power & Machines,* Faculty of Engineering (Cairo), Al-Azhar University, 2016, pp. 1–134.

37. D. Casadei, F. Profumo, G. Serra, and A. Tani, "FOC and DTC: Two viable schemes for induction motors torque control," *IEEE Transactions on Power Electronics,* vol. 17, no. 5, pp. 779–787, 2002, doi: 10.1109/TPEL.2002.802183.

Chapter 3

Electric vehicles and their charging technologies

K. Sateesh Kumar and T. Koteswara Rao

3.1 INTRODUCTION

Electric vehicle (EV) technology has emerged as a promising solution for sustainable transportation, providing lower emissions and greater energy efficiency than conventional internal combustion engines. EVs are propelled by electric motors that draw power from batteries or fuel cells. Although the technology has made significant progress, it still confronts several obstacles. The dread of running out of battery power before reaching a charging station is one of the major concerns. This difficulty is exacerbated by limited driving range and the need for a more extensive charging infrastructure.

The high initial costs of EVs, specifically the costlier battery technology, continue to hamper their widespread acceptance. In addition, batteries must be improved in terms of their durability, capacity, environmental impact, and supply chain sustainability. In addition, the infrastructure of the electrical grid must be strengthened to accommodate the increased demand for EV charging. To address these obstacles, continued research and development, investment in charging infrastructure, battery cost reduction, and policies encouraging EV adoption and sustainability are required. The purpose of this chapter is to present an overview of EVs and charging systems as well as to investigate current advancements.

3.1.1 Market of EVs in India

The EV industry in India is expanding quickly as part of the nation's ambitious targets. By 2030, India hopes to have 30% of new vehicle sales be electric, in line with the worldwide EV30 @30 program. The Indian EV market was estimated at USD 220.1 million in 2020 and is expected to increase at a CAGR of 94.4% between 2021 and 2030 as illustrated in Figure 3.1a. The government's supportive policies on EV manufacturing and procurement, along with strict emission standards like Bharat stage VI, are expected to drive market development in India.

Furthermore, India has been acknowledged as one of the best locations in the global automobile sector. Many corporations are creating production

50

DOI: 10.1201/9781003481065-3

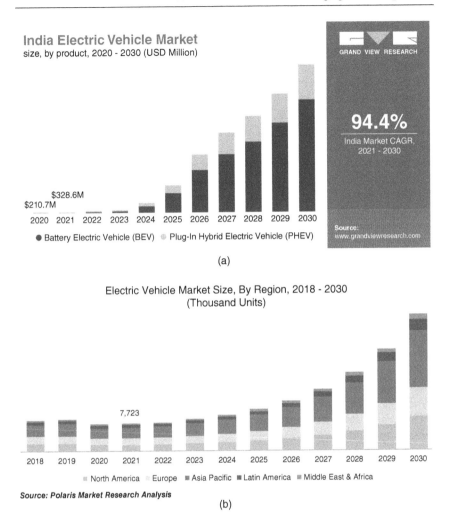

Figure 3.1   (a) India EV Market forecast [1], (b) South Asian countries EV market trends [2].

sites in India aggressively. In September 2020, for instance, Dana TM4 Inc. plans to construct a production facility in Pune, India. The new Dana TM4 factory would span 4,600 m² and be used to produce low- to high-voltage converters, electric motors, and control units. Phase II of India's Faster Adoption and Manufacturing of Electric Vehicles (FAME) Programme has similar goals, including increasing EV adoption and encouraging development in the EV manufacturing ecosystem. The FAME scheme's Phase II would be executed through the following verticals: encouraging EV demand; executing awareness efforts, including marketing and knowledge, education, and communication operations; and constructing the charging facility [2].

3.1.2 World market scenario

The worldwide EVs retail is predicted to fetch USD 7,723 million in 2021 and to increase at a Compound Annual Growth Rate (CAGR) of 21.3% during the forecast period. Increasing demand for ecologically friendly alternatives, government incentives, and high recharge capacity are driving worldwide market expansion. From 2022 to 2030, Asian EV retail is expected to develop at the speed of CAGR. This is a result of grown countries' increasing demand for passenger vehicles. In addition, the India Powered Vehicle (EV) position had the top rate of increment in the Asia-Pacific region, while South Asian countries powered vehicle industry had an exceptional retail share as shown in Figure 3.1b. Owing to local regime efforts to cut carbon emissions, Europe has the second-big retail share for powered cars, and the quick uptake of fuel-efficient vehicles has been the sector's main driver of development. The UK, Germany, and France are advanced nations that have put up to the diversification of the region [3]. Since electric cars have the biggest retail share of all EVs, the subject of four-wheelers is considered in the following subsections.

3.2 TYPES OF ELECTRIC AUTOMOBILE

Based on the energy supply for the traction motor, four-wheeler electric automobiles may be categorized into four groups: battery-powered vehicle (BEV), hybrid powered vehicle (HEV), plug-in hybrid powered vehicle (PHEV), and fuel cell powered vehicle (FCEV) [4–10]. Class structure, energy flow, and market availability are listed below:

3.2.1 Battery (powered) Electric Vehicles

Battery electric vehicles (BEVs) are regularly referred to as all-electric powered vehicles (AEVs). EVs that utilize BEV technology are driven solely by a battery-powered electric drivetrain, as illustrated in Figure 3.2 The energy required to charge the EV battery is stored in a power array pack and can be charged through a single/three-phase supply connection. The stored energy in the battery pack is then used to fuel one or more electric motors to operate the vehicle. The key components of BEVs are the electric motor, power converter, battery pack, electronic control module (ECU), and drivetrain.

To manage the vehicle's speed, the controller modulates the voltage and frequency of the AC power from the traction inverter to the EV motor. The motor is then linked to drive the wheels through a gear. When the brakes are functional or the EV is in deceleration, the motor turns to a generator and creates power, which is then returned to the battery. Participants in the BEV market include the MG ZS, TATA Tigor, Mahindra E20 Plus, Hyundai Kona, and Mahindra Verito.

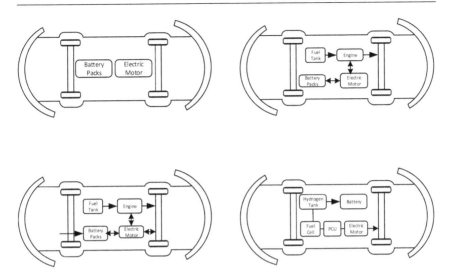

Figure 3.2 Types of EVs based on energy flow.

3.2.2 Hybrid Electric (powered) Vehicle

The vehicle's powertrain, seen in Figure 3.2, comprises a combustion engine and an electric motor, both of which are powered by batteries. Petrol engines provide propulsion, while electric motors assist the traction system under high propulsion demands. While operating in regenerative mode, the electric motor behaves as a generator to charge the fuel cell pack. The energy that has been stored in the battery will be beneficial to drive the traction motor in situations when there is a larger need for torque. Owing to their dependence on combustion engines, these cars have worse fuel efficiency than purely electric ones. In addition, HEVs need a complicated mechanical link between an electric motor and a petrol engine that needs ongoing maintenance. HEVs are thus less common in the market for EVs.

3.2.3 Plug-in Hybrid Electric Vehicle

As seen in Figure 3.2, PHEVs are also known as series hybrid EVs. An engine and an electric motor may both power the traction system. External power or regenerative mode of operation may be used to charge battery packs. It also has the option of running in all-electric mode (electric motor and fuel cell pack bestow the required energy for the traction system) or hybrid mode (in which both electricity and gasoline, as well as the battery pack, are utilized). PHEVs start their trip in an all-electric mode and stay in that manner until the power pack's ability to store energy is exhausted. At that time, the car starts using its internal combustion engine to drive.

PHEVs can be charged either by consumer supply points and/or regenerative braking as informed in the above section. Because the electric motor augments smaller engines can be used depending on the engine's power, enhancing fuel economy without sacrificing performance. Different models available in this type of EV are as follows: Toyota Prius Prime, Kia Niro Plug-in Hybrid, Hyundai Tucson, Mitsubishi Outlander, and Ford Escape.

3.2.4 Fuel Cell Electric Vehicle

FCEVs, which are sometimes called Zero-Emission Automobiles, are shown in Figure 3.2 "Fuel cell technology" is used to give the car the power it needs to move. The fuel's chemical energy is turned into electricity right away. The FCEV's main parts are an ECU, battery pack, power converter, a fuel-cell stack, and a hydrogen tank. Some ECEVs are the BMW i8, Hyundai Intrado, Maxus EUNIQ 7 Minivan, Roewe 950, and Toyota Mirai.

Other than FCEV and HEV, an electrical power source to charge the battery is needed. The next paragraph will examine several charging architectures depending on the placement of charger and power rating.

3.3 TYPES OF CHARGING ARCHITECTURES

There are two primary categories of conductive chargers used in the EVs sector. These categories are (i) On-board and (ii) Off-board chargers, which are installed on the chassis of EVs named as On-board EVs. Contemporarily, Off-board chargers are comparable to petrol stations in that they are situated outside of EVs. Power converters are the fundamental parts for energy conversion in EVs in which two-stage or multi-stage power converters are necessary to charge the battery from the AC grid in both types of chargers. The following are some of the most significant power converter configurations for EV charging (Figures 3.3–3.5):

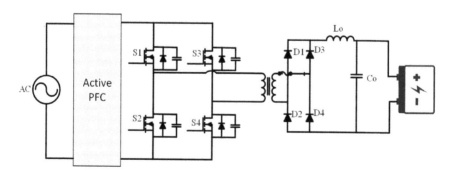

Figure 3.3 PSFBC for EV charging [11].

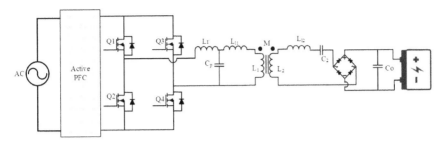

Figure 3.4 FB-LLC for EV charging [11].

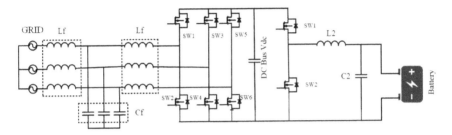

Figure 3.5 Bi-directional DC-DC converter topology [12].

Simulation results of a simple on-board EV charger connected with a single-phase AC grid are shown in Figure 3.6. Initially, the AC grid voltage is rectified to DC by the controlled rectifier. Further, a bi-directional DC-DC converter is used to charge the battery, and the corresponding results of the battery are shown in Figure 3.6c–e.

3.3.1 On-board EV charging architecture

The isolated phase shifting-based full-bridge converter (PSFBC), shown in Figure 3.3, is the most common charging converter. The isolated PSFBC operates in three stages: first, AC power is converted to DC power while the supply power factor is maintained. After that comes the step of the inverter, followed by the stage of AC-DC rectifier. Both steps employ a high-frequency transformer. As compared to traditional charging converters, phase-shifted full-bridge converters provide several advantages. These advantages include simplified control methods and less current stress on devices. In addition to this, the design of phase-shift modulation provides a further option for wide-range charging.

Despite possessing many desirable properties, the converter does have a few drawbacks, the most notable of which are high-voltage blocking on the rectifier bridge and high flow current during the freewheeling phase. To overcome the above drawbacks, full-bridge LLC resonant converter,

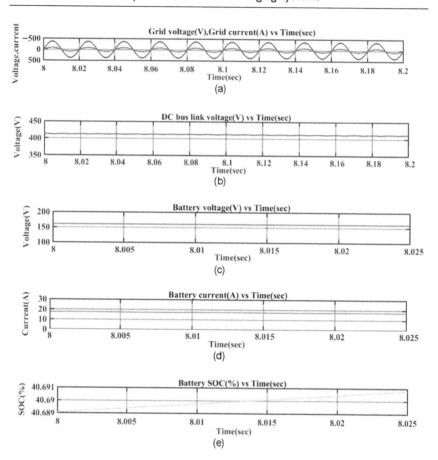

Figure 3.6 On-board EV charger for electric two-wheeler (a) supply voltage, (b) DC bus voltage, (c) battery voltage, (d) charging current, and (e) Battery State-of-Charge (SOC).

shown in Figure 3.4, is an interesting option for an EV charger on board. It offers good efficiency at high voltages and a broad operating voltage range for zero-voltage switching in power-switching devices. The pure sinusoidal current shape produced by the FB-LLC also eliminates the need for reverse recovery current and protects the rectifier diodes from voltage oscillation. Despite its many benefits, this converter architecture makes it more complex to design the filter and transformer due to the higher frequency of operation.

A two-way DC-DC converter with front end converter (three-phase model), as shown in Figure 3.5, which is used for the vehicle to grid (V2G) and Grid to Vehicle (G2V), is proposed with a battery [12]. A three-phase two-way AC-DC converter and a two-way buck-boost DC-DC converter are included in the system. This system includes an inductor connecting a three-phase AC and a two-way AC-DC converter necessary to boost DC output in order to maintain the DC bus voltage. Charging in buck mode and draining in boost mode are both possible with the DC-DC converter. The DC bus voltage must be greater than the battery voltage for the device to run in charging mode, which is buck mode. The charging current is managed by adjusting the PWM duty ratio in the buck mode. The buck-boost converter runs in boost mode when in discharge mode.

The values of passive components in various stages of the on-board charger are chosen as per the equations (3.1)–(3.9),

LCL filter design [13,14]:

$$L_i = \frac{V_{dc}}{16 * f_{sw} * \Delta I_{L\max}} \tag{3.1}$$

$$\Delta I_{L\max} = 0.10 \frac{P_n * \sqrt{2}}{3 * V_{ph}} \tag{3.2}$$

$$Z_b = \frac{V_{gl\text{-}l}^2}{P_n} \tag{3.3}$$

$$C_b = \frac{1}{\omega_g Z_b} \tag{3.4}$$

where V_{dc}=DC bus voltage, f_{sw} is the switching frequency of the three-phase bi-directional rectifier, P_n=nominal power rating of the converter, V_{ph}=phase voltage, Z_b=base impedance, and $V_{gl\text{-}l}$=line-line voltage of the grid. Filter capacitance is estimated by considering the limit of maximum power factor variation, α seen by the grid. Usually, the maximum value of $\alpha = 5\%$ as reported for grid-connected inverters is in [13,14]. Filter capacitor becomes.

$$C = \alpha C_b \tag{3.5}$$

$$L_g = r * L_i \tag{3.6}$$

where r is the relation between inverter side inductance and grid side inductance, and it is selected based on the desired ripple current attenuation. In general, it varied from 0.3 to 1 [13,14].

Design of DC bus capacitor:

$$C_{dc\min} = \frac{I_{cap,rms}}{V_{ripple} * 2 * \pi * f_{sw}} \tag{3.7}$$

where $I_{cap,rms}$=rms ripple current, V_{ripple}=ripple voltage

Design of passive components in bi-directional DC-DC converter:

$$L_b = \frac{V_b\left(V_{dc} - V_b\right)}{I_{ripple} * f_{sw} * V_{dc}} \tag{3.8}$$

$$C_b = \frac{I_{ripple}}{8 * f_{sw} * V_{ripple}} \tag{3.9}$$

where V_b=battery voltage, V_{dc}=DC bus voltage, and I_{ripple}=ripple current

In addition, researchers have been looking at several other options, like the dual-active (DAB) and triple-active bridge (TAB), with the goal of improving reliability, volume, cost, and efficiency of this on-board charging architecture. The other class of conductive charging is discussed in the next subsection.

3.3.2 Off-board EV charging architecture

Off-board charging may mitigate EVs' grid impact with proper peak demand planning and control using renewable energy sources [15–19]. Longer refilling/recharging periods, limited charging points, and a shorter driving range are all consequences of the fueling problem, which may be mitigated with a fast charger. Figure 3.7a and b depicts the two most popular types of fast charging designs: (i) the AC common bus architecture and (ii) the DC common bus architecture.

3.3.2.1 Common AC bus fast charging system

As demonstrated in Figure 3.7a, a common AC bus design may be employed in a rapid charging supply system. Each charging port has its own AC-DC (rectifier) device connected to the AC grid. Later, a DC-DC converter stage with an isolated transformer was added to manage the battery voltage. Unfortunately, each charger should connect with a separate rectification unit and inherent poor power factor performance, which may result in undesired harmonics on the AC grid. Furthermore, the connection of renewable sources in this design, namely PV panels, fuel cells, or extra energy storage devices, would need separate rectifier stages in the system. As a result, the AC bus rapid charging design has the disadvantages such as increased cost, decreased efficiency, and increased control complexity.

3.3.2.2 Common DC bus fast charging system

The alternative rapid charging system technique, as illustrated in Figure 3.7b, employs a single central rectifier with a greater power capacity to offer a shared DC bus. This enables the connection of several charging ports and gives a more viable configuration for renewable sources namely solar PV

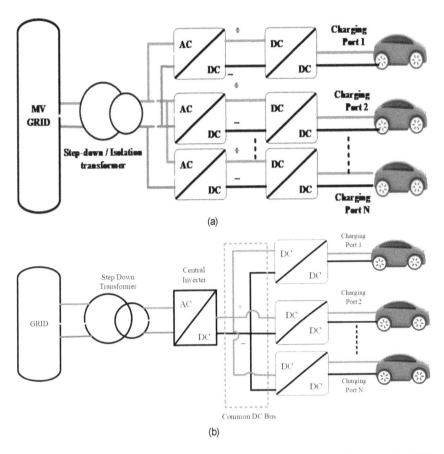

Figure 3.7 Off-grid EV charging types (a) AC common bus [20] and (b) DC common bus [21].

and fuel-cell. Moreover, there are no synchronization or reactive power concerns with the DC connection. As a result, this method enables the charging system to be capable of mitigating the detrimental consequences of EV penetration in the power grid. In comparison to the AC bus design, the system needs a high-rated central AC-DC converter and complicated protection circuitry. As a result, the decision between AC and DC rapid charging systems should be made carefully on the availability of sources and requirements.

Based on energy rating and time of charge, aforesaid charging systems are further classified into three stages, i.e., levels I, II, and III, as depicted in Figure 3.8. The power level that the charger can deliver to the battery in level I is up to 2 kW; in level II, it is up to 20 kW; and at level III, it is up to 120 kW. In addition, based on the type of power input to the EV, these chargers are further classified into AC or DC chargers. A brief comparison

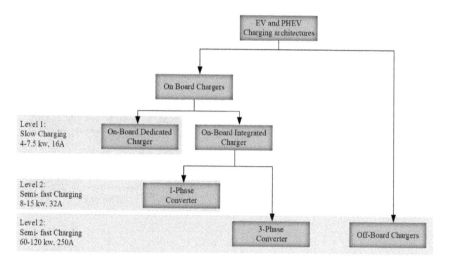

Figure 3.8 Types of EV chargers.

Table 3.1 Comparison of different levels of charging [3]

Level	Maximum power rating (kW)	Maximum ampere rating (A)
IEC standard		
AC charging		
AC level 1	4–7.5	16
AC level 2	8–15	32
AC level 3	60–120	250
DC charging		
DC fast charging	100–200	400
SAE standard (Society of Automotive Engineers)		
AC charging		
AC level 1	2	16
AC level 2	20	80
AC level 3	Above 20	-
DC charging		
DC level 1	40	80
DC level 2	90	200
DC level 3	240	400
CHAdeMO		
DC fast charging	62.5	125

of the different levels of chargers and their specifications as per standards is given in Table 3.1.

CHAdeMO was the original rapid charging standard for electric cars and plug-in hybrids established by Japanese car manufacturing companies. The word CHAdeMO is CHArge de Move, which means CHArge for MOving.

3.4 NON-CONVENTIONAL ENERGY-BASED EV CHARGING STATIONS

Renewable energy (RES)-based EV charging stations are sustainable solutions that use RES such as solar, wind, hydro, and geothermal to charge EVs [22–26]. It reduces the carbon footprint associated with charging EVs and can also provide cost savings and help balance the electricity grid. Energy storage systems, such as batteries, can store surplus energy and ensure a reliable energy supply. Government policies can encourage the development of renewable energy-based EV charging infrastructure through subsidies, tax incentives, and regulations. Solar, wind, and biomass are solutions for creating EV charging.

Several investigations are being conducted to study the large-scale, durable effect of wind energy in meeting the surplus energy demand arising from EV charging [27,28]. Nevertheless, it should be emphasized that wind energy-based systems need adequate sites and enough space for windmill installation. The difficulty is enormous in metropolitan locations, where massive structures are substantial obstacles in wind routes. Furthermore, since wind speed varies rapidly, it is less desirable for EV charging than other RE sources.

Bioelectricity differs from wind energy, and it may be simply conserved and utilized whenever needed [9]. It may be made from a variety of biomass feedstocks, including forestry and agricultural leftovers, woody energy crops, and whole tree harvesting. Several recent research studies have been published to investigate the potential use of biomass energy in EV charging. Regardless of these benefits, bioelectricity generation produces a high-contaminating environment, making it unacceptable for densely inhabited places. Similarly, sources such as tidal, hydro, and geothermal have restrictions such as availability, cost, and geographical constraints.

Solar PV power generation for EV charging is significantly more established and diverse than other renewable energy sources. This is because solar PV power allows for more freedom in connecting with the DC charging system. It also provides the opportunity to charge the EV while parked if PV panels are put on the roof of the car park [19]. Because the charging takes place during the daytime, when demand for load and power tariffs are at their highest, the cost reductions are significant.

There are different architectures of solar PV-based EV charging systems (EVCS) that are present in the literature. Solar PV-based off-grid EVCS, solar PV and fuel cell-based EVCS, and solar PV-based on-grid EVCS will be discussed in further subsections. Moreover, in all the architectures, battery energy storage systems play a vital role. as mentioned above.

3.4.1 Solar PV-based Off-grid EVCS

Solar PV-based off-grid EVCS provides a sustainable and cost-effective solution for providing EV charging infrastructure in areas without access to the electrical grid, while also contributing to the reduction of greenhouse

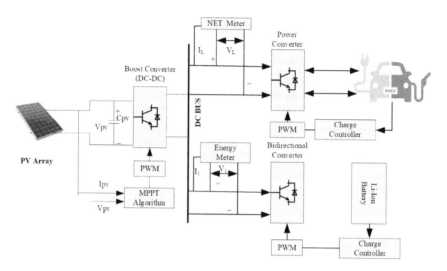

Figure 3.9 Solar PV-based Off-grid EVCS [27].

emissions and promoting energy independence [23–26]. The schematic diagram and its associated components of the solar PV-based off-grid EVCS are depicted in Figure 3.9.

They can be installed in remote areas, islands, highways, parking lots, events, and construction sites where EV drivers need a charging option and where an electrical grid connection may not be available or reliable. Among the possibilities mentioned in the literature, including battery storage is an appropriate strategy for making the proposed system sustainable. When the irradiance is variable, the PV source is effectively utilized in conjunction with the ESS. Furthermore, ESS uses the most RES possible when there is an excess of power or when EVs are not available.

3.4.2 Solar PV-based fuel cell connected Off-grid EVCS

Solar PV-based EVCS with a fuel cell connected system for EV charging is a unique and sustainable solution for providing reliable and efficient charging infrastructure for all types of EVs as depicted in Figure 3.10. The system uses solar panels to generate electricity from the Sun and stores excess energy in a battery bank [17,29–31]. The remaining solar energy can be used to produce hydrogen through an electrolyzer, which is stored in tanks and used by a fuel cell system to generate electricity for charging EVs.

In fuel-based EVs, such as those powered by hydrogen fuel cells or natural gas, a solar PV-based EV charging station with a fuel cell-connected system can also provide a reliable solution for fueling these vehicles. The solar panels would produce electricity, which is used to power an electrolyzer to produce hydrogen or to charge natural gas vehicles through an

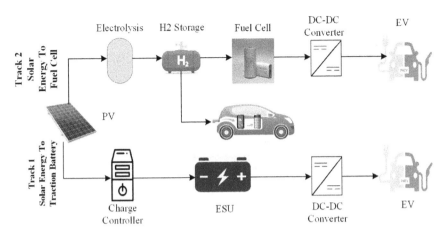

Figure 3.10 Solar PV fuel cell connected to Off-grid EV charging station [28].

on-site compressor. The stored hydrogen or natural gas can then be used by a fuel cell system or internal combustion engine to generate electricity to charge the fuel-cell-based EVs. These systems can be installed on highways, rest areas, urban and suburban areas, public spaces, and off-grid areas. This integrated system offers a sustainable and efficient solution for charging both battery-electric and fuel-based electrical vehicles, promoting energy independence and reducing environmental impact.

3.4.3 Solar PV-based On-grid EVCS

Solar PV-based grid-connected EVCS provides multiple advantages including new income streams, system stabilization, renewable energy integration, vehicle-to-grid services, and economic progress. These systems consist of various components, as shown in Figure 3.11. The PV generating system, comprising a PV array, maximum power point tracking (MPPT), and a boost converter, is the initial phase. The PV array converts solar energy into electrical energy, providing voltage V_{pv} and current I_{pv}. The boost converter adjusts V_{pv} and I_{pv} based on irradiance changes using the MPPT approach, maximizing power extraction. PWM signals from the MPPT control the boost converter's duty ratio to obtain the maximum possible extraction of solar energy.

This DC-link electricity is linked to the EV charger and ESS through the DC bus. A DC-DC bi-directional converter (BDC) is a primary device for charging and discharging batteries (either EV batteries or energy storage units). When in charging mode, the BDC functions similarly to a buck converter. When it is discharged, it functions as a boost converter. When there is too much electricity in the PV system, the ESS unit is employed to store it. During PV off-time/partial active time, the power stored in the ESS is transmitted back to the DC link. Moreover, the above description is also applied to off-grid solar PV-based EVCS (illustrated in Figure 3.8)

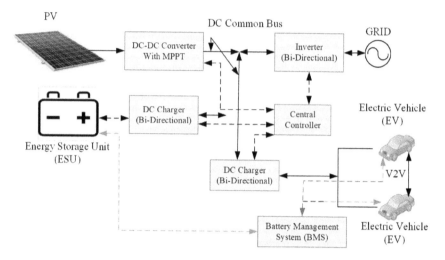

Figure 3.11 Solar PV fuel cell connected to On-grid EV charging station [27].

Further, if the PV and ESS are completely incapable of delivering any electricity (due to very low irradiation), the EV will be charged straight from the grid. The grid AC power is first transformed from alternating current to direct current using a bi-directional inverter in rectification mode. The DC charger then further conditions the DC voltage. When PV can give a certain amount of energy (but not enough for a completely independent charge), both the PV and the grid contribute to the charging. The quantity of energy obtained from the grid is proportional to the amount of energy extracted by the PV. The grid will make up the difference. Because the irradiance circumstances are very dynamic, the controller must continually check the power produced by the PV and adjust the intake from the grid to guarantee that the needed power to the EV is maintained.

Vehicle-to-grid (V2G) technology is currently gaining interest in the EV market owing to its capacity to offer grid flexibility, generate money for EV owners, boost renewable energy integration, and improve energy resilience. It enables EVs to store and deliver energy to the grid, balancing supply and demand and engaging in grid services. V2G also allows EVs to act as backup power sources in the event of an emergency and provides sophisticated fleet management. On-grid EVCS may be in residential neighborhoods, businesses, public parking lots, retail districts, roads, and public transit hubs, offering EV users with convenient charging alternatives.

3.5 CHALLENGES AND TRENDS IN EVCS

With the rapid emergence of electric cars on the market and government pressure to decrease vehicle emissions to zero by 2050, there is a significant demand for more efficient charging options [32–36]. To meet those requirements, different trends and future potentials are discussed in the EVCS namely: DC fast charging by the integration of renewable sources, static and dynamic wireless charging architectures, wide-band gap-based power converters for higher power density, improved battery technology, employment of artificial intelligent (AI) and machine learning (ML) techniques for regulating the integrated systems for realizing the low-cost solutions. Details of the above-said trends have been discussed in detail as follows:

3.5.1 DC fast charging

According to many consumer surveys, the adoption of electromobility is highly reliant on the availability and length of the charging process; high-power DC charging stations are the solution to these market needs. A typical EV can already charge roughly 80% of its battery capacity in less than 10 minutes. This is analogous to refueling a traditional automobile with an internal combustion engine. A high-power DC charger typically transforms incoming three-phase AC power into the DC voltage needed by the vehicle's battery. To transmit information about the vehicle and the level of charge of the battery, a data transmission channel is necessary. Finally, vehicle information and owner data are exchanged over a secure data link for invoicing reasons.

The key challenges in DC fast charger design are to minimize cooling efforts, provide high power density, and reduce overall system size and cost. High power density necessitates forced air conditioning, which is already typical. However, when system power density increases, the next generation of charging methods will need liquid cooling. To minimize the size of magnetic components, compact designs must explore greater switching rates ranging from 30 to 100 kHz.

3.5.2 Wireless EV charging system

Wireless charging has plenty of merits in comparison with the conventional charging methods. One of the key advantages is that the user does not require any cables and connectors, which can be damaged over time. Thus, it allows the user to charge their EV in public spaces. Since the absence of physical contact, the risk of electric shock can be eliminated. Moreover, the requirement for hardware circuit would be reduced with the wireless charging system by eliminating charging ports.

Static and dynamic wireless charging schemes are two types of wireless charging technology that can be used for EVs. Static wireless charging system includes the transfer of power from a sender coil to receiver coil which is installed beneath the EV while the vehicle is stationary. Most of the time, this technology can be seen in homes or public charging stations. Contemporarily, dynamic-based wireless charging involves the transfer of power from a transmitter coil embedded in the surface to a receiver coil installed underneath the EV as the vehicles drives over the transmitter coil. It is a more promising solution to EV owners in terms of limited range and avoiding the charging time during commutes.

3.5.3 Better battery storage technology

As EVs continue to evolve, their battery capacity is expected to increase. The advancement in power electronics technology alone cannot achieve ultra-fast charging. Some of the most interesting trends in battery technology are as follows:

a. **Higher energy density:** To enhance the driving range of EVs.
b. **Faster charging:** Development of batteries that can be charged more quickly to reduce the charging times.
c. **Longer battery lifespan:** Degradation of battery lifetime is a common problem in EVs, so the developing technologies are expected to have longer lifespans and better durability.
d. **Safer operation:** Safety of the battery should be ensured, especially in the event of a crash or other accident. Hence, the future battery technologies are expected to be safer, with less risk of fire or explosion.

3.5.4 Use of AI techniques in EV industry

AI techniques play a huge role in optimizing and enhancing the efficiency of EV charging infrastructure. Here are some key areas where AI is applied:

i. **Predictive charging:** AI algorithms can analyze historical data, weather patterns, traffic conditions, and individual driving behavior to predict the charging needs of EVs. This helps in optimizing charging schedules, managing grid load, and reducing peak demand.
ii. **Dynamic load balancing:** AI can intelligently distribute the charging load across charging stations and grid infrastructure, considering factors such as available capacity, demand patterns, and charging priorities. It ensures efficient utilization of resources and prevents overloading of the grid.
iii. **Smart charging networks:** AI enables the development of intelligent charging networks that can communicate with individual vehicles and adapt charging strategies based on real-time information. This includes features such as load management, demand response, and V2G integration.
iv. **Integration with distributed energy sources:** AI can enable the incorporation of solar and wind power into EVCS. It can optimize charging schedules based on energy availability, grid conditions, and cost considerations.

Overall, AI techniques enable intelligent decision-making, resource allocation, and automation in EV charging infrastructure, leading to improved efficiency, reduced costs, and enhanced user experience.

3.5.5 ML techniques in battery management

The use of ML approaches is essential to the management of batteries since they make effective monitoring, optimization, and predictive maintenance possible. The following is a concise and clear summary:

i. **State-of-Charge (SoC) of the battery**: The SoC, or percentage energy still accessible in the battery, may be correctly projected using ML algorithms by analyzing data from the battery voltage, current, and temperature. Having this information allows charging and discharging tactics to be optimized more effectively.

ii. **State-of-health (SoH) prediction**: ML models leverage historical battery performance data to predict the SoH, which reflects the overall health and degradation level of the battery. This enables proactive maintenance and replacement planning.

iii. **Fault detection and diagnostics**: ML techniques analyze battery data to detect anomalies, faults, or abnormalities in real time. This enables early identification of issues, allowing for timely maintenance and reducing the risk of battery performance.

iv. **Thermal management, energy management, and optimization**: ML techniques analyze the data from various sources such as thermal characteristics, energy prices, user preferences, and grid conditions to prevent overheating of battery, to optimize energy usage, and grid stability.

Overall, the use of ML techniques enhances better efficiency, prolongs battery lifespan, improves safety, and optimizes overall energy management.

3.5.6 Wide bandgap power semiconductors for EV systems

Wide bandgap (WBG) power semiconductor devices, such as silicon carbide (SiC) and gallium nitride (GaN), have drawn substantial attention in the EV applications. Compared to conventional silicon power semiconductors, WBG equipment offers several advantages, including lower losses, higher switching frequencies, and the ability to withstand higher junction temperatures. The use of WBG power semiconductors in EV power electronic systems brings about improvements in various aspects. Firstly, the lower power losses of WBG devices result in a higher range. This translates to reduced energy consumption and increased overall efficiency of the vehicle.

Secondly, the higher switching frequencies of WBG devices allow for more rapid switching operations in power electronic systems. This, in turn, enables the design of more compact and lightweight power converters. The reduced size and weight contribute to increased power density and improved packaging efficiency, which are crucial for EVs where space is often limited. Furthermore, WBG power semiconductors exhibit superior thermal properties, enabling them to operate at higher junction temperatures compared to traditional silicon-based devices.

Despite numerous benefits, the widespread adoption of WBG power semiconductors in EV faces certain challenges such as packaging, and thermal management, typical gate driver requirements, unique circuit topologies, and control strategies.

REFERENCES

1. India Electric Vehicle Market Size, Share & Trends Analysis Report By Product (BEV, PHEV), By Vehicle Type (Passenger Cars, Commercial Vehicles), And Segment Forecasts, 2021 – 2030, p. 110. Report ID: GVR-4-68039-640-4. https://www.grandviewresearch.com/industry-analysis/india-electric-vehicle-market-report.

2. Electric Vehicle Market Share, Size, Trends, Industry Analysis Report, By Power Source (Stored Electricity, On-board Electric Generator); By Vehicle Type; By Product; By Region, Segment Forecast, 2022–2030, p. 112, Jun-2022. https://www.polarismarketresearch.com/industry-analysis/electric-vehicles-ev-market.

3. Yong, J.Y.; Ramachandaramurthy, V.K.; Tan, K.M.; Mithulananthan, N. A review on the state-of-the-art technologies of electric vehicle, its impacts, and prospects. *Renew Sustain Energy Rev* 2015; 49:365–385.

4. Bhatti, A.R.; Salam, Z.; Aziz, M.J.B.A.; Yee, K.P.; Ashique, R.H. Electric vehicles charging using photovoltaic: status and technological review. *Renew Sustain Energy Rev* 2016; 54:34–47.

5. Putrus, G.; Suwanapingkarl, P.; Johnston, D.; Bentley, E.; Narayana, M. "Impact of electric vehicles on power distribution networks". In: *Proceedings of the Vehicle Power and Propulsion Conference, 2009 VPPC'09 IEEE*: IEEE; 2009, Dearborn, MI, USA. pp. 827–831.

6. Wi, Y.M.; Lee, J.U.; Joo, S.K. Electric vehicle charging method for smart homes/ buildings with a photovoltaic system. *IEEE Trans Consum Electron* 2013; 5(9):323–328.

7. Yilmaz, M.; Krein, P.T. Review of battery charger topologies, charging power levels, and infrastructure for plug-in electric and hybrid vehicles. *IEEE Trans Power Electron* 2013; 28:2151–2169.

8. Feng, H.; Tavakoli, R.; Onar, O.C.; Pantic, Z. Advances in high-power wireless charging systems: Overview and design considerations. *IEEE Trans Transp Electrif* 2020; 6:886–919.

9. Poorfakhraei, A.; Narimani, M.; Emadi, A. A review of multilevel inverter topologies in electric vehicles: Current status and future trends. *IEEE Open J Power Electron* 2021; 2: 155–170.

10. Ronanki, D.; Kelkar, A.; Williamson, S.S. Extreme fast charging technology-prospects to enhance sustainable electric transportation. *Energies* 2019; 12:3721.

11. Guo, B.; Zhang, Y.; Zhang, J.; Gao, J. Hybrid control strategy of phase-shifted full-bridge LLC converter based on digital direct phase-shift control. *J Power Electron* 2018; 18:802–816.

12. Verma, A.; Singh, B.; Shahani, D. T. Grid to vehicle and vehicle to grid energy transfer using single-phase bidirectional AC-DC converter and bidirectional DC-DC converter. *Int J Eng Sci Technol* 2011; 4:1–5. doi: 10.1109/ICEAS.2011.6147084.

13. Johnson, Brian. "Power factor correction design for on-board chargers in electric vehicles." Texas Instrum. Appl., Dallas, TX, USA, Tech. Rep. SLUA896, Jun (2018).

14. Cody Watkins, "7.4-kW EV/HEV Bidirectional On-board Charger Reference Design With GaN." Texas Instrum. Appl., Dallas, TX, USA, Tech. Rep. TIDUF18, Oct (2022).

15. Chakraborty, S.; Vu, H.-N.; Hasan, M.M.; Tran, D.-D.; El Baghdadi, M.; Hegazy, O. DC-DC converter topologies for electric vehicles, plug-in hybrid electric vehicles and fast charging stations: State of the art and future trends. *Energies* 2019; 12:1569.

16. Ahmad, A.; Alam, M.S.; Chabaan, R. A comprehensive review of wireless charging technologies for electric vehicles. *IEEE Trans Transp Electrif* 2018; 4:38–63.

17. Emadi, A.; Lee, Y.J.; Rajashekara, K. Power electronics and motor drives in electric, hybrid electric, and plug-in hybrid electric vehicles. *IEEE Trans Ind Electron* 2008; 55:2237–2245.

18. Lee, W.; Li, S.; Han, D.; Sarlioglu, B.; Minav, T.A.; Pietola, M. A review of integrated motor drive and wide-bandgap power electronics for high-performance electro-hydrostatic actuators. *IEEE Trans Transp Electrif* 2018; 4:684–693.

19. Charkhgard, M.; Farrokhi M. State-of-charge estimation for lithium-ion batteries using neural networks and EKF. *IEEE Trans Ind Electron* 2010; 57:4178–4187.

20. Bai, S.; Lukic, S.M. Unified active filter and energy storage system for an MW electric vehicle charging station. *IEEE Trans Power Electron* 2013; 28:5793–5803.

21. Rivera, S.;Wu, B.; Jiacheng, W.; Athab, H.; Kouro, S. Electric vehicle charging station using a neutral point clamped con-verter with bipolar DC bus and voltage balancing circuit. In *Proceedings of the IECON 2013-39th Annual Conference of the IEEE Industrial Electronics Society*, Vienna, Austria, 10–13 November 2013; pp. 6219–6226.

22. Brenna, M.; Dolara, A.; Foiadelli, F.; Leva, S.; Longo, M. Urban scale photovoltaic charging stations for electric vehicles. *IEEE Trans Sustain Energy* 2014; 5:1234–1241.

23. Hu, W.; Su, C.; Chen, Z.; Bak-Jensen, B. Optimal operation of plug-in electric vehicles in power systems with high wind power penetrations. *IEEE Trans Sustain Energy* 2013; 4:577–585.

24. Von Jouanne, A.; Husain, I.; Wallace, A.; Yokochi, A. Gone with the wind: Innovative hydrogen/fuel cell electric vehicle infrastructure based on wind energy sources. *IEEE Ind Appl Mag* 2005; 11:12–19.

25. Khalid, M.R.; Alam, M.S.; Sarwar, A.; Asghar, M.J. A Comprehensive review on electric vehicles charging infrastructures and their impacts on power-quality of the utility grid. *eTransportation* 2019; 1:100006.

26. Hussain, A.; Bui, V.-H.; Kim, H.-M. Optimal sizing of battery energy storage system in a fast EV charging station considering power outages. *IEEE Trans Transp Electrif* 2020; 6:453–463.

27. Traube, J. et al. Mitigation of solar irradiance intermittency in photovoltaic power systems with integrated electric-vehicle charging functionality. *IEEE Trans Power Electron* 2013; 28(6):3058–3067.

28. VanMierlo, J.; Van den Bossche, P.; Maggetto, G. Models of energy sources for EV and HEV: fuel cells, batteries, ultracapacitors, flywheels and engine-generators. *J Power Sources* 2004; 128(1):76–89.

29. Badawy, M.O.; Sozer, Y. Power flow management of a grid tied PV-battery system for electric vehicles charging. *IEEE Trans Ind Appl* 2016; 53:1347–1357.

30. Lee, B.-K.; Kim, J.-P.; Kim, S.-G.; Lee, J.-Y. A PWM SRT DC/DC converter for 6.6-kW EV onboard charger. *IEEE Trans Ind Electron* 2016; 63:894–902.

31. Peng, F.; Li, H.; Su, G.-J.; Lawler, J. A new ZVS bidirectional DC-DC converter for fuel cell and battery application. *IEEE Trans Power Electron* 2004; 19:54–65.

32. Goli, P.; Shireen, W. PV integrated smart charging of phevs based on DC link voltage sensing. *IEEE Trans Smart Grid* 2014; 5(3):1421–1428. ISSN 1949-3053. doi: 10.1109/TSG.2013.2286745.

33. Hernandez, J. C.; Sutil, F. S. Electric vehicle charging stations feeded by renewable: PV and train regenerative braking. *IEEE Latin America Trans* 2016; 14(7):3262–3269. ISSN 1548-0992. doi: 10.1109/TLA.2016.7587629.

34. Singh, M.; Kumar, P.; Kar, I.; Kumar, N. A real-time smart charging station for evs designed for v2g scenario and its coordination with renewable energy sources. In *2016 IEEE Power and Energy Society General Meeting (PESGM)*, pages 1–5, July 2016. doi: 10.1109/PESGM.2016.7741479.

35. Ehsan, A.; Yang, Q. Active distribution system reinforcement planning with EV charging stations-Part I: Uncertainty modelling and problem formulation. *IEEE Trans Sustain Energy* 2020; 11:970–978.

36. PV+Energy Storage System in EV Charging Station, Shenzhen Kstar Science & Technology Co., Ltd, April 2020. https://www.kstar.com/cn/upload/cms/www/20200701150324504.PDF.

Chapter 4

Design and implementation of solar PV-assisted sensorless predictive current controlled SPMSM LEV drive with regenerative braking

Sreejith R. and Bhim Singh

4.1 INTRODUCTION

Both the developed and developing nations are fostering transportation segment towards electrification to confront the global energy crisis, volatile crude oil prices, and climate change. Light electric vehicles (LEVs) are the most affordable EV segment, which can pave the way for easier realization of electrification with consumer acceptance. The present Asian electric three wheelers are equipped with low-voltage permanent magnet brushless direct current (PMBLDC) motors rated up to 1.2 kW peak power capacity. Although the battery technologies are evolving to improve their energy density, the lack of enough charging infrastructure and its associated initial high capital investment are retarding the growth of EV acceptance among customers. Therefore, a sustainable solution to improve the range, performance and efficiency, is vital for fast forwarding EV targets established by various government organizations.

The PMBLDC motors, utilized in electric three wheelers, work on the six-step commutation principle, have higher torque ripples, and are equipped with unreliable Hall effect sensors. Meanwhile, permanent magnet synchronous motors (PMSM) having sinusoidal distributed windings and back-EMF are highly efficient motors with almost negligible torque ripple and better voltage utilization factor. These are used in majority of the medium and high-power EV segments. Vector control and direct torque control are industry standard methods adopted for driving the permanent magnet brushless motors in EVs [1]. The preset gain parameter values of the PI controllers used for the current management by a typical vector control are susceptible to model inaccuracies, external disturbances, and parametric and load fluctuations. This degrades an EV's performance at different operating points of speed, torque and power. Because of its simplicity, optimality framework and efficacy, model predictive controller (MPC) has acquired favour for power electronic applications in machine drives and power systems [2]. The computational complexity of MPC is overcome by

DOI: 10.1201/9781003481065-4

utilizing the discrete nature of the power converter switches, leading to the most popular form of MPC known as finite control set MPC (FCS-MPC). The striking feature of MPC is that it employs an optimality paradigm that allows for the introduction of different nonlinearities and practical constraints with easiness [3]. Even different constraints can be incorporated into the cost function itself. The set stabilizability of FCS-MPC utilized for the DTC of PMSM drive is mathematically proved in Refs. [4,5]. Therefore, a stable controller with fast response is achievable with FCS-MPC as the current controller for electric drives. Even though FCS-MPC has a variable switching frequency, it mostly operates around one-fifth and one-sixth of sampling frequency [6]. Therefore, an SPMSM drive with time delay compensated predictive current controller is considered in this work, accommodating various delays that occurred during the signal processing and conditioning.

Researchers have shown immense interest in sensorless control of PMSM drive for cost reduction and reliability enhancements. Nonetheless, the sensorless techniques are hardly used in EV applications due to the non-availability of a wide speed range of operable control techniques. The flux observer and back-EMF-based estimation techniques are suitable for medium- and high-speed range, whereas the saliency-based methods are focused on the zero-speed and low-speed region [7]. Kris Scicluna et al. [8] have proposed a search-based real-time self-commissioning high frequency (HF) current injection method for zero and low speed. However, the HF methods cause acoustic noise, higher torque ripple and incur losses. Recent research on fundamental model-based position estimation methods has shown promising results in the low-speed region as well. Sliding mode observers (SMOs) are one of the most widely researched sensorless algorithms due to their robustness, simplicity, nonlinear structure and deterministic nature. Different methods adopted by the researchers to overcome the signal attenuation, phase shift, singularity and chattering effects of a conventional SMO are using adaptive second-order SMO [9], dual second-order generalized integrator-frequency locked loop [10], speed adaptive super twisting SMO-moving average filter phase locked loop (SASTSMO-MAFPLL) [11], frequency adaptive complex co-efficient filters [12], etc. Sreejith and Singh [11] have carried out an extensive comparative study on various higher order and conventional sliding mode observers and have come up with smooth second-order SMO adaptive to the motor speed with MAF-PLL. This method has achieved sensorless starting at 3.95% of the rated speed, which can be translated to almost zero linear velocity for a typical three-wheeler vehicle as discussed in the later section.

Regenerative braking is another worthwhile feature of an EV that helps recover some amount of energy during sudden braking [13]. Recent literature has reported different types of regenerative braking along with the analytical analysis [14]. It is presented that the regenerative braking energy can enhance the driving range by approximately 15%–25% or reduce the energy consumption by 20% based on the powertrain configuration, control strategy, driving speed and the driving pattern adopted [15,16]. This justifies that the utilization of the regenerated power during braking can help in significant contribution for a LEV such as two/three wheelers (2W/3W) compared to other EV segments. However, the regenerative braking is very sparsely employed in the present day 3W EVs. Moreover, battery-operated vehicles are not fully carbon emission free as the source energy is still generated mostly from fossil fuels. Therefore, different energy sources such as solar PV arrays, ultracapacitors and fuel cells can be augmented for further improvement of range in EVs based on vehicle limitations, requirements and surrounding environmental restrictions. On account of this, researchers have proposed to use the renewable energy sources for charging the vehicles using a renewable energy-based charging infrastructure [17]. Yet, it takes large-scale investment, time and planning. For low- and medium-speed LEVs such as e-rickshaws and electric auto-rickshaws, a better solution would be utilizing a rooftop solar PV array, and this has been studied in Ref. [18], quantifying its benefits, especially at a constant speed operation. Although solar electric three wheelers are studied, examined and realized in various research work [19–21], a detailed design methodology along with experimental validation illustrating different modes of operation are not discussed in the literature. According to the NREL champion photovoltaic module efficiency chart, University of New South Wales has produced a solar PV module with the highest efficiency of 40.6% [22]. With further technological advancements, the benefits of a rooftop solar PV-based EVs cannot be overlooked upon by the communities. Therefore, a systematic approach of design, control implementation and validation of a solar PV-battery-based position sensorless low-voltage PMSM LEV drive with regenerative braking functionality is presented for the first time in this work. The major advantage of this configuration is that it extends the range of the vehicle, reduces energy consumption and improves the battery life along with better efficiency as compared to conventional battery-operated LEV. Therefore, such a kind of system can accelerate the payback time to almost halves. The elucidation of the design, control and analysis of the solar PV-battery low-voltage sensorless PMSM-driven LEV configuration with experimental validation is presented for the first time in this work.

4.2 SYSTEM CONFIGURATION AND DESIGN

The system powertrain overview of an SPV-aided LV surface mounted PMSM EV drive is shown in Figure 4.1. A 48 V, 3 kW nominal continuous power-rated SPMSM with an intermittent rating of 5 kW, meeting the both rated and peak wheel power demand is selected for the study. A 41.66 V_{mpp}, 449.78 W_{mpp} solar PV array, along with 48 V_{oc}, 100 Ah, 2 C

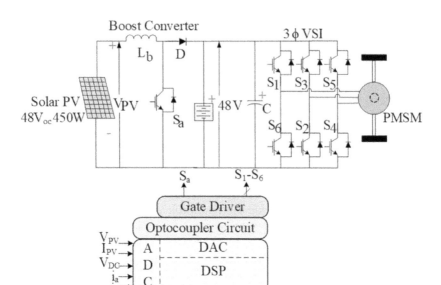

Figure 4.1 Powertrain configuration.

burst capacity battery bank provides supply to the SPMSM controlled by a three-phase IGBT-based VSI. Maximum power point tracking (MPPT) control of the solar PV array is achieved using the second-stage boost converter connected between the PV array and DC link as shown in Figure 4.1. An incremental conductance (InC) method is used for MPPT control while monitoring the battery charge to prevent over charging. The solar PV array voltage (V_{PV}), PV array current (I_{PV}), DC bus voltage (V_{DC}) and two motor phase currents (i_a and i_b) are captured and sent to the microcontroller through its analogue to digital converter (ADC) channels for the realization of the entire control algorithm. The sensorless control method estimates the speed and position information for MTPA vector control of the drive by providing optimal switching pulses (S_1–S_6) to the IGBT gate drivers of VSI through an opto-coupler-based isolation and amplification stage.

The design of powertrain components of EV drive involving the selection of solar PV array, boost converter inductor, DC-link capacitor and three-phase VSI are discussed here.

4.2.1 Solar PV array design

A solar PV array with OC voltage rating (V_{oc}) equal to that of nominal DC link voltage and a maximum power of approximately 450 W for standard temperature condition (25°C) and solar irradiance (1 kW/m²) is selected here. The solar PV array has an open-circuit voltage of 47.9 V and short circuit current of 11.49 A. Its corresponding maximum power point (MPP) voltage and MPP current values are 41.66 V and 10.8 A, respectively.

4.2.2 Boost converter design

With the help of the PV MPP voltage rating (V_{PV}) and rated V_{DC}, the boost converter duty ratio operated in a continuous mode of conduction is given as,

$$D_b = \frac{V_{DC} - V_{PV}}{V_{DC}} = \frac{48 - 41.66}{48} = 0.132 \tag{4.1}$$

For a switching frequency of $f_{sw} = 10\,kHz$, a boost inductor, L_b is designed as [23],

$$L_b = \frac{D_b \times V_{PV}}{f_{sw} \times \Delta i_L} = \frac{0.132 \times 41.66}{10,000 \times 10.778 \times 0.2} \approx 0.26\ mH \tag{4.2}$$

where Δi_L is the allowable ripple current in the inductor. This denotes that the inductor size requirement is small for a solar PV array configuration selected near to the DC link voltage.

4.2.3 Ratings of three-phase VSI

Considering a voltage safety factor of K_{vdc} for the 3-ϕ VSI, the IGBT switch voltage rating is given as:

$$V_{IGBT} = K_{vdc} \times V_{DC} = 2 \times 48 = 96 \approx 100\ V \tag{4.3}$$

Similarly, the switch current rating is selected as,

$$I_{IGBT} = K_{Idc} I_{peak} = 1.5 \times 200 = 300\ A \tag{4.4}$$

where K_{Idc} represents the factor of safety for current.
Therefore, the size of the VSI in VA is obtained as:

$$(VA)_{VSI} = V_{IGBT} I_{IGBT} = 100 \times 300 = 3\ kVA \tag{4.5}$$

4.2.4 Size of DC-link capacitor

The DC-link capacitor is selected based on the voltage ripple requirement at the battery side, and another function of the capacitor is to carry ripple current so that only DC current flows through the VSI. The minimum capacitance is calculated as [24],

$$C \geq \frac{I_{pk}}{\left(8f_{sw}\Delta v_{ripple}\right)} \geq \frac{200}{8 \times 2500 \times 48 \times 0.05} = 4166.67 \text{ μF} \quad (4.6)$$

where the I_{pk}, f_{sw}, and Δv_{ripple} are peak value of the motor current, worst-case switching frequency, and peak-to-peak ripple voltage, respectively. Therefore, the nominal DC bus capacitance is selected as 4,700 μF capacitor.

4.3 CONTROL METHODOLOGY AND MODELLING

In this section, a detailed explanation of complete control strategy of the powertrain configuration shown in Figure 4.1 is presented. It comprises the sensorless SPMSM drive control and the MPPT control algorithm of the solar PV boost converter.

4.3.1 SPMSM model

Neglecting the saturation nonlinearities, and core losses, a symmetrically balanced SPMSM modelled in stationary reference frame is given as [25],

$$V_\alpha = I_\alpha R + L\frac{dI_\alpha}{dt} + e_\alpha; \; V_\beta = I_\beta R + L\frac{dI_\beta}{dt} + e_\beta \quad (4.7)$$

$$e_\alpha = -\psi_{pm}\omega_e \sin\theta_e; \; e_\beta = \psi_{pm}\omega_e \cos\theta_e \quad (4.8)$$

$$T_e = \frac{P}{2}\frac{3}{2}\psi_{pm}\left(I_\alpha \cos\theta_e - I_\beta \sin\theta_e\right) \quad (4.9)$$

Here, $[V_\alpha \; V_\beta]^T$, $[I_\alpha \; I_\beta]^T$, and $[e_\alpha \; e_\beta]^T$ represent the terminal voltage, stator current, and back-EMF in $\alpha\beta$ reference. R, L, P, ω_e, T_e, θ_e, ψ_{pm} denote the phase resistance, phase inductance, rotor poles, electrical speed, electromagnetic torque, electrical rotor position and PM flux linkage, respectively. From the above mathematical model, the sliding mode observer is designed for the estimation of rotor position and speed.

4.3.2 PI Speed controller

The proportional integral controller (with gains, k_p and k_i) along with clamping anti-wind up method takes care of the speed control action wherein the error between the actual speed (N_{est}) and the reference speed (N_{ref}) is maintained near zero. Mathematically, the output of the speed controller is defined as:

$$T_e^*(i_q) = \left(k_p + \frac{k_i}{s} \right)(N_{ref} - N_{est}) \tag{4.10}$$

4.3.3 Model predictive control for current loop

The switching pulses for the VSI are directly provided by the inner current loop controlled by FCS-MPC after cost minimization of the squared error between reference current and actual current predicted over two two-step horizon. The discretized plant model is used for the prediction of the control variable with the least number of sensors. The entire control algorithm is fast enough to be executed within a sampling interval for generating the optimal switching pulses, and the complete flow process of the control algorithm is illustrated in Figure 4.2.

The time discretized mathematical model of an SPMSM for sampling time T_s is obtained as,

$$i_{\alpha\beta}(j+1) = \left(1 - \frac{RT_s}{L} \right)i_{\alpha\beta}(j) + \frac{T_s}{L}\left(v_{\alpha\beta}(j) - e_{\alpha\beta}(j) \right) \tag{4.11}$$

where $v_{\alpha\beta}(j)$ is voltage vector and $e_{\alpha\beta}(j)$ is the back-EMF components in the stationary reference frame

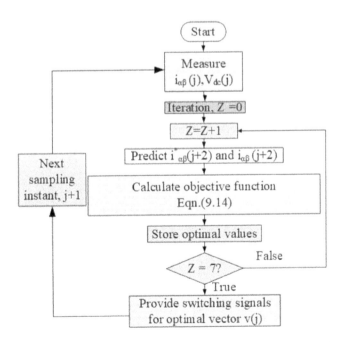

Figure 4.2 Flow process of delay compensated FCS-MPC for current control.

The two step ahead predicted value of the actual current can be recursively written as:

$$i_{\alpha\beta}(j+2) = \left(1 - \frac{RT_s}{L}\right) i_{\alpha\beta}(j+1) + \frac{T_s}{L}\left(v_{\alpha\beta}(j+1) - e_{\alpha\beta}(j+1)\right) \qquad (4.12)$$

The reference current for the $(j+2)$th instant is obtained from Lagrange interpolation method as [3],

$$i^*_{\alpha\beta}(j+2) = 6i^*_{\alpha\beta}(j) - 8i^*_{\alpha\beta}(j-1) + 3i^*_{\alpha\beta}(j-2) \qquad (4.13)$$

Two step ahead predicted values of actual and reference currents components are evaluated using (4.12) and (4.13) for every voltage vector available for a 3-ϕ inverter. This step leads to their respective squared l_2-norm cost function calculation as given by,

$$CF = \begin{cases} \left\{i^*_\alpha(j+1) - i_\alpha(j+1)\right\}^2 + \left\{i^*_\beta(j+1) - i_\beta(j+1)\right\}^2 \\ + \left\{i^*_\alpha(j+2) - i_\alpha(j+2)\right\}^2 + \left\{i^*_\beta(j+2) - i_\beta(j+2)\right\}^2 \end{cases} \qquad (4.14)$$

Irrespective of switching penalty, a choice of l_2 norm assures the stability of the system [6]. The voltage vector corresponding to a minimum CF is selected within a sampling time, and its corresponding optimal switching signals are directed to VSI.

4.3.4 Sensorless speed and position estimator

The estimation of speed and rotor position of the SPMSM drive is carried out using a modified SASTSMO-MAFPLL as shown in Figure 4.3. A continuous approximation signum function-based super twisting sliding mode observer estimates the stationary reference frame back-EMF components, from the current observer model of SPMSM, given by [11],

$$\frac{d}{dt}\hat{i}_{\alpha\beta} = -\frac{R}{L}\tilde{i}_{\alpha\beta} + \frac{1}{L}v_{\alpha\beta} + \frac{k_1\omega_e}{L}\left|\tilde{i}_{\alpha\beta}\right|^{0.5} \frac{\tilde{i}_{\alpha\beta}}{\left|\tilde{i}_{\alpha\beta}\right| + \varepsilon} + \frac{k_2\omega_e^2}{L}\int \frac{\tilde{i}_{\alpha\beta}}{\left|\tilde{i}_{\alpha\beta}\right| + \varepsilon} dt \qquad (4.15)$$

$$\hat{e}_{\alpha\beta} = -\frac{k_1\omega_e}{L}\left|\tilde{i}_{\alpha\beta}\right|^{0.5} \frac{\tilde{i}_{\alpha\beta}}{\left|\tilde{i}_{\alpha\beta}\right| + \varepsilon} - \frac{k_2\omega_e^2}{L}\int \frac{\tilde{i}_{\alpha\beta}}{\left|\tilde{i}_{\alpha\beta}\right| + \varepsilon} dt \qquad (4.16)$$

where k_1 and k_2 are the controller gains and ω_e is the estimated speed. ε is a small positive value chosen based on the smoothening requirement of the actual signum function without disturbing the robustness and control. The estimated back-EMF signals are fed into a linear phase filter-based PLL for

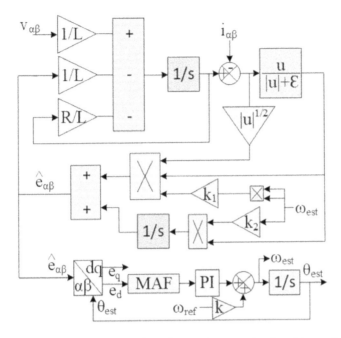

Figure 4.3 Block diagram representation of sensorless speed and position estimator.

estimating the SPMSM rotor speed and position as shown in Figure 4.3. The MAF effectively eliminates the harmonics in the direct axis back-EMF (e_d), and the lag incurred in the dynamic response is improved through an additional parallel path term comprising N_{ref} command.

4.3.5 SPV boost converter MPPT control

An InC-based MPPT control algorithm is used for the extraction of maximum power of solar PV array using the boost converter, as shown in Figure 4.4. This method overcomes the steady-state oscillation problem of the perturb and observe method and is simpler to implement. From the sensed PV voltage and current signals, reference voltage corresponding to the MPP is generated using the PWM control of the boost converter.

4.4 SIMULATION RESULTS

The performance of the presented solar PV-assisted LEV configuration is simulated using the SPMSM parameters given in Table 4.1. The entire system is modelled and simulated in MATLAB/Simulink with a sampling time of 1 μs. Figure 4.5 exhibits the sensorless control estimation and vector control

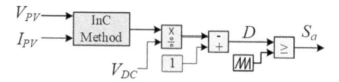

Figure 4.4 SPV boost converter maximum power point tracking control pulse generation.

Table 4.1 Complete specifications of SPMSM

Rated power	3 kW	Rated voltage	48 V_{DC}
Rated current	85 A	Back-EMF constant K_e	11.9072 $V_{pk,l-l}/k_{rpm}$
Rated speed	3,800 RPM	Torque constant K_t	0.098472 N m/A_{pk}
Rated torque	8 N m	Flux linkage	0.016412V s
Inductance	69.95 µH	Moment of inertia	0.012 kg m²
Resistance	8.5 mΩ	Viscous friction	0.00145 N m s/rad
Pole pairs	4	Dry friction	0.039 N m

operation of the predictive current controlled drive. The drive is started from the rest position and accelerated to 2,000 RPM and gradually increased to 3,000 RPM at a load torque of 4 N m. A brake is applied at 0.4s and 0.6s reducing the speed down to 200 RPM. The intermittent loading capacity of the motor is utilized for providing sufficient torque during acceleration. The drive is able to track well the reference speed over the entire speed range as it is evident from the estimated speed and estimated position matching their respective reference values using a modified SASTSMO-MAFPLL algorithm. Meanwhile, this SPMSM LEV drive is most efficiently operated by maintaining i_d at zero for maximum torque per current operation.

The SPV array-battery dynamics at the running condition of the vehicle are illustrated in Figure 4.6. It can be noted that maximum power is obtained from a solar PV array through the InC-based MPPT control regardless of varying irradiance values of 1,000, 500, and 800 W/m². This PV power is utilized for driving the vehicle during motoring operation, and it charges the battery along with the regenerated power during the braking condition. This effectively helps in improving the range of the vehicle as observed from a rise in %SOC of the battery during this period.

4.5 COST-BENEFIT ANALYSIS OF PRESENTED SOLAR PV-ASSISTED LEV CONFIGURATION WITH EXISTING EV FOR INDIAN DRIVING CYCLE

The additional benefits of regenerative braking and solar PV array assistance will be helpful in improving the range of the vehicle. Assuming a Depth of Discharge of 80% for the EV battery, the available battery energy of 48 V, 100 Ah pack=3,840 Wh.

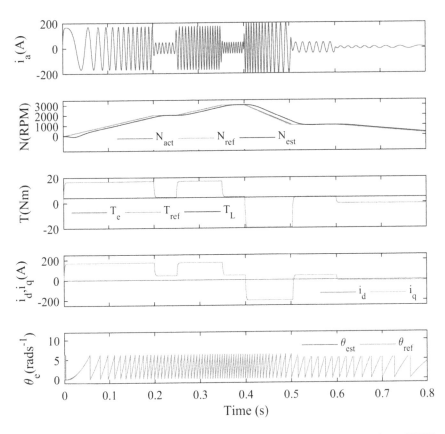

Figure 4.5 Simulated performance of SPV-assisted low-voltage sensorless PMSM driven LEV.

For Li-ion-based direct drive LEV weighing 550 kg, the observed energy consumption for IDC=44.08 Wh/km.

Now, with the additional weight of 50 kg for the rooftop solar PV array and associated connections (for the STION-150 solar PV array model of 450 W_{mpp}), the observed energy consumption for IDC=49.16 Wh/km.

Out of 108s of IDC, the deceleration/braking operation accounts for 37s. The maximum amount of energy that can be regenerated for the selected configuration is obtained as 18.77 Wh/km=1,313.9 Wh for 70 km range requirement. On average, the efficiency of regenerative braking varies from a minimum of (10% to 30%) of the battery capacity.

Therefore, the regenerated energy (assuming 30% efficiency)=394.17 Wh

For a sunny day in India, the solar PV array of 47.9 V_{mpp}, 450 W_{mpp} can generate an average energy of 2.25 kWh/day while accounting for 10% partial shading and 21% efficiency of the solar panels.

Total available energy due to battery+solar PV array+regenerative braking=3,840+394+2,250=6,484 Wh

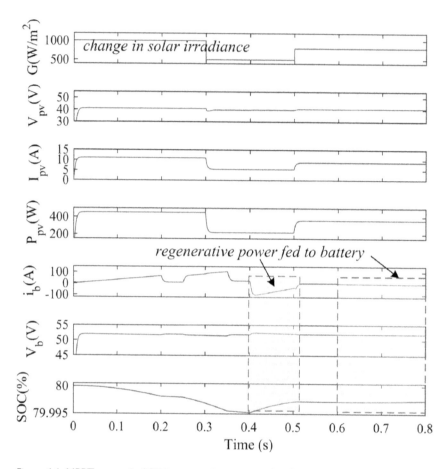

Figure 4.6 MPPT control of SPV array and corresponding battery power changes of the LEV during drive operation.

Therefore, the average range of the presented configuration for IDC=(6,484 Wh)/(49.16 Wh/km)=131.89 km.

Percentage improvement in the range compared to the existing EV=(61.89/131.89) ((131.89 – 70))/131.89 * 100%=46.92%

For IC petrol engine (Petrol rate of 101.54 Rs/L) having ARAI certified mileage of 35 km/L, INR required to cover a distance of 130 km=Rs. 377.14.

The charging price for E-rickshaw is Rs. 5/unit in Delhi. For the proposed configuration, INR required to cover a distance of 130 km=Only the price for energy consumed by the battery=3.84 kWh * 5 Rs/unit=Rs. 19.2.

Therefore, apart from the economic benefits as quantified above, the passenger comfort, performance and lifetime of the presented PMSM-based configuration are better than the existing BLDCM and IM-based e-auto rickshaws with true zero carbon emission.

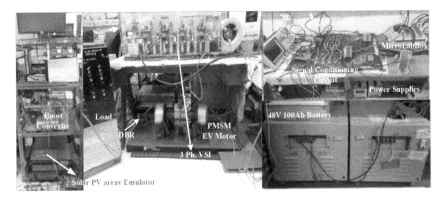

Figure 4.7 Photograph of experimental hardware prototype.

4.6 EXPERIMENTAL RESULTS

The presented EV drive configuration with its control algorithms is validated using a laboratory hardware prototype developed as shown in Figure 4.7. It comprises a 48 V 100 Ah lead acid battery source, connected to a 48 V 3 kW SPMSM through a Semikron make three-phase voltage source inverter. The solar PV array, emulated using AMETEK solar PV emulator (Model ETS600x17DPV), is connected to the DC-link through a boost converter as depicted in Figure 4.7.

The PV voltage and the DC-link battery voltage are measured using LEM make Hall effect voltage transducers (LV-25P), whereas the PV current and motor phase currents are sensed using LEM make Hall effect current transducers LA-55P and LA-125P, respectively. The sensed variables are fed into a MicroLabBox-based digital signal processor ds1202 for the implementation of control algorithms. The switching gate pulses for the boost converter and an inverter are fed into the gate drivers through an optocoupler (6N136) circuit, providing proper isolation and signal amplification. The loading arrangement is obtained by an identical coupled SPMSM connected to two parallel arranged 60 V, 80 A load boxes with the help of a three-phase diode bridge rectifier. The drive motor parameters are same as given in Table 4.1. The experimental results are captured using Keysight make mixed signal oscilloscope (InfiniiVision MSOX3024T).

4.6.1 Starting and steady-state performances of sensorless EV drive

The SPMSM is started using an *I-f* open-loop method by injecting a current signal with slowly increasing frequency corresponding to the reference speed [26]. This method is highly robust and successful without any reversal problem. The sensorless speed and position estimation performances during the starting are depicted in Figure 4.8a. As soon as the sensorless position estimate conforms to the reference position, seamless switchover takes place around 150 RPM. For a typical electric auto-rickshaw with tyre radius (r) of 0.23 m and a gear ratio (GR) of 10:1, to match the wheel speed with motor speed (N rpm) and to provide the necessary tractive force, the transition from open-loop control to sensorless closed loop operation achieved in terms of linear velocity of the vehicle (v) is calculated from angular speed of the motor (ω) as,

$$v = \frac{r\omega}{GR} = \frac{2\pi rN}{60 \cdot (GR)} = \frac{2\pi \times 0.23 \times 150}{60 \times (10)} = 0.361 \text{ m/s} = 1.3 \text{ km/h} \text{ or } 0.808 \text{ mph}$$

This clearly shows that the sensorless closed loop operation is achieved at a negligible vehicle speed and this method can be reliably used for the three-wheeler EV. The position and speed estimations at different range of speed values are shown in Figure 4.8b–d. It is evident from Figure 4.8b–d that the estimated position, θ_{est} matches exactly the reference position, θ_{ref} with a slight negligible phase delay for low, medium, and high speeds of 300, 1,000 and 2,200 RPM, respectively.

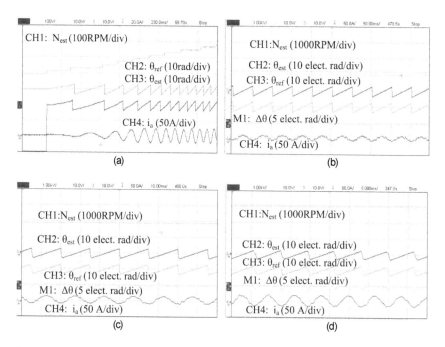

Figure 4.8 (a) Starting and steady-state operation of the sensorless SPMSM LEV drive at (b) 300 RPM, (c) 1,000 RPM, and (d) 2,200 RPM.

4.6.2 Dynamic performance of sensorless EV drive

The dynamic estimation capability of the sensorless control method during speed variation is shown in Figure 4.9a and b. The step response time for both speed increase and decrease of the drive is around 0.36 seconds with negligible overshoot. The estimated position dynamically changes according to the machine speed change, which is reflected in the phase current frequency. The field-oriented control of SPMSM using the delay compensated predictive current control is shown in Figure 4.9c and d.

It is observed that the q-component of the reference stator current, i_q^* and the actual q-component of current, i_q instantaneously match as per sudden increase and decrease in load demand while maintaining the d-axis current at zero. The independent speed and torque controls are demonstrated by the steady constant speed during the load changes. Moreover, the stability of the sensorless control operation without losing synchronism during step changes in load at 150 RPM is illustrated in Figure 4.9d. This shows the capability of the sensorless control to strongly adopt for the EV application.

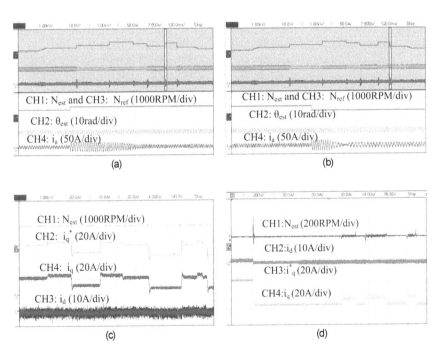

Figure 4.9 Sensorless control dynamics of the presented LEV drive during sudden (a) acceleration, (b) deceleration, (c) load steps at high speed, and (d) load steps at low speed.

4.6.3 Battery-SPV dynamics of the presented LEV drive

At different irradiance conditions considered in this work, the MPPT control achieved for a chosen PV array is illustrated in Figure 4.10a–c. Regardless of the solar irradiance, maximum powers harvested from the solar panel efficiently are indicated by the percentage MPP efficiencies 99.79%, 99.82% and 99.72% at 1,000, 750 and 1,000 W/m^2, respectively.

The detailed analysis of solar PV array and battery dynamics for various possible operating and non-operating conditions of the LEV is illustrated in Figure 4.11a–f. Various practical scenarios such as power management at solar irradiance variation, speed and load change at a constant solar irradiance, battery charging during idle/parking mode and battery charging from solar PV array and regenerated power during sudden braking operation are discussed here.

During a constant load and steady speed operation of 1,400 RPM, the battery power is reduced as the solar power keeps increasing with the increase in irradiance as shown in Figure 4.11a. This maximizes the usage of available solar power while conserving the battery power. In Figure 4.11b, irrespective of the speed changes, solar PV array is maintained at MPP for a constant irradiance of 1,000 W/m^2. Figure 4.11c illustrates the dynamics during load change when the solar PV power is at peak capacity. In this condition, as the load demand increases, the battery provides necessary power while the solar PV array is maintained at MPP. When the solar irradiance changes from 1,000 to 500 W/m^2, the battery current increases proportionately to supply the load current and thereof, provides as per the necessary load demand, shown in Figure 4.11d. During sudden fault condition of PV array or night, the solar PV array cannot provide power and the insolation becomes zero. From that instant, the battery supplies the required energy for the vehicle propulsion and this scenario is depicted in Figure 9.11e. Here, as soon as the solar power becomes suddenly unavailable, the battery current increases to provide the necessary remaining power to the vehicle.

When the vehicle is not running or parked, the energy generated at the terminals of the SPV array is utilized for recuperating the EV battery as shown in Figure 4.11f. This helps in maximum utilization of available solar power, economically benefitting the vehicle owner. Another important aspect is the regenerated power along with solar PV array power utilized for charging the EV battery during sudden start-stop or braking condition. This operation is illustrated in Figure 4.12a and b. V_b or V_{dc} is seen to increase momentarily due to the charging operation, indicated by the negative battery current during step decrement of speed.

All these detailed analyses demonstrate the benefits, significance, and effectiveness of the proposed sensorless electric three-wheeler EV

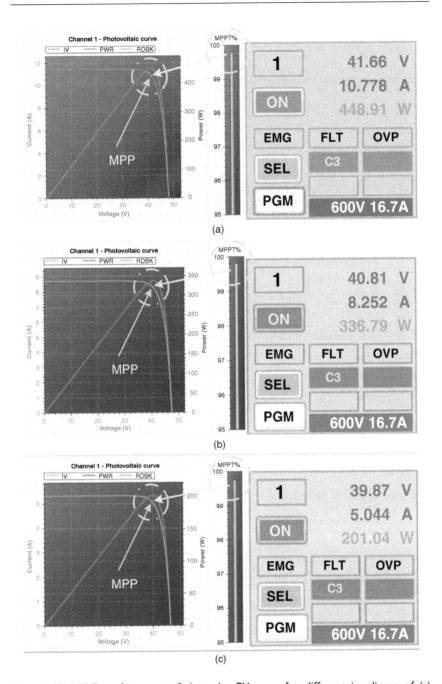

Figure 4.10 MPPT performance of the solar PV array for different irradiance of (a) 1,000 W/m², (b) 750 W/m², and (c) 500 W/m² [black line – power curve; gray line – IV curve; white dot – Operating point].

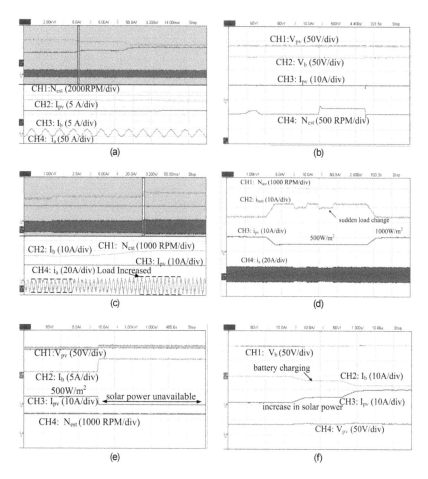

Figure 4.11 Changes in battery-SPV array during (a) steady-state operation (b) dynamic speed change (c) sudden laden (d) load changes (e) loss of solar energy (f) vehicle stop condition.

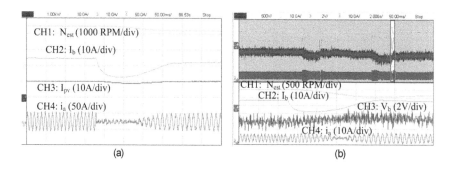

Figure 4.12 LEV battery source charging due to combined effect of solar power and regenerative power during immediate braking (a) heavy load, and (b) light load.

configuration equipped with solar PV array, having a regenerative braking feature. These discussions exemplify the scope and significance of roof-top solar PV panel for a typical e-rickshaw of 1 kW rating, in becoming a zero carbon emission vehicle with almost no running and maintenance cost. Along with the regenerative braking feature, similar benefits can be ascertained, without doubt, for a 3 kW rated electric auto-rickshaw as well.

4.7 CONCLUSION

This chapter presents modelling, design, implementation, and analysis of a two-stage SPV-assisted low-voltage position sensorless SPMSM EV drive with the help of MATLAB-based simulation and MicroLabBox dSPACE-based experimental test setup. The vector control operation of the time delay compensated FCS-MPC EV drive, evading the tuning efforts of a classical linear controller, improves its performance and efficiency. Furthermore, the cost reduction and reliability enhancement of the drive are accomplished through the estimation of position and speed information using modified super twisting SMO with MAFPLL for wide speed range starting from near zero linear vehicle velocity. An effective management of solar power and the battery energy during various steady-state and dynamic operating conditions are presented and analyzed in this work. The maximum power of the solar PV array is extracted continuously for driving the vehicle. The battery can be charged using the SPV array when the LEV is idle. Besides, the regenerative braking energy and surplus solar power during immediate braking are recuperated back into the battery. The major advantages of the presented electric auto-rickshaw configuration are that it enhances the performance of vehicle with respect to the existing ones, extends its range by approximately 47% and increases the battery life cycle.

ACKNOWLEDGEMENT

The authors are grateful to the SERB-NSC Fellowship for supporting this work.

REFERENCES

1. M. Ehsani, Y. Gao, S. Longo, and K. Ebrahimi, *Modern Electric, Hybrid Electric, and Fuel Cell Vehicles*. CRC Press, Boca Raton, 2018.
2. X. Liu, L. Zhou, J. Wang, X. Gao, Z. Li, and Z. Zhang, "Robust Predictive Current Control of Permanent-Magnet Synchronous Motors With Newly Designed Cost Function," *IEEE Transactions on Power Electronics*, vol. 35, no. 10, pp. 10778–10788, 2020.

3. J. Rodriguez and P. Cortes. *Predictive Control of Power Converters and Electrical Drives*. vol. 40. John Wiley & Sons, Hoboken, NJ, 2012.

4. M. Preindl, "Robust Control Invariant Sets and Lyapunov-Based MPC for IPM Synchronous Motor Drives," *IEEE Transactions on Industrial Electronics*, vol. 63, no. 6, pp. 3925–3933, 2016.

5. M. Preindl and S. Bolognani, "Model Predictive Direct Torque Control with Finite Control Set for PMSM Drive Systems, Part 1: Maximum Torque Per Ampere Operation," *IEEE Transactions on Industrial Informatics*, vol. 9, no. 4, pp. 1912–1921, 2013.

6. P. Karamanakos, T. Geyer and R. Kennel, "On the Choice of Norm in Finite Control Set Model Predictive Control," *IEEE Transactions on Power Electronics*, vol. 33, no. 8, pp. 7105–7117, 2018.

7. G. Wang, M. Valla and J. Solsona, "Position Sensorless Permanent Magnet Synchronous Machine Drives-A Review," *IEEE Transactions on Industrial Electronics*, vol. 67, no. 7, pp. 5830–5842, 2020.

8. K. Scicluna, C. S. Staines and R. Raute, "Sensorless Low/Zero Speed Estimation for Permanent Magnet Synchronous Machine Using a Search-Based Real-Time Commissioning Method," *IEEE Transactions on Industrial Electronics*, vol. 67, no. 7, pp. 6010–6018, 2020.

9. D. Liang, J. Li, R. Qu and W. Kong, "Adaptive Second-Order Sliding-Mode Observer for PMSM Sensorless Control Considering VSI Nonlinearity," *IEEE Transactions on Power Electronics*, vol. 33, no. 10, pp. 8994–9004, 2018.

10. R. Sreejith and B. Singh, "Sensorless Predictive Current Control of PMSM EV Drive Using DSOGI-FLL Based Sliding Mode Observer," *IEEE Transactions on Industrial Electronics*, vol. 68, no. 7, pp. 5537–5547, 2021.

11. R. Sreejith and B. Singh, "Sensorless Predictive Control of SPMSM-Driven Light EV Drive Using Modified Speed Adaptive Super Twisting Sliding Mode Observer With MAF-PLL," *IEEE Journal of Emerging and Selected Topics in Industrial Electronics*, vol. 2, no. 1, pp. 42–52, 2021.

12. Q. An, J. Zhang, Q. An, X. Liu, A. Shamekov and K. Bi, "Frequency-Adaptive Complex-Coefficient Filter-Based Enhanced Sliding Mode Observer for Sensorless Control of Permanent Magnet Synchronous Motor Drives," *IEEE Transactions on Industry Applications*, vol. 56, no. 1, pp. 335–343, 2020.

13. J. Zhang, Y. Yang, D. Qin, C. Fu and Z. Cong, "Regenerative Braking Control Method Based on Predictive Optimization for Four-Wheel Drive Pure Electric Vehicle," *IEEE Access*, vol. 9, pp. 1394–1406, 2021.

14. S. Murthy. Optimal kinetic energy recovery algorithms for electric machines. Diss. Georgia Institute of Technology, 2017.

15. S. Heydari, P. Fajri, M. Rasheduzzaman and R. Sabzehgar, "Maximizing Regenerative Braking Energy Recovery of Electric Vehicles Through Dynamic Low-Speed Cutoff Point Detection," *IEEE Transactions on Transportation Electrification*, vol. 5, no. 1, pp. 262–270, 2019.

16. V. Totev and V. Gueorgiev, "Efficiency of Regenerative Braking in Electric Vehicles," *2020 IEEE 21st International Symposium on Electrical Apparatus & Technologies (SIELA)*, Bourgas, Bulgaria, 2020, pp. 1–4.

17. B. Singh, A. Verma, A. Chandra and K. Al-Haddad, "Implementation of Solar PV-Battery and Diesel Generator Based Electric Vehicle Charging Station," *IEEE Transactions on Industry Applications*, vol. 56, no. 4, pp. 4007–4016, 2020.

18. R. Sreejith and B. Singh, "Intelligent Nonlinear Sensorless Predictive Field Oriented Control of PMSM Drive for Three Wheeler Hybrid Solar PV-Battery Electric Vehicle," *2019 IEEE Transportation Electrification Conference and Expo (ITEC)*, Detroit, MI, USA, 2019, pp. 1–6.

19. K. S. Reddy, S. Aravindhan and T. K. Mallick, "Techno-Economic Investigation of Solar Powered Electric Auto-Rickshaw for a Sustainable Transport System," *Energies*, vol. 10, pp. 754, 2017.

20. P. Mulhall, S. M. Lukic, S. G. Wirasingha, Y. Lee and A. Emadi, "Solar-Assisted Electric Auto Rickshaw Three-Wheeler," *IEEE Transactions on Vehicular Technology*, vol. 59, no. 5, pp. 2298–2307, 2010.

21. P. Mulhall, M. Naviwala, S. M. Lukic, J. Braband and A. Emadi, "Entrepreneurial Projects Program at Illinois Institute of Technology: Solar/Battery Hybrid Three-Wheel Auto Rickshaw for India," *2007 IEEE Vehicle Power and Propulsion Conference*, Arlington, TX, 2007, pp. 682–689.

22. NREL, "Champion Photovoltaic Module Efficiency Chart". Available: https://www.nrel.gov/pv/module-efficiency.html.

23. N. Mohan, T. M. Undeland, and W. P. Robbins. *Power Electronics: Converters, Applications, and Design*. John Wiley & Sons, Hoboken, NJ, 2003.

24. KYOCERA AVX catalogue, "Medium power film capacitors application notes," *AVX*, pp. 53–58, 2020.

25. J. Lee, J. Hong, K. Nam, R. Ortega, L. Praly and A. Astolfi, "Sensorless control of surface-mount permanent-magnet synchronous motors based on a nonlinear observer," *IEEE Transactions on Power Electronics*, vol. 25, no. 2, pp. 290–297, 2010.

26. Z. Wang, K. Lu and F. Blaabjerg, "A Simple Startup Strategy Based on Current Regulation for Back-EMF-Based Sensorless Control of PMSM," *IEEE Transactions on Power Electronics*, vol. 27, no. 8, pp. 3817–3825, 2012.

Chapter 5

Implementation of model predictive control of PMSM for EVPT system

*Surya Kant, Ambrish Devanshu,
and Vimal Singh Bisht*

5.1 INTRODUCTION

The electric vehicle powertrain, also known as the drivetrain, refers to the components and systems that generate and supply power to the wheels of an electric vehicle (EV) [1,2]. EVPT has several advantages over internal combustion engines, including improved efficiency, instant torque, lower maintenance costs, and reduced emissions [3–5]. In addition, the components in an EV powertrain can be more compact and lighter than those in a traditional vehicle, which helps to increase overall range and reduce vehicle weight.

The use of PMSMs in EV power trains provides several advantages over other motor types, including high torque & power density and efficiency. In addition, PMSMs have relatively simple and robust construction, making them well suited for use in EVs.

However, the control of PMSMs in EV power trains is a complex and challenging task that requires control schemes like field-oriented control (FOC) and direct torque control (DTC), to ensure efficient and reliable operation [6,7]. The success of PMSM control in EV power trains is crucial for achieving high performance, energy efficiency, and extended driving range, making it an important area of research and development in the EV industry. The primary purpose of FOC is to control the rotor's magnetic field to achieve the required torque and speed of the motor. It works by decoupling the control of torque and flux components of PMSM, allowing for precise control of the motor's performance. However, vector control still has some shortcomings such as overshoots and high dynamic performance because of using proportion integral controller. Large torque fluctuations at low speeds are the main issue of DTC.

As a result, researchers keep looking into cutting-edge and efficient control methods to enhance the efficiency of PMSM drive, i.e., internal model control [8–10], sliding mode control [11,12], state feedback control [13,14] and MPC [15–18]. Early in the 1980s, the MPC algorithm was

DOI: 10.1201/9781003481065-5

developed by Rodriguez and implemented in the PMSM drive system [19]. MPC distinguishes itself from other modern control techniques of motor by its multi-constraint control, multivariable and multi-objective as well as its simple and clear design methodology. Model predictive current control (MPCC), model predictive flux control(MPFC), model predictive torque control (MPTC), and model predictive speed control (MPSC) are four subcategories of MPC techniques according to various control variables [20–23]. MPC techniques for PMSM are categorized into two types based on control actions: finite-control-set model predictive control (FCSMPC) and continuous-control-set model predictive control (CCSMPC) [24,25]. FCSMPC uses the switching voltage of inverter as the control action directly to get quick transient characteristics of the system without requirement of modulation method by considering discrete switching states of voltage source inverter (VSI) in the prediction model. The advantages of FCSMPC also include its simple nonlinear constraint management, implementation of multivariable control, and straightforward idea.

In this chapter, a complete electric powertrain model employed PMSM as a traction motor is created using MATLAB/ Simulink. VSI used to regulate the PMSM uses the MPC technology for switching control. Modeling of the traction system is required for a complete knowledge of the dynamics of the vehicle. Simulation results validates the effectiveness of the proposed method.

5.2 MOTOR PROPERTIES FOR EVPT SYSTEMS

The main properties of electric motors that are used in different drive train configurations are cooling system, output motor power, motor torque, battery configuration used, and maximum motor speed. Permanent magnet AC machines are used as integrated systems by vehicle manufacturers including Honda, Audi, Toyota, Ford, etc., with or without internal combustion engines. Table 5.1 displays the fundamental specifications of traction motor used in EVs.

Table 5.1 Specifications of electric traction motor used in EVs

Vehicle manufacturers	Motor type	Output power (kW)	Max. torque (N m)	Battery capability (kWh)	Cooling method
Audi	Induction motor	75	330	8.8	Liquid
Volvo	Permanent magnet	150	1,200	76	Air
Honda	Permanent magnet brushless motor	135	490	4.7	Oil
Toyota	Permanent magnet	60	207	4.4	Water
Renault	Synchronous motor	90	350	22	Air
Ford	Induction motor	35	243	1.4	Liquid
Nissan	Permanent magnet	90	210	24	Air cool

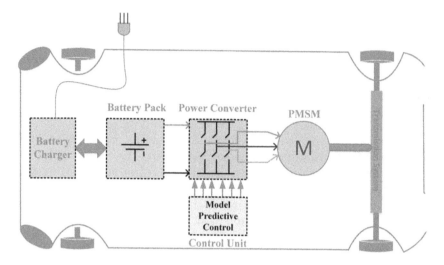

Figure 5.1 Electric Power Train System.

5.3 DESIGN OF EVPT SYSTEM

Internal combustion engines are used as the propulsion technology in traditional power train (PT) systems. The torque and speed performance of a PT exhibit strong oscillations and ripples, which are readily regulated in an electrical PT system with power electronics.

Figure 5.1 shows a complete EVPT system which includes a battery that powers the traction motor through a converter, motor coupled to the transmission system, which transfers mechanical energy to the wheels of car.

5.4 PRINCIPLE OF MODEL PREDICTIVE CONTROL FOR EVPT SYSTEM

The traditional MPC depends on characteristics to limit the switching states of converter. Through traversal, the output of the converter system is controlled under the various influences of each switching condition. To reduce the cost function and apply to the system, the ideal switching state is finally selected. Modeling of FCSMPC includes predictive model, define cost function and optimization process.

5.4.1 The predictive model of PMSM

Modeling equations in d-q axis of PMSM can be written in continuous time as [26];

$$v_d = R_s i_d + L_d \frac{di_d}{dt} - \omega_e L_q i_q \tag{5.1}$$

$$v_q = R_s i_q + L_q \frac{di_q}{dt} + \omega_e L_d i_d + \omega_e \psi_m \tag{5.2}$$

v_d, v_q, i_d, i_q, L_d and L_q are described as components of voltage, current, inductance in $d\text{-}q$ axis respectively. R_s, ψ_m and ω_e are defined as stator resistance, flux linkage, and speed of rotor respectively.

Electromagnetic torque can be derived as:

$$T_e = \frac{3}{2} p i_q \left[i_d \left(L_d - L_q \right) + \psi_m \right] \tag{5.3}$$

p is pair of poles

The mechanical speed of motor is expressed as:

$$j \frac{d\omega_m}{dt} = T_e - T_l - B_m \omega_m \tag{5.4}$$

$$\omega_e = p \omega_m \tag{5.5}$$

Where j, B_m, T_l and ω_m represent inertia, friction constant, load torque, and mechanical rotor speed respectively.

State space equation of equations (5.1) and (5.2) can be written as

$$\begin{cases} \dfrac{dx(t)}{dt} = Ax(t) + Bu(t) + C \\ y(t) = Dx(t) \end{cases} \tag{5.6}$$

where $x(t) = \begin{bmatrix} i_d(k) \\ i_q(k) \end{bmatrix}, v(t) = \begin{bmatrix} v_d(k) \\ v_q(k) \end{bmatrix}$ and $y(t)$ are defined as state variable, input variable, and output variable, respectively.

$$A = \begin{bmatrix} -R_s / L_d & \omega_e L_d / L_q \\ -\omega_e L_d / L_q & -R_s / L_q \end{bmatrix}, B = \begin{bmatrix} 1/L_q & 0 \\ 0 & 1/L_d \end{bmatrix}, C = \begin{bmatrix} 0 \\ -\omega_e \psi_m / L_q \end{bmatrix}$$

Equation (5.6) can be modified in discrete form according to forward Euler equation and expressed as:

$$\begin{cases} x(k+1) = A_0 x(k) + B_0 v(k) + C_0 \\ y(k+1) = Dx(k+1) \end{cases} \tag{5.7}$$

where k & $(k+1)$ define the value in the present state and next state, respectively.

$$A = \begin{bmatrix} 1 - T_s \dfrac{R_s}{L_d} & T_s \omega_e \dfrac{L_d}{L_q} \\ -T_s \omega_e \dfrac{L_d}{L_q} & 1 - T_s \dfrac{R_s}{L_q} \end{bmatrix}, B = \begin{bmatrix} T_s / L_q & 0 \\ 0 & T_s / L_d \end{bmatrix}, C = \begin{bmatrix} 0 \\ -T_s \omega_e \dfrac{\psi_m}{L_q} \end{bmatrix}$$

T_s is sampling time

Since SPMSM is used the inductances in both axes will be equal, i.e. $L_d = L_q = L$. Thus according to voltage equations defined in equations (5.1) and (5.2) current at next instant can be predicted by applying forward Euler method of discretization and expressed as

$$\begin{cases} i_d(k+1) = \left(1 - \dfrac{T_s R_s}{L}\right) \cdot i_d(k) + T_s \omega_e i_q(k) + \dfrac{T_s}{L} \cdot v_d(k) \\ i_q(k+1) = \left(1 - \dfrac{T_s R_s}{L}\right) \cdot i_q(k) - T_s \omega_e i_d(k) + \dfrac{T_s}{L} \cdot v_q(k) - \dfrac{T_s \omega_e \psi_m}{L} \end{cases} \qquad (5.8)$$

5.4.2 The cost function

In VSI, the basic voltage vector includes six nonzero vectors $(v_1, v_2,...,v_6)$ and two zero $(v_0$ and $v_7)$ vectors. Therefore, from equation (5.8), under various fundamental voltage vectors, the current value at $(k+1)$th instant may be predicted. The cost function is defined by substituting predicted current value and expressed as [27]:

$$C = \left| i_{q\text{ref}} - i_q(k+1) \right| + \left| i_{d\text{ref}} - i_d(k+1) \right| \qquad (5.9)$$

5.4.3 The optimization process

There are different types of optimization algorithms, which is used to minimize to cost function. For a set time N, MPC is an optimization problem that involves reducing the cost function while taking into account the system model and its constraints. It provides an N ideal vector which is required to control the VSI.

5.5 CONTROL SCHEME OF EVPT SYSTEM

Figure 5.2 shows the complete control structure of the PMSM-based EVPT system. Here, the reference for the current i_{sq}^* is generated by a PI controller, which is also utilized to manage speed. The stator current components

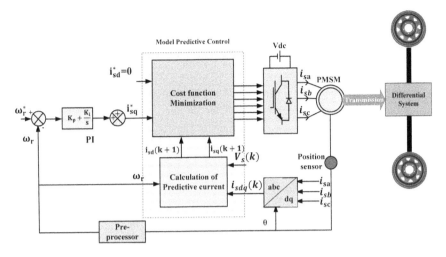

Figure 5.2 Control scheme of EVPT.

for each of the seven distinct voltage vectors generated by the inverter are predicted using the machine's discrete model. During the complete cycle of sampling time, voltage vector that reduces a cost function is picked and utilized. Electrical vehicle is driven from the traction motor through the transmission system.

5.6 RESULT AND DISCUSSIONS

Complete EVPT model is demonstrated in MATLAB/Simulink and analyzed under different modes of operation. The parameters of PMSM used in EVPT as a traction motor are given in Table 5.2, and the dynamics of vehicle are tabulated in Table 5.3.

5.6.1 Performance characteristics of traction motor

A constant speed of 314 rad/s is applied to the motor as reference initially and load is varying to examine the tracking capability of the system. Figure 5.2 shows output performance of speed of motor and vehicle, motor torque and currents. The vehicle speed (V_s) rises when the load torque of motor rises. Stator current profile of motor also tracks the load torque.

Figure 5.3 shows performance characteristics of EVPT system. Initially, the reference speed of 157 rad/s is given to the motor and at 0.15 seconds reference speed varies from 157 to 314 rad/s. A step variation of load torque from 0 to 11 N m is applied at 0.2 seconds. As the speed is varying, a fluctuation in load torque is observed. When load is applied to motor, a q-axis current generates and EVPT system starts to accelerate.

Table 5.2 Traction motor parameters

Parameters	Ratings	Parameters	Ratings
Rated power	3.4 kW	Voltage	380 V
Stator resistance	1.93 Ω	Current	6.9 A
Motor torque	11 N m	PM flux linkage	0.265 Wb
Inductances	11.4 mH	Inertia	0.11 kg m²
Pole pairs	4	Speed	314 rad/s

Table 5.3 Dynamics of vehicle

Parameter	Ratings	Parameter	Ratings
Mass	1,200 kg	Drag coefficient	0.4
Threshold velocity of wheels	0.1 m/s	Peak longitudinal force	3,500 N
Front area	3 m²	Rolling radius	3 m
Vertical load on wheels	3,000 N	Carrier to drive tooth ratio	4
Follower to base tooth ratio	2	Slip at peak load	10

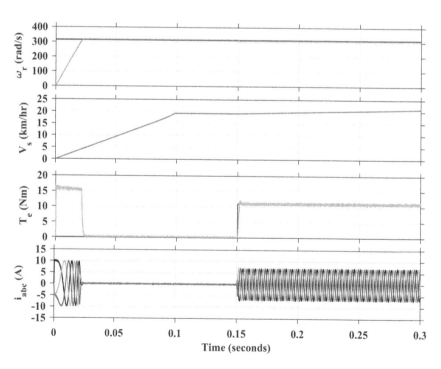

Figure 5.3 Performance of EVPT system under variable load and constant speed.

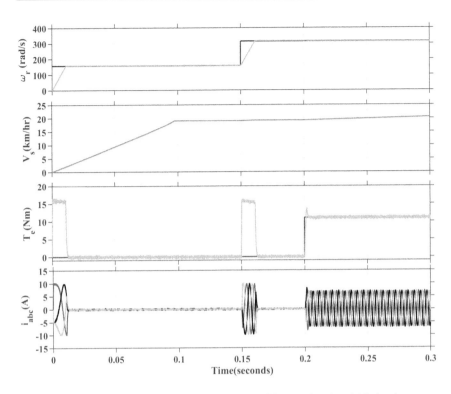

Figure 5.4 Performance of EVPT system under variable speed and variable load.

Figure 5.4 shows the performance characteristics of EVPT system under ramp speed operation. A ramp signal of slope of 30 rad/s² with respect to time is given to motor as reference. The controller produces the necessary current for controlling the motor and vehicle speed when the load torque changes by 11 N m from the no load at 0.15 seconds.

Figure 5.5 shows performance of EVPT system under load variation. Reference speed of 314 rad/s is given to the motor and variable load torque (0-5.5-11-5.5-11) N m at the time of (0-0.1-0.15-0.2-0.25) seconds is applied respectively. The required current for acceleration of EVPT is generated according to variation in load torque and the vehicle speed (V_s) rises.

5.6.2 Characteristics of EVPT system

Figure 5.6 shows vehicle speed, acceleration, tire slip and normal force on wheel characteristics under no load and constant speed operation. It is observed that the EVPT system is accelerating up to 20 m/s². This indicates

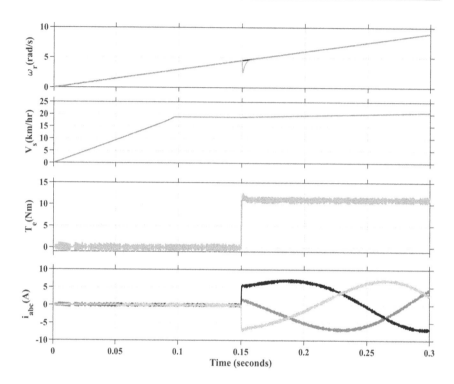

Figure 5.5 Performance of EVPT system under ramp speed.

that the electrical powertrain, which uses the PMSM as a traction motor, is picking up speed at a noticeably quicker pace. The tire of an EV should be in touch with the ground and is susceptible to slipping. The torque imparted to the wheel's axle causes the tire to push against the ground owing to friction, and the reaction force that results is then passed back to the wheel, pushing it either backward or forward (Figure 5.7).

The tire slip should be close to zero for flawless rolling [28]. Therefore, it is evident from the characteristics of tire slip that tire slip will reach zero in less than 0.1 seconds. In addition, the traction motor supplies the necessary normal force values. The overall result of all the forces and torques operating on the vehicle determines its motion. Zero pitch torque and zero normal acceleration result in zero normal force being applied to each front and back wheel. These forces help maintain the balance of forces acting on the moving vehicle [29]. Therefore, the traction system should be able to deliver sufficient performance for whole vehicle body movement.

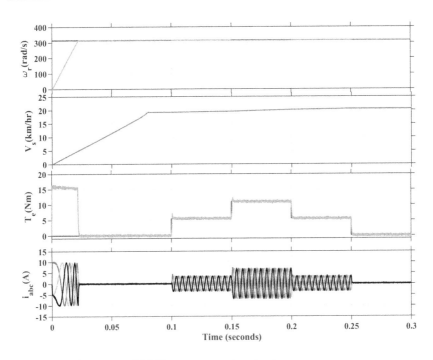

Figure 5.6 Performance of EVPT system at various load.

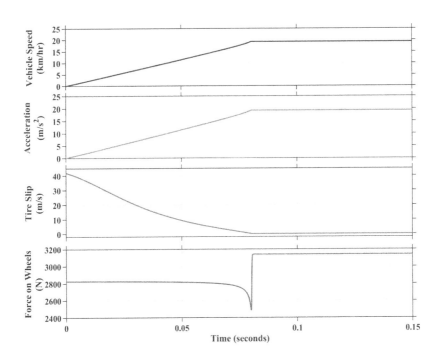

Figure 5.7 Dynamic characteristics of EVPT system.

5.7 CONCLUSION

In this chapter, an EVPT system is developed and analyzed in MATLAB/ Simulink. In the proposed EVPT system, a PMSM motor serves as the traction system, transferring the demanded energy, force, and power to the moving parts of the vehicle. The output of VSI and the powertrain's electric drive system are controlled by the model predictive control method. In this approach, the active voltage vector is only chosen for a brief period of time and for the remainder of the time, the null voltage vector is chosen. As a result, the ripples are lessened, resulting in a smooth and effective operation. Vehicle acceleration and speed are used as the foundational realization characteristics for the dynamic knowledge of electrical powertrains. The simulation findings show that the suggested scheme can attain greater performance. Owing to its enhanced features and implemented capacity, this approach may thus be regarded as a high-performance control algorithm.

REFERENCES

1. M. Karamuk, "A survey on electric vehicle powertrain systems," In *International Aegean Conference on Electrical Machines and Power Electronics and Electromotion, Joint Conference*, Istanbul, Turkey, 2011, no. September, pp. 8–10.
2. A. Emadi, Y. J. Lee, and K. Rajashekara, "Power electronics and motor drives in electric, hybrid electric, and plug-in hybrid electric vehicles," *IEEE Trans. Ind. Electron.*, vol. 55, no. 6, pp. 2237–2245, 2008, doi: 10.1109/TIE.2008.922768.
3. M. Verma, M. Sreejeth, and M. Singh, "Performance evaluation of conventional and electric powertrain," In *India International Conference on Power Electronics, IICPE*, Dec. 2018, pp. 1–6, doi: 10.1109/IICPE.2018.8709429.
4. M. Verma, M. Sreejeth, and M. Singh, "Implementation and analysis of field control on electric vehicle power train system employing PMSM as traction device," In *2018 2nd IEEE International Conference on Power Electronics, Intelligent Control and Energy Systems, ICPEICES 2018*, 2018, pp. 933–936, doi: 10.1109/ICPEICES.2018.8897480.
5. S. S. Williamson, S. M. Lukic, and A. Emadi, "Comprehensive drive train efficiency analysis of hybrid electric and fuel cell vehicles based on motor-controller efficiency modeling," *IEEE Trans. Power Electron.*, vol. 21, no. 3, pp. 730–740, 2006, doi: 10.1109/TPEL.2006.872388.
6. J. Lara, J. Xu, and A. Chandra, "Effects of rotor position error in the performance of field-oriented-controlled PMSM drives for electric vehicle traction applications," *IEEE Trans. Ind. Electron.*, vol. 63, no. 8, pp. 4738–4751, 2016, doi: 10.1109/TIE.2016.2549983.
7. R. Morales-Caporal, M. E. Leal-Lopez, J. De Jesus Rangel-Magdaleno, O. Sandre-Hernandez, and I. Cruz-Vega, "Direct torque control of a PMSM-drive for electric vehicle applications," In *2018 28th International Conference on Electronics, Communications and Computers, CONIELECOMP*, Jan. 2018, pp. 232–237, doi: 10.1109/CONIELECOMP.2018.8327204.

8. Z. Ping, Q. Ma, T. Wang, Y. Huang, and J. G. Lu, "Speed tracking control of permanent magnet synchronous motor by a novel two-step internal model control approach," *Int. J. Control. Autom. Syst.*, vol. 16, no. 6, pp. 2754–2762, 2018, doi: 10.1007/s12555-018-0255-y.
9. X. Sun, Z. Shi, L. Chen, and Z. Yang, "Internal model control for a bearing-less permanent magnet synchronous motor based on inverse system method," *IEEE Trans. Energy Convers.*, vol. 31, no. 4, pp. 1539–1548, 2016, doi: 10.1109/TEC.2016.2591925.
10. Z. Ping, T. Wang, Y. Huang, H. Wang, J. G. Lu, and Y. Li, "Internal model control of PMSM position servo system: Theory and experimental results," *IEEE Trans. Ind. Inform.*, vol. 16, no. 4, pp. 2202–2211, 2020, doi: 10.1109/TII.2019.2935248.
11. P. Gao, G. Zhang, H. Ouyang, and L. Mei, "An adaptive super twisting nonlinear fractional order PID sliding mode control of permanent magnet synchronous motor speed regulation system based on extended state observer," *IEEE Access*, vol. 8, pp. 53498–53510, 2020, doi: 10.1109/ACCESS.2020.2980390.
12. Z. Jin, X. Sun, G. Lei, Y. Guo, and J. Zhu, "Sliding mode direct torque control of SPMSMs based on a hybrid wolf optimization algorithm," *IEEE Trans. Ind. Electron.*, vol. 69, no. 5, pp. 4534–4544, 2022, doi: 10.1109/TIE.2021.3080220.
13. T. Tarczewski and L. M. Grzesiak, "Constrained state feedback speed control of PMSM based on model predictive approach," *IEEE Trans. Ind. Electron.*, vol. 63, no. 6, pp. 3867–3875, 2016, doi: 10.1109/TIE.2015.2497302.
14. A. Apte, V. A. Joshi, H. Mehta, and R. Walambe, "Disturbance-observer-based sensorless control of PMSM using integral state feedback controller," *IEEE Trans. Power Electron.*, vol. 35, no. 6, pp. 6082–6090, 2020, doi: 10.1109/TPEL.2019.2949921.
15. F. Wang, K. Zuo, P. Tao, and J. Rodriguez, "High performance model predictive control for PMSM by using stator current mathematical model self-regulation technique," *IEEE Trans. Power Electron.*, vol. 35, no. 12, pp. 13652–13662, 2020, doi: 10.1109/TPEL.2020.2994948.
16. A. M. Bozorgi, M. Farasat, and S. Jafarishiadeh, "Model predictive current control of surface-mounted permanent magnet synchronous motor with low torque and current ripple," *IET Power Electron.*, vol. 10, no. 10, pp. 1120–1128, 2017, doi: 10.1049/iet-pel.2016.0850.
17. X. Sun, M. Wu, G. Lei, Y. Guo, and J. Zhu, "An improved model predictive current control for PMSM drives based on current track circle," *IEEE Trans. Ind. Electron.*, vol. 68, no. 5, pp. 3782–3793, 2021, doi: 10.1109/TIE.2020.2984433.
18. Y. Yan, S. Wang, C. Xia, H. Wang, and T. Shi, "Hybrid control set-model predictive control for field-oriented control of VSI-PMSM," *IEEE Trans. Energy Convers.*, vol. 31, no. 4, pp. 1622–1633, 2016, doi: 10.1109/TEC.2016.2598154.
19. J. Rodríguez, J. Pontt, C. Silva, P. Cortés, U. Amman, and S. Rees, "Predictive current control of a voltage source inverter," *PESC Rec. - IEEE Annu. Power Electron. Spec. Conf.*, vol. 3, pp. 2192–2196, 2004, doi: 10.1109/PESC.2004.1355460.
20. X. Zhang, L. Zhang, and Y. Zhang, "Model predictive current control for PMSM drives with parameter robustness improvement," *IEEE Trans. Power Electron.*, vol. 34, no. 2, pp. 1645–1657, 2019.

21. O. Sandre-Hernandez, J. De Jesus Rangel-Magdaleno, and R. Morales-Caporal, "Modified model predictive torque control for a PMSM-drive with torque ripple minimisation," *IET Power Electron.*, vol. 12, no. 5, pp. 1033–1042, 2019, doi: 10.1049/iet-pel.2018.5525.

22. C. Garcia, J. Rodriguez, S. Odhano, P. Zanchetta, and S. A. Davari, "Modulated model predictive speed control for PMSM drives," *2018 IEEE Int. Conf. Electr. Syst. Aircraft, Railw. Sh. Propuls. Road Veh. Int. Transp. Electrif. Conf. ESARS-ITEC 2018*, no. 1, pp. 1–6, 2019, doi: 10.1109/ESARS-ITEC.2018.8607701.

23. R. Fu, "Robust model predictive flux control of PMSM drive using a compensated stator flux predictor," *IEEE Access*, vol. 9, pp. 136736–136743, 2021, doi: 10.1109/ACCESS.2021.3117860.

24. C. Gong, Y. Hu, M. Ma, L. Yan, J. Liu, and H. Wen, "Accurate FCS model predictive current control technique for surface-mounted PMSMs at low control frequency," *IEEE Trans. Power Electron.*, vol. 35, no. 6, pp. 5567–5572, 2020.

25. B. Wang, J. Jiao, and Z. Xue, "Implementation of continuous control set model predictive control method for PMSM on FPGA," *IEEE Access*, vol. 11, no. February, pp. 12414–12425, 2023, doi: 10.1109/ACCESS.2023.3241243.

26. M. Sreejeth, and M. Singh, "Performance analysis of PMSM drive using hysteresis current controller and PWM current controller," *2018 IEEE Int. Students' Conf. Electr. Electron. Comput. Sci. SCEECS 2018*, Bhopal, India, no. 1, pp. 1–5, 2018.

27. Suryakant, M. Sreejeth, M. Singh, and A. K. Seth, "Minimization of torque ripples in PMSM drive using PI- resonant controller-based model predictive control," *Electr. Eng.*, vol. 105, no. 1, pp. 207–219, 2023, doi: 10.1007/s00202-022-01660-y.

28. W. J. Sweeting, A. R. Hutchinson, and S. D. Savage, "Factors affecting electric vehicle energy consumption," *Int. J. Sustain. Eng.*, vol. 4, no. 3, pp. 192–201, 2011, doi: 10.1080/19397038.2011.592956.

29. M. Ferdowsi, "Plug-in hybrid vehicles - A vision for the future," *VPPC 2007-Proc. 2007 IEEE Veh. Power Propuls. Conf.*, no. 573, pp. 457–462, 2007, doi: 10.1109/VPPC.2007.4544169.

Chapter 6

Charging technology
Wired and wireless

Kantipudi V. V. S. R. Chowdary,
Kundan Kumar, and Byamakesh Nayak

6.1 INTRODUCTION

In the ever-evolving landscape of modern transportation, the quest for sustainable alternatives has brought electric vehicles (EVs) to the forefront of innovation. As the demand for cleaner and more efficient modes of transportation intensifies, the pivotal interplay between energy sources and their delivery methods becomes increasingly crucial. This chapter delves into the fascinating realm of wired and wireless charging, exploring the dual avenues through which EVs are replenished to sustain their remarkable rise. An overview of the various aspects of wired and wireless charging is presented in Table 6.1. Table 6.1 summarizes key aspects of wired and wireless charging methods. Wired charging involves a direct physical connection to a power source, offering high-speed options but necessitating plugging in. It relies on an established charging network and depends on available charging stations. This method is well integrated with EVs design but may strain local power grids. In contrast, wireless charging employs inductive coil systems, offering convenience through automatic charging without physical connections. However, it's generally slower, less efficient with energy losses, and potentially incurs higher costs for specialized systems. It appeals to users for its convenience and automation, with the Nissan Leaf being a notable commercial example of wireless charging capabilities. The global drive to curb carbon emissions and reduce dependency on fossil fuels has fueled the rapid adoption of EVs, positioning them as a pivotal solution for achieving a sustainable future. At the heart of this revolution lies the charging infrastructure, a cornerstone connecting EVs to power sources. Wired and wireless charging stand as two distinct approaches, each bearing its own set of merits and demerits, shaping the dynamics of the EV landscape [1].

Wired charging, characterized by its direct connection between the EV and a power source, offers a highly efficient and well-established method of replenishing EVs batteries. With a wide array of charging standards and

Table 6.1 Overview on the typical aspects of wired and wireless charging

Aspect	Wired charging	Wireless charging
Charging method	Direct physical connection to power source	Inductive coil systems initiate charging
Charging speed	High-speed options available	Generally slower than wired charging
Convenience	Requires plugging in	Automatic charging without physical connection
Infrastructure	Established charging network	Infrastructure still evolving
Accessibility	Depends on available charging stations	Enhanced accessibility through implanted systems
Efficiency	Efficient energy transfer	Energy losses during wireless transfer are high
Integration	Well integrated with electric vehicle design	Requires vehicle compatibility and alignment
Cost	Initial installation costs	Potential higher costs for specialized coil and supporting systems
Grid impact	Potentially strains local power grids	Dynamic charging may have less impact
User experience	Reliable and established	Convenience and automation appeal to users
Commercial example	Tesla Model S	Nissan Leaf with wireless charging capabilities

power levels, wired charging provides flexibility for users to select the optimal charging speed based on their needs. The requirement for physical connection and the need for dedicated charging stations can hinder widespread accessibility. Additionally, the deployment of high-power wired charging infrastructure demands significant investment and the potential strain on local power grids, necessitating careful planning and coordination [2]. The typical evolution of wired charging technology over the years is presented in Figure 6.1.

Wireless charging, a concept reminiscent of science fiction, has rapidly transformed into a tangible reality for EVs. By utilizing electromagnetic fields, wireless charging eliminates the need for physical connections, offering the convenience of automatic charging through inductive systems [3]. The success of the Nissan Leaf and its wireless charging capabilities showcase the potential allure of this technology, promising effortless energy replenishment without the need for plugging in. While wireless charging holds promise, it introduces its own set of challenges. Efficiency losses in power transfer, increased complexity of vehicle integration, and the need for precise alignment during charging are factors that demand careful

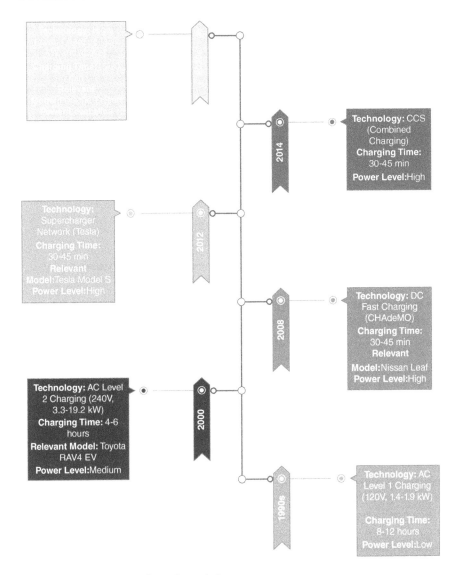

Figure 6.1 Illustrative timeline of wired charger.

consideration [4]. Figure 6.2 displays the significant contribution timeline of the wireless charging systems. over the time. As the EVs industry continues to evolve, the choice between wired and wireless charging remains a critical decision that shapes the future of transportation. The availability and development of charging infrastructure play a paramount role in determining the success of this transition.

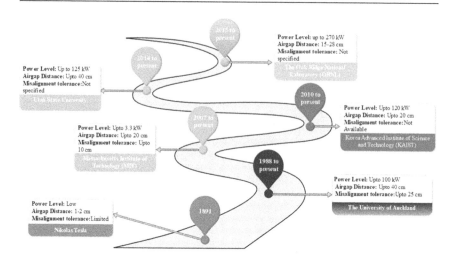

Figure 6.2 Significant contribution timeline of the wireless charging systems.

6.2 SYNOPSIS ON WIRED VERSUS WIRELESS CHARGING

As of June 30, 2021, the data released by the Central Electricity Authority revealed a count of 927 public charging stations in India. On January 14, 2022, the Ministry of Power released updated and consolidated Guidelines and Standards for EV charging infrastructure [5]. The Government of India has taken numerous steps to encourage the production and acceptance of EVs within the country. The government's strategy includes gradual expansion of coverage to additional cities. In significant urban centers and along highways, Oil Marketing Companies have revealed their intentions to establish 22,000 EV charging stations nationwide. EVs Supply Equipment (EVSE) refers to the apparatus responsible for delivering electric energy to recharge the batteries of EVs. EVSE can be categorized based on conductive or inductive methodologies, AC or DC power provisioning, unidirectional or bidirectional power transmission, as well as various power levels. Efficient and rapid charging methods are essential for EVSE to enhance battery cycle lifespan and maintain optimal charging effectiveness. Among the prevalent charging approaches are constant current (CC), constant voltage (CV), constant current-constant voltage (CC-CV), and pulse charging. The objective of the Bharat Standard is to offer an economical and domestically developed answer for EVs charging infrastructure within India [6]. The Bharat Standard outlines the subsequent types of connectors for EVSE:

Bharat AC-001: This entails a single-phase AC connector, capable of providing a maximum power of 7.4 kW. It employs an International

Electrotechnical Commission (IEC) 60309 industrial blue plug comprising three pins (L, N, PE). It accommodates electric two-wheelers, three-wheelers, and low-range four-wheelers.

Bharat DC-001: This encompasses a DC connector capable of delivering up to 15 kW of power. It employs a GB/T plug featuring two pins (+, –). It suits electric two-wheelers, three-wheelers, and low-range four-wheelers.

Bharat DC-002: This involves a DC connector with the capacity to supply up to 100 kW of power. It employs a CCS plug that integrates two DC pins (+, –) and five AC pins (L1, L2, L3, N, PE). It is designed for compatibility with electric four-wheelers equipped with high-range batteries.

Wireless charging technology, also known as inductive charging has gained prominence in recent years as a convenient and efficient method for powering electronic devices and EVs. Wireless charging operates on the principle of electromagnetic induction. It involves two main components: a transmitter (or charging pad) and a receiver (typically integrated into the device or vehicle). The transmitter generates an alternating magnetic field, which induces an electric current in the receiver's coil. This current is then converted back into electricity, which charges the device or vehicle's battery. Wireless charging systems have improved their efficiency over time, with some modern systems achieving efficiency levels similar to traditional wired charging [7,8]. Various standards exist for wireless charging, such as Qi (common for smartphones) and SAE J2954 (for EVs). Compatibility with these standards ensures interoperability. Wireless charging infrastructure may have higher upfront costs due to the need for specialized equipment like charging pads. wireless charging technology offers a versatile and convenient way to power electronic devices and is gradually making inroads into EVs charging and various other industries. While there are technical considerations like efficiency and alignment, economic factors, such as initial costs and convenience, play a significant role in its adoption. Further, the typical assessment of key attributes for wired and wireless charging is illustrated in Table 6.2 [9]. Application-oriented use cases span consumer electronics, EVs, healthcare, and industrial automation, highlighting its broad potential impact across diverse sectors. Table 6.2 provides an assessment of key attributes for wired and wireless charging systems. Wired charging boasts an established and widespread network, with over 5,000 public AC chargers and 1,500 DC fast chargers across India. Government policies support wired charging through incentives and subsidies while focusing on standardization. In contrast, wireless charging is in the early stages, mainly experimental, and has limited infrastructure. Government interest lies in promoting wireless charging, and there are incentives for research and development. However, wireless charging infrastructure may be costlier to implement, and efficiency, while improving, may still be slightly lower due to factors like alignment and distance affecting charging efficiency.

Table 6.2 The assessment of key attributes for the wired and wireless charging

Key attribute	Wired charging	Wireless charging
EV charging infrastructure	Established and widespread network of wired chargers	Developing, with fewer wireless charging stations
Government policies	Government incentives and subsidies for EV infrastructure. Focus on standardization and grid integration.	Government interest in promoting wireless charging. Incentives for R&D and deployment.
Charging methods	AC Level 1, Level 2, and DC fast charging standards. Widespread use of CCS, CHAdeMO, and type 2 connectors.	Inductive and resonant wireless charging methods. Use of Qi and other wireless charging standards.
Charger status in India	Wired chargers widely available in urban areas. Expansion to tier-2 and tier-3 cities is ongoing. over 5,000 public AC chargers and 1,500 DC fast chargers installed across India.	Wireless charging mainly in pilot and experimental stages. Limited wireless charging infrastructure.
Cost	Wired chargers generally lower in cost. Variability in installation costs. Average cost of AC Level 2 charger installation ranges from ₹30,000 to ₹50,000.	Wireless charging infrastructure may be costlier to implement. Installation costs may be higher due to equipment costs.
Efficiency	Wired chargers offer high efficiency, especially in DC fast charging. AC Level 2 chargers offer efficiencies above 90%, with DC fast chargers achieving 95% or higher.	Wireless charging efficiency has improved but may be slightly lower. Alignment and distance affect wireless charging efficiency.

6.3 WIRED CHARGING

Wired charging systems for EVs come in two primary categories: isolated and non-isolated chargers, each with its own set of technical characteristics and trade-offs. The typical schematic block diagram of the isolated and non-isolated chargers is shown in Figures 6.3 and 6.4 respectively. Isolated chargers feature electrical isolation between the grid input and vehicle output, achieved through transformers or isolation components, ensuring enhanced safety by preventing electric shock and minimizing electrical faults. These chargers often boast higher efficiency levels, exceeding 90%, and are compatible with a wide range of grid voltages [10]. On the other hand, non-isolated chargers lack this isolation, offering a more direct electrical connection between input and output. While they tend to be more cost-effective and generate less heat during operation, they may have slightly lower efficiency, typically around 85%–90%, and are often designed for specific voltage ranges, limiting their flexibility. The choice between these systems hinges on factors like

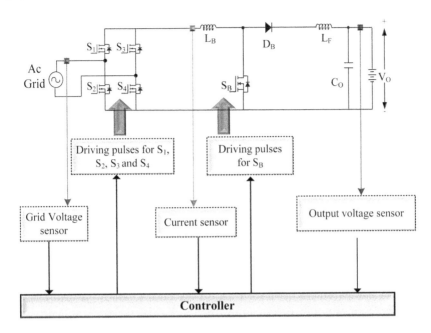

Figure 6.3 Block diagram representation of non-isolated wired charger.

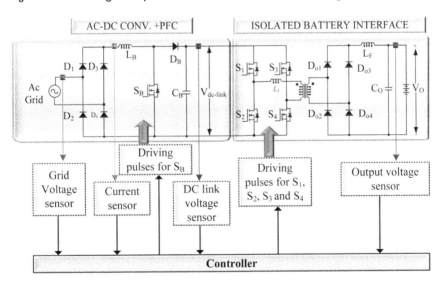

Figure 6.4 Block diagram representation of isolated wired charger.

safety requirements, cost considerations, and the intended technical application, with isolated chargers prioritizing safety and compatibility, while non-isolated chargers emphasize cost-effectiveness [11].

6.3.1 Different types of wired EV charging connectors

Various wired EV charging connectors cater to different power levels and regions. The J1772 connector (Type 1) is standard for Level 1 and Level 2 charging in North America and Japan, with examples like the Chevrolet Bolt and Nissan Leaf [12]. The Mennekes connector (Type 2) serves as Europe's Level 2 standard, used by vehicles like the BMW i3 and Hyundai Kona Electric. CCS (Combo) connectors merge J1772 or Mennekes with DC pins, offering rapid charging up to 350 kW and used by models like the Audi e-tron and Ford Mustang Mach-E. CHAdeMO is another fast-charging connector used primarily in Japan, found in vehicles like the Nissan Leaf and Kia Soul EV. Tesla, meanwhile, employs its proprietary connector for charging up to 250 kW, exclusively used in Tesla models such as the Model S, Model X, and Model Y [13].

6.3.2 Safety guidelines for wired EVs charging

To ensure safe wired charging for EVs, it's essential to follow several guidelines. Wired charging involves connecting the EV to an electric vehicle supply equipment (EVSE) using a conductive cable and plug, which can be either AC or DC chargers. Always follow the instructions from the EV and EVSE manufacturers, ensuring compatibility and avoiding damaged equipment or uncertified adapters. Handle the plug by its handle, not the cable, and avoid touching metal parts or sockets. Be cautious when charging in various conditions, especially in adverse weather, and use weatherproof equipment when needed. For home charging, consult a qualified electrician, have a dedicated circuit, and use protection devices like residual current device (RCD) or ground fault circuit interrupter (GFCI). At public stations, adhere to station operator rules, be attentive to indicators, and respect other users. Lastly, choose certified charging devices and follow manufacturer and local guidelines for safe and efficient charging [14].

6.4 WIRELESS CHARGING

Wireless charging technology has come a long way, with various methods such as inductive, resonant inductive, and magnetic resonance charging. Its primary application in EV charging presents notable advantages, including convenience, flexibility, and potential for autonomous charging. While it simplifies the charging process and enhances safety by eliminating cords, it comes with efficiency and cost considerations. Wireless charging enables devices to be powered without wires. Notable milestones in its history include Nikola Tesla's 1899 demonstration of wireless electricity transmission, the 2008 formation of the Wireless Power Consortium (Qi standard), and the 2020 introduction of Xiaomi's Mi Air Charge Technology for long-range charging. These milestones underline the evolution of wireless charging, offering the potential to revolutionize device usage, environmental sustainability, and energy sources. Different types of wireless charging methods for EVs are being explored to offer greater convenience and efficiency. Two notable approaches are quasi-dynamic wireless charging and dynamic wireless charging. Quasi-dynamic wireless charging is a wireless charging method that allows EVs to charge without plugging in, but it typically involves stationary or near-stationary charging pads or plates on the ground [15]. In this method, stationary charging pads or plates are strategically placed on the ground. These pads contain resonant coils that are tuned to the same frequency as the receiving coils on the EV. Dynamic wireless charging takes convenience to the next level by enabling EVs to charge while in motion. EVs equipped for dynamic charging have receiving coils underneath them, connected to the onboard battery system. As these vehicles move over the charging strips, they capture energy from the electromagnetic field and convert it into electric power for the battery. The circuital aspects of dynamic wireless charging encompass the coordination of embedded coils, onboard receiving coils, advanced power electronics for efficient energy transfer, and real-time control systems that adjust the power delivered based on vehicle speed and position.

The schematic diagram of the static and dynamic wireless charging is depicted in Figures 6.5 and 6.6. While dynamic wireless charging promises to eliminate the need for frequent stops at charging stations and extend the range of EVs, it presents significant challenges related to infrastructure, standardization, efficiency, and alignment. Implementing dynamic charging at scale requires substantial investment and coordination to revolutionize long-distance electric mobility. Table 6.3 summarizes key features of static, quasi-dynamic, and dynamic wireless charging systems for EVs. Static wireless charging is characterized by its convenience for stationary parking over charging pads but requires precise alignment, resulting in longer charging times and high efficiency. Quasi-dynamic systems offer some automation while still necessitating alignment and moderate charging times. Dynamic wireless charging enables continuous charging while in motion, with shorter

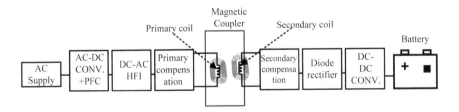

Figure 6.5 Schematic diagram of static wireless charger.

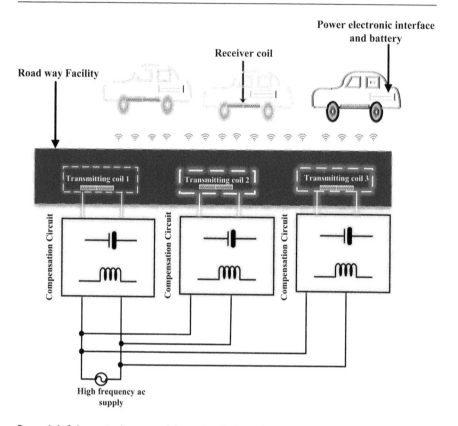

Figure 6.6 Schematic diagram of dynamic wireless charger.

charging times but higher installation costs as it's embedded in roads. It's convenient for long-distance travel but requires extensive infrastructure investment. Vehicle compatibility varies, with static systems limited to specific pads, while dynamic systems offer a wide range. Grid integration also varies, with static being grid-friendly, quasi-dynamic potentially requiring enhancements, and dynamic needing advanced grid integration. The cost-effectiveness and standardization of these systems depend on their specific use cases, with varying grid impacts from low to high. This technology involves charging infrastructure embedded in roads or tracks, allowing vehicles to charge continuously as they travel. The choice between wired and wireless charging depends on specific use cases and infrastructure availability. Misalignment issues in wireless charging systems pose significant challenges and considerations across different application scenarios. In static wireless charging, which is commonly used for stationary applications like EV charging, precision in alignment is crucial. Stricter alignment tolerances must be maintained, often with limited misalignment tolerance,

Table 6.3 Key features of static, quasi-dynamic, and dynamic wireless charging systems for electric vehicles

Features	Static wireless charging	Quasi-dynamic wireless charging	Dynamic wireless charging
Charging convenience	Stationary, requires parking over charging pad	Stationary, offers some automation but still requires alignment	Continuous charging while in motion
Alignment requirements	Precise alignment needed	Precise alignment needed	Continuous alignment required
Charging time	Longer	Moderate	Shorter
Charging efficiency	High (typically >90%)	Moderate (80%–90%)	Moderate to High (80%–95%)
Infrastructure cost	Lower installation cost compared to dynamic	Moderate installation cost	Higher installation cost, infrastructure embedded in roads
Deployment flexibility	Can be installed in various locations	Limited to specific parking areas	Requires road infrastructure
Ease of use	Convenient for parking and charging	Offers some automation, but still requires stopping	Convenient for long-distance travel
Commercial adoption	Increasing for EV fleets	Growing in public and private sectors	Emerging requires extensive infrastructure investment
Vehicle compatibility	Limited to Specific Pads	Moderate	Wide Range
Grid integration	Grid-friendly, but may require upgrades for high-power charging	Grid-friendly may require grid enhancements for high-power charging	Requires advanced grid integration for real-time power management
Energy transfer efficiency	Efficient power transfer	Efficient power transfer	Efficiency depends on real-time control and alignment
Cost-effectiveness	Cost-effective for stationary applications	Cost-effective for semi-dynamic use cases	Cost-effective for long-distance EV travel
Standardization	Standardized for some applications	Standardization emerging for specific use cases	Standards under development for broader adoption
Grid impact	Low	Moderate	High

necessitating the use of alignment guidance systems and careful design of the static charging infrastructure. In quasi-dynamic scenarios, where vehicles may have some mobility (e.g., automated guided vehicles or drones), dynamic alignment mechanisms become essential. These systems must adjust alignment in real time to accommodate vehicle movements, ensuring both efficiency and safety. In dynamic wireless charging for moving vehicles such as electric buses and trains, maintaining alignment during motion is a formidable challenge. Continuous alignment adjustments, predictive algorithms, and a balance between efficiency and alignment requirements are key considerations. Regardless of the scenario, efficient misalignment detection and correction mechanisms, employing technologies like sensors and communication protocols, are critical. Moreover, safety precautions must be integrated into the design to prevent accidents or equipment damage during alignment adjustments, especially in dynamic charging setups.

6.4.1 Different types of misalignment complexities and their tolerance of wireless charging of EVs

The complexities and tolerance of misalignment in wireless charging for EVs encompass several aspects. Lateral misalignment, resulting from widthwise coil displacement, can reduce power transfer efficiency; mitigation strategies include using multiple coils and decoupled receiving coils. Longitudinal misalignment, arising from lengthwise coil displacement, can affect alignment and efficiency; solutions involve circular or rectangular coils and adaptive tuning. Vertical misalignment, due to height differences, increases power loss; remedies include ferrite plates and shielding materials. Three types of wireless power transfer (WPT) based on operational modes are static, quasi-static/quasi-dynamic, and dynamic, each with differing misalignment challenges. Static WPT is sensitive to alignment, while quasi-static/quasi-dynamic offers moderate tolerance, and dynamic WPT provides high misalignment tolerance. Strategies for improving alignment include adaptive control algorithms and compensation networks for static and quasi-static/quasi-dynamic WPT, magnetic resonant coupling, and bidirectional communication for dynamic WPT [16].

6.4.2 Different types of safety guidelines for the wireless charging of EVs

Wireless charging for EVs employs electromagnetic induction to transfer power without cables, offering convenience, safety, and efficiency. However, it presents challenges like compatibility and interference. Various safety guidelines have been developed to address these concerns. Society of Automotive Engineers (SAE) J2954 sets criteria for wireless charging, specifying power levels and key parameters [17]. This represents a preliminary standard established by the SAE, delineating the prerequisites for wireless charging systems catering to electric and plug-in hybrid vehicles. This standard encompasses crucial criteria, including but not limited to, minimal efficiency thresholds, constraints about electromagnetic interference (EMI) and electromagnetic fields (EMF), as well as provisions for foreign object detection. Furthermore, this standard delineates four distinct power levels allocated for wireless charging, specifically 3.7, 7.7, 11, and 22 kW. The primary objective of this standard is to ensure seamless interoperability and compatibility across diverse wireless charging systems and a spectrum of vehicles.

6.5 FUTURE SCOPE AND CHALLENGES

The future of EV charging depends on factors like consumer preferences, innovation, and regulation. Improvements in efficiency, compatibility, and safety are crucial, along with standardized protocols. Hybrid systems that combine both charging methods may become more common, offering flexibility based on user needs. Overall, wired and wireless charging is essential for the widespread adoption of EVs in a sustainable transportation system.

6.5.1 Future scope for wired and wireless charging in EVs

In the realm of wired charging for EVs, the future is poised for remarkable advancements. This includes the development of ultra-fast charging systems to significantly reduce charging times, smart grid integration for efficient energy use, the establishment of universal standards for interoperability, and innovations aimed at reducing infrastructure costs [18]. These improvements will enhance the convenience and accessibility of wired charging, making it more attractive for long-distance EV travel and contributing to the broader adoption of EVs.

On the wireless charging front, the future holds exciting prospects. Advancements in resonance technology are expected to boost wireless charging efficiency, narrowing the gap with wired charging in terms of speed and energy efficiency. Dynamic wireless charging systems embedded in roads have the potential to extend EV range and reduce the reliance on large batteries. Wireless charging is also set to play a vital role in the electrification of commercial fleets and the integration of autonomous vehicles, offering convenience and efficiency gains. However, addressing challenges such as efficiency, standardization, cost, and precise alignment between charging components will be critical to realizing the full potential of wireless charging for EVs.

6.5.2 Challenges for wired and wireless charging in EVs

In the realm of wired charging, significant challenges lie in the expansion of charging infrastructure to meet the surging demand for EVs, balancing charging speed with battery health, upgrading grids to support ultra-fast charging, and ensuring a seamless user experience. These challenges involve substantial investments and careful planning to accommodate the growing EV population.

Wireless charging, while promising, faces challenges in improving charging efficiency to reduce energy loss during transmission, establishing global standards for compatibility, reducing the installation costs of wireless infrastructure, and ensuring precise alignment and positioning between charging components. Misalignment issues pose challenges in static, quasi-dynamic, and dynamic wireless charging systems. In static charging, precise parking alignment is crucial. Quasi-dynamic charging automates somewhat but still requires precise positioning. Dynamic charging faces continuous alignment challenges, including dynamic vehicle behavior and varying road conditions. These complexities necessitate advanced technologies for efficient and safe wireless charging. Overcoming these challenges will be pivotal in making wireless charging technology more competitive and practical for widespread adoption in the EVs ecosystem [19].

6.6 CONCLUSION

In conclusion, this chapter embarked on a comprehensive journey through the landscape of EVs charging technologies. It commenced with an insightful overview that is valuable for a deeper exploration. Subsequently, it delved into the intricacies of both wired and wireless charging methods, elucidating their unique strengths and limitations. Within the realm of wired charging, this chapter meticulously analyzed various charger types, all within the context of the Indian scenario. Transitioning into the wireless charging domain unravels the innovative principles that underpin this emerging technology. The distinction between static and dynamic wireless charging mechanisms underscores the versatility and potential applications of each approach. Ultimately, this chapter follows a structured progression, starting with an initial overview and then delving into the details of wired and wireless charging, encompassing isolated and non-isolated wired charging, and exploring the possibilities of static, quasi-dynamic, and dynamic wireless charging. The exploration delves into key characteristics, design considerations, challenges, and prospects, offering readers a holistic understanding of these charging techniques and their evolving role in the EVs landscape.

REFERENCES

1. A. Khaligh and S. Dusmez, "Comprehensive Topological Analysis of Conductive and Inductive Charging Solutions for Plug-In Electric Vehicles," *IEEE Transactions on Vehicular Technology*, vol. 61, no. 8, pp. 3475–3489, 2012, doi: 10.1109/TVT.2012.2213104.

2. M. Yilmaz and P. T. Krein, "Review of Battery Charger Topologies, Charging Power Levels, and Infrastructure for Plug-In Electric and Hybrid Vehicles," *IEEE Transactions on Power Electronics*, vol. 28, no. 5, pp. 2151–2169, 2013, doi: 10.1109/TPEL.2012.2212917.

3. S. Li and C. C. Mi, "Wireless Power Transfer for Electric Vehicle Applications," *IEEE Journal of Emerging and Selected Topics in Power Electronics*, vol. 3, no. 1, pp. 4–17, 2015, doi: 10.1109/JESTPE.2014.2319453.

4. A. Ahmad, M. S. Alam and R. Chabaan, "A Comprehensive Review of Wireless Charging Technologies for Electric Vehicles," *IEEE Transactions on Transportation Electrification*, vol. 4, no. 1, pp. 38–63, 2018, doi: 10.1109/TTE.2017.2771619.

5. Revised Consolidated Guidelines & Standards for Charging Infrastructure for Electric Vehicles (EV) Promulgated) Promulgated by Ministry of Power (15 JAN 2022). Retrieved on August 28, 2023, from https://pib.gov.in/PressReleasePage.aspx?PRID=1790136.

6. Bharat EV specifications for AC and DC charging - PluginIndia Electric Vehicles. Retrieved on August 28, 2023, from https://www.pluginindia.com/blogs/bharat-ev-specifications-for-ac-and-dc-charging-everything-you-need-to-know.

7. J. M. Miller, P. T. Jones, J. -M. Li and O. C. Onar, "ORNL experience and challenges facing dynamic wireless power charging of EVs," *IEEE Circuits and Systems Magazine*, vol. 15, no. 2, pp. 40–53, 2015, doi: 10.1109/MCAS.2015.2419012.

8. A. Ali, H. H. H. Mousa, M. F. Shaaban, M. A. Azzouz and A. S. A. Awad, "A Comprehensive Review on Charging Topologies and Power Electronic Converter Solutions for Electric Vehicles," *Journal of Modern Power Systems and Clean Energy*, doi: 10.35833/MPCE.2023.000107.

9. S. A. Q. Mohammed and J. -W. Jung, "A Comprehensive State-of-the-Art Review of Wired/Wireless Charging Technologies for Battery Electric Vehicles: Classification/Common Topologies/Future Research Issues," *IEEE Access*, vol. 9, pp. 19572–19585, 2021, doi: 10.1109/ACCESS.2021.3055027.

10. H. Arya and M. Das, "Fast Charging Station for Electric Vehicles Based on DC Microgrid," *IEEE Journal of Emerging and Selected Topics in Industrial Electronics*, doi: 10.1109/JESTIE.2023.3285535.

11. Q. Deng et al., "Wired/Wireless Hybrid Charging System for Electrical Vehicles With Minimum Rated Power Requirement for DC Module," *IEEE Transactions on Vehicular Technology*, vol. 69, no. 10, pp. 10889–10898, 2020, doi: 10.1109/TVT.2020.3019787.

12. Michael Schuck (Chief Editor at ThinkEV), "Types of EV Charging Connectors: Guides To EV Charging". Retrieved on October 06, 2023, from https://thinkev.com/types-of-ev-charging-connectors/.

13. By Team Biliti Electric "Different Types of Electric Vehicle Charging Connectors", 12 April 2023. Retrieved on October 06, 2023, from https://bilitielectric.com/blog/electric-vehicle-charging-connectors-types/.

14. By admin "Charging Safety Guidelines For Electric Vehicles", 31st May 2022. Retrieved on October 06, 2023, from https://www.tatacapital.com/blog/loan-for-vehicle/charging-safety-guidelines-for-electric-vehicles/.

15. A. Khaligh and M. D'Antonio, "Global Trends in High-Power On-Board Chargers for Electric Vehicles," *IEEE Transactions on Vehicular Technology*, vol. 68, no. 4, pp. 3306–3324, 2019, doi: 10.1109/TVT.2019.2897050.

16. "Communication for Wireless Power Transfer Between Light-Duty Plug-in Electric Vehicles and Wireless EV Charging Stations", Published September 29, 2020 by SAE International in United States. Retrieved on October 06, 2023, from https://www.sae.org/standards/content/j2847/6_202009/.
17. "Wireless Power Transfer for Light-Duty Plug-in/Electric Vehicles and Alignment Methodology:, Published October 20, 2020 by SAE International in United States. Retrieved on October 06, 2023, from https://www.sae.org/standards/content/j2954_202010/.
18. D. Patil, M. K. McDonough, J. M. Miller, B. Fahimi and P. T. Balsara, "Wireless Power Transfer for Vehicular Applications: Overview and Challenges," *IEEE Transactions on Transportation Electrification*, vol. 4, no. 1, pp. 3–37, 2018, doi: 10.1109/TTE.2017.2780627.
19. S. -Y. R. Hui, Y. Yang and C. Zhang, "Wireless Power Transfer: A Paradigm Shift for the Next Generation," *IEEE Journal of Emerging and Selected Topics in Power Electronics*, vol. 11, no. 3, pp. 2412–2427, 2023.

Chapter 7

Design, modelling, and control of resonant converters, resonant immittance converters, and front-end converters for EV charging

N. J. Merlin Mary and Shelas Sathyan

7.1 INTRODUCTION: BACKGROUND

One of the greatest concerns nowadays is the increase in greenhouse gases causing global warming. These gases are widely produced by the transportation sector and are harmful to the environment. Thus, in recent days, electrically driven vehicles have started to replace conventional engine vehicles. However, the charging system design for using EVs is the biggest challenge. Figure 7.1 shows the block diagram of the two-stage onboard battery charging (OBC) system. For the OBC system, the primary power source is obtained from the grid through a utility-friendly front-end AC/DC converter cascaded with a downstream isolated DC/DC converter [1]. The output of the DC/DC converter is used to charge a high-energy density battery pack. The front-end AC/DC rectifier unit causes the grid current to be distorted in nature and thus injects harmonics. Active PFC (APFC) techniques are widely employed in these charging units to follow international power quality standards such as IEC and IEEE [2].

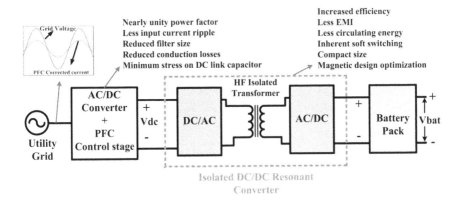

Figure 7.1 Two-stage onboard battery charging system.

DOI: 10.1201/9781003481065-7

The converters are designed and compared for the specifications given below.

  a. **Front-end stage:** 230 V_{rms} input, 50 Hz line frequency (f_l), 400 V_{DC} link voltage (V_{dc}), and 100 kHz switching frequency (f_{sw}).
  b. **DC-DC converter stage:** 320–420 V battery voltage (V_{bat}), 7.857 rated battery current (I_{bat}), and 100 kHz resonant frequency (f_r).

7.2 BATTERY CHARGING METHODS

The battery charging methods vary for different types of batteries, namely nickel metal hydride, lead-acid, and lithium-ion batteries. One widely used method for a lithium-ion battery is CC/CV charging. A lithium-ion LIR18650 rechargeable cell characteristics are given in Ref. [3]. The cell's nominal voltage is 3.7 V, the final charge voltage is 4.2 V, the standard charge current is 0.52 A, and the final charge current is 0.052 A (10% of 0.52 A). The required battery voltage and current are obtained by connecting these lithium-ion cells in series and parallel. The four main points in the charging process are shown in Figure 7.2. When connected to the charger, the battery in the discharged condition begins with CC charging. The constant current flowing into the battery increases the voltage to 370 V (nominal point) and then to rated 420 V (turning point). The charging shifts to constant voltage to prevent overcharging after the rated voltage is attained. In this mode, the current reduces drastically and reaches a final charge current of 0.7857 A. This battery charging method is safe as it allows fast charging without overcharging.

7.3 RESONANT CONVERTERS

A resonant DC-DC converter consists of an inverter, a resonant tank filter for filtering out the harmonics of the inverter output, a transformer to step up or step down the voltage, and a rectifier to obtain the DC output. The resonant

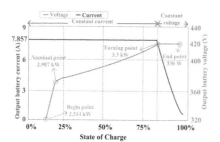

Parameter	Begin point	Nominal point	Turning point	End point
Power (W)	2514.24	2907.09	3300	330
Battery voltage (V)	320	370	420	420
Battery current (A)	7.857	7.857	7.857	0.7857
Battery resistance (Ω)	40.728	47.092	53.454	534.545

Figure 7.2 Lithium-ion battery charging profile.

converters are frequency-modulated to obtain the required DC output. The main benefit of resonant converters is minimized switching losses due to zero-voltage switching (ZVS) and zero-current switching (ZCS). The resonant tank elements are chosen such that the converter performs well at one operating point, i.e., at the resonant frequency. For a wide range of voltages and currents, optimizing the design to achieve good performance is hard. In some cases, the resonant tank current is significant even under light load causing poor efficiency. The characteristics of different resonant converters, namely series, parallel, LLC, and MSP-RC [4–9] are analyzed and compared here.

7.3.1 First Harmonic Approximation analysis

The resonant converters are analyzed by sinusoidal approximation, also known as a first harmonic approximation (FHA) [4]. This analysis assumes that the switching frequency harmonics are neglected, and the resonant tank waveforms are purely sinusoidal. Since the input voltage to the diode bridge rectifier V'_{ZW} and the filter tank current i_s are in phase with each other, the rectifier is considered as an equivalent resistance R_{ac} as shown in Figure 7.3. The graphs obtained by this analysis are primarily accurate only for high Q factors, and there is a lot of deviation for low Q factors. This is because the current is not purely sinusoidal for light load conditions (low Q). Thus, the frequency graphs obtained using this method are perfect for high Q factors. The AC equivalent resistance (R_{ac}) is the ratio of $V'_{ZW1,rms}$ (fundamental rms value of V'_{ZW}) by $i_{s,rms}$ (rms filter current). V'_{ZW} is the square-shaped rectifier input voltage with amplitude $\pm V_{bat}$. It is the sum of the DC, fundamental, and higher-order harmonic components.

$$V'_{ZW}(t) = 0 + \frac{4V'_{bat}}{\pi}\sin(\omega_s t) + \sum_{k=3,5,7...} \frac{4V'_{bat}}{k\pi}\sin(k\omega_s t) \tag{7.1}$$

where ω_s is the switching frequency, V'_{bat} is the battery voltage referred to primary and k is the harmonic number. $V'_{ZW1,rms}$ is given by $4V'_{bat}/\pi\sqrt{2}$.

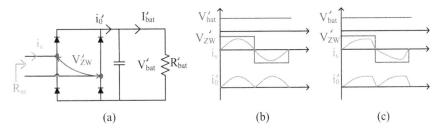

Figure 7.3 FHA analysis. (a) Diode bridge represented as R_{ac}. (b) Perfect sinusoidal current i_s at resonant frequency. (c) Imperfect sinusoidal current i_s for above resonant frequency.

The average current (I'_{bat}) through R'_{bat} (battery resistance referred to primary) is given by

$$i''_{0,avg} = I'_{bat} = \frac{1}{T_s/2} \int_0^{T_s/2} i_{s,peak} \sin(\omega_s t) dt = \frac{\sqrt{8}\ i_{s,rms}}{\pi} \tag{7.2}$$

where $i_{s,peak}$ is the filter peak current and T_s is the switching period. Thus, the AC equivalent resistance (R_{ac}) is expressed as $8R'_{bat}/\pi^2$.

7.3.2 Inductive and capacitive regions of operation

Resonant converters operate at capacitive or inductive regions based on the switching frequency of operation. Figure 7.4 shows the theoretical waveforms for capacitive and inductive modes of operation. If the input impedance of the filter tank is inductive, then the current i_s lags the inverter output voltage V_{XY}. The switches attain ZVS at turn-on, whereas, at turn-off, they are hard-switched. The antiparallel diodes are hard-switched during turn-on, whereas during turn-off, they are soft-switched. If the input impedance of the filter tank is capacitive, then the current i_s leads the voltage V_{XY}. The switches attain ZCS at turn-off, whereas at turn-on, they are hard-switched. The antiparallel diodes are hard-switched during turn-off,

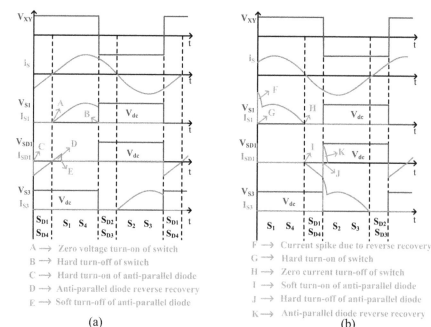

Figure 7.4 Theoretical waveforms. (a) Inductive operation. (b) Capacitive operation.

Table 7.1 Comparison of inductive and capacitive regions

Inductive region	Capacitive region
MOSFETs are preferred	IGBTs are preferred
MOSFETs do not have any tail current during turn-off. Thus, turn-off losses are less	IGBTs have a tail current during turn-off, which increases the turn-off switching losses. Thus, IGBTs are preferred for operating in regions with inherent soft switching features during turn-off
The inbuilt body diodes of MOSFETs are enough to act as antiparallel diodes, as the reverse recovery losses are zero	Fast reverse recovery antiparallel diodes are needed along with IGBTs to minimize the reverse recovery losses and the current spikes in switches
The switch turn-off losses can be minimized by paralleling small snubber capacitors	The switch turn-on losses can be minimized by paralleling small snubber capacitors

whereas during turn-on, they are soft-switched. The reverse recovery losses of the antiparallel diodes are high as they are turned off with high di/dt. This reverse recovery current affects the switch current waveform by adding an undesirable spike. The comparison between inductive and capacitive regions of operation is given in Table 7.1.

In Figure 7.4, V_S and I_S is the switch voltage and switch current, V_{SD} and I_{SD} is the antiparallel diode voltage and current. The suffix 1, 2, 3, and 4 indicates the switch numbers.

7.3.3 Series Resonant Converter (S-RC)

Figure 7.5a shows the typical circuit diagram of S-RC with DC input voltage (V_{dc}). It consists of switches S_1, S_2, S_3, and S_4 at the primary side, a transformer with N_1 and N_2 in the primary and secondary, and diodes D_1, D_2, D_3, and D_4 at the secondary side. Whenever the switching frequency equals the resonant frequency, V_{ZW} becomes equal to turn ratio ($n = N_1 / N_2$) times the battery voltage (V_{bat}). This is because, at the resonant frequency, the impedance of resonant tank elements L_a and C_a becomes equal and cancels each other. Above resonant frequency, the inductive impedance dominates, and the circuit becomes inductive in nature. R_{ac}, a function of load resistance, is in series with the resonant tank elements, as shown in Figure 7.5b. Thus, the current i_s is directly proportional to the load current. The tank current decides the reactive power losses ($P_{reactive}$) of the converter. In CC charging mode, $P_{reactive}$ are higher compared to CV charging mode. The plot of voltage versus normalized switching frequency decreases when operated away from the resonant frequency, as shown in Figure 7.6a) Thus, it is a step-down converter. The converter acts as a constant voltage source for all load conditions at the resonant frequency. The short circuit current

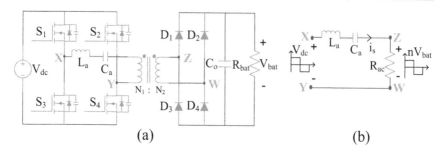

Figure 7.5 Series resonant converter. (a) Circuit diagram. (b) FHA equivalent circuit.

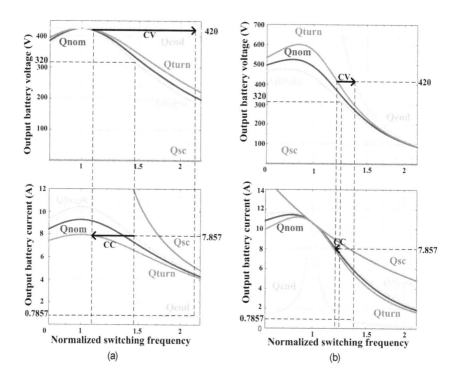

Figure 7.6 V_{bat} and I_{bat} versus f_n. (a) S-RC. (b) P-RC.

is controlled by increasing the switching frequency. The performance under light load is poor as the voltage curve for Q_{end} is almost flat. Thus, to control the voltage, the switching frequency must be increased to a larger value which increases the turn-off switching losses. At no-load conditions, the output voltage regulation is not possible by switching frequency variation.

The gain of the S-RC is given by $1 / \sqrt{\left(f_n Q - \dfrac{Q}{f_n}\right)^2 + 1}$. Q is the quality factor given by R / R_{ac}, R is the characteristic impedance, and f_n is the normalized switching frequency.

7.3.4 Parallel Resonant Converter

The parallel resonant converter (P-RC) can step up and step down the DC input voltage, as shown in the voltage versus frequency characteristics of Figure 7.6b. The typical circuit diagram and FHA equivalent circuit of P-RC are shown in Figure 7.7a and b.

As there is no inherent DC-blocking capacitor, the transformer saturation cannot be prevented. The converter acts as a constant current source for all load conditions at the resonant frequency. The current i_s is completely independent of the load current, as the current through the resonant capacitor C_a varies for different switching frequencies. During light load, i_s is higher compared to the load current. This leads to poor light load efficiency. ⅢThe P-RC has inherent short circuit protection since the current i_s is limited by the L_a impedance. The gain of the PRC is given by $1 / \sqrt{\left(1 - f_n^2\right)^2 + \left(f_n Q\right)^2}$.

7.3.5 LLC Resonant Converter (LLC-RC)

The circuit diagram of LLC-RC is shown in Figure 7.8a. The gain of the LLC-RC is $f_n^2 (m-1) / \sqrt{\left(\left(mf_n^2\right)-1\right)^2 / + f_n^2 \left(f_n^2 - 1\right)^2 (m-1)^2 Q^2}$. m is the ratio given by $(L_a + L_m) / L_a$. The steps to design the LLC resonant converter are as follows.

Step 1: Find the turns ratio (n) of the transformer from Figure 7.8b.

$$n = \frac{N_1}{N_2} = \frac{\text{Primary turns}}{\text{Secondary turns}} = \frac{M_{f@resonance} * V_{dc}}{V_{bat@nominal}} = \frac{1 * 400}{370} = 1.081 \qquad (7.3)$$

Step 2: Find the AC equivalent resistance R_{ac}.

$$R_{ac} = \frac{8n^2 R_{bat@rated}}{\pi^2} = \frac{8 * 1.081^2 * 420^2}{\pi^2 * 3,300} = 50.684 \ \Omega \qquad (7.4)$$

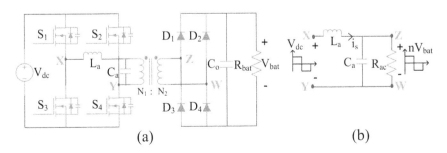

(a)   (b)

Figure 7.7 Parallel resonant converter. (a) Circuit diagram. (b) FHA equivalent circuit.

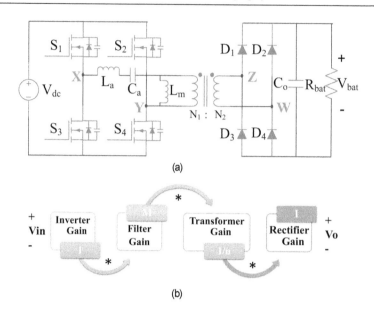

Figure 7.8 LLC resonant converter. (a) Circuit diagram. (b) Converter gain.

Step 3: At resonance,

$$R = \omega_0 L_a = 1/\omega_0 C_a \tag{7.5}$$

$$f_0 = \frac{1}{2\pi\sqrt{L_a C_a}} \text{ implies } \sqrt{L_a C_a} = 1.5924 * 10^{-6} \tag{7.6}$$

Step 4: Plot the graphs of battery output voltage versus f_n for different m values, as shown in Figure 7.9. The converter behavior for below resonant frequency is analyzed. For low values of m, higher gain is obtained for the narrow frequency range of operation. For high values of m, magnetizing inductance value is high, which leads to less circulating current and higher efficiency. Thus $m=4$ is chosen for the design. This m value is a trade-off between high efficiency and a narrow frequency range.

Step 5: Determine the Q factor at turning point. From the graph of output voltage versus f_n, Q, for which voltage crosses 420 V with slight frequency variation from the resonant frequency, is chosen as Q_{turn}.

$$Q_{turn} = \frac{R}{R_{ac}} = \frac{\omega_0 L_a}{50.684} = \frac{\sqrt{L_a / C_a}}{50.684} = 0.7 \tag{7.7}$$

Step 6: By solving equations (7.6) and (7.7), $L_a = 56.496\ \mu H$ and $C_a = 44.88\ nF$ is obtained. However, the available practical value of capacitor closer to the calculated is $C_a = 47\ nF$. For this value of C_a, the recalculated values are $L_a = 53.952\ \mu H$ and $Q_{turn} = 0.63286$.

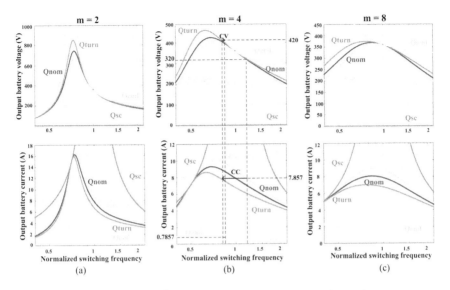

Figure 7.9 V_{bat} and I_{bat} versus f_n for LLC-RC. (a) $m=2$. (b) $m=4$. (c) $m=8$.

Step 7: Determine the value of magnetizing inductance, $L_m = mL_a - L_a = 161.856 * 10^{-6}$ H.

The performance of LLC-RC could be better in CC charging mode due to wide switching frequency variation. Also, during short circuit conditions, the frequency has to be increased to a large value to limit the load current below the rated 7.857 A.

7.3.6 Modified Series Parallel Resonant Converter (MSP-RC)

The circuit diagram of MSP-RC is shown in Figure 7.10. The gain of the MSP-RC is given by

$$\frac{f_n^3 m^4 z n^2 - f_n n^2 m^2 xyz}{\sqrt{\begin{bmatrix} -f_n^5 m^6 + f_n^4 Q m^4 z n^2 + f_n^3 m^4 \left(1 + z n^2 + y + xy\right) \\ -Q f_n^2 n^2 m^2 z \left(xy + 1 + y\right) + Q n^2 xyz - f_n m^2 xy \left(1 + z n^2\right) \end{bmatrix}^2 + \left[f_n^4 Q m^4 z n^2 - Q f_n^2 n^2 m^2 z \left(xy + 1 + y\right) + Q n^2 xyz\right]^2}} \tag{7.8}$$

where $x = L_a / L_b$, $y = C_a / C_b$, and $z = C_a / C_p$. m is factor that depends on x and y. The steps to design the MSP-RC are as follows. **Step 1 and Step 2** are same as that of LLC-RC.

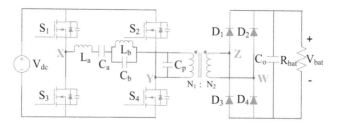

Figure 7.10 Modified series-parallel resonant DC-DC converter.

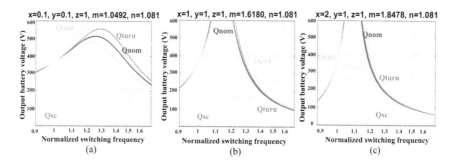

Figure 7.11 (a–c) V_{bat} versus f_n for $z=1$ and different x, y values.

Step 3: Plot the voltage graphs for different values of x and y by keeping $z=1$ as shown in Figure 7.11. For $x=2$ and $y=1$, the frequency of operation is closer to f_r.

Step 4: At resonance,

$$f_r = m / \left(2\pi \sqrt{L_a C_a} \right) \tag{7.9}$$

Step 5: Plot the output battery current, peak inverter output current, and kVA/kW rating versus f_r for different values of z by keeping $x=2$ and $y=1$ as shown in Figure 7.12. The graphs show that for the operating range of frequencies, $x=2$, $y=1$ and $z=1$ has better performance. The graphs show the converter performs well at short circuit conditions, CC, and CV charging modes. The output battery current I_{bat} for all the above converters is given by

$$I_{bat} = \text{Voltage gain} * \frac{V_{dc} 8nQ}{\pi^2 \omega_0 L_x} \tag{7.10}$$

The comparison of different resonant converters characteristics is given in Table 7.2.

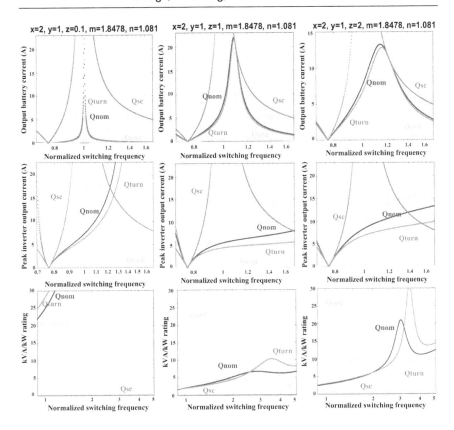

Figure 7.12 V_{bat} versus f_n for $z=1$ and different x, y values.

7.3.7 Controller implementation

The control for battery charging consists of two parallel loops, namely voltage control and current control as shown in Figure 7.13. The detected battery's state of charge (SOC) is used to enable the CC loop or CV loop. In CV charging mode, an error amplifier compares the sensed output voltage with the reference DC link voltage of 420 V. A compensator P/PI/PID is used to reduce this error, giving an output voltage signal. This signal is converted into a frequency signal and given to the gate drive logic for pulse generation. The controller operation for CC charging mode is the same as that of CV charging mode.

7.4 RESONANT IMMITTANCE CONVERTER

The RIC consists of a tank network that has impedance+admittance properties. The constant voltage source is converted to a constant current source for an immittance network and vice versa. A resonant immittance network

Table 7.2 Characteristic comparison of different resonant converters

Characteristics	S-RC	P-RC	LLC-RC	MSP-RC
Inductors	L_a =53.952μH	L_a = 53.952μH	L_a = 53.952μH L_m = 161.86μH	L_a = 262.35μH L_b = 131.18μH
Capacitors	C_a = 47 nF	C_a = 47 nF	C_a = 47 nF	C_a, C_b, C_p, = 33 nF
Turns ratio (n)	0.9411	1.081	1.081	1.081
Q factor range	1.1559~0.0882	0.8761~0.06685	0.8761~0.06685	1.4058~0.10727
Frequency range for CV charging (kHz)	108~220 (High)	118~136 (Medium)	81~86 (Less)	117~120 (Less)
Frequency range for CC operation (kHz)	108~145 (High)	118~123 (Less)	81~120 (High)	111~117 (Less)
Voltage regulation capability at highest SOC	Bad	Good	Good	Good
Short circuit protection performance	Bad	Very good	Good	Very good

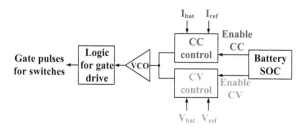

Figure 7.13 Battery charging controller implementation for resonant converters.

is a two-port network and some of the resonant immittance tanks namely LCL-T, CLC-T, LCL-π, and CLC-π are shown in Figure 7.14. These RICs have constant current characteristics.

V_a, I_a, V_b, and I_b are the input voltage, input current, output voltage, and output current of tank network. It is represented by ABCD parameters.

$$\begin{bmatrix} V_a \\ I_a \end{bmatrix} = \begin{bmatrix} A & B \\ C & D \end{bmatrix} \begin{bmatrix} V_b \\ -I_b \end{bmatrix} \tag{7.11}$$

A is the reverse voltage gain, B is the transfer impedance, C is the transfer admittance, and D is the reverse current gain. The resonant tanks exhibiting

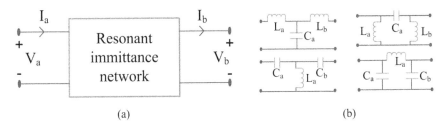

Figure 7.14 (a) Two-port resonant immittance network. (b) Types of resonant immittance tanks.

immittance property must satisfy the reciprocity theorem. The conditions for reciprocity are $A=D=0$ and $BC=1$.

Steps to find B and C parameters for LCL-T two-port network:

1. To satisfy reciprocity theorem, $A=0$. This implies $V_a / V_b = 0$ and $I_b = 0$.
2. By network theorem for $I_b = 0$ one can obtain

$$\frac{V_a}{V_b} = \frac{jX_{La} - jX_{Ca}}{-jX_{Ca}} \text{ and } \frac{I_a}{V_b} = \frac{1}{-jX_{Ca}} \tag{7.12}$$

3. Since $V_a / V_b = 0$, the impedance $X_{La} = X_{Ca}$.
4. To satisfy reciprocity theorem, $D=0$. This implies $-I_a / I_b = 0$ and $V_b = 0$.
5. By network theorem for $V_b = 0$ one can obtain

$$I_b * (jX_{Lb}) = I_{Ca} * (-jX_{Ca}); I_a = I_{Ca} + I_b \tag{7.13}$$

6. Since $-I_a / I_b = 0$, the current $I_{Ca} = -I_b$ and the impedance $X_{Lb} = X_{Ca}$.
7. Since the current I_a is also zero, the ratio B is given by

$$B = \frac{V_a}{I_b} = jX_{Lb} = jX_{Ca} \text{ and } \frac{-V_a}{I_b} = -jX_{Ca} \tag{7.14}$$

8. The ABCD parameters are obtained as follows

$$\begin{bmatrix} V_a \\ I_a \end{bmatrix} = \begin{bmatrix} 0 & -jX_{Ca} \\ \dfrac{1}{-jX_{Ca}} & 0 \end{bmatrix} \begin{bmatrix} V_b \\ -I_b \end{bmatrix} = \begin{bmatrix} 0 & \mp jZ_0 \\ \pm j\left(\dfrac{1}{Z_0}\right) & 0 \end{bmatrix} \begin{bmatrix} V_b \\ -I_b \end{bmatrix}$$

$$\tag{7.15}$$

9. where Z_0 is the characteristic impedance of the circuit at resonant frequency.

Table 7.3 Characteristic comparison of different RICs

Topology	CC charging	CV charging	Auxiliary circuit	Bidirectional
Conventional LCL-T [10]	Yes	No	No	No
LCL-T with clamp diodes [10]	Yes	Yes	Yes	No
Secondary modified LCL-T [11]	Yes	Yes	No	No
Secondary modified bidirectional CLC-T [12]	Yes	Yes	No	Yes

$$Z_1 = \frac{V_a}{I_a} = Z_0{}^2 * \frac{I_b}{V_b} = \frac{Z_0{}^2}{Z_2} = Z_0{}^2 * Y_2 \qquad (7.16)$$

$$I_b = \frac{V_a}{\pm jZ_0} \text{ and } V_b = \mp jZ_0 I_a \qquad (7.17)$$

10. The input impedance $Z_1 = V_a / I_a$ is proportional to the output admittance $Y_2 = I_b / V_b$. Hence the name immittance. I_b is proportional to V_a, and V_b is proportional to I_a.
11. The comparison of RICs is given in Table 7.3. A conventional unidirectional LCL-T RIC circuit that has CC characteristics is shown in Figure 7.15a. A modified secondary bidirectional LCL-T RIC shown in Figure 7.15b is proposed for CC/CV charging and for bidirectional power transfer.

7.4.1 Modified secondary bidirectional LCT-T RIC design

This converter acts as LCL-T resonant tank for some duration and LC resonant tank for some duration in CC charging mode. In CV charging mode, it purely acts as LC resonant tank. The diodes D_1 and D_2 does not conduct once the voltage reaches the rated value of 420 V. The gate pulses to the converter switches $(S_1, S_2, S_3, S_4, S_{1b}, \text{ and } S_{2b})$ and the analysis is similar to the proposed converter in Ref. [12]. The secondary circuit configurations for LCL and LC resonant tanks are shown in Figure 7.16. The turns ratio (n) of the transformer is given by $n = 2V_{dc} / V_{bat\_turn}$. The battery resistance R_{bat} at the crossing point of CC to CV is given by

$$R_{bat\_CC/CV} = \frac{V_{bat\_turn}{}^2}{P} = \frac{420^2}{3,300} = 53.45 \ \Omega \qquad (7.18)$$

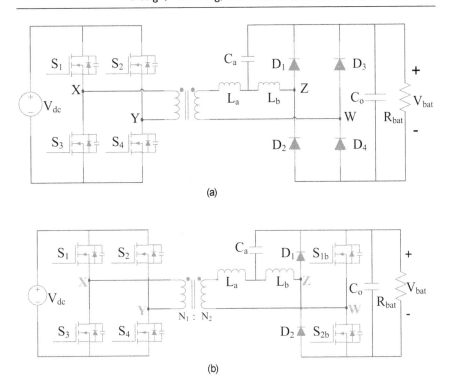

(a)

(b)

Figure 7.15 (a) Conventional LCL-T unidirectional RIC. (b) Modified LCL-T bidirectional RIC.

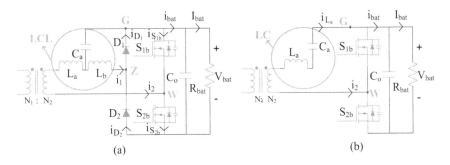

(a)   (b)

Figure 7.16 Secondary circuit configurations. (a) LCL tank. (b) LC tank.

The resonant capacitor C_a is calculated by equating the AC equivalent resistance R_{ac} at end point of CC mode and begin point of CV mode.

$$C_a = \frac{\pi^2}{2\omega_r R_{bat\_CC/CV}} = \frac{\pi^2}{2 * 2\pi * 100 * 1000 * 53.45} = 0.1469\,\mu F \qquad (7.19)$$

However, the available practical capacitor is 0.16 μF. For this C_a, L_a and L_b are calculated.

$$L_a = L_b = \frac{1}{\omega_r^2 C_a} = \frac{1}{(2\pi * 100)^2 * C_a} = 15.847 \,\mu\text{H} \qquad (7.20)$$

The magnetizing inductance of the practical transformer plays a vital role in soft switching and is assumed to be 200 μH in simulation. The charging characteristics for this design are given in Figure 7.17. The battery is represented as an equivalent resistance. The characteristics show that as the battery resistance increases and reaches the rated value, the converter automatically shifts from CC to CV charging. The simulation results during CC charging are shown in Figure 7.18. The switches attain soft switching (ZVS) for all power levels. The battery voltage and currents (V_{bat} and I_{bat}) settle down at the required values. The current i_{La} is sinusoidal. The current

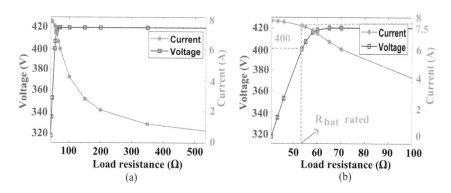

Figure 7.17 (a and b) CC/CV charging characteristics.

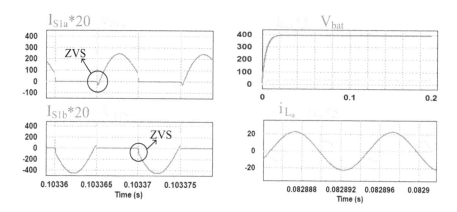

Figure 7.18 Simulation results during CC charging.

through L_b is discontinuous conducting for a short duration during CC and for CV charging, current through L_b is zero.

7.5 FRONT-END CONVERTERS

Front-end converters for power factor correction are categorized into active and passive types. Active power factor correction (APFC) converters are widely preferred due to their high efficiency, power factor, and power density. The comparison of various converter topologies adopted for PFC [13–17] is given in Table 7.4. Recently, the totem-pole PFC stage has been used widely due to its high efficiency of around 99%.

7.5.1 Totem-pole PFC stage

The totem-pole PFC using ultrafast IGBTs S_{1a} and S_{2a}, antiparallel SiC diodes, and rectifier diodes D_{1a} and D_{2a} is shown in Figure 7.19a. The DC link voltage (V_0) is compared with the reference DC voltage ($V_{0\_avg}^*$) of 400 V and the error signal (V_{err}) is given to the voltage controller. This controller output (I_m^*) multiplied with modulus of unity sinusoidal signal is the reference current for current loop. This is compared with the modulus of inductor current ($|i_L(t)| = I_m|\sin\omega_i t|$) and the error is given to the current controller for pulse generation. The open loop gate pulsing pattern and the operation modes are given in Figures 7.19b and 7.20.

   a. **Positive half input voltage cycle:** When switch S_{2a} is ON, the inductor L_x is charged by the source, and the output capacitor C_0 is supplied by the load. When switch S_{2a} is OFF, the inductor L_x discharges the energy to the load through the antiparallel SiC diode of S_{1a}.

Table 7.4 Comparison of various converter topologies for PFC

Topology	Boost	Interleaved (IL) boost	Bridgeless (BL) boost	BLIL boost	IL totem pole
No. of switches/ diodes	1/5	2/6	2/2	4/4	4/2
No. of inductors/ capacitors	1/1	2/1	2/1	4/1	2/1
Input ripple current	High	Low	High	Low	Low
Output capacitor stress	High	Low	High	Low	Low
Rectifier bridge	Yes	Yes	No	No	No
Heat management problem	Yes	Yes	No	No	No
Efficiency	Low	Low	High	High	Very high

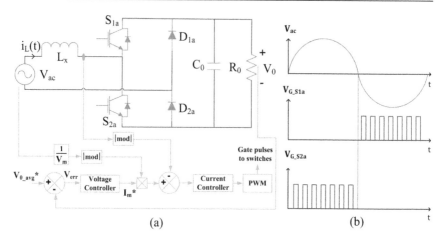

Figure 7.19 (a) Totem-pole PFC with controller implementation. (b) Open loop pulsing pattern.

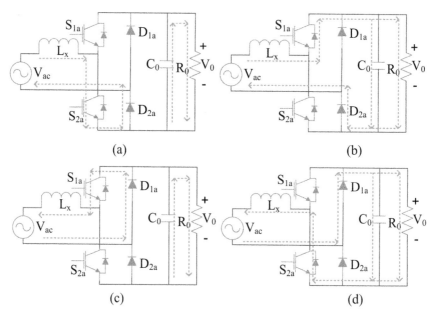

Figure 7.20 Operation modes. (a) +ve half cycle when switch ON. (b) +ve half cycle when switch OFF. (c) −ve half cycle when switch ON. (d) −ve half cycle when switch OFF.

b. **Negative half input voltage cycle:** When switch S_{1a} is ON, the inductor L_x is charged by the source, and the output capacitor C_0 is supplied by the load. When switch S_{1a} is OFF, the inductor L_x discharges the energy to the load through the antiparallel SiC diode of S_{2a}.

7.5.2 Open loop design

Step 1: Determine the duty ratio. The operation of the totem-pole PFC is the same as that of the boost converter for each half-switching period. So, the duty ratio is calculated from $V_{0\_avg} = V_{ac} / (1 - D)$. Since the input voltage V_{ac} is a 50 Hz waveform, it is assumed to be a constant for 100 kHz switching frequency (f_{sw}). The duty is calculated for the maximum AC input voltage (V_m as $D = 1 - \left(\sqrt{2} V_{rms} / V_{0\_avg} \right) = 0.1868$. $V_{rms} = V_m / \sqrt{2}$ is the rms voltage.

Step 2: Design of the input inductor. The inductor voltage is given by $V_{LX} = L_X (di / dt)$.

From this, the ripple current ΔI_L is obtained as $D \sqrt{2} V_{rms} / f_{sw} L_X$. Considering the percentage ripple as 4%, the ripple current ΔI_L is given by

$$\Delta I_L = 0.04 \left(\frac{V_{0\_avg}}{R_0 (1 - D)} \right) = \frac{D \sqrt{2} V_{rms}}{f_{sw} L_X} \tag{7.21}$$

where R_0 is the DC link resistance. From this equation, L_X is calculated as 750 µH.

Step 3: Design of the output filter capacitor.

$$\text{Rated power, } P = \frac{\text{Maximum input voltage} * \text{Maximum input current}}{2}$$

$$= \frac{V_m * I_m}{2} \tag{7.22}$$

From the above equation, I_m is calculated as $(3,300 * 2) / \left(230 \sqrt{2} \right) = 20.2908$ A.

In this chapter, the subscript 'avg' denotes the average component, subscript '2' denotes the second harmonic component, and superscript '~' denotes the small signal perturbation component.

The output voltage, $V_0 = V_{0\_avg} + v_{0\_2} + \widetilde{v_0}$ and output current, $I_0 = I_{0\_avg} + i_{0\_2} + \widetilde{i_0}$. The maximum second harmonic voltage v_{0_2m} is given by $\left(V_m * I_m \right) / \left(4 \omega_l C_0 V_{0\_avg} \right)$. The capacitor C_0 is chosen to be 1,880 µF such that v_{0_2m} is a lower value of approximately 7 V.

7.5.3 Closed loop design

The control loop design is the same as that of a conventional boost PFC. The high-power continuous conduction mode boost PFC always uses the average current control method because of its accuracy. APFC includes the outer voltage loop and the inner current loop.

7.5.3.1 Outer voltage loop

The voltage control loop and its small signal model are shown in Figure 7.21. It comprises voltage controller $\left(G_{vc}(s) \right)$, an inner closed current loop, and a

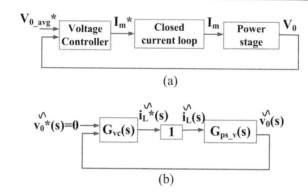

Figure 7.21 (a) Voltage control loop. (b) Small signal representation of voltage loop.

power stage ($G_{\text{ps}\_v}(s)$). The difference between the voltage reference and the sensed output voltage is given to the voltage controller, which provides the reference for the input current. The voltage loop bandwidth is chosen much lower than a current loop. Thus, the current loop gain is considered as one. The steps for designing are as follows:

Step 1: Find the transfer function of power stage, $G_{\text{ps}\_v}(s) = \tilde{v}_0(s) / \tilde{i}(s)$.

By equating input power $\left(P_{\text{in}} = \left| V_{\text{ac}} * i_L(t) \right| \right)$ to output power (P_{out}), one can get

$$V_m \left| \sin \omega_l t \right| * I_m \left| \sin \omega_l t \right| = \left(V_{0_{\text{avg}}} + v_{0_2} + \tilde{v}_0 \right) * \left(I_{0_{\text{avg}}} + i_{0_2} + \tilde{i}_0 \right) \tag{7.23}$$

The current I_m^* under dynamic conditions is equal to $I_m + i_{L2} + \tilde{i}_L = I_m - I_{m2} \cos 2\omega_l t + \tilde{i}_L$

By neglecting small signal perturbation product terms in equation (7.23), one can get

$$\frac{1}{2} V_m \tilde{i}_L = \left(\tilde{i}_0 + \frac{\tilde{v}_0}{R_0} \right) * V_{0_{\text{avg}}} \tag{7.24}$$

From boost converter small signal model [2],

$$\frac{\tilde{i}_0}{\tilde{v}_0} = \frac{1 + sR_0C_0}{R_0} \tag{7.25}$$

By equating these two equations one can get

$$G_{\text{ps}\_v}(s) = \frac{\tilde{v}_0}{\tilde{i}_L} = \left(\frac{R_0}{2 + sR_0C_0} \right) * \frac{V_m}{2V_{0_{\text{avg}}}} = \frac{19.711}{2 + s0.091} \tag{7.26}$$

Phase of $G_{\text{ps}\_v}(s)$ @ 10Hz$=-70.8°$. This frequency is considered as the bandwidth.

Step 2: Choose a voltage controller $G_{vc}(s)$ with a gain of K_v, a pole at origin, a zero at angular frequency ω_{zv} and a pole at angular frequency ω_{pv}.

$$G_{vc}(s) = \frac{K_v}{s}\left[\frac{1+\dfrac{s}{\omega_{zv}}}{1+\dfrac{s}{\omega_{pv}}}\right] \tag{7.27}$$

For a closed loop system to be stable, the phase margin needed is 60°. Phase margin is the additional lag to be added to make the total angle as –180°.

$$\left|\angle G_{vc}(s) + \angle G_{ps\_v}(s) - 60°\right|_{s=j2\pi f_{gv}} = -180° \tag{7.28}$$

$$-49.2° + 90° = \left|\tan^{-1}\left(\frac{\omega}{\omega_{zv}}\right) - \tan^{-1}\left(\frac{\omega}{\omega_{pv}}\right)\right|_{s=j2\pi 10} \tag{7.29}$$

The gain crossover frequency $f_{gv} = 10$ Hz is at the geometric mean of f_{zv} and f_{pv}. By solving the above equation, zero frequency is at 4.55 Hz and the pole frequency is at 21.97 Hz.

Step 3: By equating the compensated loop gain to one at f_{gv}, voltage gain factor K_v is calculated as 8.691.

$$\left|\frac{K_v}{s}\left[\frac{1+\dfrac{s}{\omega_{zv}}}{1+\dfrac{s}{\omega_{pv}}}\right]*1*\frac{19.711}{2+s0.091}\right|_{s=j2\pi 10} = 1 \tag{7.30}$$

7.5.3.2 Inner current loop

The current loop consists of a current controller, a pulse width modulator (PWM), and a power stage as shown in Figure 7.22. The difference between the current reference and the measured inductor current is given to the current controller, which produces a control signal $v_c(t)$. The PWM generates the pulses with duty ratio $d(t)$. The bandwidth of the current loop is very high so that the reference current is tracked with less THD as possible. The steps for designing inner current loop are as follows:

Step 1: Find the transfer function of power stage, $G_{ps\_i}(s) = \tilde{i}_L(s)/\tilde{d}(s)$ from the boost converter small signal model [2].

$$G_{ps\_i}(s) = \frac{V_{0\_avg}}{sL_x} = \frac{400}{s*750*10^{-6}} \tag{7.31}$$

$\angle G_{ps\_i}(s)$ at 10 kHz is –90°.

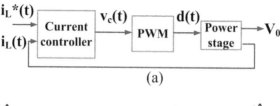

(a)

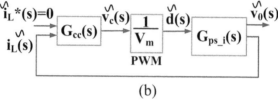

(b)

Figure 7.22 (a) Current control loop. (b) Small signal representation of current loop.

Step 2: Choose a current controller $G_{cc}(s)$ with a gain of K_c, a pole at origin, a zero at angular frequency ω_{zc} and a pole at angular frequency ω_{pc}.

$$G_{cc}(s) = \frac{K_c}{s} \left[\frac{1 + \dfrac{s}{\omega_{zc}}}{1 + \dfrac{s}{\omega_{pc}}} \right] \qquad (7.32)$$

For a closed loop system to be stable, the phase margin needed is 60°. Phase margin is the additional lag to be added to make the total angle as −180°.

$$\left| \angle G_{cc}(s) + \angle G_{ps\_i}(s) - 60° \right|_{s=j2\pi f_{gc}} = -180° \qquad (7.33)$$

$$-30° + 90° = \left| \tan^{-1}\left(\frac{\omega}{\omega_{zc}} \right) - \tan^{-1}\left(\frac{\omega}{\omega_{pc}} \right) \right|_{s=j2\pi 10000} \qquad (7.34)$$

The gain crossover frequency $f_{gcc} = 10$ kHz is at the geometric mean of f_{zc} and f_{pc}. By solving the above equation, zero frequency is at 2682.24 Hz and the pole frequency is at 37,282.27 Hz.

Step 3: By equating the compensated loop gain to one at f_{gc}, voltage gain factor K_c is calculated as 1,953.08.

$$\left| \frac{K_c}{s} \left[\frac{1 + \dfrac{s}{\omega_{zc}}}{1 + \dfrac{s}{\omega_{pc}}} \right] * \frac{1}{1} * \frac{400}{s * 750 * 10^{-6}} \right|_{s=j2\pi 10000} = 1 \qquad (7.35)$$

The bode plots of the power stage $(G_{ps\_i}(s), G_{ps\_v}(s))$, controller $(G_{cc}(s), G_{vc}(s))$, and compensated voltage and current control loops are shown in Figures 7.23 and 7.24. The open and closed loop simulation results are given in Figure 7.25. The supply current I_{ac} for open loop simulation is peaky in nature, and the output DC link voltage V_0 varies widely. For closed loop, I_{ac} is sinusoidal and is in phase with V_{ac}. The power factor is 0.998 and V_0 is regulated at 400 V with slight variation.

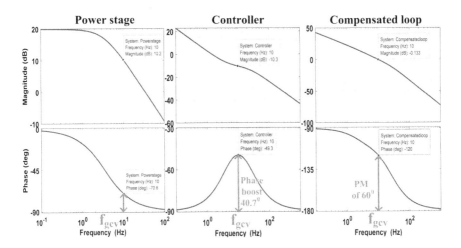

Figure 7.23 Voltage control loop bode plots.

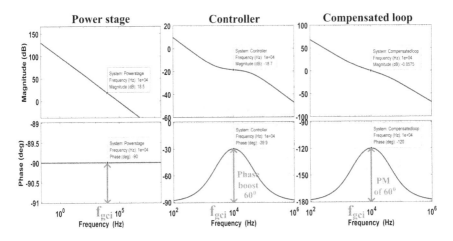

Figure 7.24 Current control loop bode plots.

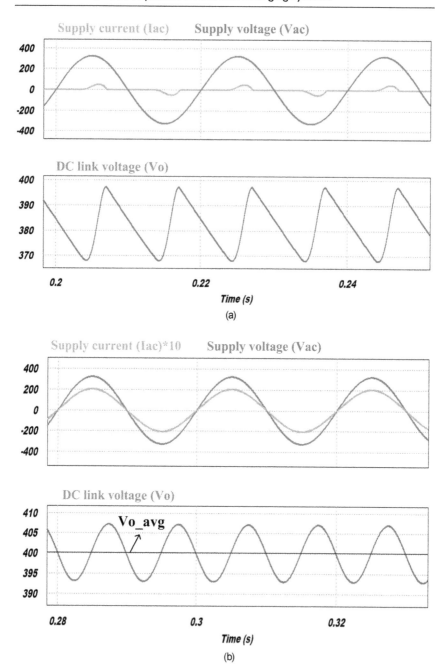

Figure 7.25 Simulation results. (a) Open loop. (b) Closed loop.

7.6 CONCLUSION

This chapter detailed the design and modeling of power electronic converters in electric vehicle two-stage battery charging systems. Various resonant DC-DC converters that require controller implementation for CC/CV charging in the second stage, namely series, parallel, LLC, and MSP-RC, were analyzed. The type of soft switching, short circuit protection performance, and frequency range of operation were discussed with graphical representation and compared. Further, the design and analysis of secondary modified resonant immittance converters with inherent CC/CV charging capability were presented. Finally, the simplified controller design procedure for PFC and DC link voltage regulation of totem-pole front-end converter is explained in detail.

REFERENCES

1. D. S. Gautam, F. Musavi, M. Edington, W. Eberle, and W. G. Dunford, "An automotive onboard 3.3-kw battery charger for PHEV application," *IEEE Transactions on Vehicular Technology*, vol. 61, no. 8, pp. 3466–3474, 2012, doi:10.1109/TVT.2012.2210259.
2. Mohan, N. Chapter 6: Power-factor-correction (PFC) Circuits and Designing the Feedback Controller. In Mohan, N. (Ed.) *First Course on Power Electronics and Drives*, 1st edition (pp. 6-1–6-11). Hoboken, NJ: John Wiley & Sons, Inc, 2012.
3. Datasheet of Li-ion Battery (Battery Model: LIR18650 2600 mAh), manufacturer EEMB Co., Ltd. https://www.ineltro.ch/media/downloads/SAAItem/45/45958/36e3e7f3-2049-4adb-a2a7-79c654d92915.pdf.
4. R. W. Erickson and D. Maksimovic, *Fundamentals of Power Electronics*, 2nd edition, ser. 10, vol. 4. USA: Kluwer Academic Publishers, Dordrecht, 2001.
5. R. L. Steigerwald, "A comparison of half-bridge resonant converter topologies," *IEEE Transactions on Power Electronics*, vol. 3, no. 2, pp. 174–182, 1988, doi: 10.1109/63.4347.
6. L. Zhao, Y. Pei, L. Wang, L. Pei, W. Cao, and Y. Gan, "Analysis and design of LCCL resonant converter based on time-domain model for bidirectional onboard charger applications," *IEEE Transactions on Power Electronics*, vol. 38, no. 8, pp. 9852–9871, 2023, doi: 10.1109/TPEL.2023.3271302.
7. J. Wu, S. Li, S. -C. Tan, and S. Y. R. Hui, "Frequency folding for LLC resonant converters in EV charging applications," *IEEE Transactions on Power Electronics*, vol. 38, no. 4, pp. 5041–5054, 2023, doi: 10.1109/TPEL.2023.3235114.
8. H. Suryawanshi and S. Tarnekar, "Improvement of power factor using modified series-parallel resonant converter," In *Power Quality '98*, doi: 10.1109/PQ.1998.710362, pp. 103–109, 1998.

9. N. J. M. Mary, S. Sathyan, and H. M. Suryawanshi, "A three-level resonant DAB converter featuring minimized circulating losses for EV battery charging," *IEEE Transactions on Industrial Electronics*, vol. 70, no. 8, pp. 7879–7890, 2023, doi: 10.1109/TIE.2023.3234135.

10. M. Borage, S. Tiwari, and S. Kotaiah, "LCL-T resonant converter with clamp diodes: A novel constant-current power supply with inherent constant-voltage limit," *IEEE Transactions on Industrial Electronics*, vol. 54, no. 2, pp. 741–746, 2007.

11. X. Li, H. Ma, S. Ren, J. Yi, S. Lu, and Q. Feng, "A novel LCL resonant converter with inherent CC-CV output for on-board chargers of plug-in electric vehicles," *IEEE Transactions on Power Electronics*, doi: 10.1109/TPEL.2022.3229025.

12. N. J. Merlin Mary and S. Sathyan, "A novel bidirectional CLC-T resonant immittance converter for CC / CV battery charging," *2023 IEEE International Conference on Electrical Systems for Aircraft, Railway, Ship Propulsion and Road Vehicles & International Transportation Electrification Conference (ESARS-ITEC)*, Venice, Italy, 2023, pp. 1–6, doi: 10.1109/ESARS-ITEC57127.2023.10114862.

13. N. J. Merlin Mary and S. Sathyan, "Design and controller implementation of 3.3 kW bridgeless boost-fed three-level resonant converter for EV battery charging. *Electrical Engineering*, 2021, doi: 10.1007/s00202-021-01416-0.

14. A. Emadi, *Advanced Electric Drive Vehicles*, 1st edition. Boca Raton, FL: Taylor & Francis Group, 2014. doi: 10.1201/9781315215570.

15. F. Musavi, W. Eberle, and W. G. Dunford, "A high-performance single-phase bridgeless interleaved PFC converter for plug-in hybrid electric vehicle battery chargers," *IEEE Transactions on Industry Applications*, vol. 47, no. 4, pp. 1833–1843, 2011, doi: 10.1109/TIA.2011.2156753.

16. Y. Jang and M.M. Jovanovic, Interleaved boost converter with intrinsic voltage-doubler characteristic for universal-line PFC front end," *IEEE Transactions on Power Electronics*, vol. 22, pp. 1394–1401, 2007.

17. J. W. M. Soares and A. A. Badin, "High-efficiency interleaved totem-pole PFC converter with voltage follower characteristics," *IEEE Journal of Emerging and Selected Topics in Power Electronics*, vol. 11, no. 2, pp. 1879–1887, 2023, doi: 10.1109/JESTPE.2022.3231131.

Chapter 8

Duty cycle charts and its application to multiport DC-DC converters in vehicular applications

S. Hajari and O. Ray

8.1 INTRODUCTION

The widespread adoption of electrification within automobiles has resulted in power distribution system connected to multiple sources and loads. Most common architectures for power distribution utilize multiple DC distribution buses with different voltage levels (e.g., 14 V dc, 42 V dc, and 380 V dc) to cater to the source (and load) requirements [1]. In addition to battery energy storage systems, hybrid power architectures have also been explored in electric vehicles through the use of auxillary power sources such as supercapacitors, fuel cells, solar panels, etc. [2–7]. In addition to power train components, the demand for more user convenience has resulted in increase in entertainment and communication loads within the electric vehicles.

Figure 8.1 shows a representative schematic of a system in which the loads connected to the DC bus are powered by two different sources: battery and solar panel. Figure 8.1a shows the power conditioning unit with dedicated converters used to interface each of the different sources [8], whereas Figure 8.1b shows the use of multiport DC-DC converter for the same purpose. In this illustration, the integrated dual-output converter [9] is considered as the power converter interface between the sources and load. The integrated multiport converter exhibits advantages such as lower number of power conversion stages, centralized controller, and fewer passive elements, which gives better dynamic performance [10]. Therefore, these converters can integrate various power sources such as batteries, solar panels, and fuel cells, aiming to extend the driving range of electric vehicles and enhance fuel efficiency in hybrid models. In addition, the vehicles may have components that operate at different voltage levels. In these cases, multiport converters can step up or step down voltage levels as needed, allowing for compatibility between various components with different voltage requirements.

The use of multiport converters to provide functionality similar to that of dedicated DC-DC converter stages results in the issue of controllability.

DOI: 10.1201/9781003481065-8

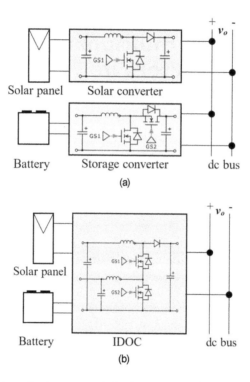

Figure 8.1 Integration of solar-storage hybrid system into DC bus. Using (a) separate converters and (b) multiport converter (integrated dual output converter).

Owing to the presence of a centralized control system, it is essential to demarcate and map each one of the control objectives to its associated control parameter. In the case of multiport converter control, multiple control objectives may exist, and the mapping of these objectives to switching intervals becomes crucial. The idea of duty cycles and duty cycle charts become quite important in this situation. Duty cycle/ratio, within a power electronics converter, is defined as the ratio of the 'ON' time of a switch to the total time of one switching cycle. It determines the behavior of the converter by influencing the power flow between source and load.

In many applications, when the same switch is being reused for multiple objectives, the duty ratio of each one of the switches is not directly associated with the control variable. For example, in [11–13], the control scheme of a three-port non-isolated converter with four control objectives has been implemented where the relation of the actual duty cycles and control objectives are dependent on the mode of operation of the converter. Similar control schemes have been observed in [14–16] with time-sharing PWM scheme as the solution to the interdependency of the duty cycles. Therefore, multiple control objectives may exist in multiport converter structures. Depending on the number of switches in a particular converter, the mapping of control objectives to switching intervals needs to be developed. In [17], a converter chart concept is introduced for high-voltage DC transmission system, providing graphical insights into various converter parameters. Furthermore, [18] proposes duty cycle charts within a phase-shifted PWM control scheme for a multiport topology, although the focus of this chapter is on introducing the charts rather than exploring their comprehensive application or addressing all possible conditions.

This chapter introduces the concept of duty cycle charts which can be used for analysis and system design for multiport DC-DC converter topologies for vehicular application. Duty cycle charts are graphical representations depicting the variation of duty cycles over specific operating conditions or control parameters. These charts provide an understanding of the relationship between different control parameters and serve as important tools for the analysis and design of multiport converters. These charts can efficiently guide the management of power flow between different ports of the converter by representing dynamic variations in duty cycles, optimizing energy distribution. The IDOC topology has been considered for illustration of the proposed concepts described in this chapter. The organization of this chapter is as follows: Section 8.2 gives an overview of the power electronic converter topology. A phase-shifted pulse width modulation scheme has been proposed for IDOC, and this has been related to the actual control duty ratios of the switching elements in the topology. Section 8.3 discusses the duty cycle charts and extends the theory of its application to the IDOC topology.

8.2 OVERVIEW OF INTEGRATED DUAL OUTPUT CONVERTER TOPOLOGY

The schematic of integrated dual output converter topology is presented in Figure 8.2. The architecture consists of three terminals where a single DC input (marked as port 1) can provide two DC outputs: one of step-up (in port 3) and one step-down type (in port 2). The converter consists of two controllable switches Q_1 and Q_2 and diode D. The converter utilizes the switch node (v_{sn}) of a conventional boost converter stage as the input for the step-down (buck) switching network. The passive elements used in the topology are inductors L_1 and L_2.

Owing to the presence of two output terminals within IDOC topology, there are two different control objectives associated with each of the terminals. These two objectives need to be realized using pulse width modulation

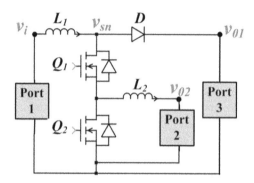

Figure 8.2 Schematic diagram of IDOC.

control of the two controllable switches Q_1 and Q_2. In addition, depending on system conditions, the power flow direction within the ports may vary. For example, port 2 is capable of bidirectional power transfer. In an electric vehicle, the converter topology can be used to interconnect two different buses at different voltage levels and integrate the bidirectional port to battery energy storage system. Hence, the converter can operate in the following modes:

- Single input dual output (SIDO), where port 1 is the input and ports 2 and 3 act as two output ports.
- Dual input single output mode (DISO), when both ports 1 and 2 act as inputs, whereas port 3 is considered as an output port.
- Single-input-single-output mode (SISO), where battery port (port 2) is idle.

The operating intervals of the converter topology are discussed in the next subsection.

8.2.1 Operating intervals of Integrated Dual Output Converter

Depending on the operation of switches, IDOC operates through three distinct switching intervals (Figure 8.3).

8.2.1.1 Interval I (duty ratio d_{ST})

The relationship between input voltage v_{in} and output v_{o1} is the same as a boost converter. Interval I (also regarded as shoot-through interval) is implemented by turning both switches (Q_1 and Q_2) 'ON' simultaneously, as shown in Figure 8.3a. The polarity of the current in inductor L_2, however, depends

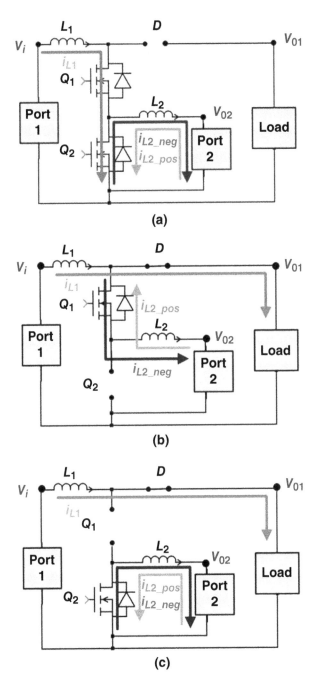

Figure 8.3 Switching intervals of IDOC: (a) Interval I (Shoot-through interval), (b) Interval II (Power interval), and (c) Interval III (Freewheeling interval).

on in which mode the converter is working. For DISO mode, the current in the inductor is freewheeling through switch Q_2, whereas for SIDO mode, the energy is getting stored in inductor L_2 from the input source at v_{o2}.

8.2.1.2 Interval II [duty ratio: d_{PW}]

In Interval II (Figure 8.3b), switch Q_1 is 'ON'. During SIDO mode, energy is transferred from source v_{in} into port v_{o2}. Since diode D is conducting during this interval, the switch node voltage is clamped to v_{o1}. In the DISO mode of operation, inductor current i_{L2} freewheels into the output v_{o1} from port 2. In the context of converter operation, the duration of this interval is equal to the freewheeling interval for storage (port 2) to DC bus power conversion (port 3).

8.2.1.3 Interval III [duty ratio: d_{FW}]

Interval III (Figure 8.3c) contributes to the boost duty ratio (in addition to Interval I) for step-up conversion between ports 2 and 3 for the DISO mode. During this interval, the current in inductor L_2 builds up while inductor current L_1 freewheels into diode D. For SIDO mode, the inductor current L_2 freewheels using switch Q_2.

8.2.1.4 Interval IV [duty ratio: $(1 - d_{ST} - d_{PW} - d_{FW})$]

Interval IV can occur when both switches are 'OFF'. However, since the switch node between switches Q_1 and Q_2 are connected to inductor L_2, for non-zero current, the circuit operates in either Interval II or III, except during zero inductor current condition.

8.2.2 Relationship between converter duty ratios

The output voltage of IDOC (v_{o1}) is higher than input v_i, whereas the magnitude of voltage v_{o2} is lower than v_i. The step-up power conversion into port 3 voltage (v_{o1}) is regulated by a shoot-through duty cycle (d_{ST}) The step-down voltage v_{o2} depends on the power interval, i.e., d_{PW}. The duty cycle d_{ST} regulates the output voltage v_{o1} by turning both switches ON simultaneously. During the SIDO mode, the control duty cycle for switch Q_1 is d_{PW} and during power reversal in DISO mode, switch Q_2 is responsible for power flow control through duty ratio d_{FW} which is the freewheeling interval. Different voltage relationships with the duty cycles have been discussed in this section for both the SIDO and DISO modes of the converter.

8.2.3 DISO mode operation of IDOC

When two sources are connected in ports 1 and 2, the expression of output voltage v_{o1} is given below with respect to duty cycle d_{ST} and d_{PW}.

$$v_{o1} = v_i / (1 - d_{ST})$$
(8.1)

$$v_{o1} = v_{o2} / d_{PW}$$
(8.2)

Therefore, from equations (8.1) and (8.2), the relationship between d_{ST} and d_{PW} is given in equation (8.3):

$$d_{PW} = (v_{o2} / v_i)(1 - d_{ST})$$
(8.3)

Equation (8.3) is a straight-line equation of d_{PW} with respect to d_{ST}, when the two source voltages are independent (for DISO mode), as shown in Figure 8.4. Since any point on that straight line can be an operating point of the converter in DISO mode, the converter can be operated with multiple combinations of operable duty ratios. In such a situation, additional operating conditions would enable the identification of operating point.

8.2.4 SIDO mode operation of IDOC

In the SIDO mode, the input voltage is v_i and two load voltages are v_{o1} and v_{o2}. So, equation (8.1) is rewritten as equation (8.4) and by replacing v_{o1} from equation (8.2), equation (8.5) has been formed.

$$v_{o1}(1 - d_{ST}) = v_i$$
(8.4)

$$v_{o2}(1 - d_{ST}) = d_{PW}v_i$$
(8.5)

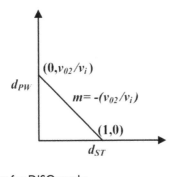

Figure 8.4 d_{PW} vs d_{ST} curve for DISO mode.

Equation (8.4) depicts the relationship between output voltage v_{o1} and duty cycle d_{ST}. Moreover, equation (8.5) shows the linear relationship between voltage v_{o2} and duty cycle d_{PW}.

8.3 PULSE WIDTH MODULATION CONTROL OF INTEGRATED DUAL OUTPUT CONVERTERS

An analysis of IDOC topology shows that output voltage v_{o1} (port 3) is higher than input v_{in} (port 1), whereas the magnitude of voltage v_{o2} (port 2) is lower than v_{in}. The step-up power conversion into port v_{o1} is regulated by shoot-through duty cycle d_{ST}. Power flow from port 2 is bidirectional in nature, where power flow into and from the port 2 is equivalent to charging and discharging operation respectively. The control of this interval is through either one of the duty ratio parameters: d_{PW} (for Interval II) or d_{FW} (for Interval III). Hence, each of the control objectives must be mapped into the duty ratio of the physical switches. The control objectives in the context of IDOC are the regulation of DC link voltage v_{o1} as well as the power balance in different ports. Figure 8.5 shows the phase-shifted pulse width modulation scheme applied for the regulation of IDOC. It can be observed that the ON time of switch Q_1 includes control duty ratios d_{PW} and d_{ST}. The width of the ON state is denoted by width W_1. Similarly, in the case of switch Q_2, the width of the pulse W_2 includes the durations d_{ST} and d_{FW}. This PWM control scheme can hence be represented as a phase-shifted pulse width modulation control with three parameters: W_1, W_2, and θ. This work explores the mapping between the control variable to the duty ratio based on the phase-shifted pulse width modulation (PS-PWM) scheme. The mapping approach is based on the pulse widths of the two switches and the corresponding phase shift angle.

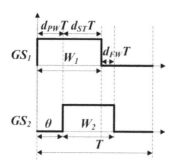

Figure 8.5 Illustration of proposed phase-shifted PWM strategy.

8.3.1 Phase shift-based PWM strategy for IDOC

The phase shift-based PWM control strategy for IDOC consists of the three parameters: W_1, W_2 and phase shift θ, as the three variables. These three parameters are the independent control variables that decide the switching instances of both the control switches Q_1 and Q_2. The control parameters of the control scheme are discussed in the subsequent part of the section.

8.3.1.1 Width of PWM signals (W_1 and W_2)

For any two-switch converter having switching pulses GS_1 and GS_2, the control signals, i.e., the duty cycles are the pulse widths (W_1 and W_2) of the respective switching pulses. The range of pulse widths varies between 0 and 1 and is defined as equation (8.6).

$$W_i = \left(\text{Time duration when the switch is gated}\right)/\left(\text{Switching Period}\right) \quad (8.6)$$

The proposed control scheme is different from the conventional phase shift PWM schemes since the value of W_i has no fixed value and may vary (theoretically) between 0 and 1.

8.3.1.2 Phase shift of PWM signals (θ)

The phase shift parameter defines the phase displacement between the pulse widths (W_1 and W_2) of the two gate signals. By design, the values of the phase shift parameters have been defined to lie within the range of 0–1.

8.4 DUTY CYCLE MAPPING IN MULTIPORT CONVERTERS

Figure 8.6a shows an illustration of direct mapping for a single control objective and a single switch system. For a SISO DC-DC converter, there is a single control objective, and the relationship is one-to-one. However, in multi-switch and multi-control objective cases also, different combinations of mapping between control objectives and control duty ratio are possible. Figure 8.6b shows the scenario when the mapping is interdependent, whereas Figure 8.6c shows the scenario for independent mapping.

For the converter under consideration, the control objectives are interdependent upon both switch-duty ratios. Table 8.1 provides expressions for the duty cycles d_{ST} and d_{PW} with variations of W_1, W_2, and θ. The expressions for the duty cycles depend upon whether ($W_1 + W_2$) is greater or less than 1. Also, it depends on the relative magnitudes of W_1 and W_2. Primarily, for different pulse width combinations, four different cases are shown in Table 8.1. Each case is divided into four zones which results in a total of 16 zones for

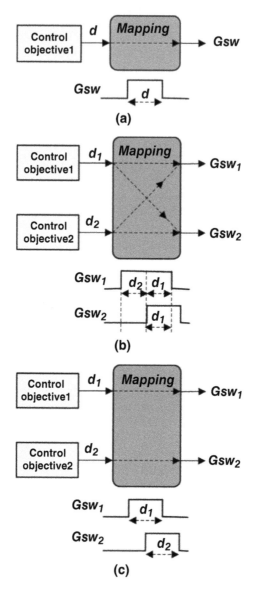

Figure 8.6 Schematic of system with (a) single control objective, (b) interdependent multiple control objective, and (c) independent multiple control objective.

4 cases. For any particular scenario if the voltage ranges are known then from that the duty cycles can be known which eventually helps to find out the feasible cases among the four cases of Table 8.1. A flowchart is shown in Figure 8.7 for the same to give an overview of finding the feasible case/cases.

Table 8.1 Duty cycle expressions considering the control parameters W_1, W_2, and θ

$$(W_1 + W_2) \leq 1$$

Case 1: $W_1 \geq W_2$

Zone	d_{ST}	d_{PW}
C1Z1: $0 \leq \theta < (W_1 - W_2)$	W_2	$W_1 - W_2$
C1Z2: $(W_1 - W_2) \leq \theta < W_1$	$W_1 - \theta$	θ
C1Z3: $W_1 \leq \theta < (1 - W_2)$	0	W_1
C1Z4: $(1 - W_2) \leq \theta < 1$	$\theta + W_2 - 1$	$1 + W_1 - W_2 - \theta$

Case 2: $W_1 < W_2$

Zone	d_{ST}	d_{PW}
C2Z1: $0 \leq \theta < W_1$	$W_1 - \theta$	θ
C2Z2: $W_1 \leq \theta < (1 - W_2)$	0	W_1
C2Z3: $(1 - W_2) \leq \theta < (1 + W_1 - W_2)$	$\theta + W_2 - 1$	$1 + W_1 - W_2 - \theta$
C2Z4: $(1 + W_1 - W_2) \leq \theta < 1$	W_1	0

$$(W_1 + W_2) > 1$$

Case 3: $W_1 \geq W_2$

Zone	d_{ST}	d_{PW}
C3Z1: $0 \leq \theta < (W_1 - W_2)$	W_2	$W_1 - W_2$
C3Z2: $(W_1 - W_2) \leq \theta < (1 - W_2)$	$W_1 - \theta$	θ
C3Z3: $(1 - W_2) \leq \theta < W_1$	$W_1 + W_2 - 1$	$1 - W_2$
C3Z4: $W_1 \leq \theta < 1$	$\theta + W_2 - 1$	$1 + W_1 - W_2 - \theta$

Case 4: $W_1 < W_2$

Zone	d_{ST}	d_{PW}
C4Z1: $0 \leq \theta < (1 - W_2)$	$W_1 - \theta$	θ
C4Z2: $(1 - W_2) \leq \theta < W_1$	$W_1 + W_2 - 1$	$1 - W_2$
C4Z3: $W_1 \leq \theta < (1 + W_1 - W_2)$	$\theta + W_2 - 1$	$1 + W_1 - W_2 - \theta$
C4Z4: $(1 + W_1 - W_2) \leq \theta < 1$	W_1	0

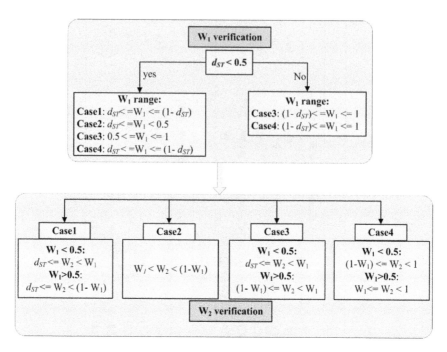

Figure 8.7 Flowchart for determining the feasible case.

8.4.1 Duty cycle vs phase shift curve: linear representation

Figures 8.8 and 8.9 are the linear representations of the variation of duty cycles d_{ST} and d_{PW}, respectively, for different combinations of W_1 and W_2. The variation has been shown for all the conditions shown in Table 8.1 with respect to the change in phase shift angle (θ).

8.4.2 Duty cycle vs phase shift curve: polar representation using Duty cycle charts

The relationship between duty cycle and phase shift of the control switch instances can be represented as polar plots, in which, the radius of the plots, varying between 0 and 1, represents the pulse width (W_1 and W_2). The phase shift (θ) is represented by angular position (per unitized), which ranges between 0 and 1. Per-unit value of phase shift represents 2°, and with respect to the time period, this is equal to the time period. In the plots, contours for values: 0.0, 0.2, 0.4, 0.5, 0.6, 0.8, and 1.0 are shown. Duty cycle charts can be developed to represent the duty cycle variation with a phase shift. In this work, these polar charts denoted as duty cycle charts form an easy mechanism to identify the operating duty cycles for a three-port converter i.e., integrated dual output converter.

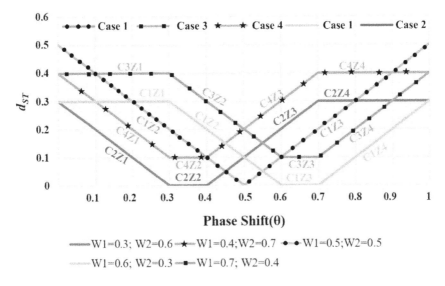

Figure 8.8 Linear representation of d_{ST} with respect to phase shift θ.

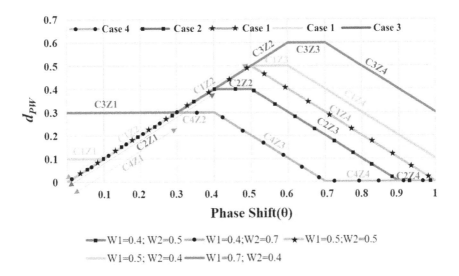

Figure 8.9 Linear representation of d_{PW} with respect to phase shift θ.

8.5 PRACTICAL EXAMPLE

This section examines an actual instance of IDOC usage in an electric vehicle. The functional diagram for the same is shown in Figure 8.10 where ports 1 and 2 are linked to the battery and solar panels, respectively, while

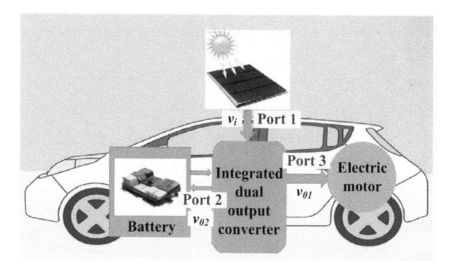

Figure 8.10 IDOC used in electric vehicle.

port 3 acts as the output port and is connected to the motor driver. In this scenario, the output voltage (v_{o1}) of the converter is standardized at 48 V. As shown in Table 8.2 with the relevant duty ratios, various input voltage (ports 1 and 2) levels have been taken into consideration.

As port 1 is the primary source, the rating of the battery has been decided considering the voltage limit of the converter $(v_{o2} <= v_i)$. Depending on the known parameters (W_1 and d_{ST}), the possible cases have also been mentioned.

However, in practice, due to the presence of non-idealities of the converter circuit, the duty cycles may vary from that of ideal cases. A schematic diagram of the non-deal converter has been redrawn in Figure 8.11, and Table 8.3 provides the values of the non-idealities of the converter.

The shoot-through and power interval duty cycles for non-ideal conditions have been considered as D'_{ST} and D'_{PW}. Using the volt-second balance equations of the converter, the relation between the duty cycles is given in equations (8.7) and (8.8).

$$D'_{PW} = \left(d_{ST} + d_{FW} \right) \left(1 - \frac{v_{ron1} + v_D}{v_{o1}} + \frac{v_{ron2}}{v_{o1}} \right) - \frac{v_{ron1} + v_D}{v_{o1}} \tag{8.7}$$

$$D'_{ST} = \frac{d_{ST}(1 + K_1) - K_2}{d_{ST}K_1 + 1 - K_2} \tag{8.8}$$

where

$$K_1 = \frac{v_d - v_{ron1} - v_{ron2}}{v_i} \text{ and } K_2 = \frac{v_d + v_{rL1}}{v_i}$$

Table 8.2 Duty cycle limits for some practical input voltage ratings of IDOC and corresponding feasible cases

Port 1 /solar PV voltage levels (v_i)	Port 2/battery voltage levels (v_{o2})	Theoretical d_{ST}	Theoretical d_{PW}	$W_1 = (d_{ST} + d_{PW})$	Possible cases
$18V < v_i < 20V$	9 V	$0.583 < d_{ST} < 0.625$	0.2	$0.783 < W_1 < 0.825$	Case 3, Case 4
	12 V		0.25	$0.833 < W_1 < 0.875$	
$30V < v_i < 36V$	9 V	$0.25 < d_{ST} < 0.375$	0.2	$0.45 < W_1 < 0.575$	Case 1, Case 2, Case 4
	12 V		0.25	$0.5 < W_1 < 0.625$	Case 1, Case 3, Case 4
	18 V		0.375	$0.625 < W_1 < 0.75$	
	24 V		0.5	$0.75 < W_1 < 0.875$	
	27 V		0.56	$0.81 < W_1 < 0.935$	Case 3
40V	9 V	0.167	0.2	0.367	Case 1, Case 2, Case 4
	12 V		0.25	0.417	Case 1, Case2, Case 4
	18 V		0.375	0.542	Case 1, Case 3, Case 4
	24 V		0.5	0.667	Case 1, Case 3, Case 4
	27 V		0.56	0.727	Case 1, Case 3, Case 4
	36 V		0.75	0.917	Case 3

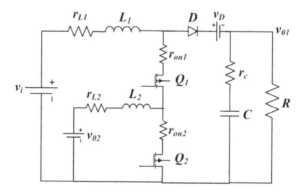

Figure 8.11 Schematic of IDOC considering non-idealities.

Table 8.3 Specifications of non-idealities of converter parameters

ESR of L_1	r_{L1}	0.13 Ω
ESR of L_2	r_{L2}	0.111 Ω
Diode voltage drop	v_D (V)	0.7 V
On state resistance of Q_1	r_{on1}	0.041 Ω
On state resistance of Q_2	r_{on2}	0.041 Ω

v_{ron1} = voltage across r_{on1} = $I_{s1}r_{on1}$ = $I_{L1}d_{ST}\,r_{on1}$
v_{ron2} = voltage across r_{on2} = $I_{s2}r_{on2}$ = $(I_{L1}d_{ST}+I_{L2}(1-d_{PW}))r_{on2}$
v_{rL1} = voltage across r_{L1} = $I_{L1}r_{L1}$
v_{rL2} = voltage across r_{L2} = $I_{L2}r_{L2}$

In equation (8.7), the modified duty cycle D'_{PW} depends on $(d_{ST}+d_{FW})$, i.e., the ON time of the switch Q_2 which is denoted as W_2. Therefore, it is evident that the duty cycle for v_{o1} to v_{o2} conversion in a non-ideal converter is dependent on W_2. Hence, the value of W_2 for which the ideal and non-ideal d_{PW} has the least error may be selected as the operating pulse width.

The representation of the duty cycle chart is shown considering v_i, v_{o1}, and v_{o2} as 30, 48, and 24 V respectively as shown in Table 8.4. From Table 8.4, it is evident that d_{ST} and d_{PW} are constant which is equivalent to W_1. So, in the following charts, W_1 is taken constant and is equal to $(d_{ST}+d_{PW})$ i.e. (0.375+0.5) (Table 8.4). The effect of non-idealities is also observed in Table 8.4.

Table 8.4 Duty cycle range considering non-idealities

Load power P_{ol} (W)	Dc link voltage v_{ol} (V)	Port 1 voltage v_i (V)	Port 2 voltage v_{o2} (V)	Current through L_1 I_{L1} (A)	Current through L_2 I_{L2} (A)	Duty cycle for ideal converter		W_2	Duty cycle for non-ideal converter		Error $(d_{PW} - D'_{PW})$
						d_{ST}	d_{PW}		D'_S	D'_{PW}	
300	48	30	24	6	5	0.375	0.5	0.375	0.346	0.35	0.15
								0.4	0.346	0.3785	0.1215
								0.45	0.346	0.428	0.072
								0.5	0.346	0.477	0.023

8.6 DUTY CYCLE CHART

The illustration of the duty cycles with respect to phase shift angle has been shown as polar plots (duty cycle charts) in this section. The polar representations are done considering W_2 (width of the switching pulse GS_1) as the radius and θ (Phase shift) as the angle. For each plot, the pulse width W_1 is considered constant. The charts are shown for the condition in Table 8.4. In the case of Table 8.4, the d_{ST} and d_{PW} are 0.375 and 0.5, respectively. Hence, $W_1 = (0.375 + 0.5) = 0.875$. To find out the feasible case/cases, Figure 8.7 is referred.

8.6.1 Determination of case

 i. $d_{ST} < 0.5$
 ii. Case 1: $d_{ST} \le W_1 \le (1 - d_{ST})$: **invalid** as $W_1 > (1 - d_{ST})$.
 iii. Case 2: $d_{ST} \le W_1 < 0.5$: **invalid** as $W_1 > 0.5$.
 iv. Case 3: $0.5 \le W_1 \le 1$: **valid**.
 v. Case 4: $d_{ST} \le W_1 \le (1 - d_{ST})$: **invalid** as $W_1 > (1 - d_{ST})$.

From the verification, it is clear that Case 3 is only the valid option so for this case the range of W_2 will be $(1 - W_1) \le W_2 < W_1$ i.e., $0.125 \le W_2 < 0.875$. So, the duty cycle charts or the polar plot of d_{ST} and d_{PW} are shown for Case 3.

8.6.2 Polar plots of d_{ST} and d_{PW} for Case 3 $((W_1 + W_2) \ge 1$ and $W_1 \ge W_2))$

Figure 8.12a and b shows the polar plots of d_{ST} and d_{PW} for Case 3. The corresponding gate pulse widths are $W_1 = 0.875$ and the W_2 as $0.125 < W_2 < 0.875$ (green-shaded area). In Figure 8.12a, the operating zone for $d_{ST} = 0.375$ is shown. Similarly, Figure 8.12b shows the d_{PW} plot. The dotted line of Figure 8.12a and b is the plot for D'_{ST} and D'_{PW}, respectively.

8.7 CONCLUSION

This work presents a comprehensive duty cycle chart for a three-port converter (IDOC), providing a detailed illustration of the operating zones of the converter in various practical applications. The duty cycle chart is specifically designed to accommodate scenarios where DC loads are connected, and both photovoltaic (PV) panels and batteries are used as energy sources. Moreover, the chart incorporates the consideration of non-idealities that may be present in the converter. By utilizing this duty cycle chart,

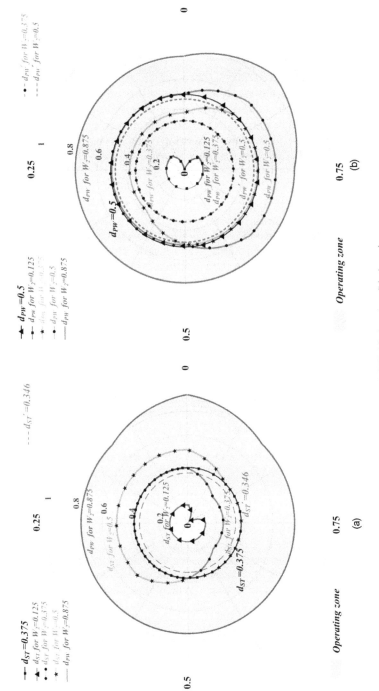

Figure 8.12 Duty cycle chart $((r, \theta) = (W_2, \theta))$ for Case 3 and $W_1 = 0.875$ (a) d_{ST} plot, (b) d_{PW} plot.

the converter's performance and behavior can be better understood and optimized under different load and energy source conditions. Analyzing duty cycle charts in vehicular applications can enable the development of control strategies in response to changing loads, and it can also help in vehicular system design by optimizing component selection, sizing, etc. Apart from vehicular technology, these charts can also have an application in renewable energy systems and industrial processes. The duty cycle study can be explored by adapting the concept for multiport converter with more number of switches and ports in non-isolated converters. Moreover, the theory can be extended by incorporating converter gain chart or power chart for enhanced insights of converter characteristics.

REFERENCES

1. A. Emadi, Y. J. Lee and K. Rajashekara, "Power Electronics and Motor Drives in Electric, Hybrid Electric, and Plug-In Hybrid Electric Vehicles," *IEEE Transactions on Industrial Electronics*, vol. 55, no. 6, pp. 2237–2245, 2008.

2. A. Emadi, K. Rajashekara, S. S. Williamson and S. M. Lukic, "Topological Overview of Hybrid Electric and Fuel Cell Vehicular Power System Architectures and Configurations," *IEEE Transactions on Vehicular Technology*, vol. 54, no. 3, pp. 763–770, 2005.

3. M. Ehsani, K. V. Singh, H. O. Bansal and R. T. Mehrjardi, "State of the Art and Trends in Electric and Hybrid Electric Vehicles," *Proceedings of the IEEE*, vol. 109, no. 6, pp. 967–984, 2021.

4. K. Gautam, M. Tariq, J. P. Pandey, K. S. Verma and S. Urooj, "Hybrid Sources Powered Electric Vehicle Configuration and Integrated Optimal Power Management Strategy," *IEEE Access*, vol. 10, pp. 121684–121711, 2022.

5. H. Yoo, S. -K. Sul, Y. Park and J. Jeong, "System Integration and Power-Flow Management for a Series Hybrid Electric Vehicle Using Supercapacitors and Batteries," *IEEE Transactions on Industry Applications*, vol. 44, no. 1, pp. 108–114, 2008.

6. A. Emadi, S. S. Williamson and A. Khaligh, "Power Electronics Intensive Solutions for Advanced Electric, Hybrid Electric, and Fuel Cell Vehicular Power Systems," *IEEE Transactions on Power Electronics*, vol. 21, no. 3, pp. 567–577, 2006.

7. K. Gautam, M. Tariq, J. P. Pandey, K. S. Verma and S. Urooj, "Hybrid Sources Powered Electric Vehicle Configuration and Integrated Optimal Power Management Strategy," *IEEE Access*, vol. 10, pp. 121684–121711, 2022.

8. Z. Yi, W. Dong and A. H. Etemadi, "A Unified Control and Power Management Scheme for PV-Battery-Based Hybrid Microgrids for Both Grid-Connected and Islanded Modes," *IEEE Transactions on Smart Grid*, vol. 9, no. 6, pp. 5975–5985, 2018.

9. O. Ray, A. P. Josyula, S. Mishra and A. Joshi, "Integrated Dual-Output Converter," *IEEE Transactions on Industrial Electronics*, vol. 62, no. 1, pp. 371–382, 2015.

10. K. Bhattacharjee, N. Kutkut and I. Batarseh, "Review of Multiport Converters for Solar and Energy Storage Integration," *IEEE Transactions on Power Electronics*, vol. 34, no. 2, pp. 1431–1445, 2019.

11. Z. Zhou, H. Wu, X. Ma and Y. Xing, "A Non-Isolated Three-Port Converter for Stand-Alone Renewable Power System," *IECON 2012-38th Annual Conference on IEEE Industrial Electronics Society*, Montreal, QC, Canada, 2012, pp. 3352–3357.

12. Y. Sato, M. Uno and H. Nagata, "Nonisolated Multiport Converters Based on Integration of PWM Converter and Phase-Shift-Switched Capacitor Converter," *IEEE Transactions on Power Electronics*, vol. 35, no. 1, pp. 455–470, 2020.

13. R. Faraji, L. Ding, M. Esteki, N. Mazloum and S. A. Khajehoddin, "Soft-Switched Single Inductor Single Stage Multiport Bidirectional Power Converter for Hybrid Energy Systems," *IEEE Transactions on Power Electronics*, vol. 36, no. 10, pp. 11298–11315, 2021.

14. D. K. Behera, I. Anand, B. Malakonda Reddy and S. Senthilkumar, "A Novel Control Scheme for a Standalone Solar PV System Employing a Multiport DC-DC Converter," *2018 9th International Conference on Computing, Communication and Networking Technologies (ICCCNT)*, Bengaluru, India, 2018, pp. 1–6.

15. V. Sheeja, R. Kalpana and B. Singh, "Time Sharing Control Based New Four Port Converter for Grid Integrated Solar PV Fed BTS Load," *2020 IEEE International Conference on Power Electronics, Drives and Energy Systems (PEDES)*, Jaipur, India, 2020, pp. 1–6.

16. S. Arun, I. A. TP, Z. V. Lakaparampil and D. Jose, "Non-Isolated Three Port Converter using Modified Time Sharing Control Scheme for PV Based LVDC Application," *2020 IEEE International Conference on Power Electronics, Drives and Energy Systems (PEDES)*, Jaipur, India, 2020, pp. 1–8.

17. E. W. Kimbark, *Direct Current Transmission*, Wiley-Blackwell, Hoboken, NJ, 1971.

18. O. Ray and S. Hajari, "Duty-Cycle Charts for Phase-Shift Controlled Impedance-Source DC-DC Converters," *2019 IEEE Industry Applications Society Annual Meeting, Baltimore*, MD, USA, 2019, pp. 1–6.

Chapter 9

Effect of misalignment issues for different coil structures in dynamic wireless charging system

Ngangoiba Maisnam, Vikram Kumar Saxena,
Kundan Kumar, and Surya Kant

9.1 INTRODUCTION

The requirement for an alternative solution has grown significantly as a result of the substantial growth in the demand for fossil fuels for road transportation and the amount of pollution emanating from conventional cars. Owing to its many benefits, the electric car offers a practical alternative to road mobility such as zero emissions of greenhouse gases, little noise pollution, less maintenance, and cheaper operating cost [1]. The major problem that electric cars have is the rechargeable battery capacities, which result in a low driving range due to their short lifespan and expensive cost. Presently, charging wires are used to carry out the battery charging procedure for an electric vehicle (EV), which increases the amount of time needed to fully charge the battery. The introduction of a dynamic wireless charging (DWC) system, which can recharge the battery while the car is still moving, is an alternate method of battery charging.

DWC systems use magnetic resonance coupling to wirelessly transfer power between a stationary charging infrastructure and a moving EV [2–6]. The efficiency of these systems is highly dependent on the alignment between the charging coil structure and the receiver coil in the vehicle [3,4]. Misalignment between these coils can result in reduced coupling efficiency, increased energy losses, and decreased overall performance of the system. The effect of misalignment issues for different coil structures in DWC systems has become a topic of great interest for researchers and industry experts [5].

Several coil structures for DWC systems have been proposed, including circular, rectangular, and hexagonal coils. Each of these structures has advantages and disadvantages regarding coupling efficiency, power transfer capability, and cost. However, regardless of the coil structure, misalignment can significantly reduce the efficiency of the system [7].

Research has shown that misalignment can be caused by various factors such as the movement of the vehicle, the distance between the charging infrastructure, and the orientation of the coils. Different strategies have

DOI: 10.1201/9781003481065-9

been proposed to mitigate these issues, including using multiple coils, integrating sensors to detect and adjust misalignment, and optimizing coil geometries to improve coupling efficiency [8–11].

Overall, the effect of misalignment issues for different coil structures in DWC systems is a crucial factor to consider for the development of efficient and reliable wireless charging infrastructure for electric vehicles [9]. Ongoing research in this area aims to address these issues and develop strategies to ensure the widespread adoption of DWC systems as a viable alternative to traditional plug-in charging.

9.2 BASIC EXPRESSION OF MISALIGNMENTS

Case 1. Lateral misalignment
The lateral misalignment of the circular spiral coil is shown in Figure 9.1. The inner coil's face is chosen for simplicity's purpose. The transmission coil (T_x) is represented by the colour blue, while the receiving coil (R_x) is

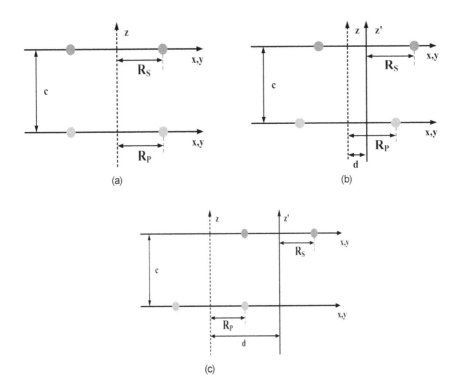

Figure 9.1 Lateral misalignment of the circular spiral coil (a) centred alignment, (b) lateral misalignment away from the centre, and (c) maximum lateral misalignment [5,6].

represented by the colour red. The mutual inductance between two circular spiral coils with lateral misalignment can be calculated as [9,10].

$$M = \frac{\mu_0}{\pi}\sqrt{R_P R_S}\int_0^{\pi}\frac{\left(1-\dfrac{d}{R_S}\cos\phi\right)\Phi(k)}{\sqrt{V^3}}\,d\phi$$

(9.1)

where

$$\alpha = \frac{R_S}{R_P},\ \beta = \frac{c}{R_P},\ k^2 = \frac{4\alpha V}{\left(1+\alpha V\right)^2+\beta^2},\ V = \sqrt{1+\frac{d^2}{R_S^2}-2\frac{d}{R_S}\cos\phi},$$

$$\Phi(k) = \left(\frac{2}{k}-k\right)K(k)-\frac{2}{k}E(k)$$

The variable c stand for the air-gap distances between the transmitter and receiver coils. R_P is the radius of the transmitting coil. The variable ϕ indicates the angle of integration at each point of the secondary coil with radius R_S, while θ signifies the angle between the coils' surfaces. $K(k)$ is used to denote the complete elliptic integral of the first kind while $E(k)$ stands in for the complete elliptic integral of the second kind [12,13]. The Legendre function of the second type and half-integral degree is $Q_{\frac{1}{2}}(x)$. The magnetic permeability of the vacuum, which is represented by the symbol μ_0, has a value of $4\pi \times 10^{-7}$ H/m.

Case 2. Angular misalignment
Figure 9.2 depicts the angular misalignment of the circular spiral coil.

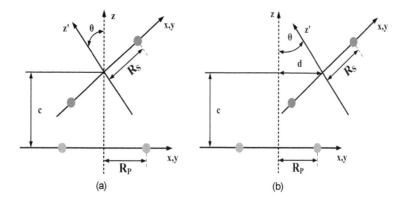

Figure 9.2 Angular misalignment of the circular spiral coil (a) axes intersect at the centre of T_x coil, and (b) axes intersect away from the centre of T_x coil [6].

The mutual inductance between two circular spiral coil with angular misalignment can be calculated as

$$M = \frac{\mu_0}{\pi} \sqrt{R_P R_S} \cos\theta \int_0^\pi \frac{\Phi(k)}{\sqrt{V^3}} d\phi \qquad (9.2)$$

where

$$V = \sqrt{1 - \cos^2\phi \sin^2\theta}, \; k^2 = \frac{4\alpha V}{1 + \alpha^2 + \beta^2 + 2\alpha\beta\cos\phi\sin\theta + 2\alpha V},$$

$$\alpha = \frac{R_S}{R_P}, \; \beta = \frac{c}{R_P}$$

$$\phi(k) = \left(\frac{2}{k} - k\right) K(k) - \frac{2}{k} E(k) = Q_{\frac{1}{2}}(x), \; x = \frac{2 - k^2}{k^2}$$

The angular misalignment of a circular spiral coil with lateral misalignment is shown in Figure 9.2b. In this case, the mutual inductance can be calculated as [6]

$$M = \frac{\mu_0}{\pi} \sqrt{R_P R_S} \int_0^\pi \frac{\left[\cos\theta - \dfrac{d}{R_S}\cos\phi\right]\phi(k)}{\sqrt{V^3}} d\phi \qquad (9.3)$$

where

$$V = \sqrt{1 - \cos^2\phi \sin^2\theta - 2\frac{d}{R_S}\cos\phi\cos\theta + \frac{d^2}{R_S^2}}, \; \alpha = \frac{R_S}{R_P}, \; \beta = \frac{c}{R_P},$$

$$k^2 = \frac{4\alpha V}{(1 + \alpha V)^2 + \xi^2}$$

$$\xi = \beta - \alpha\cos\phi\sin\theta, \; \phi(k) = \left(\frac{2}{k} - k\right) K(k) - \frac{2}{k} E(k) = Q_{\frac{1}{2}}(x), \; x = \frac{2 - k^2}{k^2}$$

The variables c and d stand for the air-gap and lateral misalignment distances, respectively, between the transmitter and receiver coils. R_P is the radius of the transmitting coil. The variable ϕ indicates the angle of integration at each point of the secondary coil with radius R_S, whereas θ signifies the angle between the coils' surfaces. $K(k)$ is used to denote the complete elliptic integral of the first kind while $E(k)$ stands in for the complete elliptic integral of the second kind. The Legendre function of the second type and half-integral degree is $Q_{\frac{1}{2}}(x)$ [12]. The magnetic permeability of the vacuum, which is represented by the symbol μ_0, has a value of $4\pi \times 10^{-7}$ H/m. These elements and concepts are crucial for the analysis and improvement of DWC systems. The radius of the transmitting coil R_P and the receiving coil R_S are kept constant throughout the computation in all expressions of the mutual inductance.

To address the misalignment challenges, a systematic approach was adopted, commencing with a meticulous design of the coil structure. The primary objective here was to minimize potential misalignment effects by optimizing the geometrical configuration of the coils. To ensure a fair and unbiased evaluation of the results, a consistent set of dimensions was maintained during the design process of both transmitting and receiving coils. By upholding uniformity in their construction, any observed differences in performance could be confidently attributed to the influence of misalignment rather than variations in coil geometry.

The final stage of the investigation involved subjecting the receiving coils to a diverse array of misalignment scenarios, encompassing different types of deviations that can manifest within the DWC system. Each identified misalignment type was methodically examined, and their respective impacts on the system's overall performance were meticulously assessed, shedding valuable light on the behaviour of the DWC system under realistic operational conditions.

9.3 MODELLING OF DIFFERENT COIL STRUCTURES

A DWC's coil structure design is one of its most important components. The coil structure plays a crucial role in influencing the system's efficiency, capacity for power transfer, and overall performance [14,15]. In DWC, a variety of coil topologies are employed, each with unique benefits and drawbacks. Different coil configurations, including circular, rectangular, and hexagonal spiral coils, have been employed for this study. Some parameters need to be determined in order to develop the coil. In Figure 9.3, these characteristics are indicated. In Figure 9.3, a cross-sectional illustration of a single circular coil with 10 conductors on each side from the centre of the coil can be observed.

To compute the dimension of the coil structure, such as inner radius, outer coil radius, and length between the centre of starting coil to the centre of the ending coil can be calculated by [16,17],

$$R = R_{in} + a = \frac{D_{in}}{2} + a \tag{9.4}$$

where D_{in} is the coil's inner diameter, R is the coil's radius, and R_{in} is its inner radius. D_{out} is the coil's outer diameter, w is the diameter of the wire,

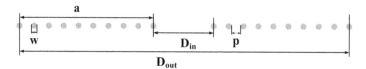

Figure 9.3 Cross-sectional diagram of a single circular coil with 10 turns.

p is the distance between consecutive wires, and a denotes the distance from the centre of the starting coil to the centre of the terminating coil.

9.3.1 Circular spiral coil

One of the most prevalent types of coils used in DWC systems are circular spiral coils. The spiral arrangement of the circular loops in these coils produces a magnetic field that can cause an electric current to flow through the receiving coil. Compared to other coil configurations, the circular spiral coil construction has a number of benefits. For instance, it is simple to construct and produces a magnetic field that is largely uniform, enabling effective power transmission. The circular form is also symmetric, which makes it less susceptible to the alignment of the receiving coil and charging pad [18–21]. The model of the circular spiral coil with a 100 mm air-gap between the transmitter and reception coils is shown in Figure 9.4. ANSYS MAXWELL 3D has been employed to develop the model.

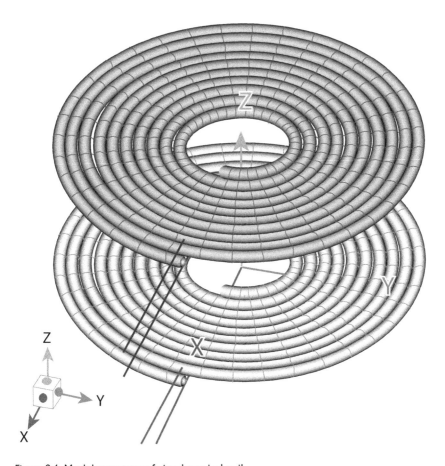

Figure 9.4 Model structure of circular spiral coil.

Both the receiver and the transmitter coils are represented by the colours red and blue, respectively. The following parameters from Table 9.1 have been utilized for the configuration of the circular spiral coil. For the purpose of this study, the transmitter and receiver coils were configured identically.

9.3.2 Rectangular spiral coil

Rectangular spiral coils are the favoured option for DWC systems because of their ability to generate a powerful and uniform magnetic field and their ease of manufacture. These spiral-shaped coils, which are made up of a number of rectangular loops, provide a higher surface area for power transfer than circular spiral coils [19]. The rectangular spiral coil type shown in Figure 9.5

Table 9.1 Dimension of the circular spiral coil

Sl. No	Parameters	Values	Unit
1.	Wire radius	2.5	mm
2.	Coil inner diameter	80	mm
3.	Coil outer diameter	278.14	mm
4.	No. of turns	10	
5.	Space between adjacent wire	1.0025	mm

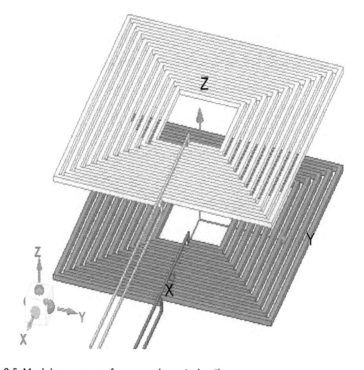

Figure 9.5 Model structure of rectangular spiral coil.

Table 9.2 Dimension of the rectangular spiral coil

Sl. No	Parameters	Values	Unit
1.	Wire radius	2.5	mm
2.	Coil inner diameter	80	mm
3.	Coil outer diameter	260	mm
4.	No. of turns	10	
5.	Space between adjacent wire	5	mm

has an air gap of 100 mm between the transmitter and reception coils. ANSYS MAXWELL 3D has been employed to develop the coil's design.

The transmitter and receiver coil have been designed identically and distinguished by the colour blue and yellow respectively. For the purpose of design, the parameters listed in Table 9.2 have been utilized.

9.3.3 Hexagonal spiral coil

A relatively new and cutting-edge coil emerging for DWC systems is hexagonal spiral coils. The spiral arrangement of the hexagonal loops in these coils produces a magnetic field that can cause an electric current to flow through the receiving coil In comparison to other coil configurations, the hexagonal spiral coil structure has a number of benefits. For situations where space is of the essence, the hexagonal shape provides for more effective use of the area that is available [20,21]. The model of a hexagonal spiral coil with a 100 mm air gap between the transmitter and reception coil is shown in Figure 9.6. ANSYS MAXWELL 3D has been used to develop the model.

The colours dark red and light purple, respectively, have been used to identify the transmitter and receiving coils. The characteristics in Table 9.3 below have been implemented for design motives.

9.4 RESULTS AND DISCUSSION

The employed numerical technique is the finite element method, with particular emphasis on ANSYS ELECTRONICS DESKTOP as the simulation tool. The simulation pertains to the magnetostatic solution, aimed at analyzing the behaviour of a transmitting coil subject to a 5 A excitation, while the receiving coil remains unpowered. Both coils are discretized using a mesh length of 40 mm, and the simulation domain spans a region of 100 mm. The subsequent analysis encompasses an examination of the outcomes under varying degrees of misalignment between the coils. Different misalignments were then introduced, including angular deviations of 5° and 10°, as well as longitudinal misalignments ranging from 0 mm (perfectly centred)

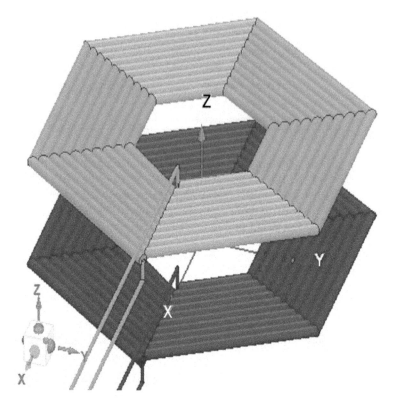

Figure 9.6 Model structure of hexagonal spiral coil.

Table 9.3 Dimension of the hexagonal spiral coil

Sl. No	Parameters	Values	Unit
1.	Wire radius	2.5	mm
2.	Coil inner diameter	80	mm
3.	Coil outer diameter	173.52	mm
4.	No. of turns	10	
5.	Space between adjacent wire	0.196	mm

up to 100 mm (maximum longitudinal misalignment of the receiver coil from the transmitter coil). To assess the effectiveness of the DWC system under various scenarios, these misalignments were examined. To maintain fairness, the inner diameter and number of turns of circular, rectangular, and hexagonal spiral coils are all kept constant [22,23].

9.4.1 Circular spiral coil

The model of the circular spiral coil with a 5° angular misalignment is shown in Figure 9.7. The simulated outcomes are depicted in Figure 9.8 when the R_x coil is 5° deviated in the x-axis. The simulated results demonstrate that different colours of curves correspond to varying air-gap lengths between the R_x coil and T_x coil, as illustrated in the legend. As we can observe from Figure 9.8a the mutual inductance between T_x and R_x coil gradually decreases as the air-gap length increases along with longitudinal distances. The magnetic flux of the transmitting coil is constant for all longitudinal misalignment changes, but the magnetic flux of the receiving coil steadily decreases as the longitudinal and vertical alignments (air-gap) are increased as shown in Figure 9.8b.

9.4.2 Rectangular spiral coil

Figure 9.9 exhibits the model of the rectangular spiral coil with a 5° angular misalignment. When the R_x coil is 5° off the x-axis, the simulated results are shown in Figure 9.10. In accordance with the legend, the simulated results show that different colours of curves correspond to varied air-gap lengths between the R_x coil and T_x coil. The mutual inductance between the T_x and R_x coils steadily reduces as the air-gap length grows along with longitudinal distances, as shown in Figure 9.10a. In comparison with the results examined in Figures 9.8a and 9.10a, the mutual inductance of the rectangular spiral coil offers a higher value than the circular spiral coil. From Figure 9.10b it can be observed that the receiving coil's magnetic flux steadily diminishes, and the transmitting coil's magnetic flux is constant for all variations in longitudinal and vertical misalignment. In the context of magnetic flux results, it can be observed that the rectangular spiral coil yields a slightly higher value than the circular spiral coil.

9.4.3 Hexagonal spiral coil

The hexagonal spiral coil model with a 5° angular misalignment is shown in Figure 9.11. The simulated outcomes are displayed in Figure 9.12 when the R_x coil is 5° off the x-axis. The simulated results demonstrate that, in line with the legend, various colours of curves represent various air-gap lengths between the R_x coil and T_x coil. As the air-gap length increases along with longitudinal distances, the mutual inductance between the T_x and R_x coils gradually decreases, as illustrated in Figure 9.10a. The mutual inductance of the rectangular spiral coil conveys a greater value than the circular and the hexagonal spiral coil when compared to the results examined in Figures 9.8a, 9.10a, and 9.12a. As seen in Figure 9.12b, the magnetic flux of the transmitting coil remains constant for all variations in longitudinal and vertical misalignment whereas that of the receiving coil gradually

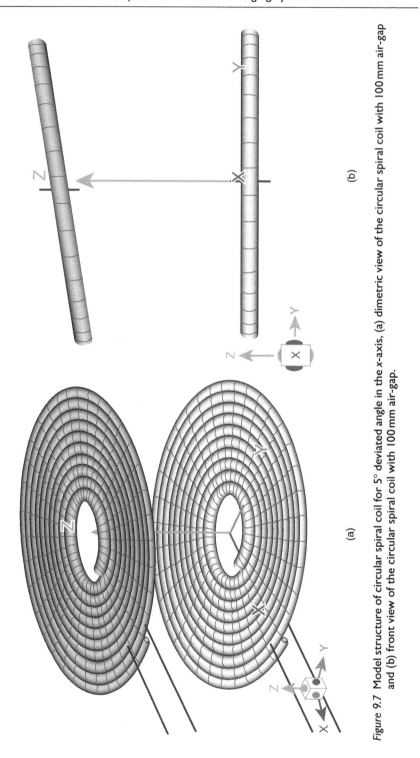

(a)

(b)

Figure 9.7 Model structure of circular spiral coil for 5° deviated angle in the x-axis, (a) dimetric view of the circular spiral coil with 100 mm air-gap and (b) front view of the circular spiral coil with 100 mm air-gap.

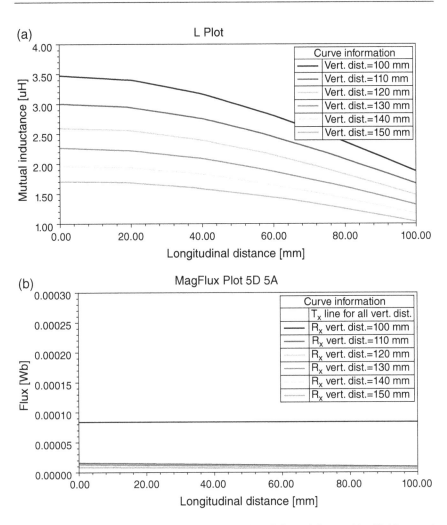

Figure 9.8 Simulated results for circular spiral coil with R$_x$ coil deviated by 5°, (a) mutual inductance and (b) magnetic flux.

decreases. The magnetic flux outcomes for hexagonal spiral coils exhibit the lowest value when compared to circular and rectangular spiral coils, according to the results examined in Figures 9.8b, 9.10b, and 9.12b.

Table 9.4 compares the outcomes of circular, rectangular, and hexagonal spiral coil with a fixed air-gap spacing of 150 mm. By assessing the mutual inductance and magnetic flux outcomes of various coil topologies, such as circular, rectangular, and hexagonal spiral coils, with varied deviation angles (i.e. 5° and 10°), while maintaining air-gap distance constant at 150 mm and varying longitudinal distance (i.e. 0–100 mm). The R$_x$ coil has no supply connected to it, whereas the T$_x$ coil is energized by a 5 A current. The ability

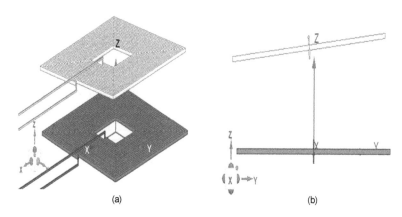

(a)   (b)

Figure 9.9 Model structure of rectangular spiral coil for 5° deviated angle in the x-axis, (a) dimetric view of the circular spiral coil with 100 mm air-gap and (b) front view of the rectangular spiral coil with 100 mm air-gap.

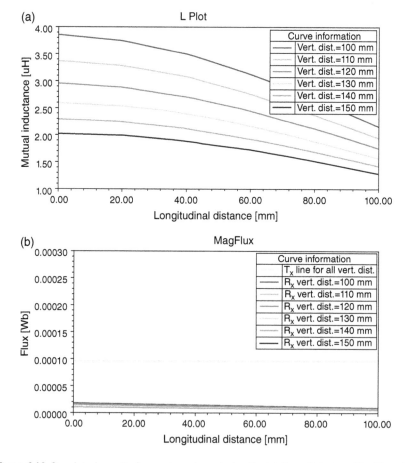

Figure 9.10 Simulated results for rectangular spiral coil with R_x coil deviated by 5° angle, (a) mutual inductance and (b) magnetic flux.

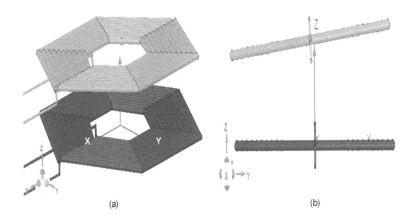

Figure 9.11 Model structure of hexagonal spiral coil for 5° deviated angle in the x-axis, (a) diametric view of the hexagonal spiral coil with 100 mm air-gap and (b) front view of the hexagonal spiral coil with 100 mm air-gap.

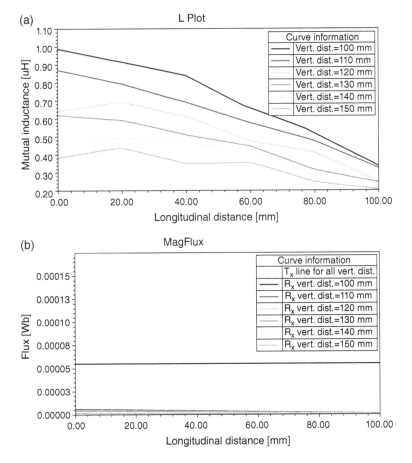

Figure 9.12 Simulated results for hexagonal spiral coil with R_x coil deviated by 5° angle, (a) mutual inductance and (b) magnetic flux.

Table 9.4 Comparative results of circular, rectangular, and hexagonal spiral coils with a constant air-gap distance of 150mm

Sl. No.	Types of coil	Angular deviation	Longitudinal distance	Mutual inductance (µH)	Magnetic flux (Wb)
1	Circular	5°	0	1.720276	0.000009
			20	1.694182	0.000008
			40	1.602948	0.000008
			60	1.456215	0.000007
			80	1.267412	0.000006
			100	1.051738	0.000005
2	Rectangular	5°	0	**2.021360**	**0.000010**
			20	1.984777	0.000010
			40	1.881868	0.000009
			60	1.721350	0.000009
			80	1.518705	0.000008
			100	1.288873	0.000006
3	Hexagonal	5°	0	0.382106	0.000002
			20	0.440554	0.000002
			40	0.352653	0.000002
			60	0.354924	0.000002
			80	0.250029	0.000001
			100	0.205469	0.000001
4	Circular	10°	0	1.733757	0.000009
			20	1.711009	0.000009
			40	1.622560	0.000008
			60	1.478773	0.000007
			80	1.293209	0.000006
			100	1.082542	0.000005
5	Rectangular	10°	0	**2.033609**	**0.000010**
			20	1.999460	0.000010
			40	1.897687	0.000009
			60	1.739853	0.000009
			80	1.537971	0.000008
			100	1.311824	0.000007
6	Hexagonal	10°	0	0.419939	0.000002
			20	0.369452	0.000002
			40	0.365936	0.000002
			60	0.314866	0.000002
			80	0.272963	0.000001
			100	0.208102	0.000001

of various coil structures to reduce power losses varies. Rectangular spiral coils appear to offer the most advantages over circular and hexagonal spiral coils, despite the fact that each coil construction, including rectangular, circular, and hexagonal spiral coils, has its own set of benefits and

Table 9.5 Comparison of different coil structure's parameter

Ref.	Coil structure	Magnetic inductance, L (in μH)	Magnetic flux, φ (in Wb)
[1]	Circular coil	0.445954	
	Rect. coil	0.5562434	-
	Hexagonal coil	0.3978252	
[5]	Circular coil (rect. cross-section)	1422.62284	
	Circular coil (rect. cross-section, solenoid type)	30.8326	-
	Circular coil (rect. cross-section, filamentary type)	7.8684	
[6]	Circular coil with inclined axis	1.7047	-
[7]	Circular coil (arbitrary shaped filaments)	0.0474028	-
[8]	Circular spiral coil	4.7	-
[9]	Coaxial circular filaments	0.2487874	-
[10]	Planar spiral coils	19.55	-
[21]	Toroidal coils	0.2513	-
Proposed work	Circular spiral coil	1.720276	0.000009
	Rect. spiral coil	2.02136	0.000010
	Hexagonal spiral coil	0.382106	0.000002

Rect.=Rectangular

drawbacks [23]. The rectangular spiral coil provides the greatest of all three coils in relation to the mutual inductance and magnetic flux value shown in the table, which is emphasized in the chart below with a value of **2.021360 μH** and **0.000010 Wb** respectively for 5° angular deviations. In the case of a 10° angular deviation, the rectangular coil exhibits a mutual inductance of **2.033609 μH** and a magnetic flux value of **0.000010 Wb**.

Table 9.5 provides comparative results in relation to the mutual inductance and magnetic flux produced between the transmitter coil and the receiving coil, in comparison to the outcomes gained from simulations undertaken by other researchers. Upon careful analysis of Table 9.5, it becomes evident that the rectangular cross-section and the rectangular spiral consistently demonstrate higher levels of mutual inductance when compared to other coil configurations. Moreover, by assessing the magnetic flux properties of the three coil shapes in the context of this investigation, it becomes apparent that the rectangular spiral coil exhibits the maximum magnetic flux.

9.5 CONCLUSION

The main issue faced in this study pertains to the impact of misalignments between the transmitter and receiver coils on the efficiency of DWC systems. Both angular and longitudinal misalignments have been identified as potential sources of power transfer losses, leading to a decrease in the overall charging mechanism's effectiveness. To address this problem, a careful examination of different coil configurations was conducted. The study focused on rectangular spiral coils, circular spiral coils, and hexagonal spiral coils. Each coil configuration was evaluated to determine its performance under various misalignment conditions. It was observed that the rectangular spiral coil demonstrated superior performance when subjected to misalignments. Its larger surface area allowed it to tolerate greater misalignments while still maintaining acceptable power transmission efficiency. On the other hand, circular spiral coils exhibited limitations in their charging range, as the magnetic field strength diminished rapidly with increasing distance between the transmitting and receiving coils. Despite being a potentially stable and reliable charging solution, hexagonal spiral coils posed challenges during production due to their complexity. Moreover, the corners of these hexagonal loops led to larger electric field concentrations, which could lead to localized heating and reduced efficiency. While the rectangular spiral coil showed promising results, there might be practical challenges in implementing it on a larger scale. The manufacturing complexity and the need for specific spatial arrangements may introduce practical difficulties in certain applications.

9.6 FUTURE WORK

In the quest for futuristic and efficient charging solutions, further research and development are essential. Pioneering efforts should focus on exploring innovative coil designs that offer heightened efficiency and ease of manufacture. Simultaneously, the exploration of advanced materials will unlock untapped potential within DWC systems. Embracing the forefront of innovation, optimizing charging system control algorithms will be critical in achieving unparalleled performance. This convergence of cutting-edge coil designs, advanced materials, and precise control algorithms promises to usher in a new era of unprecedented effectiveness and practicality in DWC, paving the way for ubiquitous, seamlessly charged devices in the future.

REFERENCES

1. T. Bouanou, H. El Fadil, A. Lassioui, O. Assaddiki, and S. Njili, "Analysis of Coil Parameters and Comparison of Circular, Rectangular, and Hexagonal Coils Used in WPT System for Electric Vehicle Charging," *World Electric Vehicle Journal*, vol. 12, no. 1, p. 45, 2021.
2. X. Mou, D. T. Gladwin, R. Zhao, H. Sun, and Z. Yang, "Coil Design for Wireless Vehicle-to-Vehicle Charging Systems," *IEEE Access*, vol. 8, pp. 172723–172733, 2020.
3. E. ElGhanam, M. Hassan, A. Osman, and H. Kabalan, "Design and Performance Analysis of Misalignment Tolerant Charging Coils for Wireless Electric Vehicle Charging Systems," *World Electric Vehicle Journal*, vol. 12, no. 3, p. 89, 2021.

4. L. Zhao, et al., "A Misalignment-Tolerant Series-Hybrid Wireless EV Charging System with Integrated Magnetics," *IEEE Transactions on Power Electronics*, vol. 34, no. 2, pp. 1276–1285, 2019.

5. C. Akyel, S. Babic, and M. Mahmoudi, "Mutual Inductance Calculation for Noncoaxial Circular Air Coils with Parallel Axes. *Progress in Electromagnetics Research*, vol. 91, pp. 287–301, 2009. doi: 10.2528/PIER09021907.

6. S. I. Babic and C. Akyel, "Calculating Mutual Inductance between Circular Coils with Inclined Axes in Air," *IEEE Transactions on Magnetics*, vol. 44, no. 7, pp. 1743–1750, 2008.

7. S. S. Kumar, C. H. Lee, E. Mamleyev, and K. Poletkin, "Calculation of Mutual Inductance between Circular and Arbitrary Shaped Filaments: Segmentation Method," In *ACTUATOR 2022; International Conference and Exhibition on New Actuator Systems and Applications*, Mannheim, Germany, 2022, pp. 1–4.

8. J. P. K. Sampath, A. Alphones, and D. M. Vilathgamuwa, "Coil Optimization against Misalignment for Wireless Power Transfer," In *2016 IEEE 2nd Annual Southern Power Electronics Conference (SPEC)*, Auckland, New Zealand, 2016, pp. 1–5, doi: 10.1109/SPEC.2016.7846159.

9. K. V. Poletkin and J. G. Korvink, "Efficient Calculation of the Mutual Inductance of Arbitrarily Oriented Circular Filaments via a Generalisation of the Kalantarov-Zeitlin Method," *Journal of Magnetism and Magnetic Materials*, vol. 483, 2019, pp. 10–20.

10. I. Hussain and D. Woo. "Inductance Calculation of Single-Layer Planar Spiral Coil," *Electronics*, vol. 11, no. 5, p. 750, 2022.

11. I. Hussain and D. Woo. "Simplified Mutual Inductance Calculation of Planar Spiral Coil for Wireless Power Applications," *Sensors*, vol. 22, no. 4, p. 1537, 2022.

12. M. Abramowitz and I. A. Stegun, *Handbook of Mathematical Functions*. Washington, DC: National Bureau of Standards, 1972.

13. S. Gradshteyn and I. M. Rhyzik, *Tables of Integrals, Series and Products*. New York: Dover, 1972.

14. K. Kumar, K. V. V. S. R. Chowdary, B. K. Nayak, and V. Mali, "Performance Evaluation of Dynamic Wireless Charging System with the Speed of Electric Vehicles," In *Proceedings of IEEE Indian Council International Conference (INDICON-2022)*, Kochi, India, 24–26 November, 2022, pp. 1–6.

15. K. Kumar, K. V. V. S. R. Chowdary, V. Mali, and R. R Kumar, "Analysis of Output Power Variation in Dynamic Wireless Charging System for Electric Vehicles," In *Proceedings of IEEE International Conference on Smart Technologies for Power, Energy and Control (STPEC 2021)*, Bilaspur, India, 19–22 December, 2021, pp. 1–6.

16. F. W. Grover, *Inductance Calculations*: New York: Dover, 1964.

17. M. R. R. Razu, et al., "Wireless Charging of Electric Vehicle While Driving," *IEEE Access*, vol. 9, pp. 157973–157983, 2021.

18. K. V. V. S. R. Chowdary and K. Kumar, "Assessment of Dynamic Wireless Charging System with the Variation in Mutual Inductance," *Proceedings of IEEE Indian Council International conference (INDICON-2022)*, Kochi, India, 24–26 November, 2022, pp. 1–6.

19. D. S. Filip and D. Petreus, "Simulation of an Inductive Coupled Power Transfer System," In *IECON 2016-42nd Annual Conference of the IEEE Industrial Electronics Society*, Florence, Italy, 2016, pp. 6559–6564.

20. H. Liu et al., "Dynamic Wireless Charging for Inspection Robots Based on Decentralized Energy Pickup Structure," *IEEE Transactions on Industrial Informatics*, vol. 14, no. 4, pp. 1786–1797, 2018.
21. M. R. Alizadeh Pahlavani and H. A. Mohammadpour, "Impact of Depth of Penetration on Mutual Inductance and Electrical Resistance of Individual Toroidal Coils Using Analytical and Finite Element Methods Applicable to Tokamak Reactors," *IEEE Transactions on Plasma Science*, vol. 38, no. 12, pp. 3380–3386, 2010.
22. M. Grzeskowiak, et al. "Coils for Ingestible Capsules: Near-Field Magnetic Induction Link." *Comptes Rendus Physique*, vol. 16, no. 9, pp. 819–835, 2015.
23. K. V. V. S. R. Chowdary, K. Kumar, R. K. Behera, and S. Banerjee, "Overview and Analysis of Various Coil Structures for Dynamic Wireless Charging of Electric Vehicles," In *2020 IEEE International Conference on Power Electronics, Smart Grid and Renewable Energy (PESGRE2020)*, Cochin, India, 2020, pp. 1–6.

Chapter 10

Power quality issues in EV charging station

Pradeep Kumar

10.1 INTRODUCTION

Nowadays, electric vehicles (EVs) are a relatively new transportation concept. EVs are becoming increasingly popular due to several advantages such as reduced environmental pollution, lesser transportation prices, and lesser petroleum usage [1]. In India, as in other established countries, the use of EVs such as E-bike, E-rickshaw, electric scooter, and electric car is rapidly increasing, accounting for more than nine lakh registered EVs as of 2022. To run these EVs, electric motor is employed with power from battery pack. EVs are more efficient than internal combustion vehicles. Even if EVs use electricity generated from fossil fuels, their overall efficiency is higher and their pollution is lower. Noise pollution is a problem in some Indian cities. Some Indian cities have the worst levels of noise pollution in the world. EVs are much quieter and may help to reduce noise pollution in cities. In India, the charging infrastructure for EVs is still under development. As a result, the EV owner is forced to charge their batteries unlawfully from a residential connection, causing system failure in the power sector [2]. Key challenges perceived while transforming to EVs include power quality (PQ) problems [3–5]. Due to EV establishment on the distribution side, PQ difficulties for instance voltage inequality, source current harmonics, transformer failure, and associated problems are expected. The negative impact of harmonics on PQ difficulties has been explained in Refs. [6–9]. A DC supply is needed to charge the EV battery, and the charging unit is linked to the power system via an AC/DC power conversion system. The harmonics are generated from this power conversion system, which has a negative impact on PQ when the harmonics exceed the system's adequate limits. The total harmonic distortion (THD) is a tool that can be useful for the measurement of harmonics in percentage. It can be either current THD or voltage THD. Investigation about the impact of EV charging on PQ issues is studied with the Monte Carlo approach as per literature [10,11]. Masoum et al. [12] presented a novel structure of load tap chargers and capacitors to reduce EV's harmonic effluence. To deliberate the consequence of EV charging on transformer life, Gomez and Morcos [13] generated a computer program by considering load, EV charging start time, and charging duration. Due to EV charging, unbalance and harmonics have been achieved and it has been mentioned by Kutt et al. [14]. It is also proposed that the power company concentrate on the PQ issues generated by EV charging. The consequences of EVs, photovoltaic systems, and EV-PV hybrids on PQ are also examined in Ref. [4]. The PQ improvement of the EV charging station can be performed by the Custom power devices i.e. DSTATCOM, DVR, and UPQC. The DSTATCOM can mitigate current-based PQ issues. In this chapter, the EV charging-based DSTATCOM with D-Q control technique is implemented in MATLAB/Simulink and PQ performances have been examined. The novelty of the chapter is to establish a DSTATCOM system with D-Q-based control in EV charging site and with the help of DSTATCOM, current-related PQ difficulties such as grid current THD can be mitigated.

10.2 EV CHARGING STATION

Figure 10.1 shows a pictorial view of an EV charging station. This charging station consists transformer, filter, AC-DC, and DC-DC converter.

The capacity of charging station can be estimated from overload factor K, No. of slots at charging station N_{slot}, peak power at each EV P_{EV} and power factor $\cos\varnothing$ as [15]

$$S_{rated} = \frac{K_{load}N_{slot}P_{EV}}{\cos\varnothing}\, kVA \qquad (10.1)$$

The detailed discussion on the components of EV charging station is as follows:

10.2.1 Choice of grid voltage [16]

The charging station is connected to 415 V of distribution grid. 120 kV transmission line is transformed to 415 V distribution grid through 120 kV/3.3 kV and 3.3 kV/415 V power transformers.

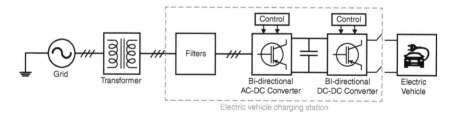

Figure 10.1 EV charging station.

10.2.2 Transformer rating selection [16]

The transformer rating is evaluated based on the rating of charging station capacity. The transformer of 3.3 kV/415 V at 50 Hz frequency is selected.

10.2.3 Battery design [16]

The most significant component of an EV is the battery. For proper charging and discharging purpose, exact modelling of battery is desired. The most popular batteries which are employed in EV are Li-ion, NiCad, NiMh, lead acid, etc. The parameters to be noted for battery selection are nominal voltage, capacity, cost, weight, energy density, and life cycle. Due to its high energy density and life cycle, the Li-ion battery is the most preferred option.

10.2.4 Converter design [16]

There are two converters AC-DC and DC-DC converter which is the part of EV charging stations. IGBT switches with PWM control are employed in AC-DC converters. The PWM approach consumes less power. The Buck converter is another type of DC-DC converter that can be used for large voltage to small voltage conversion.

The AC-DC converter output voltage is evaluated from line voltage V_{L-L} of 415 V and modulation index m of 0.9.

$$V_{dc} = \frac{2\sqrt{2}\,V_{L-L}}{\sqrt{3}\,m} \tag{10.2}$$

10.3 DSTATCOM

The configuration of DSTATCOM is represented in Figure 10.2. A DSTATCOM is one of the members of custom power family and it is

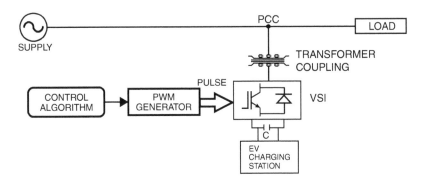

Figure 10.2 DSTATCOM configuration.

located at the point of common coupling with shunted from the distribution network [17,18].

A DSTATCOM is a shunt compensation device that offers an efficient method of compensating reactive power and regulating voltage. A voltage source inverter (VSI), a DC capacitor, EV charging station, a coupling transformer, and a control algorithm are all part of it. The DSTATCOM is regulated so that it only exchanges reactive power with the grid. This is accomplished by injecting current in quadrature with grid voltage. The reactive power is provided to the grid when DSTATCOM voltage is larger than the grid voltage, and DSTATCOM works as a capacitive manner. The reactive power is provided to the DSTATCOM when grid voltage is larger than the DSTATCOM voltage and DSTATCOM works as an inductive manner. If the grid and DSTATCOM voltages are the same value, then no reactive power exchange between the grid and the DSTATCOM will achieve, and the DSTATCOM is in the floating position. The DSTATCOM contains a VSI in its core, which can be used for a variety of applications with proper control algorithms. The control mechanism utilised to extract the reference current components determines the DSTATCOM's performance. The PWM module generates the switching pulses by using the same reference signal.

10.3.1 D-Q control technique

The primary purpose of the control technique is to provide the switching pulses for the inverter switches. In this chapter, D-Q-based control technique (shown in Figure 10.3) is proposed for the DSTATCOM system [19]. The *a-b-c* to *d-q-0* transformation converts the three-phase load currents to the *d-q-0* component of load currents. These *d-q-0* component of load currents are fed to second-order low pass filter (LPF). The filtered output signal is again converted to three-phase reference current via the *d-q-0* to *a-b-c* transformation. The three-phase PLL is synchronised with the PCC voltage and produces phase angle for the transformation block.

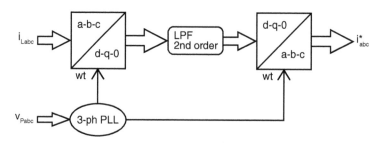

Figure 10.3 D-Q control.

The following mathematical manipulation has been performed during the entire process:

$$\begin{bmatrix} iLd \\ iLq \\ iL0 \end{bmatrix} = \frac{2}{3} \begin{bmatrix} \cos(wt) & \cos\left(wt - \frac{2\pi}{3}\right) & \cos\left(wt + \frac{2\pi}{3}\right) \\ -\sin(wt) & -\sin\left(wt - \frac{2\pi}{3}\right) & -\sin\left(wt + \frac{2\pi}{3}\right) \\ \frac{1}{2} & \frac{1}{2} & \frac{1}{2} \end{bmatrix} \begin{bmatrix} iLa \\ iLb \\ iLc \end{bmatrix}$$

$$\tag{10.3}$$

$$\begin{bmatrix} i_a^* \\ i_b^* \\ i_c^* \end{bmatrix} = \begin{bmatrix} \cos(wt) & -\sin(wt) & 1 \\ \cos\left(wt - \frac{2\pi}{3}\right) & -\sin\left(wt - \frac{2\pi}{3}\right) & 1 \\ \cos\left(wt + \frac{2\pi}{3}\right) & -\sin\left(wt + \frac{2\pi}{3}\right) & 1 \end{bmatrix} \begin{bmatrix} i_d^* \\ i_q^* \\ i_0^* \end{bmatrix} \tag{10.4}$$

10.3.2 Parameter design of DSTATCOM

In this section, various parameters of the DSTATCOM have been designed.

10.3.2.1 Determination of a DC capacitor [20]

The DC capacitor of the VSI-based DSTATCOM is determined by the DSTATCOM's instantaneous energy accessible during transients. Here, the notion of energy conservation is used.

$$\frac{1}{2} C_{DC} \left(V_{DC}^2 - V_{DC1}^2 \right) = k_1 3 V a I t \tag{10.5}$$

Here, V_{DC} is the DC voltage's reference value and V_{DC1} is the DC bus's least voltage point, a is the overloading ratio, V and I are the phase voltage and current, and t is the time necessary to regain the DC bus voltage.

10.3.2.2 Determination of an AC inductor [20]

The AC inductance (L_r) of DSTATCOM is determined from the current ripple $I_{cr,pp}$, switching frequency f_s, modulation index m, overloading ratio a and DC voltage (V_{DC}).

$$L_r = \sqrt{3}\, m V_{DC} / \left(12\, a f_s\, I_{cr,pp} \right) \tag{10.6}$$

10.3.2.3 Determination of switches rating in terms of voltage and current [20]

The voltage rating (V_{sw}) of the Inverter switches can be estimated as

$$V_{sw} = V_{DC} + V_d \tag{10.7}$$

Under dynamic conditions, V_d is the 10% overshoot of DC voltage.
The current rating (I_{sw}) of the Inverter switches can be estimated as

$$I_{sw} = 1.25\left(I_{cr,pp} + I_{peak}\right) \tag{10.8}$$

These equations can be used to calculate the voltage and current ratings of IGBT switches.

Table 10.1 shows the values for the DSTATCOM parameters. In Table 10.1, the values on the supply side and load side are rated values which remains constant for the Indian power systems. The DC capacitor (C_{dc}) and AC inductance (L_f) values are obtained from equations (10.5) and (10.6) respectively. The rest parameters are predesigned values. The DC voltage is evaluated from equation (10.2).

10.4 DEVELOPMENT OF EV CHARGING STATION WITH DSTATCOM

Extensive simulation studies are performed for the validation of the proposed system. Figure 10.4 represents EV charging-based DSTATCOM. This figure will be converted into MATLAB/Simulink platform. The simulation time is 1 sec with a variable-step solver. The D-Q-based control algorithm for the DSTATCOM is also modelled by power system

Table 10.1 DSTATCOM parameters

Parameter	Values
Supply side	$V_s=415V, f=50\,Hz$ $R_s=1.18\,\Omega, L_s=30\,mH$
Load side (nonlinear load-DC side)	$R_d=120\,\Omega, L_d=20\,mH$
DSTATCOM	$V_{dc}=400V, C_{dc}=6{,}000\,\mu F$ $L_f=35mH$
D-Q control technique	PLL's minimum frequency$=45\,Hz$, Filter cut-off frequency$=25\,Hz$ PWM generator$=$Three-phase bridge (6 pulses)
PWM carrier frequency	$1{,}620\,Hz$
Sample time	$T_s=50e\text{-}06$ seconds

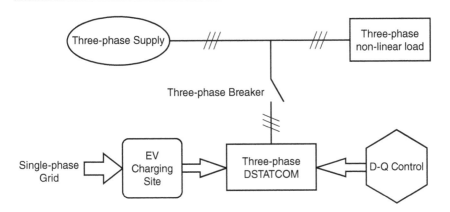

Figure 10.4 EV charging-based DSTATCOM.

blocksets of MATLAB/Simulink. Table 10.1 lists the parameters utilised in the simulation. The three-phase distribution system has a diode-based nonlinear load. The EV charging-based DSTATCOM is connected at the PCC of the distribution system through a three-phase breaker and two-winding transformer. The FFT analysis can be achieved from the powergui block. The various waveforms of voltage, current, and PWM pulses can be depicted with the help of scope. A three-phase *V-I* measurement block is employed on the both source and load side to measure the voltage and current simultaneously.

10.5 RESULTS AND DISCUSSION

The objective of the section is to demonstrate the MATLAB/Simulink-based results of the proposed system in terms of PQ improvement. The discussion has been made under without compensation and with compensation with the help of a three-phase breaker.

10.5.1 Performance of EV charging based DSTATCOM under without compensation

Figure 10.5 depicts the waveshapes of three-phase voltage and current on the source side when the DSTATCOM is not connected to the power system. The nonlinear load creates a non-sinusoidal shape of source current however the source voltage waveform has some ripple with sinusoidal. The performances have been observed for the interval $t=[0.6–0.7$ seconds].

Figure 10.6 denotes the waveshapes of three-phase voltage and current on the load side when the DSTATCOM is not connected to the power system.

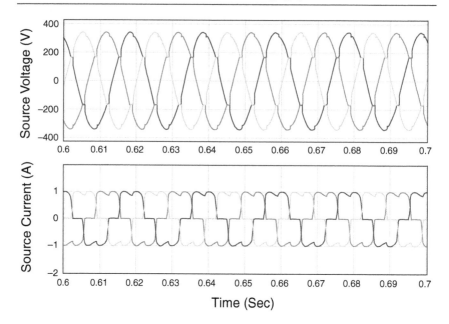

Figure 10.5 Uncompensated source voltage and source current waveform.

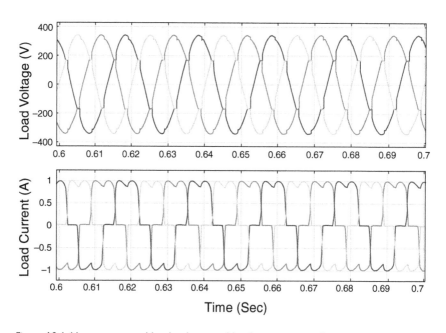

Figure 10.6 Uncompensated load voltage and load current waveform.

The power system has a nonlinear load. Due to non-linearity, non-sinusoidal load current appears. The load voltage waveform is sinusoidal with some ripples. The performances have been observed for the interval $t=[0.6-0.7$ seconds]. It has been observed that there is similarity of waveshapes in Figures 10.5 and 10.6 under without compensation.

Figure 10.7 denotes DC voltage waveform of the inverter of the DSTATCOM under without compensation. In this waveform, the proposed DC voltage of 400 V is not achieved which concludes poor DC Voltage Regulation by the DSTATCOM. The performance has been observed for the interval $t=[0-1$ seconds].

Figure 10.8 represents compensating current waveform under without compensation. In this case, the compensating current is zero i.e. no compensation occurs. The performance has been observed for the interval $t=[0-1$ seconds].

Under without compensation, the pulse generated by the PWM generator has been depicted in Figure 10.9. The waveform has been observed for the interval of $t=[0.6-0.61$ seconds].

Figure 10.10 shows the FFT analysis of the source current in terms of percentage THD. The THD is a tool for harmonic measurement. In case of without compensation, the THD of source current is 26.43% as per Figure 10.10.

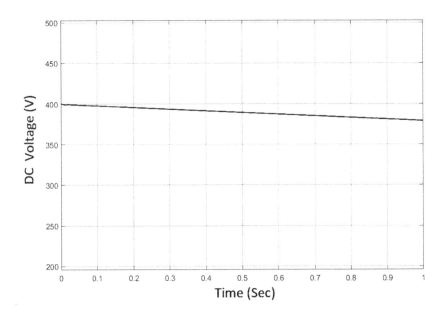

Figure 10.7 DC voltage regulation under without compensation.

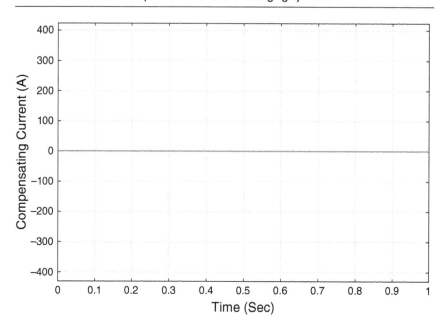

Figure 10.8 Compensating current waveform under without compensation.

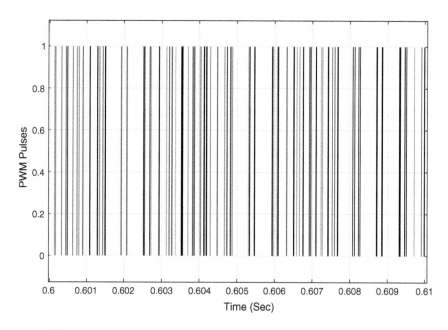

Figure 10.9 PWM pulses under without compensation.

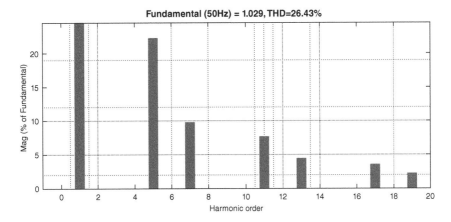

Figure 10.10 Uncompensated source current THD.

10.5.2 Performance of EV charging based DSTATCOM under with compensation

Figure 10.11 depicts the waveshapes of three-phase voltage and current on the source side when the EV charging-based DSTATCOM is connected to the power system. There is a sinusoidal shape of source current due to the DSTATCOM effect even though load is nonlinear. The source voltage waveform has some ripple with a sinusoidal shape. The performances have been observed for the interval $t=[0.6–0.7$ seconds].

Figure 10.12 denotes the waveshapes of three-phase voltage and current on the load side when the DSTATCOM is connected with the power system. The power system has a nonlinear load. Due to non-linearity effect, non-sinusoidal load current appears always. The load voltage waveform is sinusoidal with some ripples. The performances have been observed for the interval $t=[0.6–0.7$ seconds].

Figure 10.13 shows the compensating current waveform when DSTATCOM is connected to the power system. The compensating current is the injecting current provided by the DSTATCOM. Its amplitude is 8A and sinusoidal in nature. The compensating currents have been observed for the interval $t=[0.6–0.7$ seconds].

Under with compensation, the pulse generated by the PWM generator has been depicted in Figure 10.14. The waveform has been observed for the interval of $t=[0.6–0.61$ seconds]. This pulse is provided to switching devices of the DSTATCOM.

Figure 10.15 denotes the DC voltage waveform of the inverter of the DSTATCOM under with compensation. In this waveform, the proposed DC voltage of 400 V is achieved perfectly which concludes better DC

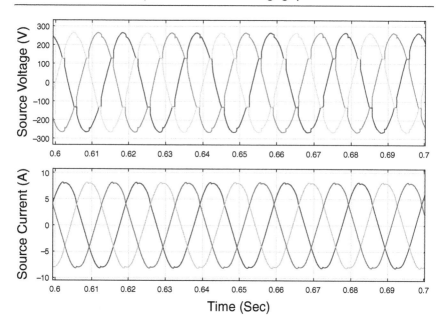

Figure 10.11 Compensated source voltage and source current waveform.

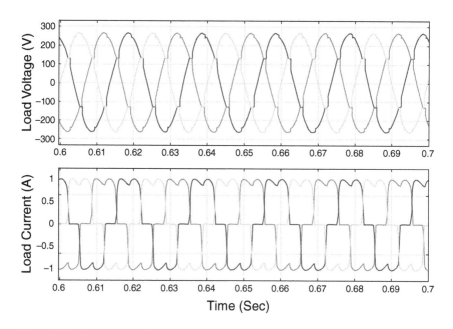

Figure 10.12 Compensated load voltage and load current waveform.

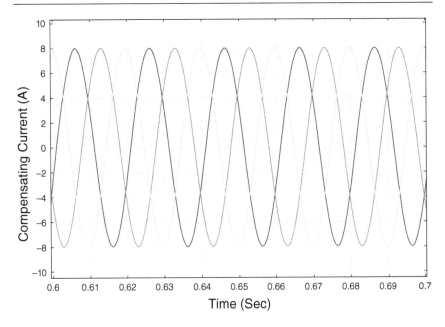

Figure 10.13 Compensating current waveform under with compensation.

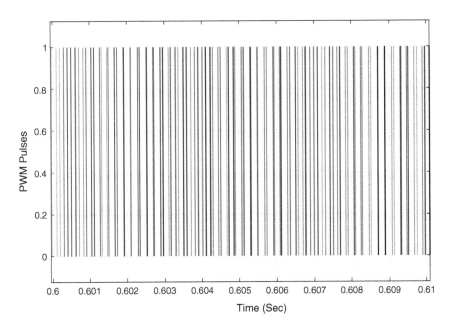

Figure 10.14 PWM pulses under with compensation.

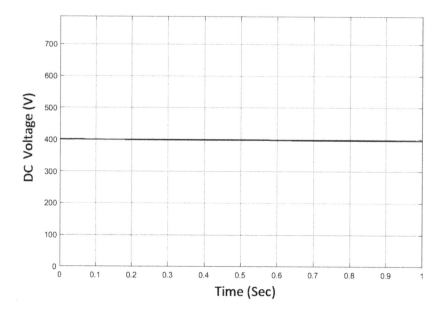

Figure 10.15 DC voltage regulation under with compensation.

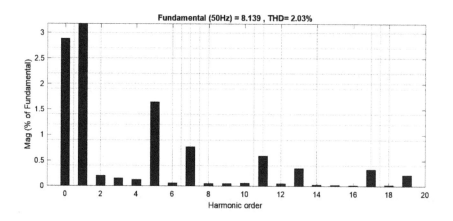

Figure 10.16 Compensated source current THD.

Voltage Regulation by the DSTATCOM. The DC voltage regulation has been observed for the interval $t=[0-1$ seconds]. Figure 10.16 shows the FFT analysis of the source current in terms of percentage THD when the DSTATCOM is connected to the power system. In this case, the THD of source current is 2.03% as per Figure 10.16. The percentage THD value satisfies the IEEE-519 harmonic standard efficaciously [20].

Table 10.2 Source current THD (%)

Compensation	THD value
Without compensation	26.43
With compensation	2.03

Table 10.3 Comparison of compensated source current THD (%)

Present contribution	Reference [2]	Reference [16]	Reference [21]	Reference [22]
2.03	4.82	2.68	29.16	3.54

Table 10.2 represents a summary of THD measurement of source current in percentage. The measurement has been depicted for without and with compensation cases.

Table 10.3 represents a comparison of compensated source current THD for present contribution and existing literature where the lowest % THD of 2.03% has been achieved in the proposed work.

10.6 CONCLUSION AND FUTURE SCOPE

In this chapter, the PQ improvement of the distribution grid by the EV charging-based D-STATCOM has been proposed. The proposed DSTATCOM system has been controlled by the D-Q technique. The complete EV charging-based D-STATCOM has been designed and implemented in MATLAB/Simulink. After execution, the performances have been observed under without compensation and with compensation. In case of without compensation, poor DC voltage regulation and harmonic distortion in source current have been achieved but after compensation, the DC voltage is regulated perfectly and there is no distortion in the source current waveform. The FFT analysis of the source current has been studied to examine the source current THD in without and with compensation cases. It has been concluded that the percentage THD of source current is below 5% in the case of with compensation which conforms IEEE-519 harmonic standard. This work can be further extended in the following manner:

i. Comparative PQ analysis can be performed by adopting more than two control techniques for the DSTATCOM.
ii. The inverter topologies can be modified as multi-level, multi-step, current source inverter, Z-source inverter, etc.
iii. The performances can be examined with other nonlinear loads such as arc furnace, induction furnace, etc.

REFERENCES

1. Sivakumar, P., Sandhya Devi, R. S., Vidhya Shree, S., & Keerthanaa, K. (2018). Electric vehicles-benefits and challenges. *Ecology, Environment and Conservation*, vol. 24, pp. 410–414.
2. Karmaker, A. K., Roy, S., & Ahmed, M. R. (2019). Analysis of the impact of electric vehicle charging station on power quality issues. *International Conference on Electrical, Computer and Communication Engineering*, Cox's Bazar, Bangladesh (pp. 1–6).
3. Khan, A., Memon, S., & Sattar, T. P. (2018). Analyzing integrated renewable energy and smart-grid systems to improve voltage quality and harmonic distortion losses at electric-vehicle charging stations. *IEEE Access*, vol. 6, pp. 26404–26415.
4. Saritha, M. & Manitha, P. V. (2022). Power quality issues on the integration of RES-EV to grid: A review. *International Conference on Innovations in Science and Technology for Sustainable Development* (pp. 347–352), Kollam, India.
5. Verma, A. & Singh, B. (2021). AFF-SOGI-DRC control of renewable energy based grid interactive charging station for EV with power quality improvement. *IEEE Transactions on Industry Applications*, vol. 57, no. 1, pp. 588–597.
6. De la Rosa, F. C. (2006). *Harmonics and Power Systems*. CRC Press, Boca Raton, FL.
7. Jain, S. K. & Singh, S. N. (2011). Harmonics estimation in emerging power system: Key issues and challenges. *Electric Power Systems Research*, vol. 81, no. 9, pp. 1754–1766.
8. Acharya, S., Ghosh, R. & Halder, T. (2016). An adverse effect of the harmonics for the power quality issues. *International Conference on Computational Techniques in Information and Communication Technologies (ICCTICT)* (pp. 569–574), New Delhi, India.
9. Arrillaga, J. & Watson, N. R. (2003). *Power System Harmonics*. John Wiley & Sons Ltd, Hoboken, NJ.
10. Chen, J., Torquato, R., & Salles, D., (2014). Method to assess the power quality impact of plug-in electric vehicles. *IEEE Transactions on Power Delivery*, vol. 29, no. 2, pp. 958–965.
11. Gray, M. K. & Morsi, W. G. (2015). Power quality assessment in distribution systems embedded with plug-in hybrid and battery electric vehicles. *IEEE Transactions on Power Systems*, vol. 30, no. 2, pp. 663–671.
12. Masoum, M. A. S., Deilami, S., & Islam, S. (2010). Mitigation of harmonics in smart grids with high penetration of plug-in electric vehicles. *IEEE PES General Meeting*, Minneapolis, MN, USA (pp. 1–6).
13. Gomez, J. C. & Morcos, M. M. (2003). Impact of EV battery chargers on the power quality of distribution systems. *IEEE Transactions on Power Delivery*, vol. 18, no. 3, pp. 975–981.
14. Kutt, L., Saarijarvi, E., Lehtonen, M., et al. (2013). A review of the harmonic and unbalance effects in electrical distribution networks due to EV charging. *International Conference on Environment and Electrical Engineering* (pp. 556–561), Wroclaw, Poland.

15. Varghese, A. S., Thomas, P., & Varghese, S. (2017). An efficient voltage control strategy for fast charging of plug-in electric vehicle. *Innovations in Power and Advanced Computing Technologies (i-PACT)*, pp. 1–4.
16. Chaturvedi, V., Ahmed, S. Z., Kumar, A., & Jaiswal, S. (2022). Power quality improvement of grid-connected EV charging station using DSTATCOM. *IEEE Students Conference on Engineering and Systems (SCES)* (pp. 1–5), Prayagraj, India.
17. Singh, B., Jayaprakash, P., Kothari, D. P., Chandra, A., & Haddad, K. A. (2014). Comprehensive study of DSTATCOM configurations. *IEEE Transactions on Industrial Informatics*, vol. 10, no. 2, pp. 854–870.
18. Bai, Z. et al. (2023). A capacitive-coupling winding tap injection DSTATCOM integrated with distribution transformer for balance and unbalance operations. *IEEE Transactions on Industrial Electronics*, vol. 70, no. 2, pp. 1081–1093.
19. Sepulveda, C. A., Munoz, J. A., Espinoza, J. R., Figueroa, M. E., & Melin, P. E. (2013). All-on-chip dq-frame based D-STATCOM control implementation in a low-cost FPGA. *IEEE Transactions on Industrial Electronics*, vol. 60, no. 2, pp. 659–669.
20. Singh, B., Chandra, A., & Al-Haddad, K. (2015). *Power Quality Problems and Mitigation Techniques*. John Wiley and Sons Ltd, Hoboken, NJ.
21. Sabarimuthu, M. et al. (2021). Measurement and analysis of power quality issues due to electric vehicle charger. *IOP Conference Series: Materials Science and Engineering*, vol. 1055, p. 012131.
22. Irfan, M. M., Rangarajan, S. S, Collins, E. R., & Senjyu, T. (2021). Enhancing the power quality of the grid interactive solar photovoltaic-electric vehicle system. *World Electric Vehicle Journal*, vol. 12, no. 3, p. 98.

Chapter 11

Sign Least Mean Kurtosis and Least Mean Forth (SLMFK/LMF)-based power quality analysis in grid tied EV SPV system

Subhranshu Sekhar Puhan, Renu Sharma, and Pabitra Mohan Patra

LIST OF SYMBOLS AND ABBREVATIONS

SPV:	Solar Photovoltaic
LMF:	Linear Mean Fourth
DSTATCOM:	Distribution Static Compensator
PCC:	Point of Common Coupling
P & O:	algorithm Perturb and Observe algorithm
V_t:	Terminal voltage
V_{sa}, V_{sb}, V_{sc}:	Source voltage of phase a, b, c respectively
u_{pa}, u_{pb}, u_{pc}:	In-phase unit template of phase a, b, c respectively
V_{dc}:	DC bus voltage
V_{dcref}:	Reference DC bus voltage
e:	Error quantities
P_{pv}:	PV power
w_{pa}, w_{pb}, w_{pc}:	Active weight component of load current of phase a, b, c respectively
w_{sp}:	Total weights of fundamental active components
wLpa:	Average weights of active fundamental load current

11.1 INTRODUCTION: BACKGROUND AND DRIVING FORCES

The global campaign EV 30@30, Faster adoption of Manufacturing of Hybrid Electric Vehicle (FAME-II scheme) and budgetary support for design and operation of quality charging station encourage manufacturer and researchers in an indirect fashion in India. Even the Government of India along with organisation like Bureau of Indian Standard (BIS)

DOI: 10.1201/9781003481065-11

have prescribed the standard, operation and procedure for design of EV, charging infrastructure for EVs and schematic representation of plug in hybrid electric vechicle. The Government of India has another arrangement to generate 500 GW of Power from non-fossil-based energy by 2030 and 280 GW (roughly 60%) solar energy installation target by 2030, which gives motivations and appropriations to the establishment of solar photovoltaic based environmentally friendly power projects [1]. In emerging market trends arena, renewable energy-assisted charging infrastructure is an attractive option for manufacturer and consumer. The unpredictability of RE sources along with stability and power qualities issues associated after multiple RE sources penetration empowers to think or charging infrastructure for EVs [2,3]. Several topologies are described by authors in Refs. [4,5]. The topologies used in Refs. [4] and [5] are of unidirectional DC/DC converter for battery which does not allow the flow of energy from vehicle to grid. The control methodology for vehicle to grid energy transfer and use the energy in EV during standstill mode of EV is depicted in Refs. [6,7]. The charging of EVs using the grid is not a good idea as it consumes an enormous amount of power from the grid. Therefore, an alternate source of energy is required for EV battery charging. The renewable energy sources prove to be a better alternative for EV charging instead of the grid [8]. The intermittent and uncertainty nature of SPV system can be overcome by introduction of whole SPVEV system with grid as depicted in Ref. [9]. Where as, Compensation of reactive power required by the grid is provided by VSC.

Here the authors have proposed sign least mean kurtosis/LMF based approach for bidirectional power flow (V2G and G2V). The proposed algorithm in this manuscript is a combination of sign least mean kurtosis along with least mean forth algorithm for VSC control. The proposed algorithm (SLMFK) algorithm has minimal power quality variation, and the grid current is purely within IEEE-519 standard.

11.2 SYSTEM LEVEL DIAGRAM

The block diagram of the EV charging station assisted with solar PV(SPV) is demonstrated in Figure 11.1. The bidirectional converter used along with battery decides the mode of operation of EV (Charging/discharging). The PV array is coupled to DC-link through a capacitor. Moreover, through the DC-link capacitor, SPV array is connected to the DC bus and both of them connected to the utility after a VSC based inverter. The detailed schematic diagram of the above-mentioned test case system is depicted in Figure 11.1. When SPV is not operating, i.e. in DSTATCOM mode, the battery is just providing power to the DC load connected locally to the EV battery combination.

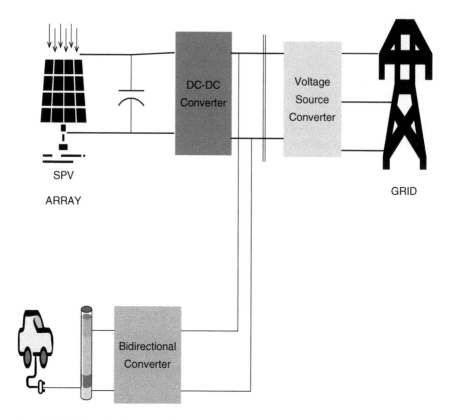

Figure 11.1 Schematic diagram of system.

11.3 CONTROLLER DESIGN FOR TEST CASE SYSTEM

The charging station controller is divided into three parts:

   i. MPPT controller details
  ii. VSC switching for gate pulse generation
 iii. EV charging/discharging strategies

11.3.1 MPPT controller details

Here the authors have used perturb and observe method for maximum power generation from the SPV array. As the SPV array taken in to picture is single stage, there is no DC/DC converter after SPV array.

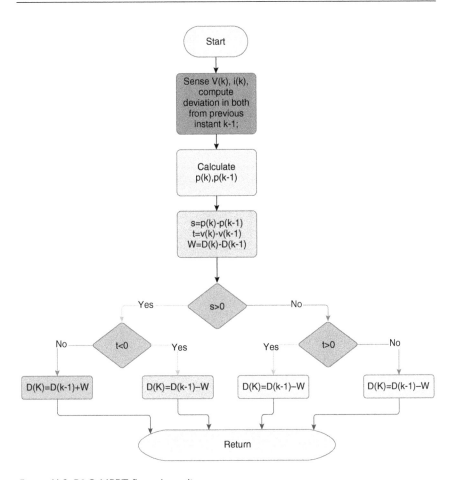

Figure 11.2 **P&O MPPT flow chart diagram.**

The MPPT algorithm used in SPV array decides the reference DC bus voltage generation. Steps involved in MPPT is described as mentioned in Figure 11.2.

11.3.2 Charge controller details

The charging and discharging mode of battery is depicted in Figure 11.3. DC bus reference and DC bus voltage are evaluated and passed through a PI controller to get the battery current. The state of charge and its reference are passed through a PI controller, and its difference is compared through a saw tooth waveform. The input from battery current and battery state of charge is passed through an AND gate and other through a NOT and AND gate.

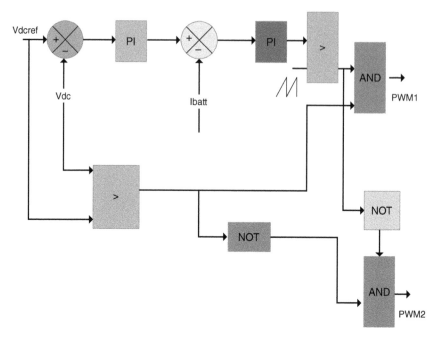

Figure 11.3 BESS control strategies.

11.3.3 VSC controller details

VSC control strategies is depicted in Figure 11.4. The switching strategies for VSC is illustrated with the help of sign least mean kurtosis-based method along with least mean forth algorithm. The combined algorithm is called as SLMFK control algorithm. The mathematical expression for SLMFK algorithm is described as follows:

$$v_{sa} = \frac{2v_{sab} + v_{sbc}}{3}; v_{sb} = \frac{-v_{sab} + v_{sbc}}{3}; v_{sc} = \frac{-v_{sab} - 2v_{sbc}}{3} \quad (11.1)$$

The source voltage of phase *a*, *b*, *c* is depicted in equation (11.1). The terminal voltage at VSC terminal is depicted in equation 11.2. Here the authors have used the format of unit template rather than only terminal voltages to decrease the fluctuation in terminal voltages. The error component is mentioned as in equation 11.5.

Similarly, the active weight component of phase *a*, *b* and *c* (w_{pa}, w_{pb} & w_{pc}) is illustrated in equations (11.4), (11.7), and (11.8), respectively. Here the authors have used combined LMF and sign least regressor mean kurtosis algorithm for switching control of VSC to reduce the total harmonic distortion. The reactive weight component of different phases can be calculated just by referring the in-phase component active weight (Table 11.1).

Table 11.1 Overview of existing control algorithm for VSC

	Order	Domain	Error	Complexity	Noise cancellation
SRF-PLL	NA	Time	Highest	High	NA
FOGI-FLL	4	Frequency	Less than SRF-PLL	High	Better as compared to SRF-PLL
LMS	2	Adaptive filter	Lesser	Still high	Better
LMF	4	Adaptive filter	Lesser	Easy	Better
SLMFK	4	Adaptive filter	Least	Easy	Good

$$v_t = \sqrt{\frac{2}{3}\left(v_{sa}^2 + v_{sb}^2 + v_{sc}^2\right)} \tag{11.2}$$

$$u_{pa} = \frac{v_{sa}}{V_t}; u_{pb} = \frac{v_{sb}}{V_t}; u_{pc} = \frac{v_{sc}}{V_t} \tag{11.3}$$

$$w_{pa}(n+1) = w_{pa}(n) + 4\mu \cdot \text{sign}\left\{3\sigma(n) - e_{pa}^2(n)\right\} \cdot e_{pa}(n) u_{pa(n)} + e_{pa}^3(n) \tag{11.4}$$

$$e_{pa} = i_{La}(n) - w_{pa}(n) u_{pa}(n) \tag{11.5}$$

$$\sigma_{ea}^2(n) = \beta\sigma_{ea}^2(n-1) + e_{pa}^2(n) \tag{11.6}$$

$$w_{pb}(n+1) = w_{pb}(n) 4\mu \cdot \text{sign}\left\{3\sigma_{eb}^2(n) - e_{pb}^2(n)\right\} \cdot e_{pb}(n) u_{pb}(n) + e_{pb}^3(n) \tag{11.7}$$

$$w_{pc}(n+1) = w_{pc}(n) 4\mu \cdot \text{sign}\left\{3\sigma_{ec}^2(n) - e_{pc}^2(n)\right\} \cdot e_{pc}(n) u_{pb}(n) + e_{pc}^3(n) \tag{11.8}$$

$$i_{sa}^* = w_{sp} \cdot u_{pa}; i_{sb}^* = w_{sp} \cdot u_{pb}; i_{sc}^* = w_{sp} \cdot u_{pc} \tag{11.9}$$

$$w_{sp} = w_{cp} + w_{Lpa} - w_{pv} \tag{11.10}$$

The PV feed forward term is taken into account as depicted in equation (11.12). The reactive component of load component can be calculated as in equation (11.11).

$$w_{Lpa}(n) = \frac{1}{3}\left\{w_{pa}(n) + w_{pb}(n) + w_{pc}(n)\right\} \tag{11.11}$$

$$w_{pv} = \frac{2P_{pv}}{3V_t} \tag{11.12}$$

11.4 RESULT AND ANALYSIS

The steady-state behaviour of proposed SLMFK algorithm is shown in Figures 11.4–11.12. The solar insolation throughout the operation is considered as 1,000 w/m². The DC bus voltage is kept constant by the help of battery converter. In ideal case, the grid current and voltage are maintained sinusoidal, and both are within the limit of IEEE-519 format. During grid mode of operation, the EV assisted with battery is charging as the total power required by the EV is lesser than SPV output. The difference of SPV and EV power is depicted into grid. So the grid power is negative. During normal mode of operation, the THD as mentioned in Figure 11.11. Figures 11.4–11.11 deals with charging mode of operation, and in this case the battery power is negative as mentioned in figure and hence the SOC is increasing from the original SOC. In this phase of operation, only a nonlinear Diode bridge rectifier is on AC side.

When the solar insolation is zero, i.e., in DSTACOM mode of operation, the battery-assisted EV is providing power to a dummy DC load as present. Hence from supporting a DC load for a short span of time allowed to identify the battery as vehicle to grid mode of operation. In each of the case, the DC voltage is constant, and the grid voltage and current are within IEEE-519 format and sinusoidal. The detailed result and analysis

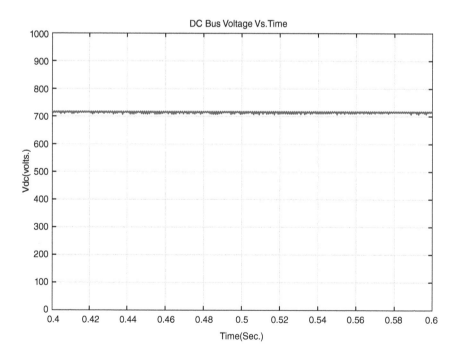

Figure 11.4 DC bus voltage vs. time.

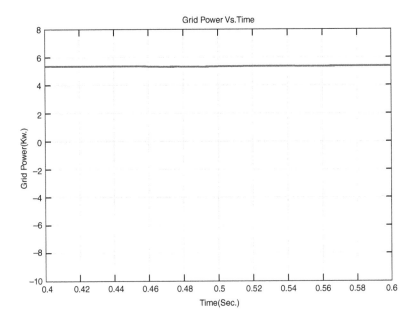

Figure 11.5 Grid power vs. time (charging mode).

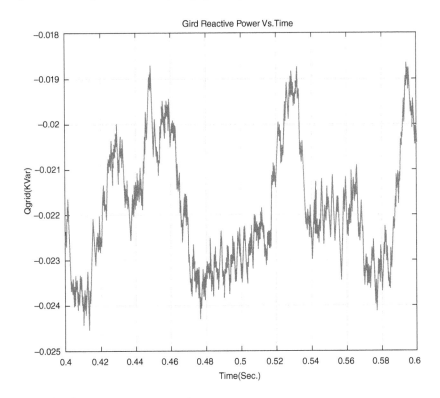

Figure 11.6 Grid reactive power vs. time.

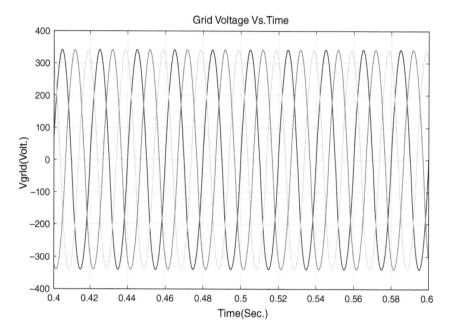

Figure 11.7 Grid voltage vs. time.

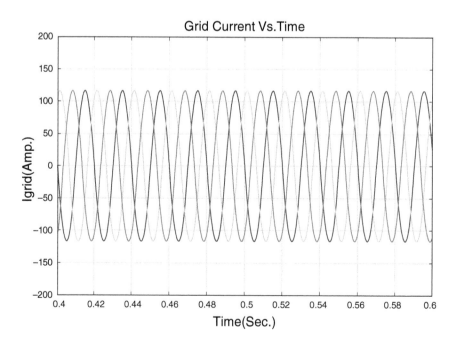

Figure 11.8 Grid current vs. time.

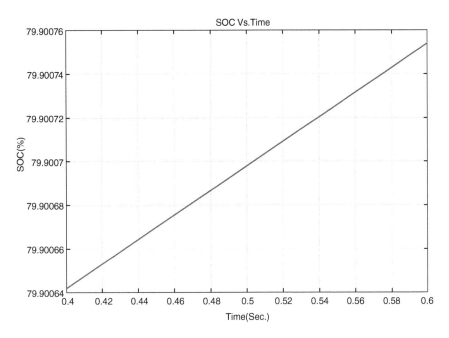

Figure 11.9 Battery SOC vs. time.

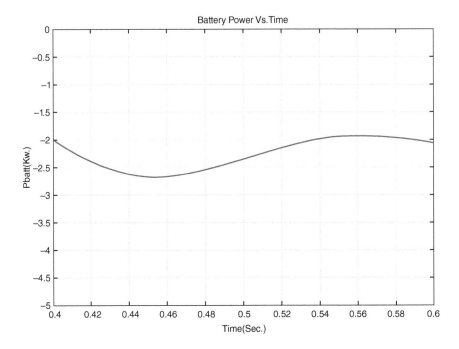

Figure 11.10 Battery power vs. time.

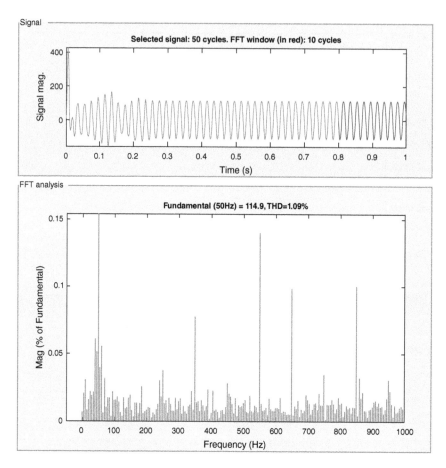

Figure 11.11   THD analysis of grid current.

is illustrated in figure section in Figures 11.12–11.16. In both charging mode and DSTATCOM mode of operation, the grid reactive power is near to zero, and hence VSC operates at unity power factor of operation. In DSTATCOM mode of operation (night time), a dummy resistive load is taken at DC side along with nonlinear load at AC side.

11.5 CONCLUSION

This manuscript illustrates a sign least mean kurtosis along with least mean forth control algorithm for VSC switches, P & O for MPPT control, BESS control strategies as mentioned in Figure 11.3. The proposed control algorithm is tested in MATLAB/SIMULINK environment for the test case

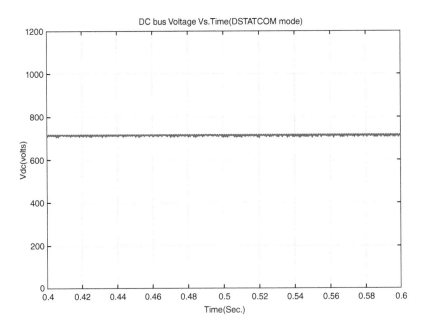

Figure 11.12 DC bus voltage vs. time (DSTATCOM mode).

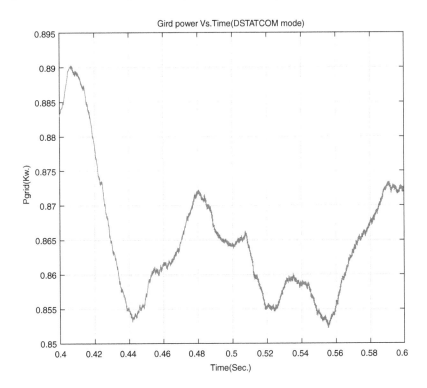

Figure 11.13 Grid power vs. time (DSTATCOM mode).

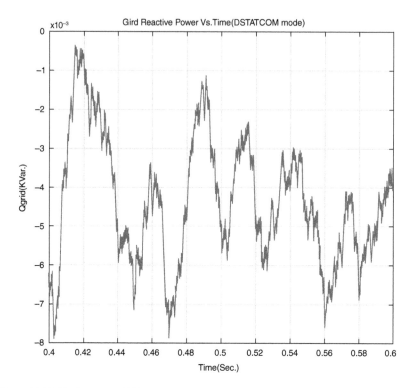

Figure 11.14 Grid reactive VAR vs. time.

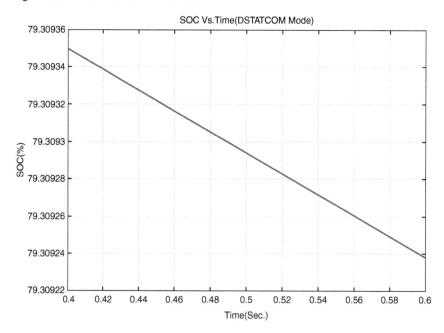

Figure 11.15 SOC (%) vs. time (DSTATCOM mode).

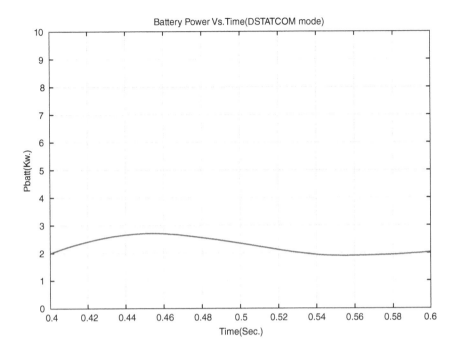

Figure 11.16 Battery power vs. time (DSTATCOM mode).

system as shown in Figure 11.1. In both charging mode of operation and DSTATCOM mode of operation, the DC bus voltage is maintained constant, and the grid current THD is well below the permissible limit of 5% as in IEEE-519 standard. Moreover, the proposed algorithm used the combined benefits of least mean forth algorithm (lesser complexity) and least mean kurtosis (better steady-state response).

REFERENCES

1. R. H. Ashique, Z. Salam, M. J. B. A. Aziz and A. R. Bhatti, "Integrated photovoltaic-grid dc fast charging system for electric vehicle: A review of the architecture and control," *Renewable and Sustainable Energy Reviews*, vol. 69, 2017, pp. 1243–1257, ISSN 1364-0321, doi: 10.1016/j.rser.2016.11.245.
2. K. Hou et al., "A reliability assessment approach for integrated transportation and electrical power systems incorporating electric vehicles," *IEEE Transactions on Smart Grid*, vol. 9, no. 1, pp. 88–100, 2018, doi: 10.1109/TSG.2016.2545113.
3. D. M. Nguyen, M. A. Kishk and M. S. Alouini, "Toward sustainable transportation: Accelerating vehicle electrification with dynamic charging deployment", *IEEE Transactions on Vehicular Technology*, vol. 71, no. 9, pp. 9283–9296, 2022.

4. R. Prasad, C. Namuduri and P. Kollmeyer, "Onboard unidirectional auto-motive G2V battery charger using sine charging and its effect on Li-ion batteries," *Proceedings of IEEE Energy Conversion Congress and Exposition*, Montreal, QC, Canada, pp. 6299–6305, 2015.

5. B. Singh, G. Bhuvaneswari and V. Garg, "Improved power quality AC-DC converter for electric multiple units in electric traction," *Proceedings of IEEE Power India Conference*, New Delhi, India, pp. 1–6, 2006.

6. T. Na, X. Yuan, J. Tang and Q. Zhang, "A review of on-board integrated electric vehicles charger and a new single-phase integrated charger," *CPSS Transactions on Power Electronics and Applications*, vol. 4, no.4, pp. 288–298, 2019, doi: 10.24295/CPSSTPEA.2019.00027.

7. V. T. Tran, M. R. Islam, K. M. Muttaqi and D. Sutanto, "An efficient energy management approach for a solar-powered EV battery charging facility to support distribution grids," *IEEE Transactions on Industry Applications*, vol. 55, no. 6, pp. 6517–6526, 2019, doi: 10.1109/TIA.2019.2940923.

8. V. Jain, S. Kewat and B. Singh, "Three phase grid connected PV based EV charging station with capability of compensation of reactive power," *IEEE Transactions on Industry Applications*, vol. 59, no. 1, pp. 367–376, 2023, doi: 10.1109/TIA.2022.3213530.

9. M. Kazemi Eghbal and G. Alipoor, "LMSK: A robust higher-order gradient-based adaptive algorithm," *IET Signal Processing*, vol. 13, no. 5, pp. 506–515, 2019.

Chapter 12

Modified damped SOGI-based controller for grid interfaced solar system with multifunctional capabilities

Dinanath Prasad and Piyush Pandey

12.1 INTRODUCTION

The use of traditional energy sources causes global warming, which impacts the entire planet's system. It is accomplished by the combustion of fossil fuels, which emit hazardous gases that impact living organisms as well. Renewable energy-based SPV panels are utilized widely for creating electricity [1]. Also, it is not linked to any form of pollution as well, and not any kind of hazardous gas is emitted into the environment. However, an SPV array demands a significant initial expenditure, but once built, no more investment is necessary. The SPV array contains no moving parts for energy extraction. As a result, creating energy through an SPV plant is a low-cost option source. Also, solar energy is plentiful and may be used in a variety of ways such as cooking heating watermarked food (photosynthesis and agriculture), and for electricity, etc. In addition, there are several concerns with the use of solar energy harvesting, and, some of the effects are mentioned in the works of literature [2,3]. Nowadays grid-connected mode is a widely accepted mode over economical operation since it doesn't need any kind of storage (batteries). As a result, grid support in SPV systems is maintained effectively. In addition, integrating electric vehicle (EV) propulsion drives with grid-connected PV systems offer opportunities for cleaner transportation and better utilization of renewable energy resources. The specific implementation and level of integration depend on the infrastructure, technology, and requirements of the system being developed. The PV-integrated charging stations-based approach involves integrating SPV panels directly into EV charging stations. These stations can be grid-connected and equipped with PV panels, allowing them to generate electricity from the Sun. The PV panels supply power to charge the EVs connected to the station, and any excess energy can be fed back to the grid or used for other purposes. The grid-connected modes and their various topologies with energy storage devices have been published in Refs. [4–7]. Moreover, the grid-integrated challenges and their solutions have been addressed in various papers [8,9].

The MPPT technique is utilized for the maximum utilization of solar energy from a solar-fed plant. In this respect, various authors reproduce literature in the MPPT algorithms from the extraction of peak power from the SPV system [10]. Some of the MPPT algorithms such as perturb and observe (P&O) and incremental conductance (INC)-based MPPT are widely used because they are simple to construct and ease employability [11,12].

In this chapter, we utilized a three-phase grid-connected SPV system with linear and nonlinear loads. The nonlinear loads include uninterruptible power supply (UPS), magnetic ballast fluorescent bulbs, light-emitting diode, etc. These nonlinear loads create power quality (PQ) issues such as distortions in power supply, power factor reductions, and load unbalancing [13,14]. Moreover, these mentioned PQ issues solutions are mentioned in the literature [15–17]. In addition, in the concern of grid-connected systems, the role of power electronics-based converters play a major role [18–22]. Also, PQ problems are an ongoing concern due to the use of electronic instruments such as information technology gadgets. To mitigate the utility grid's PQ concerns, the voltage source converter (VSC) operates as a shift grid-supporting converter, delivering energy to the grid. The comparison of alternative control algorithms for controlling grid-connected VSCs is reported in Ref. [23]. The strategies described here are based on estimating reference current from contaminated load current.

Various control strategies are adopted to cope up with the above-mentioned issue for the improvement in PQ. Also, various literature studies offered shunt active power filter (SAPF)-based compensation control techniques for distorted load currents. It is desired that the compensating control techniques should be fast and accurate, and they should have better filtering capabilities. A common control approach such as synchronous reference frame concepts (SRFT), Instantaneous reactive power theory (IRPT) is commonly employed for controlling the grid converter given in these literatures [24,25]. It is intended to decrease high switching ripples. But it suffers from poor dynamic performance.

SOGI and damped-SOGI-based methods are used in power electronics and power systems for different uses such as grid syncing, harmonic predictions, and control of grid-connected functions [26,8]. Both of these algorithms are based on a second-order integrator structure and can track signals with high accuracy and fast response. The stability study of these algorithms is important to ensure that they can work safely and correctly over a range of operating situations. The stability study of the damped-SOGI algorithm is similar to that of the SOGI algorithm, but with an extra damper factor that changes the root point. However, SOGI and damped SOGI suffer from poor DC offset rejection capability. Various conventional

Table 12.1 Conventional controllers and their behavior

Control algorithm	Behavior
SRFT, IRPT, and GI	Poor dynamic performance
SOGI	Poor DC offset rejection capabilities
SOGI-FLL	Inadequate higher-order harmonic filtering capability

algorithms and their behavior are tabulated in Table 12.1. For the DC offset rejection from the SOGI algorithm is well presented in the literature [27] for single-phase S-DTATCOM. Modified damped SOGI algorithm that has add-on features of DC offset rejection capability, as well as this algorithm, possesses a more stable response compared to the SOGI algorithm. Overall the proposed technique shows accurate and robust behavior with the multifunctional features of grid-connected SPV systems. The suggested system configuration with a modified damped SOGI algorithm is modeled in a MATLAB environment. Most important is that the presented system fulfills the IEEE-519 standard.

12.1.1 Background of the research work

The literature review indicates that various techniques have been utilized in grid-interfaced solar energy conversion systems. This is a type of SPV system that is connected to the electrical grid. It allows solar-generated electricity to be used on-site while also enabling any excess power to be exported to the grid. In addition, grid-tied solar systems are popular for both residential and commercial applications. They offer an efficient and cost-effective way to harness solar energy while remaining connected to the grid for additional power needs. PQ improvement techniques are methods used to enhance the quality of electrical power, ensuring that it meets the desired standards and is free from disturbances or abnormalities. Many PQ improvement techniques are available in the literature for PQ improvements. SRF and IPRT are the older techniques, also known as the dq0 or Park's transformation, which are mathematical techniques used in power systems for analyzing and controlling electrical quantities in three-phase systems. It is commonly employed in PQ improvement strategies. Moreover, the SRF theory is based on the idea of rotating reference frames and is particularly useful in situations where the control and correction of PQ issues such as voltage sags, harmonics and reactive power are needed. By changing the three-phase system into a two-coordinate orthogonal reference frame (dq or Park's frame), it improves the study and control of power flow and quality. The SOGI algorithm is known for its simplicity, accuracy, and ability to handle non-ideal conditions such as distorted waveforms and frequency variations. It has found widespread application in renewable energy systems, where accurate frequency synchronization is essential for efficient power conversion and grid integration. It's worth noting that the specific implementation details of the SOGI algorithm may vary depending on the application and the desired level of accuracy.

By employing this theory, PQ issues can be detected, analyzed, and compensated in real time. This enables power systems to mitigate voltage distortions, reactive power imbalances, and harmonic problems, ultimately leading to improved PQ for connected loads. It's important to note that the field of power systems and PQ is vast, and there may be more specific techniques. Therefore, it's always recommended to consult updated literature and domain experts for the latest developments in PQ improvement techniques.

12.2 SYSTEM TOPOLOGY

The utilized system shown in Figure 12.1, and the 22-kW solar PV system is interfaced with a three-phase grid. A solar PV array, MPPT controller, boost converter, DC bus capacitor, grid-interfaced inductors, ripple filter, and loads are included in the recommended system. Appendices include detailed construction data for the suggested system as well as the characteristics of solar data. The overall system is linked to a three-phase power grid,

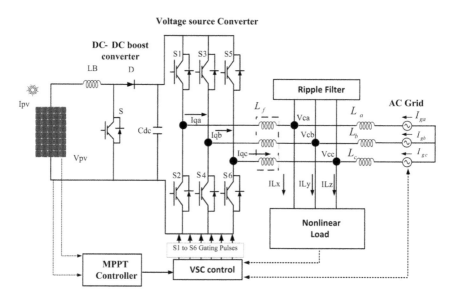

Figure 12.1 Proposed system of design.

as well as linear and nonlinear loads, through series resistance. The VSCs are used to turn the DC voltage made by the PV panels into AC voltage that can feed into the electricity grid. The VSC ensures that the AC voltage output from the PV system is synced with the grid. Filters are coupled at the point of common coupling (PCC) to eliminate switching ripples.

The whole system's behavior is mostly determined by how the control initiatives are constructed. The recommended system control method is intended for SPV arrays, boost converters, and VSC switching. Boost converter duty ratios are modified using an MPPT approach based on the INC technique. The MPPT technique based on the incremental conductance method is described in Figure 12.2.

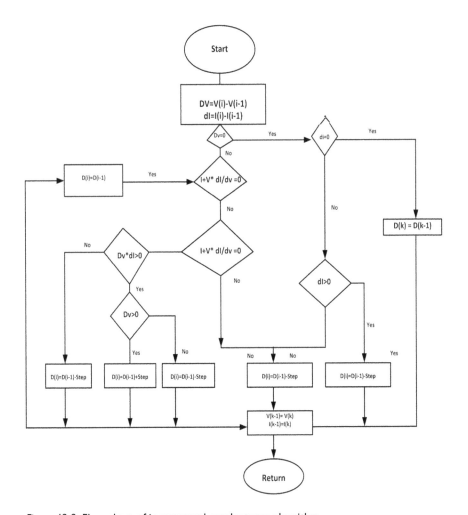

Figure 12.2 Flow chart of incremental conductance algorithm.

12.3 MPPT TECHNIQUE

MPPT is an approach used in photovoltaic (PV) systems to improve the power flow from solar panels. The goal of MPPT is to ensure that the PV system operates at its maximum power point (MPP) under changing weather conditions, such as changes in sunlight strength or temperature.

Solar panels have a characteristic voltage-current (V-I) curve that represents their power output at different operating points. The MPP is the point on this curve where the panel provides the highest possible power for a given set of variables. To maximize the energy collected from the solar panel, the MPPT method is applied to constantly track and change the working point of the panel to stay at or near the MPP. The choice of the MPPT method relies on factors such as system complexity, cost, efficiency, and weather variables. MPPT is commonly used in solar power systems, including grid-connected systems and standalone solar applications, like solar-powered water pumps and streetlights, to maximize power output and increase overall system efficiency.

12.3.1 Incremental conductance

Incremental conductance is a control method used MPPT systems for SPV panels. The goal of an MPPT system is to take the maximum power possible from a PV panel by constantly watching the MPP, which refers to the point at which the panel produces the highest output power. The incremental conductance method constantly measures the voltage and current output of the PV panel and generates the incremental conductance, which is the change in output power concerning change in voltage. By comparing the increasing conductance to zero, the program can determine whether the panel is working at the MPP or not. If the increasing resistance is negative, the program keeps the panel operating at the current voltage. If the incremental conductance is positive, it means that the panel is not yet working at the MPP and the voltage needs to be addressed. Conversely, if the incremental conductance is negative, it means that the panel has already passed the MPP and the voltage needs to be decreased. The incremental conductance algorithm is a popular choice for MPPT systems because it can track the MPP quickly and accurately, even in rapidly changing environmental conditions such as cloud cover or shading. This results in a more efficient and reliable solar power system. The graphical flow of incremental conductance is described in Figure 12.2.

12.4 PROPOSED MODIFIED DAMPED SOGI ALGORITHM

The proposed modified damped SOGI algorithm controller is presented in Figure 12.3. The objective of the modified damped SOGI algorithm

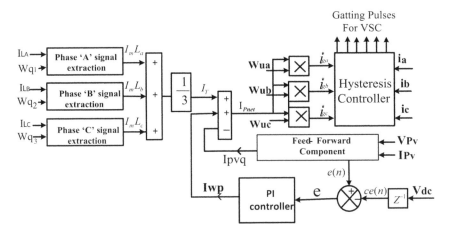

Figure 12.3 Modified damped SOGI algorithm.

controller control scheme is utilized to generate pulses for the inverter. The loop known as feed-forward (FF) is employed for the referencing current (I_{PVq}), which assists in dynamic characteristic enhancement. Moreover, solar photovoltaic power (P_{pv}) and interconnected voltages (V_{te}) are employed for calculating the reference current. The FF component of PV, current (I_{wp}), quadrature unit template (W_{q1}, W_{q2}, W_{q3}), and the in-phase unit template signals (W_{ua}, W_{ub}, W_{uc}) are employed for the VSC switching method. The PV-based FF component is approximated as,

$$I_{PVq} = \frac{2}{3} * \frac{P_{pv}}{V_{te}} \tag{12.1}$$

where V_{te}: is the terminal voltage magnitude is computed as,

$$V_{te} = \sqrt{\frac{2\left(V_{ga}^2 + V_{gb}^2 + V_{gc}^2\right)}{3}} \tag{12.2}$$

In-phase unit templates are,

$$W_{ua} = \frac{V_{ga}}{V_{te}}, \quad W_{ub} = \frac{V_{gb}}{V_{te}}, \quad W_{uc} = \frac{V_{gc}}{V_{te}} \tag{12.3}$$

The quadrature unit template is estimated as,

$$W_{q1} = \frac{W_{uc} - W_{ub}}{\sqrt{3}}, \quad W_{q2} = \frac{W_{ua} - W_{uc}}{\sqrt{3}}, \quad W_{q3} = \frac{W_{ub} - W_{ua}}{\sqrt{3}} \tag{12.4}$$

12.4.1 Fundamental active current component estimation

The magnitude and frequency of the fundamental load current (I_{fa}) are to be computed for the realization of the modified damped SOGI control scheme. Further, from figure 12.6 extaction of fundamental load current extaction presented.

$$I_1 = g_1 * e$$

where error $e = \left(I_{LA} - I_{fa} \right)$

$$\text{So, } I_1 = g_1 * \left(I_{LA} - I_{fa} \right) \tag{12.5}$$

$$I_2 = I_1 - I_3$$

$$I_2 = \left\{ g_1 * \left(I_{LA} - I_{fa} \right) \right\} - I_3 \tag{12.6}$$

where $I_6 = I_2 * I_5$

$$I_6 = \left\{ g_1 * (I_{LA} - I_{fa}) - I_3 \right\} * I_5 \tag{12.7}$$

$$I_5 = I_{fa} * W_c$$

where $W_c = I_4 + W_n$

$$I_4 = e * I_3 * \frac{g_2}{S} \tag{12.8}$$

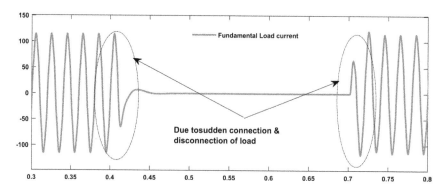

Figure 12.4 Fundamental load current waveform.

$$I_5 = I_{fa} * (I_4 + W_n)$$

$$= I_{fa} * \left(e * I_3 * \frac{g_2}{S} + W_n \right) \tag{12.9}$$

$$I_3 = \frac{1}{S} * I_5$$

$$I_3 = \frac{1}{S} * \left\{ I_{fa} * \left(e * I_3 * \frac{g_2}{S} + W_n \right) \right\} \tag{12.10}$$

where $I_{fa} = I_6 * \dfrac{1}{S}$

So, $I_{fa} = \dfrac{1}{S} * \left\{ g_1 * (I_{LA} - I_{fa}) - I_3 \right\} * I_5$

$$I_{fa} = \frac{1}{S} \left\{ g_1 * (I_{LA} - I_{fa}) - I_{fa} \left(\frac{e * I_3 * g_2 + W_n * S}{S^2} \right) \right\} * I_{fa} \left(\frac{e * I_3 * g_2}{S} + W_n \right) \tag{12.11}$$

The fundamental load current (I_{fa}), is in the same phase as the PCC voltage which can be represented mathematically in equation (12.12), and it can also be depicted in Figure 12.4 as,

$$I_{fa} = I_{max} \sin(W_c t - \phi_p)$$

$$= I_{max} \cos(\phi_p) \tag{12.12}$$

Figure 12.4 shows that the extracted fundamental load current is sinusoidal in nature as well as free from the harmonics. Also, it is noticed that in this figure the nature of fundamental current when one of the phase 'a' is suddenly disconnected on the duration of time $t=0.4$–0.7 seconds. But, in the load current components of harmonics are present on it and the nature of the load currents is in quasi square shape. Figure 12.5 depicts the nature of the quasi square form.

Also, for the extraction of constant active components value $(I_m L_a)$ of phase "a" from the input Sample & Hold (S & H), zero cross detector (ZCD) and quadrature vector components (W_{q1}) are utilized. Similarly, phase "b" and phase "c" can be extracted in similar manners. Now, equivalent component (I_T) can be estimated by all the three-phase divided by three. So, an equivalent three-phase current can be estimated as,

$$I_T = \frac{(I_m L_a + I_m L_b + I_m L_c)}{3} \tag{12.13}$$

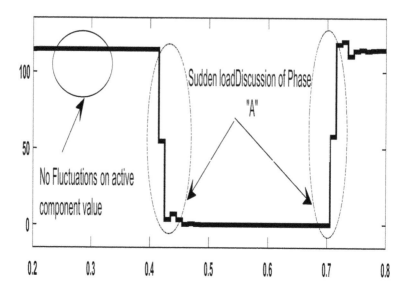

Figure 12.5 Nature of load current on sudden load discussion.

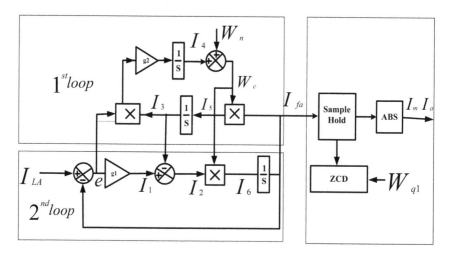

Figure 12.6 Block diagram for phase 'a' for modified damped SOGI.

12.4.2 Active loss component estimations

The active loss components (I_{Pnet}) are calculated as:-

$$I_{Pnet} = I_{Wp} + I_T - I_{PVq} \tag{12.14}$$

where I_{Wp}: DC bus voltage controller, I_T: Equivalent component of load current and I_{PVq}: FF output. Furthermore, the grid reference currents $(i_{ga}^*, i_{gb}^*, i_{gc}^*)$ are estimated by using the template of unit phase as,

$$i_{ga}^* = I_{Pnet} * W_{ua}, \ i_{gb}^* = I_{Pnet} * W_{ub}, \ i_{gc}^* = I_{Pnet} * W_{uc} \tag{12.15}$$

Likewise,

$$i_{ea} = i_{ga}^* - i_{ga}$$

$$i_{eb} = i_{gb}^* - i_{gb} \tag{12.16}$$

$$i_{ec} = i_{gc}^* - i_{gc}$$

where (i_{ea}, i_{eb}, i_{ec}) is the current error and (i_{ga}, i_{gb}, i_{gc}) is sensed grid current.

These assessed current error values are supplied into the hysteresis controller, which produces three getting signals. A NOT logic gate is used to convert these three signals to six gate pulses, which are then used to regulate the grid-connected VSC.

12.5 RESULTS AND DISCUSSION

Using MATLAB/Simulation software, the simulation is run with varied operating conditions to demonstrate the behavior of the suggested technique. The results were obtained by considering loads that are nonlinear at the location where there is common coupling. Simulation results are incorporated in the performance analysis of the proposed system. Following notations indicating in the shown waveforms as: solar irradiation (I_r), DC link bus voltage (V_{dc}), SPV current (I_{pv}), SPV power (P_{pv}), AC grid current (I_{gabc}), compensatory currents (I_{ca}, I_{cb}, I_{cc}) and load current (i_{La}, i_{Lb}, i_{Lc}).

12.5.1 The behavior of the system under constant irradiance with faulty conditions of load

Figure 12.7 demonstrates the nature of a solar PV system under nonlinear load with invariable irradiation. Also, with various circumstances of the waveforms represented as I_r, V_{dc}, I_g, i_{La}, i_{Lb}, i_{Lc}, i_{ca}, i_{cb}, and i_{cc}. It is shown that for the constant solar irradiance of 1,000 w/m², the DC link voltage is maintained constant at 700 V with very minute variations observed.

Figure 12.7 also depicts the behavior of an SPV system when one phase is purposefully unbalanced under nonlinear load conditions. The waveforms of I_r, V_{dc}, I_g, i_{La}, i_{Lb}, i_{Lc}, i_{ca}, i_{cb}, and i_{cc}, and V_t are shown in Figure 12.7. Suppose that the solar array continues to operate at 1,000 W/m² insolation but that phase '*a*' is purposefully removed at (*t*=0.6–0.7 seconds). Grid currents are stated to be precisely sinusoidal and balanced in both steady-state (before *t*=0.6 seconds and after *t*=0.7 seconds) and unbalanced (*t*=0.6–0.7 seconds) circumstances. During the unbalancing phase, the SPV-producing system satisfies the criteria for active power demand and load balancing. Yet, in this unbalanced scenario, the VSC DC bus voltage remains constant at 700 V.

12.5.2 The behavior of the system under varied solar irradiance

Figure 12.8 shows the behavior of a solar PV system, the solar irradiance initially on the duration of time at *t*=0–0.2 seconds is 600 W/m². But, just at *t*=0.2 seconds the solar irradiance intensity changed from 600 to 1000 W/m². On the other hand, the solar temperature is operated at 25 °C. It is observed with the above-mentioned variable conditions the DC link voltage is again constant as well as the grid current is purely balanced and sinusoidal in nature.

12.5.3 The behavior of the system under varied frequency variations

Figure 12.9 depicts the variation of frequency at different times of instants. As we can see the frequency varied at *t*=0.4 seconds and at *t*=0.5 seconds. At *t*=0.4 seconds the frequency is operated at 49.5 Hz and *t*=0.5 seconds the frequency is operated at 50.5 Hz. Under these circumstances, the DC

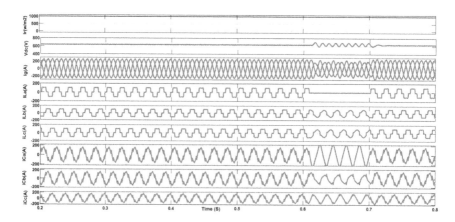

Figure 12.7 Solar PV system under nonlinear load for constant irradiance.

connection voltage remains constant at 700 V, and the grid current is similarly sinusoidal.

Figure 12.10 represents the FFT analysis for the number of cycles for 5, and the fundamental frequency of 50 Hz. It is shown that the THD of the source current is 1.78%. Therefore, it is concluded that the THD of grid current well follow the standard of IEEE, i.e., less than 5%.

12.6 CONCLUSION

The modified damped-SOGI method is effectively built and employed with the SPV system for gird interfaced mode. The designed modified damped-SOGI technique has been proven to be better than SOGI or other conventional algorithms due to its strong frequency response and high convergence rate. A brief mathematical analysis is presented for the estimation of the fundamental current from the load current. The SPV system has been shown to offer excellent response characteristics under variable insolation circumstances. Moreover, the SPV system's response at nonlinear loads was shown to be well adequate. Grid current harmonic analysis has been analyzed under varied solar irradiance, sudden load fluctuations, and faulty condition in the proposed system.

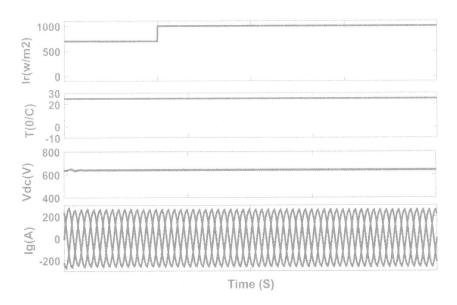

Figure 12.8 Solar PV system under varied solar irradiance.

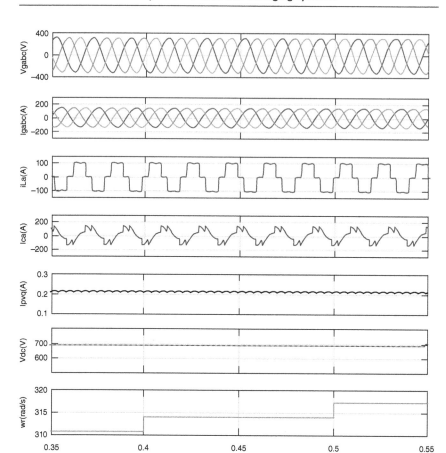

Figure 12.9 Variation of frequency.

APPENDIX

Solar capacity=22 kW, V_{oc}=46 V, I_{sc}=6 A, V_{mp}=40, N_p=40, N_s=4,
    Other Parameters:- V_{gabc} (V) (grid voltage)=415 V; V_{dc} (V)=700 V; filters values:- R=5 Ω, C=50 μF; connecting inductor=0.1 mH; loads value, R=4 Ω, L=20 mH.

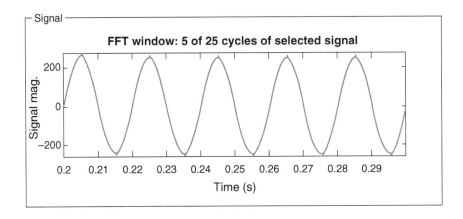

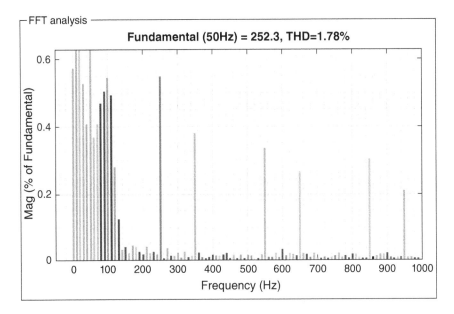

Figure 12.10 FFT analysis.

REFERENCES

1. S. Rahman, "Alternative energy sources: The quest for sustainable energy," *IEEE Power Energy Mag.*, vol. 5, no. 2, pp. 82–83, 2007.
2. Y. Li, S. S. Choi, C. Yang, and F. Wei, "Design of variable-speed dish Stirling solar-thermal power plant for maximum energy harness," *IEEE Trans. Energy Convers.*, vol. 30, no. 1, pp. 394–403, 2015.
3. M. Malinowski, J. I. Leon, and H. Abu-Rub, "Solar photovoltaic and thermal energy systems: Current technology and future trends," *Proc. IEEE*, vol. 105, no. 11, pp. 2132–2146, 2017, doi: 10.1109/JPROC.2017.2690343.

4. D. Barater, C. Concari, G. Buticchi, E. Gurpinar, D. De, and A. Castellazzi, "Performance evaluation of a 3-level ANPC photovoltaic grid-connected inverter with 650-V SiC devices and optimized PWM," *IEEE Trans. Ind. Appl.*, vol. 52, no. 3, pp. 2475–2485, 2016.

5. S. B. Kjaer, J. K. Pedersen, and F. Blaabjerg, "A review of single-phase grid-connected inverters for photovoltaic modules," *IEEE Trans. Ind. Appl.*, vol. 41, no. 5, pp. 1292–1306, 2005.

6. M. Das and V. Agarwal, "Novel high-performance standalone solar PV system with high-gain high-efficiency DC-DC converter power stages," *IEEE Trans. Ind. Appl.*, vol. 51, no. 6, pp. 4718–4728, 2015.

7. B. Xiao, L. Hang, J. Mei, C. Riley, L. M. Tolbert, and B. Ozpineci, "Modular cascaded H-bridge multilevel PV inverter with distributed MPPT for grid-connected applications," *IEEE Trans. Ind. Appl.*, vol. 51, no. 2, pp. 1722–1731, 2015.

8. B. Singh, S. Dwivedi, and C. Jain, "Damped-SOGI based control algorithm for solar PV power generating system," *IEEE Trans. Ind. Appl.*, vol. 53, no. 3, pp. 1780–1788, doi: 10.1109/TIA.2017.2677358.

9. S. Harb, M. Mirjafari, and R. S. Balog, "Ripple-port module-integrated inverter for grid-connected PV applications," *IEEE Trans. Ind. Appl.*, vol. 49, no. 6, pp. 2692–2698, 2013.

10. P. Sharma, S. P. Duttagupta, and V. Agarwal, "A novel approach for maximum power tracking from curved thin-film solar photovoltaic arrays under changing environmental conditions," *IEEE Trans. Ind. Appl.*, vol. 50, no. 6, pp. 4142–4151, 2014.

11. F. Paz and M. Ordonez, "High-performance solar MPPT using switching ripple identification based on a lock-in amplifier," *IEEE Trans. Ind. Electron.*, vol. 63, no. 6, pp. 3595–3604, 2016.

12. K. S. Tey and S. Mekhilef, "Modified incremental conductance algorithm for photovoltaic system under partial shading conditions and load variation," *IEEE Trans. Ind. Electron.*, vol. 61, no. 10, pp. 5384–5392, 2014.

13. A. R. Malekpour, A. Pahwa, A. Malekpour, and B. Natarajan, "Hierarchical architecture for integration of rooftop pv in smart distribution systems," *IEEE Trans. Smart Grid*, vol. 9, no. 3, pp. 2019–2029, 2017.

14. D. Prasad, N. Kumar, and R. Sharma, Shunt active power filter based on synchronous reference frame theory connected to SPV for power quality enrichment. In: Tomar, A., Malik, H., Kumar, P., Iqbal, A. (eds) *Machine Learning, Advances in Computing, Renewable Energy and Communication*. Lecture Notes in Electrical Engineering, vol. 768. Springer, Singapore, 2022. doi: 10.1007/978-981-16-2354-7_26.

15. B. Singh, A. Chandra, and K. A. Haddad, *Power Quality: Problems and Mitigation Techniques*. London: Wiley, 2015.

16. M. Bollen and I. Guo, *Signal Processing of Power Quality Disturbances*. Hoboken, NJ: Johm Wiley, 2006.

17. D. Prasad, N. Kumar, and R. Sharma, "Grid interfaced solar-wind hybrid power generating systems using fuzzy-based TOGI control technique for power quality improvement," *J. Intell. Fuzzy Syst.*, vol. 42, no. 2, pp. 1127–1139, 2022, doi: 10.3233/JIFS-189777.

18. J. M. Carrasco et al., "Power-electronic systems for the grid integration of renewable energy sources: A survey," *IEEE Trans. Ind. Electron.*, vol. 53, no. 4, pp. 1002–1016, 2006, doi: 10.1109/TIE.2006.878356.

19. J. M. Peter, "Main future trends for power semiconductors from the state of the art to future trends," presented at the *PCIM*, Nürnberg, Germany, Jun. 1999, Paper R2 667–671.

20. J. Rodriguez, J.-S. Lai, and F. Z. Peng, "Multilevel inverters: A survey of topologies, controls, and applications," *IEEE Trans. Ind. Electron.*, vol. 49, no. 4, pp. 724–738, 2002.

21. P. Jayaprakash, B. Singh, D. Kothari, A. Chandra, and K. Al-Haddad, "Control of reduced-rating dynamic voltage restorer with a battery energy storage system," *IEEE Trans. Ind. Appl.*, vol. 50, no. 2, pp. 1295–1303, 2014.

22. R. C. Portillo et al., "Modeling strategy for back-to-back three-level converters applied to high-power wind turbines," *IEEE Trans. Ind. Electron.*, vol. 53, no. 5, pp. 1483–1491, 2006, doi: 10.1109/TIE.2006.882025.

23. B. Singh and J. Solanki, "A comparison of control algorithms for DSTATCOM," *IEEE Trans. Ind. Electron.* vol. 56, no. 7, pp. 2738–2745, 2009.

24. J. Sul, K. Ljokelsoy, T. Midtsund, and T. Undeland, "Synchronous reference frame hysteresis current control for grid converter applications," *IEEE Trans. Ind. Appl.*, vol. 47, no. 5, pp. 2183–2194, 2011.

25. F. Wu, L. Zhang, and J. Duan, "A new two-phase stationary-frame-based enhanced PLL for three-phase grid synchronization," *IEEE Trans. Circuits Sys. II, Exp. Briefs*, vol. 62, no. 3, pp. 251–255, 2015.

26. S. Prakash, J. K. Singh, R. K. Behera, and A. Mondal, "Comprehensive Analysis of SOGI-PLL Based Algorithms for Single-Phase System," *2019 National Power Electronics Conference (NPEC)*, Tiruchirappalli, India, 2019, pp. 1–6, doi: 10.1109/NPEC47332.2019.9034724.

27. Smadi, I. A. and B. H. Bany Fawaz, DC offset rejection in a frequency-fixed second-order generalized integrator-based phase-locked loop for single-phase grid-connected applications. *Prot Control Mod. Power Syst.*, vol. 7, no. 1, pp. 1–13, 2022, doi: 10.1186/s41601-021-00223-w.

Chapter 13

An adaptive Reinforcement Learning MPPT technique applied to standalone solar PV system

Aurobinda Bag, Pratap Sekhar Puhan, and T. Anil Kumar

13.1 INTRODUCTION

Owing to the increasing demand for electrical energy for industrial and modern living standards, there is a need to supplement power for renewable energy as an alternative to conventional source of electric energy such as solar PV system, wind electrical system, fuel cell, biomass, etc. However, maximum power extraction from the solar PV system is a challenging task. A number of MPPT algorithms have been applied for the extraction of maximum output power from the solar PV system [1]. Some indirect methods, such as curve fitting, look-up table, open circuit voltage, and short circuit current MPPT algorithms, are available [2]. These MPPT methods are not suitable under changing environmental conditions.

Further, there are some direct algorithms such as hill climbing (HC) [3], Perturb and Observe (P&O) [4], and Incremental Conductance (IC) [5]. However, P&O and HC methods encounter serious problems due to continuous perturbation at the operating point with reduction in efficiency [6]. Another demerit of the P&O algorithm is the sensitiveness toward atmospheric changes as in Refs. [7–9]. Further, IC-MPPT algorithm suffers from significant recursion near the MPP are reported in Refs. [10,11].

In lieu of this, artificial intelligence-based MPPT control schemes, such as neural network (NN), particle swarm optimization (PSO) and fuzzy logic (FL), and sliding mode control (SMC), have been depicted in Refs. [12–16]. FL controller requires expert knowledge to design it properly. However, these are offline MPPT schemes which have fix problem applications.

The above-mentioned problem can be conquered using RL-based MPPT controller, which enables one to reach the MPP faster and quickly respond to change in atmospheric condition after learning. In the literature [17], the RL-based MPPT scheme is proposed to extract maximum output power from a wind electrical system. The reinforcement learning MPPT controller is implemented for a solar PV system as given in the literature [17–19].

DOI: 10.1201/9781003481065-13

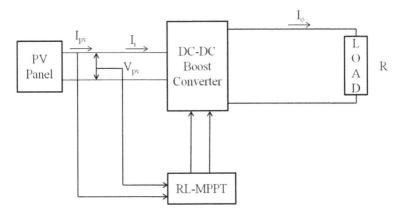

Figure 13.1 Configuration for isolated solar PV system.

Further, reinforcement learning MPPT controller is introduced in the literature [20] with a novel state definition.

However, in this chapter, a RL-MPPT algorithm is proposed for the
extraction of maximum output power from solar PV system during variable solar insolation and temperature conditions. The performance of the
RL-MPPT algorithm is evaluated in simulation and experimental setup
in comparison to IC-MPPT algorithm during changing environmental
conditions. The configuration of an isolated solar PV system is shown in
Figure 13.1.

13.2 REINFORCEMENT LEARNING
CONTROL ALGORITHM

In case of reinforcement learning algorithm, the agent is trained from its
personal experience with directly interrelating through conditions such as
states, actions and rewards. Reinforcement learning algorithm focuses for
mapping from states to actions to optimize rewards. In this algorithm, the
agent gets reward and accordingly takes step for transition from a state
$s \in S$ to another state $s' \in S$ on the way to the optimized output. Some of the
RL algorithms such as temporal difference learning, Q-learning associated
with finite Markov's Decision Process. Mostly finite Markov's Decision
Process is defined as a set of state S, set of action A, transition probability
function T, which defines the transition probability from the state $s \in S$ to
s' in which an action $a \in A$ is taken and the reward R which obtains after
every state transformation.

In reinforcement learning algorithm, the agent obtains a state response
that stands in for the states $s \in S$ of the surroundings. The agent takes an
action $a \in A$ in accordance to the mapping. Further, the action is extracted

in accordance to the action choosing strategy such as ε-greedy or soft-max. Just after one sample time, as the response of the action $a \in A$, state transformation causes from s to s' in accordance of the action choosing policy. After that, the agent gains the award $r \in R$, in accordance to the immediate outcome of the action 'a' of the exchange of the state. Then goal of the agent in case of RL control scheme is to attain action choosing policy to optimize the subsequent award.

13.3 REINFORCEMENT LEARNING MPPT SCHEME FOR SOLAR PV SYSTEM

Applying the reinforcement learning algorithm, for harvesting optimum power from the solar PV panel, the following three things, namely, state space, action space and reward, are required to be defined. The agent discovers the state of the conditions $s \in S$ that defines the point of operation for the solar PV panel and in accordance makes out a distinct control action $a \in A$ applying action choosing policy. The ε-greedy action choosing policy is used. Then the PV panel goes in for another point of operation. Concurrently, a reward r is obtained by an agent to refurbish the foregoing state action value. For obtaining optimum possible output power from solar photovoltaic panel, every instant a higher action should be selected with a higher probability.

a. **State:** The state, that narrates the situation of PV panel, is very important, in order to exhibit better performance for RL scheme. The state should have enough description and contain much information for describing system state. Further, large information leads to a much larger state space and lengthy learning time, whereas deficient information leads to increased learning inaccuracy.

The described state space for applying RL-MPPT is splitted into several states $s_1, s_2, s_3, s_4...s_n$ as defined in equation (13.1).

$$S = \left[s_1, s_2, s_3, s_4 \ldots s_n \right] \tag{13.1}$$

b. **Action:** The action area A could be defined by several numbers of required perturbations, which are implemented on the solar PV system for bringing the swap of the functioning of the PV system. The definition of action space is as follows:

$$A = \left\{ -2\Delta v, \Delta v, 0, \Delta v, 2\Delta v \right\} \tag{13.2}$$

Here, the big change is $2\Delta v$, little change as Δv and no change as 0 defined in photovoltaic panel voltage output. Further in every state, the agent has five numbers of actions in order to change the PV system operating point. Each time, an agent chooses an action according to detection of state and action picking strategy from the action area for extraction of maximum possible power from the solar PV panel.

c. **Reward:** After finishing the action choosing policy, the agent gets award for evaluating the choosing action. The defined reward function is as follows:

$$R = \begin{cases} +1, & \text{if } P_{pv,t+1} - P_{pv,t} > \delta \\ 0, & \text{if } P_{pv,t+1} - P_{pv,t} < \delta \\ -1, & \text{if } P_{pv,t+1} - P_{pv,t} < -\delta \end{cases} \tag{13.3}$$

in which $P_{pv,t+1}$ and $P_{pv,t}$ signify the power output of solar PV during consecutive time steps $t+1$ and t separately. δ stands in for a small valued positive number. The reward +1 signifies action which is required to take an augmentation of P_{pv} for agent; on the other hand, the reward –1 is meant for reduction of P_{pv} and 0 represents as no change.

13.4 REINFORCEMENT LEARNING ALGORITHM TO EXTRACT MPPT FROM SOLAR PV SYSTEM

The reinforcement learning scheme learns through its own occurrence with interrelating constantly with surrounding and executes the finest action after accomplishment of learning time in accordance with its comeback. The control scheme for drawing out of MPP from PV panel is a deterministic issue as the PV transitions would be similar for each state-action composition under the similar surroundings. So a deterministic strategy could be assimilated, and the applied discovery policy does not have to be persistent to acquire the latest model. Therefore, arbitrary investigation is required for state-action area prior to strategy investigation. The control scheme investigates for a definite round in accordance with the action area. Number of investigation steps may be determined by $i = a \times m$, in which 'a' represents different actions taken and the 'm' represents multiplier. For a large number of state and action steps, the 'm' should be chosen large. As soon as the total numbers of state action steps are discovered, the control scheme may be saturated for merging toward optimized strategy. The flowchart for the suggested reinforcement learning MPPT scheme is displayed in Figure 13.2, which is depicted below.

The Q-learning table is established simply putting zero to all starting value. After that, during every round, of assimilation V_{pv}, P_{pv} are sensed to

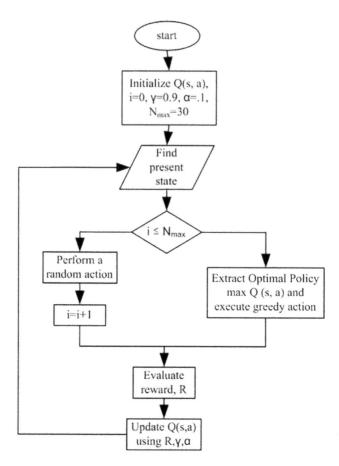

Figure 13.2 Flowchart for reinforcement learning-based MPPT algorithm for solar PV system.

calculate the indexes of state in the Q-learning table. Then action '*a*' is cho-sen arbitrarily from the area of action. Concurrently, the variable is incre-mented by 1. RL-MPPT control scheme begins by discovering the various state actions as late as '*m*' number of investigation steps per state is finished. At the starting every time step, a current state is realized. The reward *R* as in equation (13.3) can be computed with calculating the distinction among consecutive solar PV power outputs. The optimum value in the successive state is taken out and conveyed as $\max_{a'} = Q_{(s', a')}$.

Q-learning current rule can be evaluated by the state action values as follows:

$$Q'_{(s,a)} = Q_{(s',a')} + \alpha \left[R + \gamma \max_{a'} Q'_{(s',a')} - Q_{(s,a)} \right] \tag{13.4}$$

in which α represents the learning rate where as γ represents the discount factor.

Larger learning rates follow fast convergence, but it may cause fluctuation at non-optimized value. So, choosing a smaller value of α can cause convergence. On the other hand, γ equals to 1, which could result the better reward for future. In the final investigation, an optimized strategy should be chosen for finest state action combinations.

13.5 INCREMENTAL CONDUCTANCE MPPT SCHEME

The IC-MPPT control scheme is well known for its better MPPT characteristics [10]. Figure 13.3 depicts the flowchart for the IC-MPPT scheme. IC-MPPT scheme differentiates the incremental conductance to instantaneous conductance. When the operating point reaches at MPP, then perturbation stops and PV operation holds at this point. When the operating

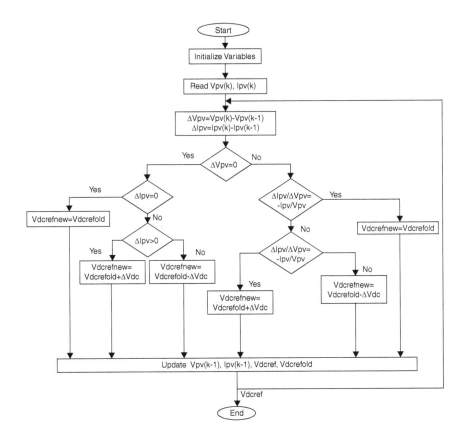

Figure 13.3 Incremental conductance MPPT control scheme.

current changes, the control scheme is in such a way that, voltage can be increased or decreased to achieve a new operating point corresponding to the maximum power point. The MPP can be tracked quickly choosing the correct step size. The optimized point of operation for the P-V curve is at the left side of the MPP indicates $(\Delta I_{pv}/\Delta V_{pv})+(I_{pv}/V_{pv})>0$, the voltage of PV panel needs to improve to obtain MPP. Further this point comes under right to the MPP, i.e., $(\Delta I_{pv}/\Delta V_{pv})+(I_{pv}/V_{pv})<0$, then the PV output PV panel voltage requires to reduce for achieving MPP.

13.6 SIMULATED OUTPUT AND DISCUSSIONS

Figure 13.4 shows that in the first case the solar irradiance and temperature remain constant. Figure 13.4a–c describes the input power, current and voltage to DC-DC boost converter, which is out from the solar PV system at constant solar irradiance and temperature condition. When we compare them with their output from DC-DC boost converter, there will be rise in voltage and fall in current to keep the power to be constant as depicted in Figure 13.4d–f, respectively. The input and output power remains unchanged for the DC-DC converter, and it boosts the given voltage from 110 to 210 V and at the same time fall in current from 23 A to nearly 12 A and the power remains unchanged before and after applying to converter, i.e., 2,400 W.

Further in the second case, the temperature of the solar cell is changing and keeping the irradiance as constant as in Figure 13.5a. It is observed that if the temperature of the module increases, then there will be fall in produced power of the solar cell which results in decreasing the overall power produced at normal conditions. As we can clearly see from Figure 13.5 when the temperature increases from 297° to 323° Kelvin in 0.6 seconds, the current produced by PV cell also reduces initially producing 23 A and it falls to 21 A because of rise in temperature. Further, the temperature increased to 335° Kelvin at 0.8 seconds, and the current will reduce to 19 A as observed from Figure 13.5b and e. Similarly, the power and voltage of the system also decrease, which can be observed from Figure 13.5c, d, f, and g. The panel will work efficiently at 295°K.

In the third case, the temperature is kept constant by varying the irradiation of the solar cell as in Figure 13.6a. As the irradiance of the module decreases then the power produced also decreases which can be seen in Figure 13.6. During irradiance 1,000 W/m², the power generated will be 2,400 W at an instant 0.5 seconds, the irradiance was reduced to 750 W/m² and then automatically the power generated also reduced to 1,500 W, as shown in Figure 13.6c and f. Further, it reduced to 500 W/m² at 0.75 seconds, and the power generated will be 750 W. Similarly, the input and output voltages and currents of the converter will be decreased, which is observed from Figure 13.6b, d, e, and g, respectively.

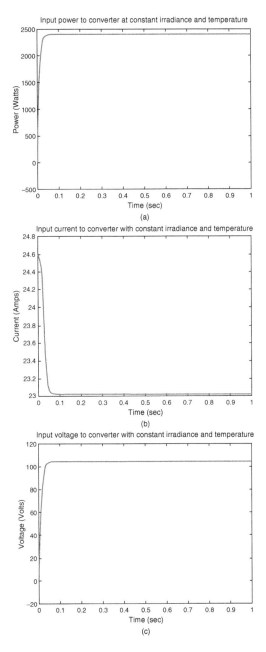

Figure 13.4 (a) Input power to converter during constant solar irradiance and temperatures, (b) Input current to converter during constant solar irradiance and
temperatures, (c) Input voltage to converter during constant solar irradiance
and temperatures, (d) Output power from converter during constant solar
irradiance and temperatures, (e) Output current from converter during constant solar irradiance and temperatures, (f) Output voltage from controller
during constant solar irradiance and temperatures.

(Continued)

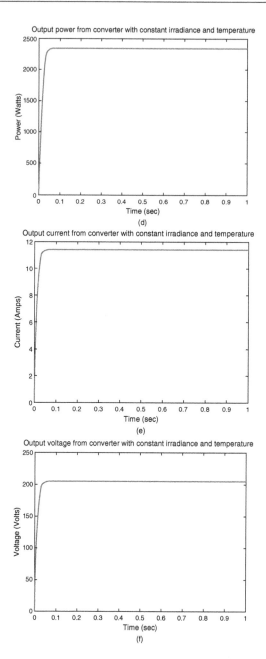

Figure 13.4 (Continued) (a) Input power to converter during constant solar irradiance and temperatures, (b) Input current to converter during constant solar irradiance and temperatures, (c) Input voltage to converter during constant solar irradiance and temperatures, (d) Output power from converter during constant solar irradiance and temperatures, (e) Output current from converter during constant solar irradiance and temperatures, (f) Output voltage from controller during constant solar irradiance and temperatures.

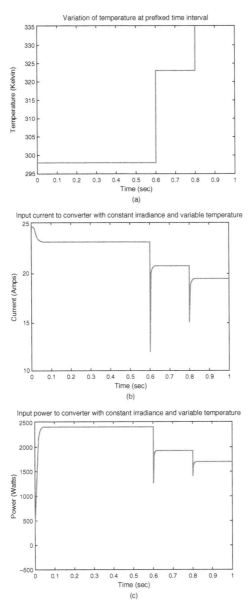

Figure 13.5 (a) Variation of temperature of solar PV system, (b) Input current to converter during constant solar irradiance and variable temperatures, (c) Input
power to converter during constant solar irradiance and variable temperatures, (d) Input voltage to converter during constant solar irradiance and
variable temperatures, (e) Output current to converter during constant solar
irradiance and variable temperatures, (f) Output power to converter during
constant solar irradiance and variable temperatures, (g) Output voltage to
converter during constant solar irradiance and variable temperatures.

(Continued)

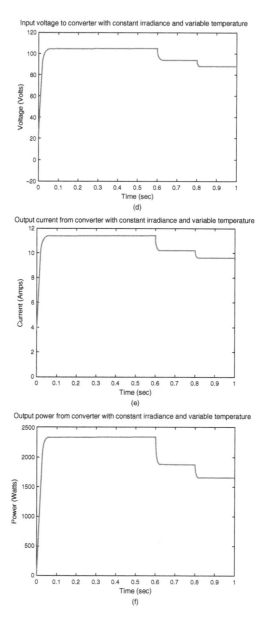

Figure 13.5 (Continued) (a) Variation of temperature of solar PV system, (b) Input current to converter during constant solar irradiance and variable temperatures, (c) Input power to converter during constant solar irradiance and variable temperatures, (d) Input voltage to converter during constant solar irradiance and variable temperatures, (e) Output current to converter during constant solar irradiance and variable temperatures, (f) Output power to converter during constant solar irradiance and variable temperatures, (g) Output voltage to converter during constant solar irradiance and variable temperatures.

(Continued)

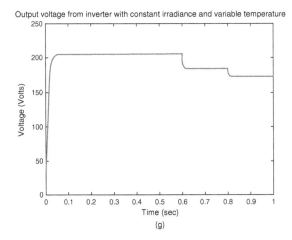

Figure 13.5 (Continued) (a) Variation of temperature of solar PV system, (b) Input current to converter during constant solar irradiance and variable temperatures, (c) Input power to converter during constant solar irradiance and variable temperatures, (d) Input voltage to converter during constant solar irradiance and variable temperatures, (e) Output current to converter during constant solar irradiance and variable temperatures, (f) Output power to converter during constant solar irradiance and variable temperatures, (g) Output voltage to converter during constant solar irradiance and variable temperatures.

From Figure 13.7a, it is seen that for the RL-MPPT control scheme 0.09 seconds is required for reaching the steady-state conditions, which is earlier in IC-MPPT (0.07 seconds) at starting (during training). But when the RL-MPPT scheme is learned properly, it then tracks MPPT faster than the IC-MPPT scheme during variation in solar irradiance as shown in Figure 13.8. This may be due to the learning ability of the RL-MPPT scheme. Fewer ripples reflected in the RL-MPPT scheme in comparison to the IC-MPPT scheme after learning.

As shown in Figure 13.7b, in RL-MPPT, it takes 0.09 seconds to reach the steady-state position. But for IC-MPPT, it takes 0.07 seconds to reach the MPP. After learning RL-MPPT tracks faster than IC-MPPT during change in temperatures. Fewer ripples reflect in the RL-MPPT scheme in comparison to IC-MPPT just after change in temperature when the RL algorithm is properly learned. The simulation results validate the effective learning ability of the RL-MPPT scheme in comparison to the IC-MPPT scheme. Consequently, the RL-MPPT scheme gives better result as compared to the IC-MPPT scheme.

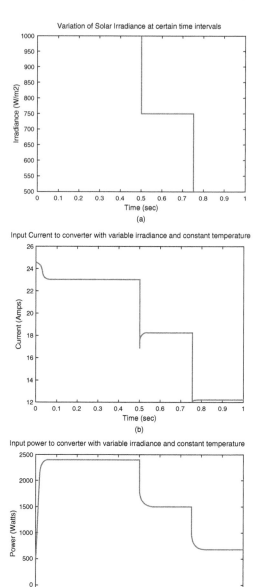

Figure 13.6 (a) Variations of irradiance of solar PV system, (b) Input current to converter during variable solar irradiance and constant temperatures, (c) Input power to converter during variable solar irradiance and constant temperatures, (d) Input voltage to converter during variable solar irradiance and constant temperatures, (e) Output current to converter during variable solar irradiance and constant temperatures, (f) Output power to converter during variable solar irradiance and constant temperatures, (g) Output voltage to converter during variable solar irradiance and constant temperatures.

(Continued)

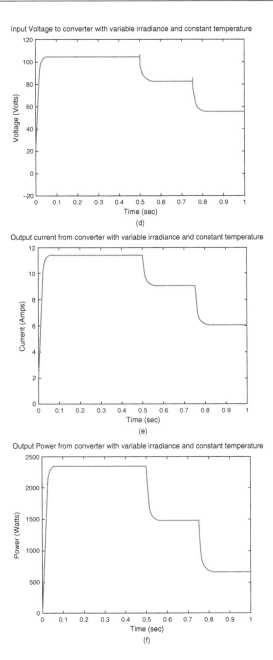

Figure 13.6 (Continued) (a) Variations of irradiance of solar PV system, (b) Input current to converter during variable solar irradiance and constant temperatures, (c) Input power to converter during variable solar irradiance and constant temperatures, (d) Input voltage to converter during variable solar irradiance and constant temperatures, (e) Output current to converter during variable solar irradiance and constant temperatures, (f) Output power to converter during variable solar irradiance and constant temperatures, (g) Output voltage to converter during variable solar irradiance and constant temperatures.

(Continued)

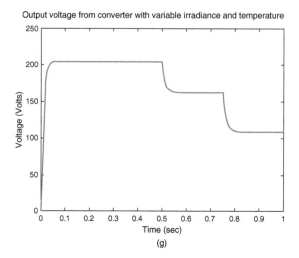

Figure 13.6 (a) Variations of irradiance of solar PV system, (b) Input current to converter during variable solar irradiance and constant temperatures, (c) Input power to converter during variable solar irradiance and constant temperatures, (d) Input voltage to converter during variable solar irradiance and constant temperatures, (e) Output current to converter during variable solar irradiance and constant temperatures, (f) Output power to converter during variable solar irradiance and constant temperatures, (g) Output voltage to converter during variable solar irradiance and constant temperatures.

13.7 EXPERIMENTAL RESULTS

The RL-MPPT control scheme is implemented in the experimental setup, which consists of a solar array simulator. The output of the solar array simulator is connected to the DC-DC boost converter. The RL-MPPT and IC-MPPT algorithm is proposed in the DC-DC boost converter using the dSPACE 1103 control platform. The MPPT tracking performance of the experimental setup is shown in Figure 13.8. As shown in Figure 13.8a and b, it is observed that implementing the RL-MPPT scheme in experimental setup, 99.8% of MPPT has to be obtained as compared to the IC-MPPT scheme, which is 98.6%. So in the experimental setup, the RL-MPPT scheme exhibits outstanding performance as compared to the IC-MPPT scheme due to the learning ability of the RL control scheme. The comparison of the RL-MPPT scheme with the IC-MPPT scheme is tabulated in Table 13.1.

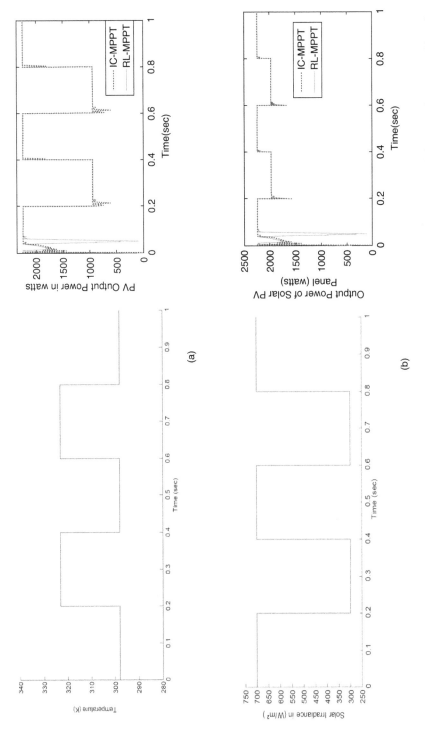

Figure 13.7 (a) Comparison of output PV power during variable solar temperatures, (b) Comparison of output PV power during variable solar irradiance.

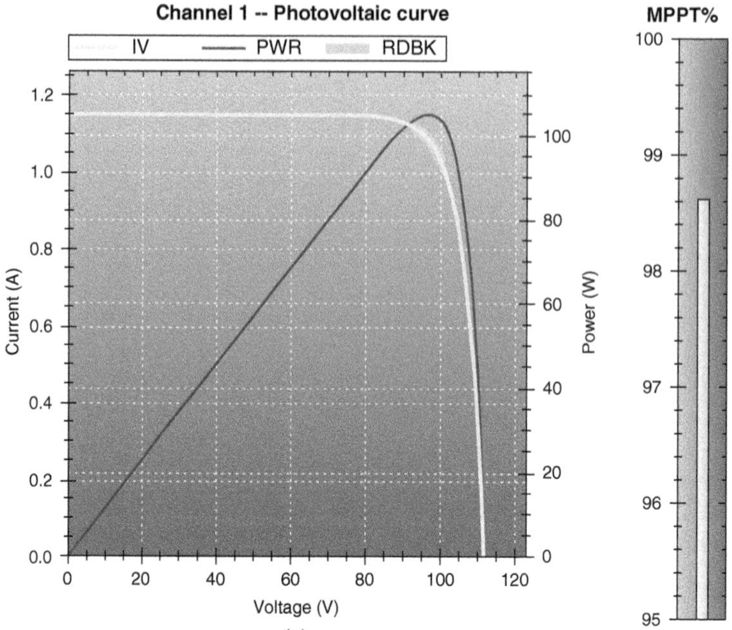

Figure 13.8 (a) Performance of Maximum Power Point Tracking in RL-MPPT scheme, (b) Performance of Maximum Power Point Tracking in IC-MPPT scheme algorithm.

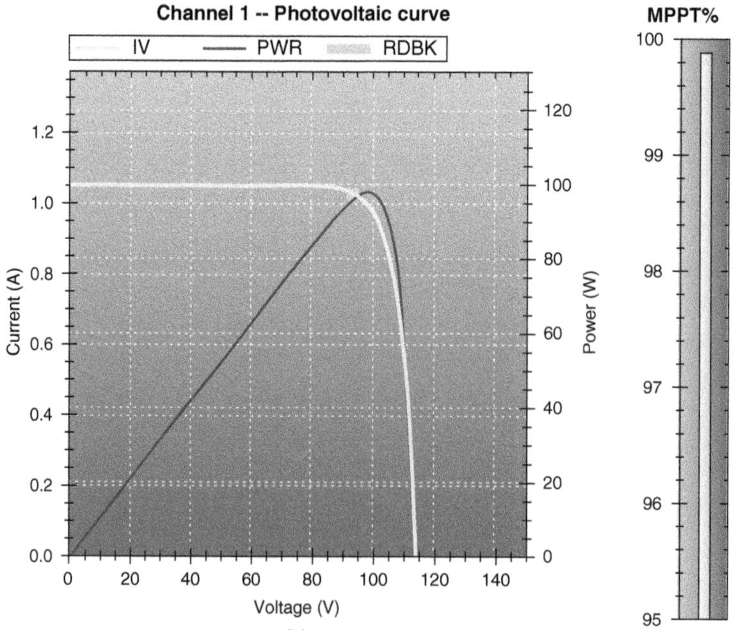

Table.13.1 Comparison of RL-MPPT and IC-MPPT Controllers

Type	RL-MPPT	IC-MPPT
Online learning ability	Yes	No
MPPT tracking performance % (experimental)	99.8	98.6
Duration (seconds) for sustain of ripple in PV output power during change in irradiance (after learning)	0.02	0.025
Duration (seconds) for sustain of ripple content in PV output power during change in temperature (after learning)	0.01	0.02

13.8 CONCLUSION

RL-MPPT control scheme is proposed on a standalone solar photovoltaic system for deriving the maximum output power at different environmental conditions like change in solar irradiance and temperature. The RL-MPPT scheme is implemented on the solar photovoltaic system in MATLAB/Simulink as well as on the developed experimental setup. The RL-MPPT algorithm incorporates with online learning ability, which results in better MPPT tracking efficiency under changing environmental conditions. So the performance of the RL-MPPT scheme is computed by comparing the conventional IC-MPPT algorithm in simulation and experimental setup developed. It is observed that in simulation and experimental setup, the RL-MPPT algorithm exhibits outstanding performance like fast MPPT as compared to the IC-MPPT algorithm during variable solar irradiance and temperature conditions when it is properly learned.

REFERENCES

1. B. Subudhi and R. Pradhan, "A comparative study on maximum power point tracking techniques for photovoltaic power systems", *IEEE Transactions on Sustainable Energy*, vol. 4, no. 1, pp. 89–98, 2013.
2. P. Das, "Maximum power tracking based open circuit voltage method for PV system", *Energy Procedia*, vol. 90, pp. 2–13, 2016.
3. C. B. N. Fapi, P. Wira, M. Kamta, A. Badji, and H. Tchakounte, "Real-time experimental assessment of Hill Climbing MPPT algorithm enhanced by estimating a duty cycle for PV system", *International Journal of Renewable Energy Research*, vol. 9, 1180–1189, 2019.
4. M. Kamran, M. Mudassar, M. R. Fazal, M. U. Asghar, M. Bilal, and R. Asghar, "Implementation of improved Perturb & Observe MPPT technique with confined search space for standalone photovoltaic system", *Journal of King Saud University-Engineering Sciences*, vol. 32, no. 7, pp. 432–441, 2020.
5. H. Siva and S. Balaraman, "Step incremental conductance MPPT for solar PV system based on fuzzy logic controller", *Journal of Trends in Computer Science and Smart Technology*, vol. 4, no. 1, pp. 23–29, 2022.
6. M. A. Elgendy, B. Zahawi, and D. J. Atkinson, "Assessment of perturb and observe MPPT algorithm implementation techniques for PV pumping applications", *IEEE Transactions on Sustainable Energy*, vol. 3, no. 1, pp. 21–33, 2012.

7. N. Femia, G. Petrone, G. Spagnuolo, and M. Vitelli, "Optimization of perturb and observe maximum power point tracking method", *IEEE Transactions on Power Electronics*, vol. 20, no. 4, pp. 963–973, 2005.

8. M. A. Elgendy, B. Zahawi, and D. J. Atkinson, "Operating characteristics of the perturb and observe algorithm at high perturbation frequencies for stand-alone PV systems", *IEEE Transactions on Energy Conversion*, vol. 30, no. 1, pp. 189–198, 2015.

9. M. A. G. De Brito, L. Galotto, L. P. Sampaio, G. D. A. e Melo, and C. A. Canesin, "Evaluation of the main MPPT techniques for photovoltaic applications", *IEEE Transactions on Industrial Electronics*, vol. 60, no. 3, pp. 1156–1167, 2013.

10. M. A. Elgendy, B. Zahawi, and D. J. Atkinson, "Assessment of the incremental conductance maximum power point tracking algorithm", *IEEE Transactions on Sustainable Energy*, vol. 4, no. 1, pp. 108–117, 2013.

11. K. Visweswara, "An investigation of incremental conductance based maximum power point tracking for photovoltaic system", *Energy Procedia*, vol. 54, pp. 11–20, 2014.

12. A. I. Dounis, P. Kofinas, G. Papadakis, and C. Alafodimos, "A direct adaptive neural control for maximum power point tracking of photovoltaic system", *Solar Energy*, vol. 115, pp. 145–165, 2015.

13. A. Mellit and S. A. Kalogirou, "MPPT-based artificial intelligence techniques for photovoltaic systems and its implementation into field programmable gate array chips: Review of current status and future perspectives", *Energy*, vol. 70, pp. 1–21, 2014.

14. K. Ishaque, Z. Salam, M. Amjad, and S. Mekhilef, "An improved particle swarm optimization (PSO)-based mppt for pv with reduced steady-state oscillation", *IEEE Transactions on Power Electronics*, vol. 27, no. 8, pp. 3627–3638, 2012.

15. P. Singh, D. Palwalia, A. Gupta, and P. Kumar, "Comparison of photovoltaic array maximum power point tracking techniques", *International Journal of Advanced Research in Science, Engineering and Technology*, vol. 2, no. 1, pp. 401–404, 2015.

16. C. C. Chu and C. L. Chen, "Robust maximum power point tracking method for photovoltaic cells: A sliding mode control approach", *Solar Energy*, vol. 83, no. 8, pp. 1370–1378, 2009.

17. C. Wei, Z. Zhang, W. Qiao, and L. Qu, "Reinforcement-learning-based intelligent maximum power point tracking control for wind energy conversion systems", *IEEE Transactions on Industrial Electronics*, vol. 62, no. 10, pp. 6360–6370, 2015.

18. R. C. Hsu, C. T. Liu, W. Y. Chen, H. I. Hsieh, and H. L. Wang, "A reinforcement learning-based maximum power point tracking method for photovoltaic array", *International Journal of Photo-Energy*, vol. 2015, pp. 1–12, Mar 2015.

19. A. Youssef, M. E. Telbany, and A. Zekry, "Reinforcement learning for online maximum power point tracking control", *Journal of Clean Energy Technologies*, vol. 4, no. 4, pp. 245–248, 2016.

20. P. Kofinas, S. Doltsinis, A. Dounis, and G. Vouros, "A reinforcement learning approach for MPPT control method of photovoltaic sources", *Renewable Energy*, vol. 108, pp. 461–473, 2017.

Chapter 14

Technical and economic evaluation of renewable powered electric vehicle charging loads for New Delhi region

Mohd Bilal, Fareed Ahmad,
Arshad Mohammad, and M. Rizwan

14.1 INTRODUCTION

The transportation sector in India plays an utmost role in the production of harmful gases, primarily in the form of CO_2. In addition, CO_2 emissions are accelerated by the energy and agricultural sectors. The increasing population has resulted in considerable increase in the number of automobiles, exacerbating pollution and fuel consumption. To tackle this issue, the adoption of EVs is steadily increasing as they generate lower pollution levels. However, the rapid proliferation of EVs has placed a considerable demand on the utility grid, particularly as EV users charge their vehicles in residential areas without generating revenue for the electrical sector. Consequently, India's grid infrastructure is facing strain. To alleviate this burden, a viable plan for electricity generation is necessary, and this research aims to explore the deployment of RE sources in conjunction with the grid to meet the growing EV load requirements. Such research endeavours have been scarce in previous studies. Globally, the adoption of EVs is on the rise, resulting in increased interest in the energy consumption sector as a burgeoning field of investigation. This subsection examines the current state of charging infrastructure, electricity generation from renewables for EV charging, energy costs, and the potential decrease in harmful emissions through the deployment of alternative mode of charging the EVs. The energy and transport sectors are major contributors to global carbon footprints. While renewable energy (RE) resources mitigate the release of harmful gases into the atmosphere, grid-powered EVs can significantly reduce the carbon footprint in the transportation market. By integrating RE sources with EVs, there is great potential to address both economic and environmental challenges. Numerous studies have explored the functionality of EVs and RE sources within system configurations, including ideal hybrid setups such as Solar/Wind/Diesel/Battery systems. Among these, solar photovoltaics (SPV)

DOI: 10.1201/9781003481065-14

255

systems have proven to be more practical and cost-effective compared to wind turbine (WT) systems [1]. The importance of designing RE systems appropriately cannot be overstated, given the significant growth and adoption of such systems in the past decade. It is crucial to ensure that these systems are designed with reliability in mind while also maintaining reasonable costs [2]. Failing to appropriately size a configuration can result in technical constraints being violated and resource scarcity, while an oversized system can become excessively costly. Therefore, it is essential to employ optimization strategies based on metaheuristics to fix the optimal number of decision variables for system design. As part of this sizing approach, the element of the interconnected system needs to be assembled and interconnected to assess its efficiency under specific climatic conditions. This involves evaluating the power generation from RES and monitoring the charge state of BES. Existing literature discusses various sizing approaches, including recursive strategies [3] and software platforms including HOMER [4]. The utilization of traditional strategies that rely on recursion, numerical calculations, or statistical techniques has significantly declined. In contrast, there has been a growing interest in employing optimization techniques as alternatives, which offer great promise for addressing optimization challenges. Metaheuristics, in particular, have proven to be highly effective in this regard [5]. Numerous studies [6] have been carried out in an attempt to apply these algorithms for achieving optimal sizing of RE units [6]. The study investigates the realistic boundaries of the EV sector in China and analyses the impact of subsidies on an automaker's optimum generation and price choices [7]. A comprehensive survey of placing EV load in distribution and transportation network is performed [8,9]. Using the HOMER software application, a feasibility analysis of an SPV-powered EV charging station in Shenzhen, China is conducted. This predicted solution solves grid-related power concerns by combining SPV and satisfying the future demands for EVs [10]. Several studies see the inclusion of RES, including SPV, into charging infrastructure as the optimal strategy for increasing the fiscal and ecological benefits of EVs and supporting the concept of a smart grid [11]. The implementation of an AI-based algorithm for improving the design parameters of a distribution network [12]. The authors of Ref. [13] explain several parts of the formulation of the issue, selecting the design variables and the creation of a probability distribution function to enhance efficiency and efficacy. A hybrid model of two optimization algorithms, i.e., genetic algorithm and particle swarm optimization, is developed to perform the optimal charging and discharging of EV load for reducing the losses, improvement in voltage fluctuations and minimization of charging cost [14]. The authors of Ref. [15] introduced an improved optimization strategy to effectively determine the proper node for placing the EV load in the IEEE 33-bus system. The amount of solar power generation to power the EV load has been estimated using artificial intelligence-based techniques. In Ref. [16], the hybrid model of SPV and WT integrated with grid has been developed to meet the demand of shopping malls and EV load. Using an artificial colony of bees and PSO, the different components are optimally sized to acquire minimum energy cost and component cost. This research will show the optimal approach and operations of a RES-powered EV charging station aiming to make reduction in emission and energy cost. The hybrid model suggested consists of SPV, WT, bio-gas, batteries, and DG units [17]. The authors of Ref. [18] developed a cost-based model for placing EV load considering uncertainties associated with EV arrival and departure time. In Ref. [19], the evaluation of technical possibility of building an independent fast electric vehicle charging station (EVCS) in Qatar comprising WT, SPV, bio-generator as RES, and numerous storage systems is presented. Using the HOMER programme, the envisioned architecture is developed, analyzed, and simulated to identify the optimal techno-economic configuration for the daily rapid charging of 50 EVs. Spatial limitations, the predictable nature of EV load, and the weather circumstances of the place under consideration are all considered. The SPV power is supplied to EVs, and surplus electricity is sold to the utility on the HOMER platform. The author developed a modelling scheme for an SPV/Wind/BES for a desolate terrain using genetic algorithms [20]. The authors employed the GWO algorithm for the deployment of EV load in highly populated regions of South Delhi, India [21]. A multi-objective PSO is proposed for sizing and analysis of an SPV/WT/hydroelectric power plant in connection to a pumped-storage powered system [22].

The energy sources for the hybrid system in this study are SPV modules, battery units, and the utility grid. To evaluate the effectiveness of the suggested framework with that of a standard model, the framework is built as a simple microgrid. The primary purpose of this chapter is to address the issue of component sizing by lowering the cost of the various components as well as the cost of energy while keeping in mind that the reliability constraint must not exceed the established limitations. The levelized energy cost (LCOE) is another metric used to evaluate the performance of an integrated system. The optimization method is based on a year's worth of real-time data of sun intensity and ambient temperature.

14.2 MATHEMATICAL MODELLING OF SYSTEM COMPONENTS

This section deals with the interconnection of different system components and their mathematical modelling. The hybrid energy system being studied consists of an SPV panel, battery, inverter, and backup grid. A schematic representation of the proposed grid-connected system is illustrated in Figure 14.1.

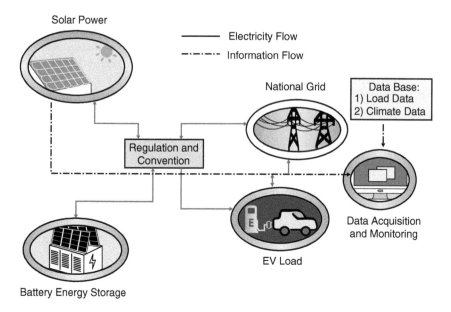

Figure 14.1 Schematic diagram of different system components.

14.2.1 Modelling of solar array

The energy generation from SPV relies on several factors, including the dimensions of the installed solar panel, the amount of solar radiation incidenting on the peripherals of the solar array, the ambient temperature of the solar cell, and the geographical position of the solar panel. These factors can be mathematically expressed using equation (14.1).

$$P_{\text{SPV}}(t) = \eta_{\text{SPV}} A_{\text{SPV}} I_h(t) \{1 - 0.005(T_c - 25)\} \tag{14.1}$$

where η_{SPV} and A_{SPV} denotes the efficiency and area of solar panels respectively, $I_h(t)$ denotes the solar radiation incidenting on the peripherals of the solar array and T_c is the ambient temperature of solar cell. The basic input factors for the SPV module are listed in Table 14.1.

14.2.2 Battery energy storage

Owing to the unpredictable pattern of SPV production, it is crucial to size the batteries correctly in order to meet the load requirements. The charging and discharging cycles of the battery depend on its current charge level.

In certain cases, the battery's condition fluctuates based on its power production and load profile. The exchange of power between the RES and load is properly managed by employing the highly efficient BES. The BES is said to be in a charging state when electrical energy generated by RES exceeds

Table 14.1 Input parameters for system component [24]

Components	Characteristics	Values
Solar PV panel	Maximum capacity	325 W
	Capital cost	950 $/kW
	Replacement cost	900 $/kW
	Operation & maintenance cost	10 $/kW
	Time	25 years
Battery	Capital cost	235 $/kW
	Replacement cost	190 $/kW
	Operation and maintenance cost	2 $/kW/year
Bidirectional converter	Capital cost	171 $/kW
	Replacement cost	171 $/kW
	Operation and maintenance cost	4 $/kW/year
Utility grid	Grid acquisition price	0.12 $/kWh
	Grid selling price	$/kWh

the load requirement. The state of charging of the BES at instant τ may be expressed as follows [23]:

$$SOC_{bat}(\tau+1) = SOC_{bat}(\tau)(1-\sigma) + \left[P_{SPV}(\tau) - P_{EVCS\text{-}dem}(\tau) \right] * \eta_{bat} \quad (14.2)$$

On the other hand, when RES are insufficient to supply the EV charging demand, the battery serves as a reserve to supply the load and operates in a draining condition. The discharge state of the BES at instant τ can be described as follows:

$$SOC_{bat}(\tau+1) = SOC_{bat}(\tau)(1-\sigma) - \frac{\left[P_{EVCS\text{-}dem}(\tau) - P_{SPV}(\tau) \right]}{\eta_{bat}} \quad (14.3)$$

where $SOC_{bat}(\tau)$ and $SOC_{bat}(\tau+1)$ stands for the SOC of BES at instant (τ) and $(\tau+1)$ respectively, σ determines the rate at which battery discharges, η_{bdinv} is the efficiency of inverter, $P_{SPV}(\tau)$ are the power output of SPV and η_{bat} is the round trip efficiency of the BES.

14.2.3 Modelling of bidirectional inverter

The bidirectional inverter is deployed for transforming DC quantity to AC and vice versa. The energy extracted from SPV panels is in DC form, which is further fed to the EVs. The output of the bidirectional inverter is transformed into DC/AC using equation (14.4):

$$P_{AC} = \eta_{bdinv} * P_{DC} \quad (14.4)$$

P_{AC} and P_{DC} represents the AC and DC power, η_{bdinv} represents the efficiency of bidirectional inverter.

The suggested system assumes a 97% bidirectional inverter efficiency.

14.2.4 Utility grid

In situations, when the output power from RES and battery output are inadequate to satisfy the power demand of load, the energy deficit may be met by borrowed energy from the grid network, as shown in equation (14.5):

$$P_{Purc}^{grid}(t) = P_D^{EV}(t) - \left[P_{SPV\text{-}out}^{total}(t) + \left[\left(P_{SPV\text{-}out}^{total}(t) + \left(SOC_{bat}(t) - SOC_{bat}^{min}(t) \right) \right) \times \eta_{bdinv} \right] \right]$$

(14.5)

where $P_{Purc}^{grid}(t)$ denotes the power taken from the grid network and $SOC_{bat}^{min}(t)$ represents the lower limit on SOC of BES, $P_D^{EV}(t)$ denotes the total power demand.

On the other hand, when power produced by RES is adequately high and BES is completely charged, the surplus electricity is resold to the power grid, as indicated by equation (14.6)

$$P_{Sell}^{grid}(t) = \left[P_{SPV\text{-}out}^{total}(t) + \left[\left(P_{SPV\text{-}out}^{total}(t) - \left(SOC_{bat}^{max}(t) - SOC_{bat}(t) \right) \right) \times \eta_{bdinv} \right] \right] - P_D^{EV}(t)$$

(14.6)

where $P_{Sell}^{grid}(t)$ denotes the extra electricity sold to the grid and $SOC_{bat}^{max}(t)$ represents the maximum charging status of EV battery.

14.3 OBJECTIVE FUNCTIONS

It is necessary to find the ideal number of solar panels, denoted by N_{SPV}, and batteries, denoted by N_{bat}, to guarantee that the grid-connected SPV-based system fulfils the power need of EVs. The LCOE and the total net present cost (TNPC) are regarded as the objectives that need to be minimized.

14.3.1 Total net present cost

The TNPC of an interconnected system represents its overall cost. The TNPC of the system encompasses all costs and revenues generated over the entire lifespan of the system. This covers the upfront expenditures for purchasing system components, operating-system replacement prices, and maintenance costs. For the optimal arrangement, the number of SPV panels and BES are selected as the two key choice factors. Hence, the following mathematical equations are constructed for the NPC of different system components:

$$TNPC(\$) = NPC_{SPV} + NPC_{bat} + NPC_{bdinv} + C_P^{grid} - C_S^{grid} \tag{14.7}$$

14.3.2 Levelized cost of energy

The LCOE is a measure of the system's average cost per kWh of energy produced. The LCOE is calculated as the ratio of yearly price for energy production by the yearly power output. LCOE depends on capital recovery factor (CRF), as shown in equation (14.8) [4]:

$$LCOE = \frac{TNPC \times CRF}{\sum_{t=1}^{T} P_{gen}(t)} \ \$/kW \tag{14.8}$$

CRF may be further computed using equation (14.9) as follows:

$$CRF = \frac{R(1+R)^{\Omega}}{\left((1+R)^{\Omega} - 1\right)} \tag{14.9}$$

$P_{gen}(t)$ is the total power generated by energy sources, R is the lifetime of the project and Ω denotes the interest rate.

Several factors affect LCOE, including initial investment, solar radiation, longevity, operating and maintenance costs, CRF, etc.

14.4 OPTIMIZATION TECHNIQUE

Traditional optimization algorithms excel at finding optimal solutions for continuous and differentiable functions with unconstrained maximum and minimum values. However, their applicability in real-world scenarios is limited as they do not consider the need for continuous or discrete objectives. To achieve optimal results for specific problems, more sophisticated and complex optimization strategies are required. The proposed EBEA optimizes the number of decision variables, i.e., SPV units used to meet the EV load requirement by minimizing the LCOE and TNPC.

14.4.1 Enhanced bald eagle algorithm

The enhanced bald eagle algorithm (EBEA) method relies on the prior bald eagle algorithm (BEA) method and impacts the hunting behaviour of bald eagles [25]. As part of the hunt tactics, space selection, scouring, and swooping in on the quarry are all employed.

Space selection: The bald creates the amount of space arbitrarily using the previously sought information using equation (14.10).

$$Q_{n,j} = Q_b + \alpha \times r \left(Q_{\text{mean}} - Q_j \right) \tag{14.10}$$

As in the earlier BEA, an updated parameter, α, is used to resolve location shifts and can be conveyed using equation (14.11) is similar to a predetermined weight.

$$\alpha = \frac{\left(1.5 \times \left(\max_{\text{iter}} - t + 1 \right) \right)}{\max_{\text{iter}}} \tag{14.11}$$

This suggested parameter influences the exact position of bald eagles and enhances the exploration and exploitation features of EBEA. r is an integer whose value lies between 0 and 1, Q_b indicates the best search and Q_n denotes the new search, Q_{mean} indicates that the eagles have retained all the information from the previous search.

Scouring stage: To expedite their hunt for prey in the designated area, bald eagles move in a circular path using equation (14.13). The position of bald eagle is adjusted at every moment using equations (14.14)–(14.17).

$$Q_{j,n} = Q_j + n(j) \times \left(Q_j - Q_{j+1} \right) Q_b + m(j) \times \left(Q_j - Q_{\text{mean}} \right) \tag{14.12}$$

$$m(j) = \frac{mr(j)}{\max|mr|} \quad n(j) = \frac{nr(j)}{\max|nr|} \tag{14.13}$$

$$mr(j) = r(j) \times \sin \left(\delta(j) \right) \quad nr(j) = r(j) \times \cos \left(\delta(j) \right) \tag{14.14}$$

$$\delta(j) = \alpha \times \pi \times \text{rand} \tag{14.15}$$

$$r(j) = \delta(j) \times R \times \text{rand} \tag{14.16}$$

where α lies between 5 and 10, R varies within the range of 0.5 and 2.

Swooping stage: In this stage, the eagles begin to swoop towards their quarry from an optimal search posture using equations (14.18)–(14.20).

$$Q_{j,n} = \text{rand} \times Q_b + m_1(j) \times \left(Q_j - C_1 \times Q_{\text{mean}} \right) + n_1(j) \times \left(Q_j - C_1 \times Q_b \right) \tag{14.17}$$

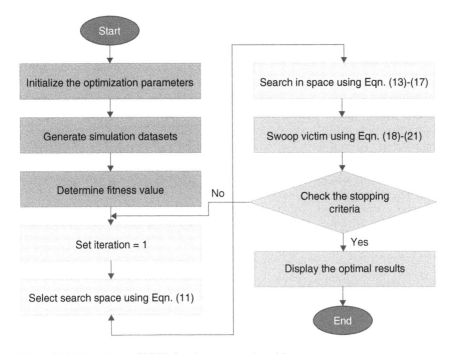

Figure 14.2 Flow chart of EBEA for the proposed problem.

$$m_1(j) = \frac{mr(j)}{\max|mr|} \ n_1(j) = \frac{nr(j)}{\max|nr|} \qquad (14.18)$$

$$mr(j) = r(j) \times \sinh(\delta(j)) \ nr(j) = r(j) \times \cosh(\delta(j)) \qquad (14.19)$$

$$\delta(j) = \alpha \times \pi \times \text{rand}, \ r(j) = \delta(j) \qquad (14.20)$$

The values of C_1 and C_2 lie between 1 and 2. The steps involved in the implementation of EBEA are displayed in Figure 14.2.

14.5 RESULT AND DISCUSSION

14.5.1 Description of research region, sources and load

The important components, geographical position of studied area and load requirement framework are presented in this section.

14.5.1.1 Area under study

The planned research is undertaken in Delhi's northwestern district. The geographic coordinates of the region under study are 28.7408°N (latitude) and 77.1126°E (longitude). The research region is shown from a geographical aspect as shown in Figure 14.3.

Owing to the high level of education and employment among residents in this area, electric vehicles (EVs) have become their primary mode of daily transportation. It is assumed that around 130–160 EVs running on the road of selected location, which are stored and charged at 15 different locations. The owners of these facilities have expressed concerns about the exorbitant cost of charging EVs, as these vehicles rely on grid power for their energy supply.

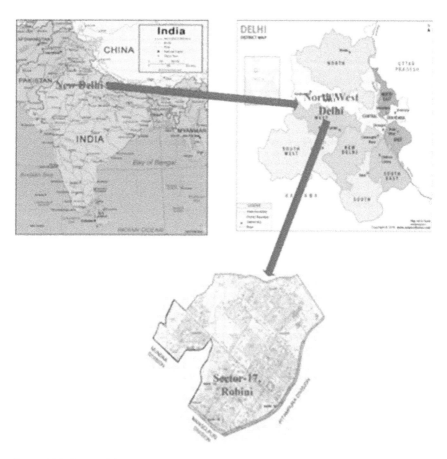

Figure 14.3 Selected location on map.

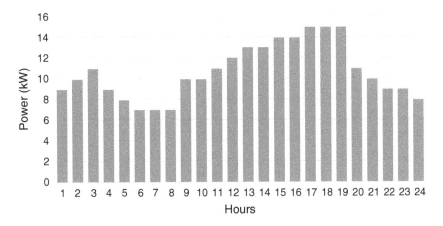

Figure 14.4 EVCS load profile on daily basis [24].

14.5.1.2 Description of the EV load in the studied zone

In this study, the system load is represented by e-rickshaws, which are three-wheeled electric vehicles. Each three-wheeled vehicle is equipped with four lead-acid batteries, with their capacities ranging from 150 to 160 Ah and operating at 12 V. When considering a 12-V, 180-Ah battery, the theoretical energy capacity amounts to 2.2 kWh. Typically, the EV battery is re-energized up to 92% of its maximum rating, resulting in an actual energy capacity of 1.94 kWh.

The analysis indicates that the mean daily energy consumption amounts to 241 kWh, with an average power consumption of 10.24 kW and a peak load of 26.92 kW. Figure 14.4 provides an hourly visualization of the EVCS load.

14.5.2 Important outcomes and discussion

This scenario investigates the technological, economic, and environmental implications of grid and SPV-powered integrated energy system. In this approach, when SPV systems are unable to meet power requirements, grid electricity is employed as an alternative source. The extra amount of electricity is injected into the grid, needing limited storage capacity while taking advantage of the substantial surplus energy generated by hybrid energy solutions. For this analysis, a fixed grid power price of $0.10/kWh and a fixed grid sell-back price of $0.06/kWh are assumed. Table 14.2 provides a comparison of results obtained using the EBEA, PSO, and GWO techniques.

Table 14.2 Comparison of achieved outcomes using different metaheuristic techniques

Methods used	EBEA	PSO	GWO
SPV	232	218	196
Grid purchase	51,155	52,671	54,367
Grid sales	77,135	76,432	76,197
Converter	2	2	2
TNPC ($)	263,377	276,543	298,654
LCOE ($/kWh)	0.119	0.143	0.217
Computational time (seconds)	29,812.873	30,341.457	32,349.952

In the case of the grid-connected SPV system, when there is zero grid purchase (indicating equal electricity consumption and supply to the grid), battery storage units are not required. Despite featuring 232 PV modules with 325 W of rated capacity and a bidirectional converter of rating 49.4 kW, the grid-powered integrated system has minimal energy costs and does not require battery storage. This is primarily due to its significantly lower Levelized Cost of Energy (LCOE) of 0.119 $/kWh. Notably, EBEA outperforms PSO and GWO, exhibiting lower LCOE (0.119 $/kWh) and TNPC of $263,377. The convergence characteristics of the three algorithms are presented in Figure 14.5.

However, it should be noted that the additional power generated by the grid-based designing of energy system is comparatively lesser than other alternative configurations. This is because a sizable proportion of excess energy is sent back into the utility grid and only a small number of storage devices are required to satisfy demand at times when solar PV electricity is not available.

In situations where solar energy is not available, load demands are met by grid electricity. Figure 14.6 indicates that during the spring season, there is considerable reliance on grid energy due to heightened power requirements. As a tropical nation, India benefits from consistent sunlight throughout the year. However, despite expectations of higher SPV output during the summer, the presence of wet days results in a decrease in SPV energy production compared to other times of the year.

Solar energy meets approximately 71.3% of the overall energy demand, with the remaining 28.7% being fulfilled by grid electricity. The power contribution by different energy sources in meeting the EV load demand is depicted in Figure 14.7.

Figure 14.8 presents the cost breakdown of various components in the proposed system. The SPV panel and battery account for a substantial portion of the total system cost, as they are considered expensive investments. It is important to keep in mind that even though the BES has

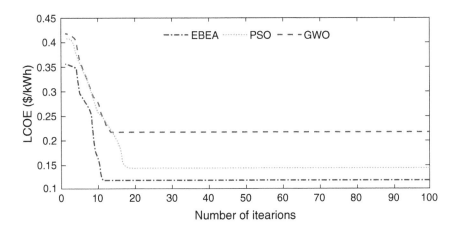

Figure 14.5 Convergence curve of the EBEA, PSO and GWO.

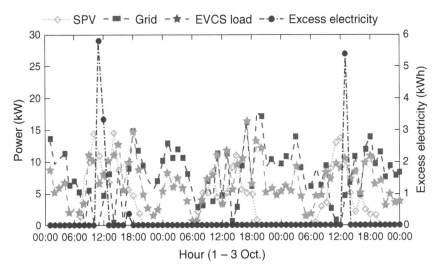

Figure 14.6 Power analysis on hour basis for grid-and-solar PV-based EVCS.

high replacement costs throughout the course of the project, the total resource cost outweighs the original investment. As a result, this hybrid energy system necessitates a consistent capital input to ensure proper functionality.

Figure 14.9 illustrates the monthly electricity transactions between the system and the electric grid. One noteworthy observation is that the system generates an excess of electricity, even after meeting the annual demand. This surplus power is transferred back to the utility. However, during

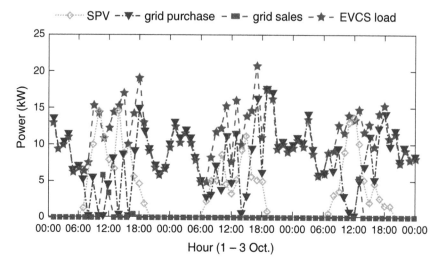

Figure 14.7 Hourly load demand satisfaction using grid and SPV.

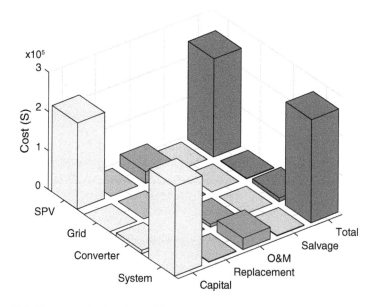

Figure 14.8 The cost-wise breakup of different component of the proposed system [24].

August and December, when SPV electricity production is insufficient, the system relies heavily on grid power to meet the demand. In contrast, the system uses very little electricity from the grid in May and other months with high RE generation.

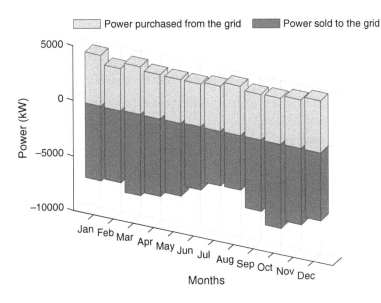

Figure 14.9 Grid energy purchase and sold on monthly basis.

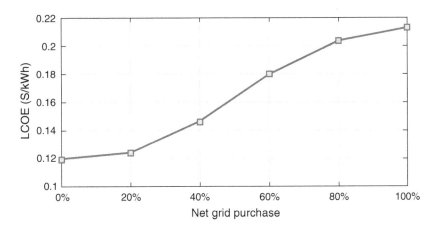

Figure 14.10 Impact of net grid purchase on LCOE.

14.5.3 Effect of energy purchased from grid on LCOE

In this section, we delve into the impact of grid energy purchases and grid energy sell-back on the LCOE, examining how these factors influence the overall cost. When there is a net grid purchase of 0%, meaning an equal amount of energy is purchased from and returned to the grid, the LCOE remains stable. Figure 14.10 shows that while the rise in grid sell-back brings about a decline in LCOE, an elevation in grid purchases causes an increase in the LCOE. The findings presented in Figure 14.10 demonstrate that when there is a higher reliance on grid energy to meet load demands, the LCOE rises accordingly. For instance, a significant 36% rise in the LCOE results from a 50% rise in electricity from the grid purchases compared to grid energy sell-back.

14.6 CONCLUSION

Hybrid energy systems offer efficient and reliable energy solutions for both grid-powered and non-grid locations. Integrating RE components into the grid enhances the overall system efficiency. This chapter describes a comprehensive framework for the design of a grid-connected SPV-based EV charging station in the northwestern part of Delhi, India. The economic, technical, and environmental impacts of the grid-connected SPV-based EV charging station are extensively examined. Metaheuristic techniques, including EBEA, PSO, and GWO, are employed to optimize the decision variables. Notably, EBEA proves to be a robust framework that facilitates model development. The results demonstrate that EBEA outperforms PSO and GWO, achieving lower LCOE at $0.119/kWh and TNPC of $263,377. The SPV and grid-based EV charging station exhibit significant cost reductions compared to PSO and GWO approaches. In addition, a system with equal energy procurement and sell-back can be advantageous commercially. When the grid sell-back price exceeds the grid acquisition cost, the LCOE decreases. The findings indicate that a 50% rise in the grid sell-back price can lead to a 44% reduction in LCOE.

REFERENCES

1. Fares D, Fathi M, Mekhilef S. Performance evaluation of metaheuristic techniques for optimal sizing of a stand-alone hybrid PV/wind/battery system. *Appl Energy* 2022;305:117823. https://doi.org/10.1016/j.apenergy.2021.117823.
2. Bernal-Agustín JL, Dufo-López R. Techno-economical optimization of the production of hydrogen from PV-Wind systems connected to the electrical grid. *Renew Energy* 2010;35:747–58. https://doi.org/10.1016/j.renene.2009.10.004.
3. Giallanza A, Porretto M, Puma GL, Marannano G. A sizing approach for stand-alone hybrid photovoltaic-wind-battery systems: A Sicilian case study. *J Clean Prod* 2018;199:817–30. https://doi.org/10.1016/j.jclepro.2018.07.223.
4. Halabi LM, Mekhilef S, Olatomiwa L, Hazelton J. Performance analysis of hybrid PV/diesel/battery system using HOMER: A case study Sabah, Malaysia. *Energy Convers Manag* 2017;144:322–39. https://doi.org/10.1016/j.enconman.2017.04.070.

5. Lian J, Zhang Y, Ma C, Yang Y, Chaima E. A review on recent sizing methodologies of hybrid renewable energy systems. *Energy Convers Manag* 2019;199:112027. https://doi.org/10.1016/j.enconman.2019.112027.

6. Al Busaidi AS, Kazem HA, Al-Badi AH, Farooq Khan M. A review of optimum sizing of hybrid PV-Wind renewable energy systems in Oman. *Renew Sustain Energy Rev* 2016;53:185–93. https://doi.org/10.1016/j.rser.2015.08.039.

7. Zheng X, Lin H, Liu Z, Li D, Llopis-Albert C, Zeng S. Manufacturing decisions and government subsidies for electric vehicles in China: A maximal social welfare perspective. *Sustainability* 2018;10:1–28.

8. Bilal M, Rizwan M. Electric vehicles in a smart grid: a comprehensive survey on optimal location of charging station. *IET Smart Grid* 2020;3:267–79. https://doi.org/10.1049/iet-stg.2019.0220.

9. Ahmad F, Ashraf I, Iqbal A, Marzband M, Khan I. A novel AI approach for optimal deployment of EV fast charging station and reliability analysis with solar based DGs in distribution network. *Energy Reports* 2022;8:11646–60. https://doi.org/10.1016/j.egyr.2022.09.058.

10. Ye B, Jiang J, Miao L, Yang P, Li J, Shen B. Feasibility study of a solar-powered electric vehicle charging station model. *Energies* 2015;8:13265–83. https://doi.org/10.3390/en81112368.

11. Filote C, Felseghi R, Raboaca MS, Aşchilean I. Environmental impact assessment of green energy systems for power supply of electric vehicle charging station. *Int J Energy Res* 2020;44:10471–94. https://doi.org/10.1002/er.5678.

12. Bilal M, Rizwan M, Alsaidan I, Almasoudi FM. AI-based approach for optimal placement of EVCS and DG with reliability analysis. *IEEE Access* 2021;9:154204–24. https://doi.org/10.1109/ACCESS.2021.3125135.

13. Niccolai A, Bettini L, Zich R. Optimization of electric vehicles charging station deployment by means of evolutionary algorithms. *Int J Intell Syst* 2021;36:5359–83. https://doi.org/10.1002/int.22515.

14. Mozafar MR, Moradi MH, Amini MH. A simultaneous approach for optimal allocation of renewable energy sources and electric vehicle charging stations in smart grids based on improved GA-PSO algorithm. *Sustain Cities Soc* 2017;32:627–37. https://doi.org/10.1016/j.scs.2017.05.007.

15. Ahmad F, Khalid M, Panigrahi BK. An enhanced approach to optimally place the solar powered electric vehicle charging station in distribution network. *J Energy Storage* 2021;42:103090. https://doi.org/10.1016/j.est.2021.103090.

16. Singh S, Chauhan P, Jap Singh N. Feasibility of grid-connected solar-wind hybrid system with electric vehicle charging station. *J Mod Power Syst Clean Energy* 2021;9:295–306. https://doi.org/10.35833/MPCE.2019.000081.

17. Aldhanhani T, Al-Durra A, El-Saadany EF. Optimal design of electric vehicle charging stations integrated with renewable DG. *2017 IEEE Innov. Smart Grid Technol. - Asia, IEEE; 2017, p. 1–6. https://doi.org/10.1109/ISGT-Asia.2017.8378428.

18. Ahmad F, Iqbal A, Asharf I, Marzband M, Khan I. Placement and capacity of EV charging stations by considering uncertainties with energy management strategies. *IEEE Trans Ind Appl* 2023:1–10. https://doi.org/10.1109/TIA.2023.3253817.

19. Wahedi A Al, Bicer Y. Techno-economic assessment of a renewable energy-based electric vehicle fast-charging station in Qatar, 2021, pp. 1629–34. https://doi.org/10.1016/B978-0-323-88506-5.50252-7.

20. Abdelkader A, Rabeh A, Mohamed Ali D, Mohamed J. Multi-objective genetic algorithm based sizing optimization of a stand-alone wind/PV power supply system with enhanced battery/supercapacitor hybrid energy storage. *Energy* 2018;163:351–63. https://doi.org/10.1016/j.energy.2018.08.135.

21. Bilal M, Rizwan M. Intelligent algorithm based efficient planning of electric vehicle charging station: A case study of metropolitan city of India. *Sci Iran* 2023;30(2):559–576. https://doi.org/10.24200/sci.2021.57433.5238.

22. Xu X, Hu W, Cao D, Huang Q, Chen C, Chen Z. Optimized sizing of a stand-alone PV-wind-hydropower station with pumped-storage installation hybrid energy system. *Renew Energy* 2020;147:1418–31. https://doi.org/10.1016/j.renene.2019.09.099.

23. Bilal M, Ahmad F, Rizwan M. Techno-economic assessment of grid and renewable powered electric vehicle charging stations in India using a modified metaheuristic technique. *Energy Convers Manag* 2023;284:116995. https://doi.org/10.1016/j.enconman.2023.116995.

24. Bilal M, Alsaidan I, Alaraj M, Almasoudi FM, Rizwan M. Techno-economic and environmental analysis of grid-connected electric vehicle charging station using AI-based algorithm. *Mathematics* 2022;10:924. https://doi.org/10.3390/math10060924.

25. Ahmad F, Ashraf I, Iqbal A, Khan I, Marzband M. Optimal location and energy management strategy for EV fast charging station with integration of renewable energy sources. *2022 IEEE Silchar Subsect. Conf.*, IEEE; 2022, pp. 1–6. https://doi.org/10.1109/SILCON55242.2022.10028897.

Chapter 15

Energy storage system optimum sizing in battery electric vehicle

The role of battery modelling

Sakshi Bansal, Ashish Khandelwal, and Munmun Khanra

15.1 INTRODUCTION

Electric vehicles (EVs) are becoming more popular owing to their ability to reduce greenhouse gas emissions, air quality, energy efficiency, operating costs, and maintenance. This is a growing concern for individuals, governments, and companies [1]. The higher upfront cost of EVs compared to internal combustion engine (ICE) vehicles, range anxiety, lack of charging infrastructure, lack of public awareness about switching to EVs due to concerns about their performance and convenience, and difficulties in producing and supplying EV components like batteries, electric motors, etc. are some factors which limit the adaptability and affordability of EVs [2,3].

Most of the hurdles are connected to EVs' ESS. Choosing the right size and type of ESS is essential for EVs to perform well and reliably, particularly when compared to ICE vehicles. The size of the ESS impacts the range and power of EVs. A bigger ESS increases the vehicle's weight and range, but it may lower efficiency. It might raise the vehicle's pricing. In contrast to this, a compact ESS will have a limited range, but could be more cost-effective. Therefore, the ESS size should be selected based on a balance between driving range, performance, cost, and practicality [4,5]. The optimal size of ESS in EVs relies on several parameters, including vehicle weight, driving range, charging infrastructure, driving conditions, cost, ESS type, temperature, ESS degradation, vehicle design, power requirements, charging times, ESS models, etc. This study examines how ESS modelling affects optimum capacity selection in EVs.

The ESS models are used to capture the dynamics of ESS. These models aid in determining the performance and lifetime of the ESS as well as optimizing its design and control [6]. This study considers the Lithium-ion Battery (LIB) to be the sole ESS used to power the vehicle. To simulate the behaviour of batteries, several modelling approaches have been investigated in previous research, with electrochemical models, equivalent circuit models, empirical models, data-driven models, etc. being the most commonly used models [7,8]. Different battery models can have varying degrees of accuracy and computational complexity, which can impact their applicability for various applications. For instance, a simple empirical model may be adequate for some applications, while others may require a more complex physics-based model. The optimal size of the ESS may also be affected by the battery model chosen. A more accurate model can provide more accurate predictions of the battery's performance and behaviour, allowing for more accurate and optimal sizing of the ESS. In contrast, a less accurate model may result in sub-optimal sizing of the ESS, which can reduce the EV's range and performance. Consequently, it is essential to choose a battery model that is suitable for the application and provides enough accuracy for the desired level of application. Zhang et al. [9] provided a comprehensive review of the battery models that can be used to understand and analyze the battery's behaviour in EVs, including the electrochemical model (EChM), the equivalent circuit model (ECM), the empirical model, and the black box model. It is suggested that, as the EChM is the most accurate and complex, it should be used for battery design, whereas the empirical model, which is the least accurate and complex, should only be used for constant operating conditions. However, it is further recommended that ECM achieves a reasonable balance between accuracy and complexity and therefore should be used for real-time control and State of Charge (SoC) estimation. Fotouhi et al. [10] reviewed three models for use in EV applications: the mathematical model, the EChM, and the ECM. It is observed that, unlike the other two models, the reduced order EChM provides strong internal battery insights and can therefore be used for EV range prediction and battery management. Similarly, Adaikkappan and Sathiyamoorthy [11], and Saldaña et al. [12] carried out a comprehensive comparison between three models to investigate their applicability in EV applications: EChM, ECM, and a data-driven model. It is concluded that EChM is computationally complex and therefore is not recommended for online control roles. Despite having the lowest interpretability, ECM is recommended for use in real time because of its computational efficacy. Seaman et al. [13] discussed ECM and EChM in detail, as well as battery models suitable for real-time simulation and control, SoC and State-of-Health (SoH) estimation, thermal impact, and high-fidelity modelling for EV and hybrid EV applications. Researchers observed that choosing a model to utilize in an application is dependent on the constraints of the application and the quantities of interest being simulated [14,15].

As per the literature, it is observed that EChM being highly accurate should be used for ESS design purposes in EVs. Despite this, the majority of published works utilized ECM because of its high computational efficiency and simplicity to determine optimal ESS sizes and evaluate the performance of ESS in vehicular applications. Researchers in Refs. [16–18] employed multiple ECM versions to compute the optimal battery and supercapacitor (SC) sizes for EVs and HEVs. Pinto et al. [19] investigated the influence of battery models and sizing strategies for EVs and HEVs. Researchers found that higher order battery models result in fewer battery cells in battery EV (BEV).

It is important to observe that the sizing of an ESS in an EV is typically performed offline. This indicates that the ESS sizing calculations are performed before the ESS is installed in the vehicle and are based on a variety of parameters, including the intended vehicle range, battery chemistry, powertrain specifications, environmental conditions, etc. The optimal sizing of ESS in EVs must take ambient temperature into account, with a focus on understanding the temperature range the vehicle will come across and its influence on battery performance and safety. Consequently, model complexity can be a secondary concern. Accuracy and reliability should be prioritized so that the derived ESS size is more reliable in real-world scenarios. Therefore, in this study, the effect of ESS modelling on the sizing of ESS at varying ambient temperatures is investigated for EV. Specifically, a battery-powered city bus is taken into account. The daily bus route is predetermined and covers 240 km with multiple stops. Next, an optimal ESS sizing problem is formulated by taking into account two widely accepted models, the ECM and the EChM. The optimal battery capacities are computed using the particle swarm optimization (PSO) algorithm, taking into account various constraints at three distinct ambient temperatures. The results are subsequently compared and analyzed. Finally, recommendations are made regarding the optimal battery model for the economic and reliable capacity of the ESS in EV.

This chapter is organized as follows: Section 15.2 describes the system description, including driving cycle, powertrain, input demand power, and battery modelling information. Section 15.3 describes the formulation of the optimal sizing problem. The results of this investigation are presented and discussed in Section 15.4. Section 15.5 finally presents the conclusions derived from this research.

15.2 SYSTEM DESCRIPTION

This section provides a summary of the system under investigation. The subsequent subsections describe the electric powertrain, driving cycle, input demand power, and battery cell models.

15.2.1 Electric powertrain and driving cycle

In this research, a battery-powered city bus is considered. The electric powertrain of the city bus is shown in Figure 15.1, and its specifications are listed in Table 15.1. The battery module (BM) is connected to the DC bus of the DC-AC converter utilizing a passive configuration.

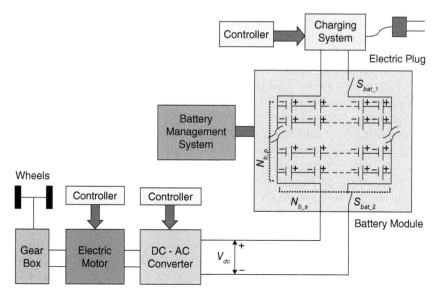

Figure 15.1 Electric powertrain of battery city bus [21].

Table 15.1 City bus specifications and their corresponding values [21]

Parameter	Value
Mass of bus without storage system (mass$_{bus}$)	11,000 kg
Mass of passengers (mass$_p$)	2,000 kg
Mass of ESS (mass$_{ess}$)	(Total no. of cells × mass of a cell) kg
Total bus mass (m)	$\left(mass_{bus} + mass_p + mass_{ess}\right)$
Gravitational acceleration (g)	9.8 m/s^2
Coefficient of friction (μ)	$0.005 + \left(\dfrac{14.696}{\rho}\right) \times \left(0.001 + 0.0095 \left(\dfrac{v}{27.778}\right)^2\right)$
Tyre pressure (ρ)	36 psi
Drag coefficient (C_d)	0.79
Air density (ρ_a)	1.202 kg/m^3
Frontal area of bus (A)	7.316 m^2
Wind speed against vehicle's movement (v_{wind})	2 m/s

The BM is made by connecting N_{b_s} number of battery cells in series in 1 branch and N_{b_p} number of such parallel branches as shown in Figure 15.1. Consequently, the total number of cells in the BM is equal to the product of N_{b_s} and N_{b_p}. The urban dynamometer driving schedule (UDDS) [20],

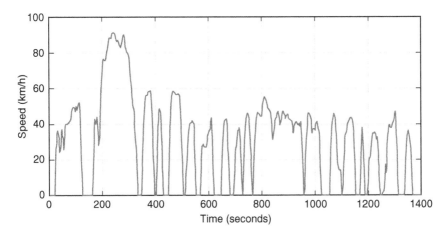

Figure 15.2 Driving cycle- Urban Dynamometer Driving Schedule (UDDS)

as shown in Figure 15.2, is used for creating the entire journey of the city bus. The UDDS cycle travels a total distance of 12 km. The complete route of the city bus consists of 20 successive runs of UDDS and 19 repetitions of a 1,200 waiting period in between two UDDS trips. Throughout each waiting period, the BM can be charged from the grid. In this way, a total of 240 km distance was covered by the bus.

15.2.2 Vehicle power demand calculation

Figure 15.2 depicts the driving cycle that is utilized as the key input for determining the required amount of power to operate the vehicle. The power demand P_d of the vehicle during the course of the run is computed using longitudinal vehicle dynamics in (15.1) [22], which is based on the speed versus time information of the driving cycle and the different forces acting on the vehicle. Thus, the following variables and parameters are used in P_d computations:

$$P_d = P_a + P_g + P_r + P_w + P_{aux} \tag{15.1}$$

$$P_d = \left(m\frac{dv}{dt} + mg\sin\theta + \mu mg\cos\theta + 0.5C_d\rho A(v+v_{wind})^2 \right)v + P_{aux} \tag{15.2}$$

where P_a represents the power due to acceleration, P_g represents the gravitational power, P_r represents power due to rolling friction, P_w represents the aerodynamics power, and P_{aux} represents the auxiliary power to run the auxiliary sources of the bus like AC, door, music system, lights, etc. The specifications of the parameters along with their values involved in (15.2) are listed in Table 15.1.

15.2.3 Battery modelling

An A123 ANR26650 LiFePO$_4$ cylindrical battery cell is considered in this work [23]. The specifications of the battery cell are listed in Table 15.2. The behaviour of LIBs may be simulated using a variety of models, including the EChM, the ECM, and data-driven. Following are descriptions of the two widely established battery models utilized in this work: the ECM and the EChM.

15.2.3.1 Equivalent circuit model of battery

In this study, a two-RC branch ECM is utilized to capture the dynamics of battery cell because it offers a reasonable balance between complexity and accuracy in capturing battery dynamics in practical applications [24]. The ECM is shown in Figure 15.3. The ECM consists of open circuit voltage V_{ocv},

Table 15.2 Specifications of A123 ANR26650MI Lithium-ion battery [23]

Specifications	Value
Nominal capacity (Cap)	2.3 Ah
Nominal voltage (V_t)	3.V
Maximum voltage (V_t)	3.6 V
Maximum continuous discharge current (I)	70 A
Pulse discharge at 10 seconds	120 A
Operating temperature range	−30°C to +60°C
Mass	0.07 kg

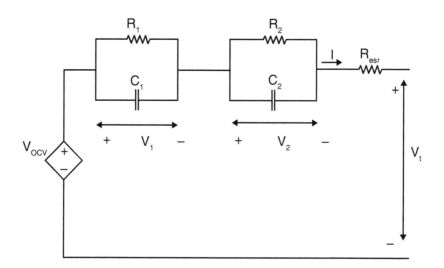

Figure 15.3 Equivalent circuit model (ECM) of Li-ion battery.

an equivalent series resistor R_{esr}, and two parallel RC networks. The transient behaviour of the battery may be captured using the two RC branches. The accumulation of charge across the electrode-electrolyte interface and the internal redistribution of charge within the active electrode of a battery cell is described by the two RC networks. The resistance offered by the current collectors, electrolytes, electrode pores, and so on is represented by R_{esr}. The mathematical model corresponding to Figure 15.3 is presented in (15.3)–(15.16) as:

$$\frac{dV_1}{dt} = \frac{-1}{R_1 C_1} V_1 + \frac{1}{C_1} I \tag{15.3}$$

$$\frac{dV_2}{dt} = \frac{-1}{R_2 C_2} V_2 + \frac{1}{C_2} I \tag{15.4}$$

$$V_t = V_{ocv} - V_1 - V_2 - I R_{esr} \tag{15.5}$$

$$\frac{dSoC}{dt} = \frac{-1}{3,600 \times \text{Capacity}} I \tag{15.6}$$

$$R_{esr\_ch} = 0.0055 \exp\left(\frac{22.2477}{T_{amb} + 11.5943}\right) \tag{15.7}$$

$$R_{esr\_dch} = 0.0048 \exp\left(\frac{31.0494}{T_{amb} + 15.3253}\right) \tag{15.8}$$

$$R_{1\_ch} = \left(0.0016 - 0.0032(SoC) + 0.0045(SoC)^2\right)$$
$$\exp\left(\frac{159.2819}{T_{amb} + 41.4548}\right) \tag{15.9}$$

$$R_{1\_dch} = \left(\begin{array}{c} 7.1135e - 4 - 4.3865e - 4(SoC) \\ + 2.3788e - 4(SoC)^2 \end{array}\right)$$
$$\exp\left(\frac{347.4707}{T_{amb} + 79.5816}\right) \tag{15.10}$$

$$R_{2\_ch} = \left(0.0113 - 0.027(SoC) + 0.0339(SoC)^2\right)\exp\left(\frac{17.0224}{T_{amb}}\right) \tag{15.11}$$

$$R_{2\_dch} = \left(0.0288 - 0.073(SoC) + 0.0605(SoC)^2\right)\exp\left(\frac{16.6712}{T_{amb}}\right) \tag{15.12}$$

$$C_{1\_ch} = 523.215 + 6.4171e + 3(SoC) - 7.5555e + 3(SoC)^2$$

$$+ \left(50.7107 - 131.2298(SoC) + 162.4688(SoC)^2\right)T_{amb} \qquad (15.13)$$

$$C_{1\_dch} = 335.4518 + 3.1712e + 3(SoC) - 1.3214e + 3(SoC)^2$$

$$+ \left(53.2138 - 65.4786(SoC) + 44.3761(SoC)^2\right)T_{amb} \qquad (15.14)$$

$$C_{2\_ch} = 6.2449e + 4 - 1.055e + 5(SoC) + 4.4432e + 4(SoC)^2$$

$$+ \left(198.9753 + 7.5621e + 3(SoC) - 6.9365e + 3(SoC)^2\right)T_{amb}$$
$$(15.15)$$

$$C_{2\_dch} = 3.1887e + 4 - 1.1593e + 5(SoC) + 1.0493e + 5(SoC)^2$$

$$+ \left(60.3114 + 1.0175e + 4(SoC) - 9.5924e + 3(SoC)^2\right)T_{amb}$$
$$(15.16)$$

The parameters involved in (15.3)–(15.16) are in their SI units except T_{amb} which is in °C.

15.2.3.2 Electrochemical model of battery

The EChM of the battery, which is based on electrochemical principles, provides more precise information about the battery's internal states. The reported works on optimal sizing of ESS in EVs rarely make use of electrochemical models because of their computational inefficiency and complexity. Additional research is being conducted to find ways to reduce computational inefficiencies by refining electrochemical models. One such model that is employed in this study is the single particle model (SPM), a reduced order electrochemical model that is both computationally efficient and incorporates the essential battery design factors [25,26]. This study adopts the reduced order SPM of A123 ANR26650 LiFePO$_4$ cylindrical battery cell in Ref. [25] and shown in Figure 15.4. The SPM is based on the assumption that each electrode of the LIB cell is modelled as a single spherical particle with a surface area proportional to that of the respective electrodes, and that the charge dynamics in the solid material are neglected. The SPM includes partial differential equations (PDEs) to represent the mass conservation in each electrode. The terminal voltage of the LIB cell is derived using Butler-Volmer kinetics and is dependent on the thermodynamic potential of each electrode, overpotentials, and ohmic drop. The PDEs, their boundary conditions, and cell voltage are presented in (9.17)–(9.22). The description of the

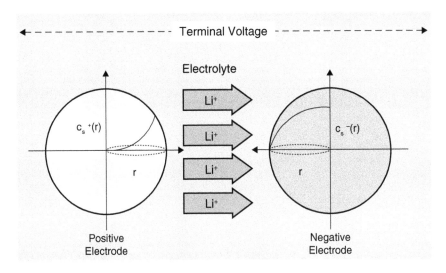

Figure 15.4 Electrochemical model (EChM) of Li-ion battery.

Table 15.3 Description of the parameters used in (9.17)-(9.22) and their values [25]

Parameter	Symbol (unit)	Negative electrode	Positive electrode	Separator
Electrode thickness	δ (m)	3.4×10^{-5}	8×10^{-5}	2.5×10^{-5}
Particle radius	R_s (m)	5×10^{-6}	5.0×10^{-8}	-
Active material volume fraction	ε_s	0.58	0.374	0.55
Filler volume fraction	ε_f	0.0326	0.0535	-
Electrode plate area	A (m²)	1.8×10^{-1}	1.8×10^{-1}	-
Maximum solid phase concentration	$c_{s,max}$ (mol/m³)	30,555	22,806	-
Stoechiometry at 0% SOC	$y_0\%, x_0\%$	0.0132	0.74	-
Stoechiometry at 100% SOC	$y_{100}\%, x_{100}\%$	0.811	0.035	-
Average electrolyte concentration	c_e (mol/m³)	-	-	1200
Bruggman exponent	B_{rugg}	1.5	1.5	1.5
Exchange current density	j_0 (A/m²)	0.5	5×10^{-2}	-
Charge transfer coefficients	$\alpha_{ox}, \alpha_{red}$	0.5	0.5	-
Solid phase Li diffusion	D_s (m²/s)	3.0×10^{-15}	5.9×10^{-20}	-
Electrolyte phase Li⁺ diffusion	D_e (m²/s)	-	-	2.0×10^{-10}

parameters used in (15.17)–(15.22) along with their values is listed in Table 15.3.

$$\frac{\partial}{\partial t}c_s - \frac{1}{r^2}\frac{\partial}{\partial r}\left(r^2 D_s \frac{\partial}{\partial r}c_s\right) = 0 \qquad (15.17)$$

Boundary conditions:

$$D_s \frac{\partial}{\partial r} c_s \bigg|_{r=0} = 0; \quad -D_s \frac{\partial}{\partial r} c_s \bigg|_{r=R_s} = \frac{jf}{a_s F}; \quad a_s = \frac{3\varepsilon_s}{R_s} \tag{15.18}$$

$$V(t) = \Phi_s(L) - \Phi_s(0) = U_p - U_n + \eta(L) - \eta(0) + \Phi_e(L) - \Phi_e(0) \tag{15.19}$$

$$\theta_p^b = \frac{C_{s,p}^b}{c_{s,p,\max}} \text{ and } \theta_n^b = \frac{C_{s,n}^b}{c_{s,n,\max}} \tag{15.20}$$

$$SOC_{bat} = 100 \left(\frac{\theta_n^b - \theta_{n,0\%}^b}{\theta_{n,100\%}^b - \theta_{n,0\%}^b} \right) \tag{15.21}$$

$$V(t) = U_p \left(\frac{c_{s,p}^s}{c_{s,p,\max}} \right) - U_n \left(\frac{c_{s,n}^s}{c_{s,n,\max}} \right)$$

$$+ \frac{RT}{\propto F} l_n \left(\frac{\frac{-R_{s,p}}{6\varepsilon_{s,p} i_{0,p} A \delta_p} I + \sqrt{\left(\frac{R_{s,p}}{6\varepsilon_{s,p} i_{0,p} A \delta_p} \right)^2 + 1}}{\frac{-R_{s,n}}{6\varepsilon_{s,n} i_{0,n} A \delta_n} I + \sqrt{\left(\frac{R_{s,n}}{6\varepsilon_{s,n} i_{0,n} A \delta_n} \right)^2 + 1}} \right)$$

$$+ (1 - t_+) \frac{2RT}{F} \ln \frac{c_e(L)}{c_e(o)} - \frac{I}{2A} \left(\frac{\delta_n}{k_n^{eff}} + 2 \frac{\delta_{sep}}{k_{sep}^{eff}} + \frac{\delta_p}{k_p^{eff}} \right) \tag{15.22}$$

15.3 OPTIMAL ESS SIZING PROBLEM FORMULATION

In this section, the optimal sizing problem of ESS is formulated. The optimal sizing of LIB in the city bus is a nonlinear integer programming problem. The generalized representation of a nonlinear integer programming consists of an objective function that should be maximized or minimized depending on the application under the equality and in-equality constraints. The information about the input variables, optimization variables, equality constraints, and inequality constraints needed to keep the city bus running smoothly and reliably is detailed in the following subsections.

15.3.1 Input variables (I)

In an optimization problem, an input variable is defined as a variable whose values are already known or fixed. The key input to the system is driving cycle using which the power demanded by the bus is calculated using (15.2).

Along with this, the cost of the one LIB cell is also given as input to the system. The per cell cost of LIB is \$9.25 [27].

$$I = [P_d, \text{cost\_cell}] \tag{15.23}$$

15.3.2 Optimization variables (O)

The optimization variable is defined as a variable that can be altered within predetermined limits in order to optimize the objective function. In this study, the total number of cells that is N_{b_s} and N_{b_p} required to make a BM as shown in Figure 15.1 are considered as optimization variables.

$$O = [N_{b\_s}, N_{b\_p}] \tag{15.24}$$

15.3.3 Objective function (Z)

The objective function in a given problem is defined as a mathematical expression that specifies the variable to be optimized. It is primarily a function of optimization variables, and, in some cases, a function of input variables. In this study, the objective is to investigate the influence of ESS modelling on ESS optimal sizing in a city bus. Thus, the objective function only considers the minimization of initial BM cost.

$$Z = \min(N_{b\_s} \times N_{b\_p} \times \text{cost\_cell}) \tag{15.25}$$

15.3.4 Equality constraints (Cons$_{eq}$)

In an optimization problem, an equality constraint is a mathematical expression or statement that must be exactly satisfied by the values of the optimization variables in order to determine the optimal solution. Meeting the power demanded by the vehicle on the DC bus by the BM is the only equality constraint considered in this work. There will be losses due to drive train components such as DC-AC converter, electric motor, and gearbox before the power from the BM reaches the wheels of city bus. Thus, the net power from BM on the DC bus is:

$$\text{Cons}_{eq} = \alpha \frac{P_d}{\eta_d} + (1 - \alpha)(P_d \times \eta_d) \tag{15.26}$$

where the value of α can be either 1 or 0 representing motoring and regenerative actions. η_d is defined as the drivetrain efficiency and is equal to the product of the efficiency of DC-AC converter, electric motor, and gearbox. The power rating of the electric motor and the DC-AC converter is

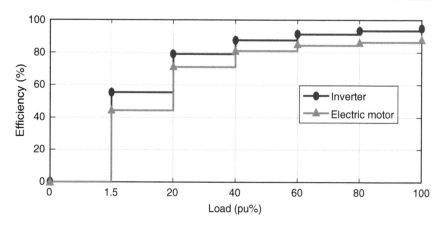

Figure 15.5 Efficiency of DC-AC converter (inverter) and electric motor [28].

determined by the maximum amount of power required by the gearbox and electric motor. The efficiency of the DC-AC converter and electric motor depends on the load, whereas the efficiency of the transmission is constant, as shown in Figure 15.5 [28].

15.3.5 In-equality constraints (Cons$_{\text{in-eq}}$)

Inequality constraints are mathematical expressions that provide higher or lower limitations on the values of the different variables of the system, therefore restricting the number of feasible solutions. In this work, inequality constraints are viewed as the limits imposed on some performance measures of BM so that BM can securely meet the drivability requirements of the city bus. Thus, the in-equality constraints considered in this work are:

$$V_{t-\min} \leq V_t \leq V_{t-\max} \tag{15.27}$$

$$I_{\min} \leq I \leq I_{\max} \tag{15.28}$$

$$P_{b-\min} \leq P_b \leq P_{b-\max} \tag{15.29}$$

$$SoC_{\min} \leq SoC \leq SoC_{\max} \tag{15.30}$$

$$V_{bus-\min} \leq V_{bus} \leq V_{bus-\max} \tag{15.31}$$

where the V_t is terminal voltage, I is current, and P_b is power of the LIB. The minimum- maximum values of DC bus voltage V_{bus} and SoC of LIB considered in this study are 200–600 V and 30%–90% respectively. Rest all the minimum and maximum values of parameters shown in (15.27)–(15.31) are to be maintained in their respective limits as per Table 15.2.

15.4 RESULTS AND DISCUSSION

In this section, the simulation results obtained in order to understand the influence of LIB modelling on optimal capacity selection of ESS in city buses are presented and discussed. The input power required by the city bus is computed using (15.2). In Section 15.3, the optimal ESS sizing problem is then formulated. Owing to the presence of so many constraints and differential equations that must be discretized at each time instant, the optimal sizes are then determined using the PSO algorithm, a well-established meta-heuristic optimization algorithm. The economic sizing of ESS in EVs is a complex problem that requires consideration of a range of factors, including battery dynamics, drive train dynamics, etc. Thus, evolutionary algorithms have the potential to offer more accurate, efficient, and robust solutions for the economic sizing of ESS in EVs, particularly when dealing with complex, nonlinear relationships between input and output variables. The advantages of PSO such as simplicity, efficiency, fast convergence, robustness against local optima, and versatility make it a competitive and widely used optimization algorithm in various fields including transportation. In the following subsections, the derived results for each scenario are presented.

15.4.1 Performance of models of LIB under non-uniform current profile

In this subsection, the performance of both LIB models, ECM and EChM, under an EV load profile is analyzed. The current profile used to demonstrate the behaviour of the models is a scaled-down version of the standard UDDS driving cycle-based EV load profile. The behaviour of the terminal voltages and SoC of both the models corresponding to the load profile is shown in Figure 15.6.

Figure 15.6b and c demonstrate that the pattern, beginning point, and end point of both plots are identical. However, there is a significant gap between the beginning and end points. The voltage and SoC plots of the ECM and EChM of a LIB can differ due to the numerous assumptions and simplifications made for their respective models. The diffusion and polarization effects within ECM are represented by two RC branches. In contrast, the EChM describes the detailed electrochemical processes, including the kinetics and diffusion of lithium ions, the electrode-electrolyte interface reactions, and the transport of electrons and ions within the battery.

15.4.2 Optimal sizes of ECM and EChM at different ambient temperatures

This section presents and discusses the optimal sizes determined by both models (ECM and EChM) at three ambient temperatures: 5°C, 25°C, and 45°C. Note that neither the thermal nor ageing dynamics of LIB are taken (see Appendix for the flowchart used to calculate ESS sizes) into account.

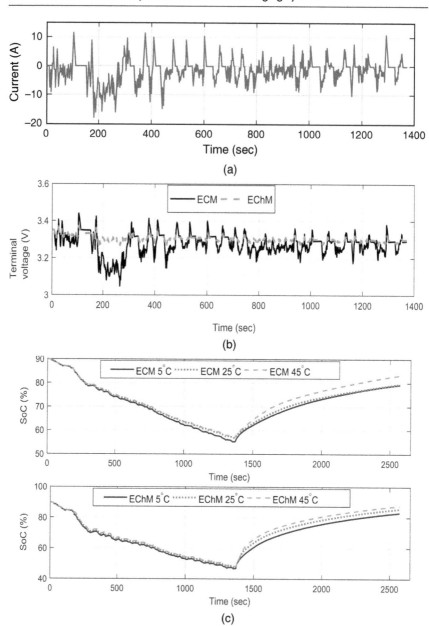

Figure 15.6 Performance of ECM and EChM under EV load profile: (a) EV load current profile, (b) Terminal voltage variation, and (c) SoC variation.

Consequently, the thermodynamic and degradation dynamics that affect the parameters during battery operation are not examined.

In Table 15.4, the optimal sizes of ESS for both models at various ambient temperatures are provided. It can be observed from Table 15.4 that

Table 15.4 Optimal sizes of the battery using ECM and EChM at different ambient temperatures with UDDS driving cycle

Ambient temperature (°C)	Series (N_{b_s})		Parallel (N_{b_p})		Capacity (Ah)		Energy (kWh)		Cost ($)	
	ECM	EChM	ECM	EChM	ECM	EChM	ECM	EChM	ECM	EChM
5	103	80	86	137	197.8	315.1	73.3	90.7	81,937	101,380
25	82	78	143	131	328.9	301.3	97.1	84.6	108,466	94,517
45	74	149	136	66	312.8	151.8	83.3	81.4	93,092	90,965

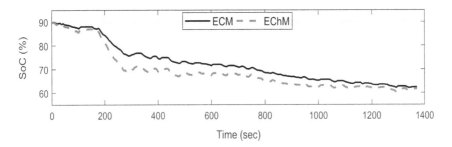

Figure 15.7 SoC variation of ECM and EChM for 1 cycle at different ambient temperatures.

there is a significant difference between the optimal sizes obtained by the two models. Table 15.4 additionally indicates that the size variation trends of the two models are different. This is because the phenomenon of capturing the internal dynamics of the battery is very different in both models, as described in subsection 15.4.1. In particular, the charging of BM during the waiting period of the bus plays a significant role in meeting the drivability requirements for subsequent cycles. This is observable by comparing the SoC variation of both models. Figure 15.7 shows a sample of the SoC variation between the two models during the first cycle. In this study, the first cycle refers to when a LIB undergoes its initial discharge and charge between 90% and 30% SoC. This also denotes the end of the initial UDDS trip and waiting period. The SoC after completing one UDDS trip at 5°C is less than at 45°C. This is due to the fact that, at lower temperatures, the chemical reactions occurring within the LIB are more sluggish, necessitating a greater capacity to meet the power requirements than at 45°C. However, it is well known that the optimal efficacy of LIB is obtained between 23°C and 25°C. This can be more clearer by analyzing the performance of both models in future by including thermal and ageing dynamics of LIB during optimal sizing. Therefore, from the present study, it can be stated that the modelling of ESS has a significant impact on optimal sizing in vehicular applications. Also, it is widely believed that EChM captures

Table 15.5 Optimal sizes of the battery using ECM and EChM at different ambient temperatures with NYCC and SC03 driving cycles

Ambient temperature (°C)	Series (N_{b_s})		Parallel (N_{b_p})		Capacity (Ah)		Energy (kWh)		Cost ($)	
	ECM	EChM	ECM	EChM	ECM	EChM	ECM	EChM	ECM	EChM
NYCC										
5	142	81	26	47	59.8	108.1	30.57	31.52	34,151	35,215
25	101	140	39	26	89.7	59.8	32.61	30.14	36,436	33,670
45	96	81	40	43	92	98.9	31.80	28.84	35,520	32,218
SC03										
5	146	111	49	66	112.7	151.8	59.24	60.66	66,175	67,766
25	126	74	59	96	135.7	220.8	61.55	58.82	68,765	65,712
45	132	66	55	104	126.5	239.2	60.11	56.83	67,155	63,492

the LIB dynamics more precisely than ECM and is therefore regarded as a more realistic model than ECM for complex processes like ESS sizing in EVs. Finally, given that sizing is an offline process, this study suggests that a more realistic model should be used during optimal sizing calculations.

The simulation studies are also performed to demonstrate the effect of battery modelling on ESS sizing for two different driving cycles, namely New York City Cycle (NYCC) and SC03. The results are presented in Table 15.5. It is observed from Table 15.5 that the trend of ESS size change in relation to battery model change is in line with what has been observed for UDDS. Consequently, it is found that battery modelling has a significant impact on the optimal ESS size for this city bus.

15.5 CONCLUSION

The growing availability of charging infrastructure and the improvement of battery technology have led to an increase in consumer interest in EVs. The performance of an EV heavily depends on its ESS. An ESS model that can accurately explain the dynamics of the ESS during EV operation is essential for choosing the proper ESS size for an EV to optimize its performance. Hence, in this study, the effect of ESS modelling on optimal ESS sizing for an urban city bus is investigated. The results from this study indicate that (i) battery modelling has a significant impact on the optimal sizing of ESS for city bus; (ii) ambient temperature also influences the optimal sizing of ESS in city bus; and (iii) Since EChM is the most accurate and robust model, it is recommended to use it for EV battery size calculations.

APPENDIX

See Figure 15.8

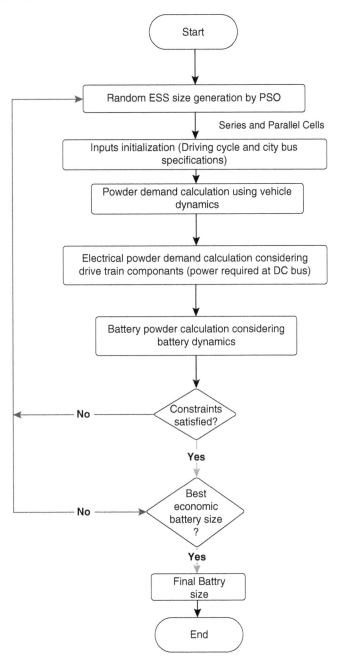

Figure 15.8 Flowchart of proposed work.

REFERENCES

1. Kumar, R. R. & Alok, K. (2020). Adoption of electric vehicle: A literature review and prospects for sustainability. *Journal of Cleaner Production*, 253, 119911.
2. Sanguesa, J. A., Torres-Sanz, V., Garrido, P., Martinez, F. J., & Marquez-Barja, J. M. (2021). A review on electric vehicles: Technologies and challenges. *Smart Cities*, 4(1), 372–404.
3. Li, Z., Khajepour, A., & Song, J. (2019). A comprehensive review of the key technologies for pure electric vehicles. *Energy*, 182, 824–839.
4. Hasan, M. K., Mahmud, M., Ahasan Habib, A. K. M., Motakabber, S. M. A., & Islam, S. (2021). Review of electric vehicle energy storage and management system: Standards, issues, and challenges. *Journal of Energy Storage*, 41(December 2020), 102940.
5. Hannan, M. A., Wali, S. B., Ker, P. J., Rahman, M. S. A., Mansor, M., Ramachandaramurthy, V. K., Muttaqi, K. M., Mahlia, T. M. I., & Dong, Z. Y. (2021). Battery energy-storage system: A review of technologies, optimization objectives, constraints, approaches, and outstanding issues. *Journal of Energy Storage*, 42(May), 103023.
6. Shen, M. & Gao, Q. (2019). A review on battery management system from the modeling efforts to its multiapplication and integration. *International Journal of Energy Research*, 43, 2–33.
7. Tamilselvi, S., Gunasundari, S., Karuppiah, N., Abdul Razak, R. K., Madhusudan, S., Nagarajan, V. M., Sathish, T., Shamim, M. Z. M., Saleel, C. A., & Afzal, A. (2021). A review on battery modelling techniques. *Sustainability*, 13(18), 10042.
8. Billy, W., Dhammika, W., Shichun, Y., & Xinhua, L. (2020). Battery digital twins: Perspectives on the fusion of models, data and artificial intelligence for smart battery management systems. *Energy and AI*, 1,100016, ISSN 2666-5468.
9. Zhang, C., Li, K., McLoone, S., & Yang, Z. (2014). Battery modelling methods for electric vehicles - A review. *2014 European Control Conference, ECC 2014*, Strasbourg, France, pp. 2673–2678.
10. Fotouhi, A., Auger, D. J., Propp, K., Longo, S., & Wild, M. (2016). A review on electric vehicle battery modelling: From Lithium-ion toward Lithium-Sulphur. *Renewable and Sustainable Energy Reviews*, 56, 1008–1021.
11. Adaikkappan, M & Sathiyamoorthy, N. (2022). Modeling, state of charge estimation, and charging of lithium-ion battery in electric vehicle: A review. *International Journal of Energy Research*, 46(3), 2141–2165.
12. Saldaña, G., Martín, J. I. S., Zamora, I., Asensio, F. J., & Oñederra, O. (2019). Analysis of the current electric battery models for electric vehicle simulation. *Energies*, 12(14), 2750.
13. Seaman, A., Dao, T. S., & McPhee, J. (2014). A survey of mathematics-based equivalent-circuit and electrochemical battery models for hybrid and electric vehicle simulation. *Journal of Power Sources*, 256, 410–423.
14. Thiruvonasundari, D. & Deepa, K. (2020). Electric vehicle battery modelling methods based on state of charge- review. *Journal of Green Engineering*, 10(1), 24–61.

15. Naseri, F., Barbu, C., & Sarikurt, T. (2022). Optimal sizing of hybrid high-energy/high-power battery energy storage systems to improve battery cycle life and charging power in electric vehicle applications. *Journal of Energy Storage*, 55(Part D), 105768, ISSN 2352-152X.
16. Lu, X. & Wang, H. (2020). Optimal sizing and energy management for cost-effective PEV hybrid energy storage systems. *IEEE Transactions on Industrial Informatics*, 16(5), 3407–3416.
17. Mamun, A.-A., Liu, Z., Rizzo, D. M., Onori, S., & Member, S. (2019). An integrated design and control optimization framework for hybrid military vehicle using Lithium-ion battery and supercapacitor as energy storage devices. *IEEE Transactions on Transportation Electrification*, 5(1), 239–251.
18. Pourabdollah, M., Egardt, B., Murgovski, N., & Grauers, A. (2017). Effect of driving, charging, and pricing scenarios on optimal component sizing of a PHEV. *Control Engineering Practice*, 61, 217–228.
19. Pinto, C., Barreras, J. V., de Castro, R., Araújo, R. E., & Schaltz, E. (2017). Study on the combined influence of battery models and sizing strategy for hybrid and battery-based electric vehicles. *Energy*, 137, 272–284.
20. Dynamometer Drive Schedules. www.epa.gov. Available at: https://www.epa.gov/vehicle-and-fuel-emissions-testing/dynamometer-drive-schedules (accessed on August 5, 2023).
21. Bansal, S., Dey, S., & Khanra, M. (2021). Energy storage sizing in plug-in Electric Vehicles: Driving cycle uncertainty effect analysis and machine learning based sizing framework. *Journal of Energy Storage*, 41(February), 102864.
22. Gillespie, T.D. *Fundamental of Vehicle Dynamics*, Society of Automotive Engineers, Inc., Reading, MA, 1992.
23. A123Systems. (2006). ANR 26650 high power Li-Ion Cell (datasheet). *Datasheet*, 617, 100001.
24. Perez, H. E, Siegel, J. B., Lin, X., Stefanopoulou, A. G., Ding, Y., & Castanier, M. P. (2012). "Parameterization and validation of an integrated electro-thermal cylindrical LFP battery model." *Proceedings of the ASME 2012 5th Annual Dynamic Systems and Control Conference joint with the JSME 2012 11th Motion and Vibration Conference.* Volume 3. Florida, USA. October 17-19, pp. 41–50.
25. Prada, E., Di Domenico, D., Creff, Y., Bernard, J., Sauvant-Moynot, V., & Huet, F. (2012). Simplified Electrochemical and thermal model of LiFePO 4-graphite Li-Ion batteries for fast charge applications. *Journal of the Electrochemical Society*, 159(9), A1508–A1519.
26. Di Domenico, D. (2010). Lithium-ion battery state of charge and critical surface charge estimation using an extended Kalman filter. *Journal of Dynamic Systems, Measurement, and Control*, 132, 1–11.
27. The Lithium Werks ANR26650M1B. buyA123batteries.com. Available at: https://www.buya123products.com/goodsdetail.php?i=6 (accessed on August 5, 2023).
28. Bansal, S., Nambisan, P., Saha, P., & Khanra, M. (2022). Effect of supercapacitor modelling and unit cell capacitance selection towards economic sizing of energy storage system in electric vehicle. *Journal of Energy Storage*, 51(February), 104517.

Chapter 16

Multiport DC-DC converters to integrate multiple energy storages for electric vehicles

Pratim Bhattacharyya, Raghu Selvaraj, Siddheswar Sen, and Santu Kumar Giri

16.1 INTRODUCTION

As the world is aiming towards carbon neutrality, the development of sustainable technologies for green transportation systems is gaining momentum at a brisk pace. A recent study by International Energy Agency (IEA) predicts that nearly 60% of on-road vehicles are needed to be electrified by 2030 [1]. In the commercial EVs sector, battery-operated electric vehicles (BEVs) have the highest production rate and market share in comparison with other EV technologies [2]. However, the major drawback in adoption of BEVs for transportation is the requirement of high-power density (W/kg) and energy density (Wh/kg) to cover an extended range of travel. Regardless of that, numerous setbacks such as high battery cost, reliability, range anxiety, prolonged charging time and life cycle of battery are withholding rapid commercialization of BEVs in the consumer's perspective [3–6]. Apart from that, the reliability and efficiency of power electronics components, converter topologies, electronic circuits and electric motors are also influencing vehicles cost. Presently, to achieve a higher driving range in BEVs, the battery capacity needs to be increased, which inadvertently increases the kerb weight and chassis dimension of the vehicle [7]. The power requirement for vehicles usually depends on the type of driving cycle (UDDS, NEDC, MIDC, etc.) and in some cases, complementing the energy or power density of battery with a secondary energy storage is preferred as a viable alternative [8–10]. Incorporation of a secondary energy storage in conjunction with the battery helps enhance the lifespan, mitigates thermal runaway, limits the charging/discharging rate and improves reliability [11]. In the future, the adoption of MES for EVs can outperform existing battery technologies, improve driving range, enhance efficiency and lower vehicle cost [12,13]. To ensure effective operation and better utilization of the MES, advanced power electronic converters like multiport DC-DC converters in conjunction with an optimal power management strategy need to be developed. In this chapter, insightful information on energy storage technologies for EVs is discussed. Besides, state-of-the-art on EV categories

DOI: 10.1201/9781003481065-16

and its possibility to incorporate MES are provided for enlightening the researchers. Furthermore, conceptualization on MES integration and critical evaluation on multiport DC-DC converter configurations are discussed to understand practical implications in future research directions.

16.2 ENERGY STORAGE SYSTEMS FOR ELECTRIC VEHICLES

Figure 16.1 shows a powertrain architecture of an EV with major components. Here, the traction inverter, electric motor and gear transmission form the part of electric propulsion unit, while the energy storage system (ESS), high voltage (HV) DC-DC converter and onboard charger forms a part of the electrical power unit. ESS forms a pivotal entity of the electric power unit, so it must be designed proficiently to ensure optimum EV performance. There are certain parameters, which govern the selection of a suitable ESS for EV powertrains like high energy density (Wh/kg), high power density (W/kg), fast charging capability, high dynamic response, prolonged cycle life, ease of maintenance, optimal size & volume, etc. [14]. In the present scenario, battery (Li-ion), ultracapacitor (UC) and fuel cell (FC) are popularly considered ESS for EV applications [8]. Particularly from an energy density perspective, battery has a maximum energy density of 265 Wh/kg with a 'tank to wheel' operational efficiency of 81% [15]. Therefore, it is suitable for on-road vehicles (2W, 3W, 4W (passenger cars)) to provide continuous power. While focusing on off-road vehicles, the terrain operation demands a high-power density, which shall be provided by an UC. On the other hand, heavy-duty vehicles (bus, truck) require a higher driving range (>800 km) with a lower kerb weight, where FCs are a preferable choice. The detailed characteristics of battery, UC and FC are discussed in

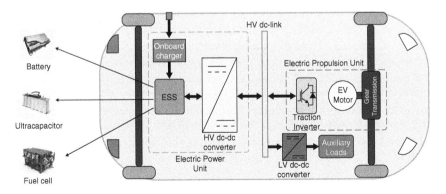

Figure 16.1 EV powertrain architecture [4].

Table 16.1 Parametric comparison between battery, ultracapacitor and fuel cell [17,18]

Parameters	Battery (lithium-ion)	Ultracapacitor	Fuel cell
Energy density (Wh/kg)	High, 100–265	Low, 1–5	Very high, >1,400
Power density (W/kg)	100–3,500	>4,000	~ 1,600
Efficiency	Nearly 90% at light loads, Nearly 50% at high loads	Almost 95% at high loads	Almost 50% at rated power
Cost per kWh	500–1,000 USD (large system)	2,500–6,000 USD (typical)	15,000–20,000 USD (typical)
Dynamic response	Medium	Very fast	Slow
Lifetime (no of cycles)	500–2,000	>100k	2,000–4,000
Operating temperature (°C)	0–50	−45 to 65	−35 to 45
Maintenance	Less, once replaced in vehicle lifetime	Not required	Fuel storage tank needs a routine check-up
Cell balancing requirements	Active balancing	Passive balancing	Balance of Plant (BoP)

number of literature studies [16–19]. A parametric comparison between the three types of energy storages is enumerated in Table 16.1 [17,18].

16.3 INTEGRATION OF MULTIPLE ENERGY STORAGES FOR EVS

In practical aspects, load profile of an EV is highly dynamic in nature with frequent variations in power demand during acceleration/deceleration. During such operational period, an ESS with high power density is essential to meet the varying power demand. Several studies reveal that single ESS is incapable to fulfil dynamic power variations during various driving scenarios [17,20]. These practical challenges introduce the concept of integrating two or more ESS with complementary characteristics is termed as a hybrid energy storage system (HESS). A combination of battery and UC can offer a trade-off between the desired criteria of high energy density and high-power density with longer lifetime [9,10]. On the other hand, the slow dynamic response of a FC can be compensated by integrating battery or UC with FC [21,22]. The key benefits of HESS are pointed out below:

- Improvement of peak power delivering capability of ESS.
- Enhancement in regenerative power recuperation capability.

- Augmentation in the dynamic performance of EV.
- Overall size and weight of the ESS is reduced by eliminating the requirement of oversized single energy storage.
- Improvement in the reliability and lifespan of ESS.

Based on the above research intervention, the present ESS technology and preferred HESS technology for different EV segments are tabulated in Table 16.2 [23,24]. The HESS technology is most suitable for E-2W (sports) and E-4W (passenger and sports car) [23]. The combination of Li-ion+UC shall be adopted for low voltage (48–96 V) and high voltage (300–800 V) system with the aim to improve the lifespan of a Li-ion battery. Most of the commercial FCEVs employ a combination of FC+Li-ion to tackle the dynamic power variations [24]. However, the addition of UCs in FCEVs shall further improve the operational characteristics of FC. Incorporation of MES into EV powertrain becomes challenging because it needs to be effectively controlled to ensure the proper power sharing among energy storages. Therefore, an appropriate configuration for hybridization is required to be selected to deal with the fluctuating power demand of EVs.

The dynamic performance, control flexibility, efficiency and lifetime of the ESS rely on the type of HESS configuration. The selection of a HESS configuration vastly varies depending upon the EV drivetrain power requirements [8–10]. The configurations of HESS can broadly be classified into five different categories, as illustrated in Figure 16.2 [8].

Among the conventional HESS configurations, the passive configuration (Figure 16.3a) is the simplest approach to interconnect MES without employing any power electronic converters [25,26]. However, such configurations suffer from practical shortcomings like ineffective utilization of energy storages, and uncontrolled power-sharing due to the absence of power management, thereby hampering their market penetration. The active configurations, on the other hand, offer much superiority in terms of overall system performance due to independent control of MES. The parallel active HESS (Figure 16.3b) is the most popular and versatile approach for commercialization among the conventional HESS configurations [27,28]. The cascaded configuration is another active approach for interconnecting MES as illustrated through variant 1 (Figure 16.3c) and variant 2 (Figure 16.3d) [29,30]. The semi-active HESS is a slight modification from the parallel active configuration, where one of the power electronic converters is usually eliminated for the sake of space and size reduction. For battery-UC HESS, the semi-active HESS can further be categorized as battery semi-active (Figure 16.3e) and UC semi-active (Figure 16.3f) configurations [31–33]. Table 16.3 provides a concise idea on the key features of different HESS configurations [25–33].

Table 16.2 Parametric comparison between different EV segments [23,24]

Categories	Sub-categories	Driving range and top speed	Motor power rating (kW)	ESS voltage rating (V)	Present ESS technology	Preferred HESS technology	Key vehicle models
Battery electric vehicles (BEVs)	E-2W	Upto 150km and 90 kmph	1–5	24–48	Battery (Li-ion)	NA	Hero Electric Photon HX (1.8kW), Turbowheel Lightning (2kW), Bajaj Chetak (4kW)
	E-3W	Upto 130km and 30 kmph	≤2 (L-3)	24–48	Li-ion	NA	YC electric yatri deluxe (1.4kW), Mahindra treo yaari (2kW), Safar smart (1.2kW)
		Upto 200km and 60 kmph	1.5–12 (L-5)	48–72	Li-ion	NA	Piaggo Apecity (5kW), Euler Hiload DV (11kW), Altigreen NeEV (8.25kW)
	E-4W	Upto 150km and 90 kmph	≤30 Hatchback	48–72	Li-ion	Li-ion+UC	Mahindra e2o plus (19kW),
		Upto 320km and 110 kmph	≤55 Sedan	72	Li-ion	Li-ion+UC	Tata Tigor EV (55kW), Mahindra Everito (31kW)
		Upto 460km and 170 kmph	90–250 SUV	300–400	Li-ion	Li-ion+UC	Tata Nexon EV (96kW), Hyundai Kona Electric (100kW)
		Upto 400km and 100 kmph	100–500 Bus	300–800	Li-ion	Li-ion+UC	Tata motors Starbus EV (245kW), Ashok Leyland 12m EV (150kW)
FCEVs	E-4W	Upto 1,000km and 200 kmph	80–150 SUV/Sedan	280–420	FC+Li-ion	FC+Li-ion/ FC+UC	Hyundai Tucson (100kW),Toyota Mirai (114kW)
		Upto 600km and 120 kmph	80–250 Bus	400–580	FC+Li-ion	FC+Li-ion+UC	Wright Street Deck Hydroliner FCEV (85kW), Sentient Lab Hydrogen FCEV
Sports EVs	E-2W	Upto 150km and 130 kmph	≥5	48–96	Li-ion	Li-ion+UC	Dualtron Thunder 2 (5.4kW), Rion RE 90 (10kW)
	E-4W	Upto 1,000km and 260 kmph	185–500	400–800	Li-ion	Li-ion+UC	Tesla Roadstar (185kW), Porsche Taycan Turbo S (460kW)

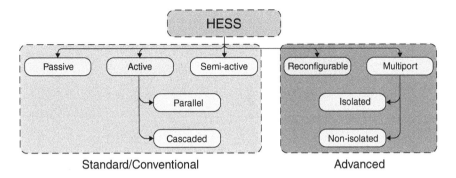

Figure 16.2 Categorization of HESS configurations [8].

16.4 MULTIPORT CONVERTER TOPOLOGIES FOR HESS IN EV APPLICATIONS

To address the inadequacies of conventional HESS configurations in EV powertrains, researchers are motivated to develop HESS configurations for optimal utilization of MES with enhanced power density and improved efficiency. By reconfiguring the conventional HESS (passive, active and semi-active) based on dynamic power scenarios, the effective utilization of MES can be achieved. Although research studies on reconfiguration techniques for ESS have been reported, but their applicability for HESS in EV applications is yet to be explored [34,35]. On the contrary, the advent of multiport DC-DC converters has paved the way for integrating MES through a unified power electronic platform. Multiport DC-DC converters offer numerous advantages in terms of high integration through component sharing, centralized power management and higher power density [36–38].

16.4.1 Categorization of multiport DC-DC converters

The different types of multiport DC-DC converters reported in literature studies can be categorized into four types in terms of isolation, structure, direction of power flow and gain based on EV powertrain operational requirements. In general, multiport DC-DC converters are commonly categorized as isolated, non-isolated and partially isolated in existing literature studies. Figure 16.4 represents the detailed classification of multiport DC-DC converters [38].

16.4.1.1 Isolated multiport DC-DC converters [39,40]

This converter topology inherently provides an isolation between the MES and output ports by employing a multi-winding transformer, as can be

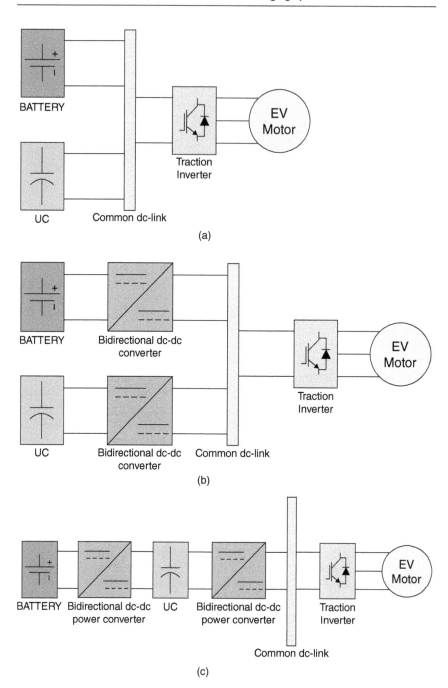

Figure 16.3 Conventional configurations of HESS (a) Passive HESS [25,26] (b) Parallel active HESS [27,28] (c) Cascaded active HESS (variant 1) [29] (d) Cascaded active HESS (variant 2) [30] (e) Battery semi-active HESS [31,32] (f) UC semi-active HESS [33].

(Continued)

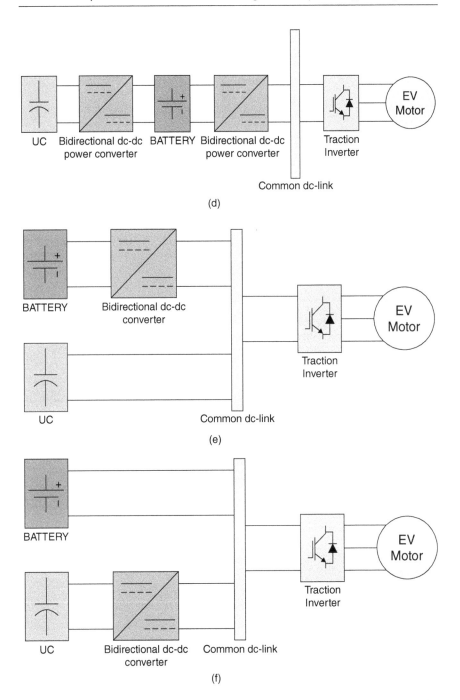

Figure 16.3 (Continued) Conventional configurations of HESS (a) Passive HESS [25,26] (b) Parallel active HESS [27,28] (c) Cascaded active HESS (variant 1) [29] (d) Cascaded active HESS (variant 2) [30] (e) Battery semi-active HESS [31,32] (f) UC semi-active HESS [33].

Table 16.3 Parametric comparison of conventional HESS configurations [25–33]

Parameters	Passive [25,26]	Active [27–30]	Semi-active [31–33]
Cost	Low	High	Moderate
Flexibility	No	Full	Partial
Range of control strategies adoption	Low	High	Moderate
DC-link voltage fluctuation	Yes	No	Yes, for battery semi-active HESS
Fault tolerance	No	Yes	Only for the ESS connected through DC-DC converter
Space	Less	High	Intermediate
Control complexity	Low (devoid of controller)	High (increased computational complexity due to power management of multiple energy storages)	Moderate (due to power management of single energy storage)
Remarks	Recommended when cost is the deciding factor in small systems	Suitable for large capacity systems which require a superior dynamic power management	Recommended when the size of the ESS is of main concern

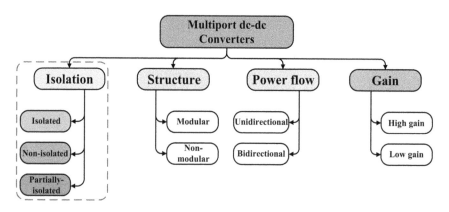

Figure 16.4 Categorization of multiport DC-DC converters [38].

seen in Figure 16.5a [39,40]. The incorporation of an isolation transformer reduces the risk of electrical shocks/hazards, which ensures the safety of an EV. In addition, the high-frequency transformer transfers energy between MES and DC-link capacitor in buck or boost modes with a high conversion ratio. This topology is quite beneficial for 400 V and 800 V EV systems,

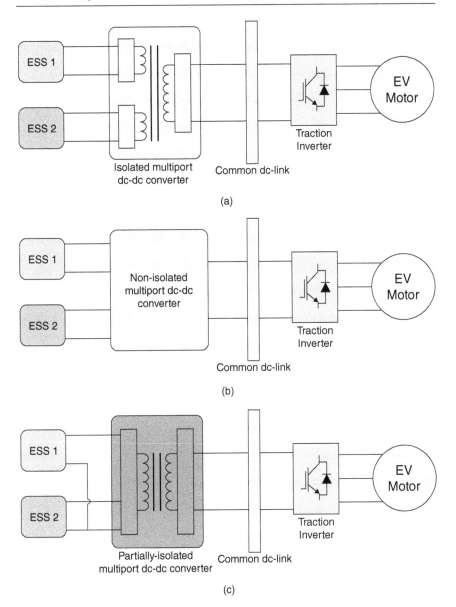

(a)

(b)

(c)

Figure 16.5 Generalized block level representation of (a) Isolated multiport DC-DC converter [39,40] (b) Non-isolated multiport DC-DC converter [42–47] and (c) Partially isolated multiport DC-DC converter [41].

whichever is driven by a low-voltage MES. Furthermore, this topology is mostly preferable for UC-based HESS, since stacking of UCs at high voltages is not recommended due to the complexity in balancing circuitry. During an occurrence of fault in MES or any of the ports (input/output), the faulty port can easily be isolated and other healthy ports shall continue their operation in a compromised manner. Despite its favourable benefits to EV powertrain, this topology suffers with higher cost, complicated magnetics design requirements and greater number of power electronic components leading to higher volume and size.

16.4.1.2 Non-isolated multiport DC-DC converters [42–47]

In general, non-isolated multiport DC-DC converters (Figure 16.5b) eliminate the high-frequency transformer requirements with less design complications and higher power density [42–47]. As a part of this, the entire power components such as power switches, controllers and passive components are reduced. This component reduction influences the size and volumetric ratio, which facilitates for the implementation in EV powertrains. In practical aspects, this topology offers a relatively higher efficiency in comparison with isolated topology, due to the absence of parasitic losses and leakage inductances of a transformer. Moreover, this topology requires a controller with minimum memory allocation and optimum processing speed. The major drawbacks of the non-isolated converters are the limited voltage conversion ratios and the absence of galvanic isolation between the input and output ports. Besides, the non-isolated converter suffers from safety and reliability issues, since a fault that occurs at any of the ports may get transmitted to the other healthy ports causing a downtime in HESS operation.

16.4.1.3 Partially isolated multiport DC-DC converters [41]

The partially isolated or electromagnetically coupled multiport converters (Figure 16.5c) are considered as a trade-off between the isolated and non-isolated topologies [41]. In this topology, usually the input ports are interconnected electrically, while galvanic isolation is provided between the output and input ports. The merits of this topology are higher voltage gain with a wider range of voltage operations. This operational feature achieves the power conversion efficiency relatively lesser than non-isolated topology. To improve the efficiency in partially isolated topology, either modifications in power circuitry or soft switching control scheme is needed to be implemented.

16.4.2 Evaluation of multiport converter topologies for HESS in EV powertrains

In this section, five benchmarking multiport converter configurations for HESS in EV powertrain applications are discussed while highlighting their merits and demerits.

16.4.2.1 Bidirectional non-isolated multi-input converter [42]

The bidirectional three-port non-isolated multiport converter in Ref. [42] can accommodate multiple input ports by integrating individual converter module. As depicted in Figure 16.6a, the input port (V_1 or V_2) along with the assembly of an active switch (S_1 or S_2), diode (D_1 or D_2) and inductor (L_1 or L_2) forms a buck converter module. This configuration provides independent control over individual energy storage. However, this topology operates with double-stage conversion during power transfer between two input ports involving both inductors, which results in reduced efficiency. Apart from that, the topology offers limited voltage gain because of its cascaded structure (input buck and output boost converter).

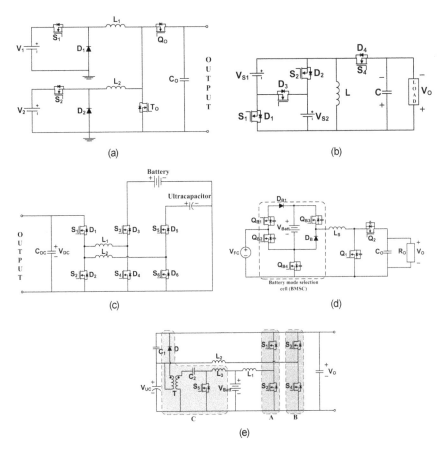

Figure 16.6 Circuit configuration of (a) Bidirectional non-isolated multi-input converter [42] (b) Non-isolated bridge type multiport converter [43] (c) Modular multi-input bidirectional converter [44] (d) Integrated multi-mode converter [45] and (e) Reduced rating multi-input converter [46].

16.4.2.2 Bridge-type multiport converter [43]

In Ref. [43], a non-isolated bridge-type dual input DC-DC converter (Figure 16.6b) employing single inductor (L) and four switches ($S_1 \sim S_4$) is discussed. One of the salient features of this topology is reduction of conduction losses due to the absence of diode in the circuit. Although the presence of a single inductor facilitates overall size reduction and minimizes the critical electromagnetic interference (EMI) issues, it lacks independent control over each energy storage. Besides, the converter generates an inverted voltage at the output port, which raises the concern of uncommon grounding between the input and output ports.

16.4.2.3 Modular multi-input bidirectional converter [44]

A non-isolated bidirectional DC-DC converter (Figure 16.6c) comprising two inductors (L_1 and L_2) and six number of PWM controlled switches (S_1–S_6) is presented in Ref. [44]. Apart from the merits of operating at relatively higher efficiency, this topology offers the provision of independent as well as simultaneous control over MES. Furthermore, the three ports of this converter are bidirectional, which enables the storage of regenerative power. However, one of the shortcomings of this topology is that the power flow between the two input ports involves a series path of both the inductors which slightly reduces the efficiency.

16.4.2.4 Integrated multi-mode converter [45]

The single inductor-based multi-mode converter (Figure 16.6d) presented in Ref. [45] consists of a battery mode selection cell (BMSC) composed of switches (Q_{B1}–Q_{B4}) and two diodes (D_{B1}, D_B) that are connected to the battery. Having a single inductor offers certain advantages like minimization of magnetically induced losses, lower magnetic interferences and reduction in size and volume of the converter. In addition, this topology also aims to reduce voltage stress on semiconductor devices because the switches Q_{B1}–Q_{B4} and diode D_B are clamped to the lower voltage terminals (V_{FC} or V_{Batt}). However, the topology deficits in providing independent control over the FC and battery due to lack of separate inductors. Furthermore, the charging of the battery through FC cannot be technically possible owing to the absence of inductor in the charging path.

16.4.2.5 Reduced rating multi-input converter [46]

A two-input DC-DC converter [46] can be considered as a unification of three types of converter as shown in Figure 16.6e. Converters A and B are bidirectional buck-boost converters while converter C is an isolated SEPIC converter. The UC is interfaced to the load through the series connected converter C, which assists the UC by generating a voltage, to compensate the drop in UC voltage that occurred during surge power delivery. This topology offers advantages like the presence of all bidirectional ports and independent control through separate inductors. The first and foremost drawback of this topology is that the voltage rating of UC needs to be matched with DC-link voltage, which necessitates UC to be overrated. Moreover, the UC practically remains underutilized since it cannot be discharged up to a much lower voltage level due to the absence of a regulated high-power DC-DC conversion path between the UC and DC-link. Furthermore, the topology exploits an additional SEPIC converter, which inadvertently increases the overall size and volume.

16.5 A FLEXIBLE BIDIRECTIONAL MULTIPORT CONVERTER FOR EVS [47]

Addressing the challenges of the prior configurations, a flexible bidirectional multiport converter (Figure 16.7) for battery-UC HESS has been presented in Ref. [47]. This dual input (V_B and V_{UC}) single output (V_{DC}) converter, as illustrated in Figure 16.7, comprises two inductors (L_{UC}, L_B), five PWM switches (S_{B1}, S_{UC1}, S_{B2}, S_{UC2}, and S_{CL}), a single diode (D_{CL}) and a non-PWM changeover switch (S_C). The converter uniquely consists of two dedicated yet flexibly re-allocable power flow paths for facilitating the flow of high and low currents, namely the high current path (HCP) and low current path (LCP). The components associated with the HCP including the inductor (L_{UC}) and bidirectional assembly of PWM switches (S_{UC1} and S_{UC2}) are rated at high power according to the peak current operating capability of the converter. In contrast, the inductor (L_B) and PWM switches (S_{B1} and S_{B2}) associated with LCP are rated as per the nominal current handling capability. The switch S_{CL} in the configuration acts as the main PWM switch to

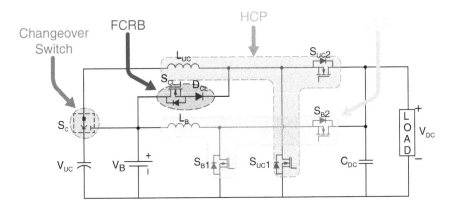

Figure 16.7 Circuit configuration of flexible non-isolated multiport converter [47].

enable the charging operation of UC from the battery. The switch S_{CL} is connected in series with a diode D_{CL} forming a forward conducting reverse blocking (FCRB) pair to prevent the battery against the inadvertent power flow from the UC terminals. This topology offers the feature of flexibly re-allocating the battery and UC to a desired power transfer path (HCP or LCP) depending on the dynamic load scenario. Flexibility of re-allocation is highly desirable for multiport converters in EV powertrain applications to ensure a superior power flow management to improve energy storage utilization and for enhancing the recuperation of regenerative braking energy. The flexibility of the configuration is achieved by virtue of a changeover switch S_C, which allows the dynamic coupling and decoupling of either of the energy storage with the HCP. The operation of the converter is diversified into seven distinct modes corresponding to possible dynamic load power scenarios prevalent in an EV drive cycle as enumerated in Table 16.4.

16.5.1 Results and analysis

The flexible multiport converter is simulated in MATLAB/Simulink platform to verify the operation of the converter across seven distinct modes mentioned in Table 16.4. A load profile consisting of forward powering (steady speed and acceleration) and regenerative braking events is selected, corresponding to possible dynamic events encountered in an EV. The simulation parameters and different component values are listed in Table 16.5.

Table 16.4 Conditions and modes of operation of flexible multiport converter

Condition	Operation	PWM switch	Position of S_c
Steady load demand	Battery to load through LCP	S_{B1}	Coupled with UC
Peak load demand	Battery to load through LCP	S_{B1}	Coupled with UC
	UC to load through HCP	S_{UC1}	
Peak load demand with UC in discharged condition	Battery to load through HCP	S_{UC1}	Coupled with battery
Steady load demand with UC in discharged condition	Battery to load through LCP	S_{B1}	Coupled with UC
	Battery charging UC	S_{CL}	
Load regeneration	UC recuperating regenerative power through HCP	S_{UC2}	Coupled with UC
Load regeneration with UC in fully charged condition (low power)	Battery recuperating regenerative power through LCP	S_{B2}	Coupled with UC
Load regeneration with UC in fully charged condition (high power)	Battery recuperating regenerative power through HCP	S_{UC2}	Coupled with battery

Table 16.5 Simulation parameters and component values

Parameters/components	Value
Battery	LiFePO$_4$, 25.2V (nominal), 20 Ah
Ultracapacitor	16.2V (full charged), 116.67 F
L_{UC}	30 μH, 90 A (saturation current)
L_B	60 μH, 50 A (saturation current)
C_{DC}	1,500 μF
V_{DC}	48V
V_{UC}	16.2 V ~ 12.8V
V_B	27.5 V ~ 25V
Steady load current threshold limit (through LCP)	9 A
SOC$_{UC}$ (lower threshold)	75%
f_S (switching frequency)	100 kHz

The simulation is performed in two different scenarios based on the SOC of UC. At the beginning of scenario 1, the UC is at a fully charged state with a SOC of greater than 95% (V_{UC}=16.2 V), while the battery too remains at a SOC of 95% (V_B=27.5 V). The load profile selected during scenario 1 is composed of three different events commencing with a steady load demand for 3 seconds (0–3) followed by a regenerative braking event of 3.2 seconds (3–6.2) and concluding with a dynamic event (composed of steady load and multiple peak load intervals) of 6 seconds (6.2–12.2). The different current and voltage waveforms related to the operation of the converter during scenario 1 are illustrated in Figure 16.8a. It is quite evident from the obtained results that, during the first steady load interval, the converter is operated in mode 1 to allow the battery for supplying the steady load current through LCP. The UC, on the other hand, remains idle during this interval at a fully charged state. However, the next regenerative interval displays an interesting scenario of transition between mode 6 and mode 7 of converter operation. At the beginning of the event, when the load starts regenerating, the regenerative power is required to be recuperated by the battery since the UC is already in a fully charged state. Thus, the converter shifts its operation to mode 6 for recuperating the regenerative power through LCP. As the regenerative current begins to increase beyond the predefined threshold current limit of the LCP (9 A), the converter immediately transits to mode 7 to recuperate the total regenerative current in battery through HCP, thereby demonstrating flexibility in operation. Towards the end of the regenerative interval, when the regenerative current reduces below the threshold limit, the converter reverts back to operate in mode 6 till the end of the interval. The last dynamic event with fluctuating load current demands reveals the converter operation through multiple transitions between mode 1 and mode 2 in close succession. The event begins with the converter operating

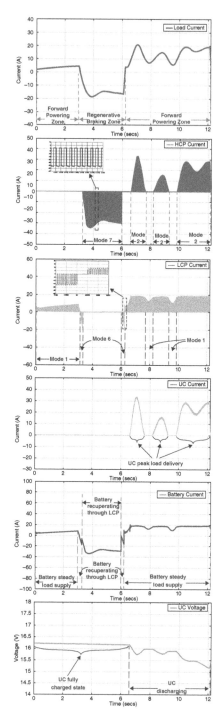

Figure 16.8 Simulation waveforms corresponding to (a) Scenario 1 (SOC$_{UC}$=95%) (b) Scenario 2 (SOC$_{UC}$=77%).

(Continued)

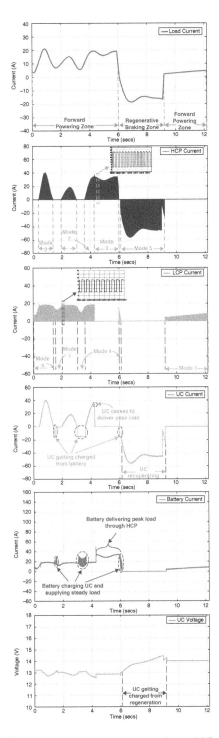

Figure 16.8 (Continued) Simulation waveforms corresponding to (a) Scenario I (SOC$_{UC}$=95%) (b) Scenario 2 (SOC$_{UC}$=77%).

in mode 1 as the battery supplies the increasing load current through LCP. Gradually, as the load current increases beyond the threshold limit (9 A), the UC comes into action to deliver the peak load power with the converter shifting its operation to mode 2. It is evident from Figure 16.8a, that UC discharges during successive peak load intervals by contributing maximum portion of the peak load current through HCP while the battery supplies a nearly steady load current throughout the duration of peak load event. The smooth transition between mode 1 and mode 2 verifies the dynamic flexibility of the configuration.

In scenario 2, the UC is partially discharged to a SOC of nearly 77% (13.2 V) while the load profile is slightly altered as the fluctuating load current event occurring at the beginning for 6 seconds (0–6) followed by the regenerative period of 3.2 seconds (6–9.2) and concluding with the steady load demand for 3 seconds (9.2–12.2). The dynamic transitions of the converter across multiple modes (mode 1 to mode 5) are revealed in this scenario as depicted in Figure 16.8b. At the start of the event, the converter operates in mode 1 with the battery supplying the load demand through LCP until the arrival of the first peak load instant. Here, just like the previous case, the UC delivers a maximum portion of the load current through HCP while the battery supplies a nominal current as the converter operates in mode 2. After the peak load diminishes, the UC is discharged below the threshold limit of 76%, which initiates the converter operation in mode 4 with the battery recharging the UC (by controlling S_{CL}) while simultaneously supplying the steady load current through LCP till the onset of the next peak load interval. The second peak load interval also encounters a similar operation as the converter reverts to mode 2 with the UC supplying the peak load current. As the event ends, the UC is again recharged from the battery through a constant current with the converter altering its operation to mode 4. However, in the third peak load interval, an interesting scenario is observed, where the converter initially starts by operating in mode 2 with the UC delivering load power through HCP till the SOC_{UC} falls below the threshold limit (here predefined as 75% at $V_{UC}=12.8$ V). As the UC terminates to deliver the peak load current in spite of the continuing load demand, the converter promptly alters its operation to mode 3, by engaging the battery to deliver the peak load current through HCP for the remaining duration. This flexibility of operation ensures an uninterrupted supply of peak load even during the non-availability of UC. After the end of peak load interval, the converter reverts back to mode 4 for charging the UC from battery till the initiation of the regeneration event. During the regenerative event, the UC is prioritized to recuperate the total regenerative energy through HCP with the converter operating in mode 5 while the battery remains idle throughout the entire duration. In the final steady load demand interval, the converter again operates at mode 1 with the battery supplying the required power.

The obtained simulation results verify the flexible operation of converter across multiple modes and also validate the capability of the converter in achieving smooth transition between multiple operating modes even during transient load power scenarios.

16.5.2 Comparison with other multiport converter topologies

The flexible multiport converter [47] has been compared with other popular multiport topologies discussed in the previous section based on certain topological parameters as depicted in Table 16.6. It can be inferred that the flexible multiport converter offers a range of the following distinct functionalities that are pertinent for EV powertrain applications.

a. The flexible multiport converter allows charging of one energy storage from other and provides single-stage power processing in every possible power flow paths, unlike the topologies reported in Refs. [42,44,46] where the charging of energy storage can only be accomplished through a double-stage conversion path involving both the inductors.

b. The single inductor-based configurations in Refs. [43,45] achieve single-stage power conversion similar to the flexible configuration, but lack independent control over each energy storages due to the absence of a separate inductor. On the contrary, the flexible converter provides independent power control over both battery and UC through dedicated inductors. Besides, the configurations in Refs. [43,45] neither offer the possibility of charging between energy storages nor provide the facility of simultaneous power transfer.

c. The flexible multiport converter, unlike the prior works ([42–46]), offers the flexibility to dynamically allocate the battery either with the LCP or with HCP depending on the diverse operating conditions. This unique feature helps in coupling the battery easily to L_{UC}, when the UC is not available for peak power delivery or recuperation of energy. Thus, the selection of L_B can be done judiciously based on the steady power level, which eliminates the necessity for oversized high current rated inductors.

16.6 CHALLENGES AND FUTURE RESEARCH DIRECTIONS

16.6.1 Development of high-gain multiport DC-DC converters

In the present scenario, the DC bus voltage for an EV powertrain is being upgraded from 400 to 800 V in relation to implement fast charging option. This requirement is needed for the development of non-isolated multiport DC-DC converters with high conversion ratios.

Table 16.6 Comparison table of flexible multiport converter with other multiport topologies

Topology	Bidirectional non-isolated multi-input converter [42]	Bridge type multiport converter [43]	Modular multi-input bidirectional converter [44]	Integrated multi-mode converter [45]	Reduced rating multi-input converter [46]	Flexible non-isolated multiport converter [47]
Ports	3	3	3	3	3	3
Bidirectional ports	3	3	3	3	3	3
Inductors	2	1	2	1	3	2
PWM switches	4	4	6	3	5	5
Non-PWM switches	0	0	0	3	0	1
Diodes	2	0	0	2	1	—
Capacitors	1	1	1	1	3	—
Independent control	Yes	No	Yes	No	Yes	Yes
Single stage power conversion	All except one	All modes	All except one	Yes	All except one	All modes
Charging between energy storages	Two stage path	Not possible	Two stage path	Not possible	Two stage path	Yes
Simultaneous power transfer	Yes	Not possible	Yes	Not possible	Yes	Yes
Flexibility of re-allocation	No	No	No	No	No	Yes

Challenges: Higher conversion ratio operation of a multiport DC-DC converter results in high input current ripples at the MES. This necessitates the requirement of high power rated passive components and power switches. Therefore, the minimization of input ripple current is an important research aspect, which needs to be addressed for commercialization.

16.6.2 Implementation of fault-tolerant strategies

The reliability of the EV powertrain components is one of the important factors to ensure safety. The switching components of multiport converters are prone to frequent failures during dynamic operational scenarios. To qualify the automotive standards, fault diagnosis and tolerant operation of multiport converters are needed to be implemented.

Challenges: The fault identification time and reconfiguration time need to be minimal to avoid detrimental failure of the EV powertrain. To ensure the fail-safe operation of multiport converter, the controller must process, compute and execute the fault-tolerant scheme within a single operating cycle.

16.6.3 Development of a single-stage multiport converter and inverter

A standard EV powertrain architecture is a double-stage power conversion system from ESS to the EV motor, comprising a DC-DC conversion stage interfaced with a DC-AC inverter stage. Shifting from the standard double-stage power conversion system to a unified single-stage power conversion eliminates the requirement for an inverter stage, thereby enhancing the overall power conversion efficiency and power density of the EV powertrain.

Challenges: One of the major technical difficulties in implementing a single-stage power conversion is the higher controller burden, design complexity and electromagnetic interference (EMI) issues. To solve these issues, printed circuit boards (PCBs) must be critically designed with optimal placement of components.

16.6.4 Development of wide band gap device-based high-frequency multiport converters

With the aim of size miniaturization, the multiport converters must be designed to operate at higher switching frequencies. However, at such high frequencies, the switching losses of the converters tend to increase considerably, which reduces the overall efficiency. To minimize the switching losses, wide band gap (WBG) power semiconductor devices must be selected for designing the multiport converters by replacing the conventional Si-based devices. Among the WBG devices, the Gallium Nitride (GaN) is best suited for the design of high-frequency converters owing to their minimum switching losses, smaller chip area and lower heat dissipation. Thus, the development of high-frequency multiport converters employing GaN power semiconductor switches is one of the promising research arenas.

Challenges: One of the critical design challenges associated with high-frequency operation (>100 kHz) is the increased EMI issues. Therefore, maintaining the equilibrium between the high switching frequency and electromagnetic compatibility of the system requires optimal component placement and skilled design of PCBs.

16.7 CONCLUSION

This chapter summarizes the concept of MES integration for EV powertrains and provides insightful knowledge on various multiport HESS configurations. The state-of-the-art multiport DC-DC converters are evaluated from the perspective of their applicability for EV powertrains. The merits and demerits of the configurations are pointed out with respect to pertinent parameters like number of active switches and passive components, availability of bidirectional ports, provision of single-stage power conversion, ability of independent control over energy storages, simultaneous power transferring capability, etc. Further, addressing the drawbacks of the prior works, a flexible bidirectional multiport converter is analyzed through simulation based on various dynamic load power scenarios of an EV. Finally, to promote the development of energy-efficient multiport converter topologies, challenges in market adoption with next-generation design considerations are put forward, and future research directions are also prospected to further enhance the knowledge. In a nutshell, this chapter aims to provide a 'one-stop' information source on the said subject for students, researchers, academicians and application engineers.

REFERENCES

1. International Energy Agency, "By 2030 EVs represent more than 60% of vehicles sold globally, and require an adequate surge in chargers installed in buildings," https://www.iea.org/reports/by-2030-evs-represent-more-than-60-of-Vehicles-Sold-Globally-and-Require-an-Adequate-Surge-in-Chargers-Installed-in-Buildings, pp. 1–5, 2022.
2. A. Mahmoudzadeh Andwari, A. Pesiridis, S. Rajoo, R. Martinez-Botas, and V. Esfahanian, "A review of Battery Electric Vehicle technology and readiness levels," *Renew. Sust. Energy Rev.*, vol. 78, no. May, pp. 414–430, 2017.
3. S. Manzetti and F. Mariasiu, "Electric vehicle battery technologies: From present state to future systems," *Renew. Sust. Energy Rev.*, vol. 51, pp. 1004–1012, 2015.

4. M. A. Hannan, M. M. Hoque, A. Mohamed, and A. Ayob, "Review of energy storage systems for electric vehicle applications : Issues and challenges," *Renew. Sust. Energy Rev.*, vol. 69, no. September 2015, pp. 771–789, 2017.

5. S. F. Tie and C. W. Tan, "A review of energy sources and energy management system in electric vehicles," *Renew. Sust. Energy Rev.*, vol. 20, pp. 82–102, 2013.

6. J. Deng, C. Bae, A. Denlinger, and T. Miller, "Electric vehicles batteries: Requirements and challenges," *Joule*, vol. 4, no. 3, pp. 511–515, 2020.

7. M. Safayatullah, M. T. Elrais, S. Ghosh, R. Rezaii, and I. Batarseh, "A comprehensive review of power converter topologies and control methods for electric vehicle fast charging applications," *IEEE Access*, vol. 10, pp. 40753–40793, 2022.

8. T. S. Babu, K. R. Vasudevan, V. K. Ramachandaramurthy, S. B. Sani, S. Chemud, and R. M. Lajim, "A comprehensive review of hybrid energy storage systems: Converter topologies, control strategies and future prospects," *IEEE Access*, vol. 8, pp. 148702–148721, 2020.

9. A. Ostadi and M. Kazerani, "A comparative analysis of optimal sizing of battery-only, ultracapacitor-only, and battery-ultracapacitor hybrid energy storage systems for a city bus," *IEEE Trans. Veh. Technol.*, vol. 64, no. 10, pp. 4449–4460, 2015.

10. F. Ju, Q. Zhang, W. Deng, and J. Li, "Review of structures and control of battery-supercapacitor hybrid energy storage system for electric vehicles," *Adv. Batter. Manuf. Serv. Manag. Syst.*, pp. 303–318, 2016.

11. M. J. Lencwe, S. P. D. Chowdhury, and T. O. Olwal, "Hybrid energy storage system topology approaches for use in transport vehicles: A review," *Energy Sci. Eng.*, vol. 10, no. 4, pp. 1449–1477, 2022.

12. S. Bansal, S. Dey, and M. Khanra, "Energy storage sizing in plug-in Electric Vehicles: Driving cycle uncertainty effect analysis and machine learning based sizing framework," *J. Energy Storage*, vol. 41, p. 102864, 2021.

13. R. Hema and M. J. Venkatarangan, "Adoption of EV: Landscape of EV and opportunities for India," *Meas. Sensors*, vol. 24, p. 100596, 2022.

14. E. Roshandel, A. Mahmoudi, S. Kahourzade, A. Tahir, and N. Fernando, "Propulsion system of electric vehicles: Review," In *2021 31st Australasian Universities Power Engineering Conference (AUPEC)*, Perth, Australia, Sep. 2021, pp. 1–6.

15. L. B. Van Leeuwen, "Hydrogen or battery tractors: What potential for sustainable grape growing?" *IVES Tech. Rev. Vine Wine*, 2020. https://doi.org/10.20870/IVES-TR.2019.4381

16. S. Vazquez, S. M. Lukic, E. Galvan, L. G. Franquelo, and J. M. Carrasco, "Energy storage systems for transport and grid applications," *IEEE Trans. Ind. Electron.*, vol. 57, no. 12, pp. 3881–3895, 2010.

17. A. Emadi, *Handbook of Automotive Power Electronics and Motor Drives.* CRC Press, Boca Raton, FL, 2017.

18. S. K. Biradar, R. A. Patil, and M. Ullegaddi, "Energy storage system in electric vehicle," In *Power Quality '98*, Hyderabad, India, pp. 247–255.

19. M. K. Hasan, M. Mahmud, A. K. M. Ahasan Habib, S. M. A. Motakabber, and S. Islam, "Review of electric vehicle energy storage and management system: Standards, issues, and challenges," *J. Energy Storage*, vol. 41, p. 102940, 2021.

20. A. Emadi, *Advanced Electric Drive Vehicles.* CRC Press, Boca Raton, FL, 2014.

21. F. Tao, L. Zhu, Z. Fu, P. Si, and L. Sun, "Frequency decoupling-based energy management strategy for fuel cell/ battery/ultracapacitor hybrid vehicle using fuzzy control method," *IEEE Access*, vol. 8, pp. 166491–166502, 2020.

22. P. K. Pathak, A. K. Yadav, S. Padmanaban, P. A. Alvi, and I. Kamwa, "Fuel cell-based topologies and multi-input DC-DC power converters for hybrid electric vehicles: A comprehensive review," *IET Gener. Transm. Distrib.*, vol. 16, no. 11, pp. 2111–2139, 2022.

23. M. S. H. Lipu et al., "Review of electric vehicle converter configurations, control schemes and optimizations: Challenges and suggestions," *Electronics*, vol. 10, no. 4, pp. 1–37, 2021.

24. Z. Fu, H. Wang, F. Tao, B. Ji, Y. Dong, and S. Song, "Energy management strategy for fuel cell/battery/ultracapacitor hybrid electric vehicles using deep reinforcement learning with action trimming," *IEEE Trans. Veh. Technol.*, vol. 71, no. 7, pp. 7171–7185, 2022.

25. A. Lahyani, P. Venet, A. Guermazi, and A. Troudi, "Battery/supercapacitors combination in Uninterruptible Power Supply (UPS)," *IEEE Trans. Power Electron.*, vol. 28, no. 4, pp. 1509–1522, 2013.

26. J. P. Zheng, T. R. Jow, and M. S. Ding, "Hybrid power sources for pulsed current applications," *IEEE Trans. Aerosp. Electron. Syst.*, vol. 37, no. 1, pp. 288–292, 2001.

27. S. K. Kollimalla, M. K. Mishra, A. Ukil, and H. B. Gooi, "DC grid voltage regulation using new HESS control strategy," *IEEE Trans. Sustain. Energy*, vol. 8, no. 2, pp. 772–781, 2017.

28. U. Manandhar, N. R. Tummuru, S. K. Kollimalla, A. Ukil, G. H. Beng, and K. Chaudhari, "Validation of faster joint control strategy for battery- and supercapacitor-based energy storage system," *IEEE Trans. Ind. Electron.*, vol. 65, no. 4, pp. 3286–3295, 2018.

29. O. Onar and A. Khaligh, "Dynamic modeling and control of a cascaded active battery/ultra-capacitor based vehicular power system," In *2008 IEEE Vehicle Power and Propulsion Conference*, Sep. 2008, pp. 1–4.

30. I. J. Cohen, D. A. Wetz, J. M. Heinzel, and Q. Dong, "Design and characterization of an actively controlled hybrid energy storage module for high-rate directed energy applications," *IEEE Trans. Plasma Sci.*, vol. 43, no. 5, pp. 1427–1433, 2015.

31. Q. Zhang and G. Li, "Experimental study on a semi-active battery-supercapacitor hybrid energy storage system for electric vehicle application," *IEEE Trans. Power Electron.*, vol. 35, no. 1, pp. 1014–1021, 2020.

32. Z. Song, H. Hofmann, J. Li, X. Han, X. Zhang, and M. Ouyang, "A comparison study of different semi-active hybrid energy storage system topologies for electric vehicles," *J. Power Sources*, vol. 274, pp. 400–411, 2015.

33. P. Bhattacharyya, A. Banerjee, S. Sen, S. K. Giri, and S. Sadhukhan, "A modified semi-active topology for battery-ultracapacitor hybrid energy storage system for EV applications," *2020 IEEE International Conference on Power Electronics, Smart Grid and Renewable Energy (PESGRE2020)*, Cochin, India, 2020, pp. 1–6.

34. M. Momayyezan, B. Hredzak, and V. G. Agelidis, "Integrated reconfigurable converter topology for high-voltage battery systems," *IEEE Trans. Power Electron.*, vol. 31, no. 3, pp. 1968–1979, 2016.

35. S. Ci, N. Lin, and D. Wu, "Reconfigurable battery techniques and systems: A survey," *IEEE Access*, vol. 4, pp. 1175–1189, 2016.

36. A. Affam, Y. M. Buswig, A. K. B. H. Othman, N. Bin Julai, and O. Qays, "A review of multiple input DC-DC converter topologies linked with hybrid electric vehicles and renewable energy systems," *Renew. Sust. Energy Rev.*, vol. 135, no. January 2020, p. 110186, 2021.

37. K. Jyotheeswara Reddy and S. Natarajan, "Energy sources and multi-input DC-DC converters used in hybrid electric vehicle applications - A review," *Int. J. Hydrogen Energy*, vol. 43, no. 36, pp. 17387–17408, 2018.

38. A. K. Bhattacharjee, N. Kutkut, and I. Batarseh, "Review of multiport converters for solar and energy storage integration," *IEEE Trans. Power Electron.*, vol. 34, no. 2, pp. 1431–1445, 2019.

39. X. Pan, H. Li, Y. Liu, T. Zhao, C. Ju, and A. K. Rathore, "An overview and comprehensive comparative evaluation of current-fed-isolated-bidirectional DC/DC converter," *IEEE Trans. Power Electron.*, vol. 35, no. 3, pp. 2737–2763, 2020.

40. B. Zhao, Q. Song, W. Liu, and Y. Sun, "Overview of dual-active-bridge isolated bidirectional DC-DC converter for high-frequency-link power-conversion system," *IEEE Trans. Power Electron.*, vol. 29, no. 8, pp. 4091–4106, 2014.

41. M. Uno, M. Sato, Y. Tada, S. Iyasu, N. Kobayashi and Y. Hayashi, "Partially isolated multiport converter with automatic current balancing interleaved PWM converter and improved transformer utilization for EV batteries," *IEEE Trans. Transport. Electrific.*, vol. 9, no. 1, pp. 1273–1288, 2023.

42. F. Akar, Y. Tavlasoglu, E. Ugur, B. Vural, and I. Aksoy, "A bidirectional nonisolated multi-input DC-DC converter for hybrid energy storage systems in electric vehicles," *IEEE Trans. Veh. Technol.*, vol. 65, no. 10, pp. 7944–7955, 2016.

43. S. Athikkal, G. Guru Kumar, K. Sundaramoorthy, and A. Sankar, "A non-isolated bridge-type DC-DC converter for hybrid energy source integration," *IEEE Trans. Ind. Appl.*, vol. 55, no. 4, pp. 4033–4043, 2019.

44. A. Hintz, U. R. Prasanna, and K. Rajashekara, "Novel modular Multiple-Input Bidirectional DC-DC Power Converter (MIPC) for HEV/FCV application," *IEEE Trans. Ind. Electron.*, vol. 62, no. 5, pp. 3163–3172, 2015.

45. J. -Y. Kim, B. -S. Lee, Y. -J. Lee, and J. -K. Kim, "Integrated multi mode converter with single inductor for fuel cell electric vehicles," *IEEE Trans. Ind. Electron.*, vol. 69, no. 11, pp. 11001–11011, 2022.

46. S. Kurm and V. Agarwal, "Hybrid energy storage system based on a novel reduced rating multi-input converter," *IEEE Trans. Power Electron.*, vol. 35, no. 11, pp. 12133–12142, 2020.

47. P. Bhattacharyya, S. Ghorai, S. Sen, and S. K. Giri, "A flexible non-isolated multiport converter to integrate battery and ultracapacitor for electric vehicle applications," *IEEE Trans. Circuits and Systems II: Express Briefs*, vol. 70, no. 3, pp. 1044–1048, 2023.

Index

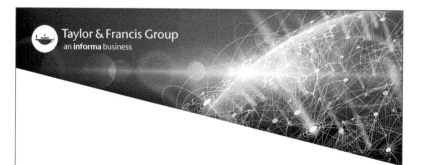